Aesthetics and Analysis in Writing on Religion

Aesthetics and Analysis in Writing on Religion

Modern Fascinations

Daniel Gold

UNIVERSITY OF CALIFORNIA PRESS
Berkeley · Los Angeles · London

University of California Press
Berkeley and Los Angeles, California

University of California Press, Ltd.
London, England

Most of chapter 4 was previously published as
"Making UFO's Move: Aesthetics and Argument in
Writing on Religion," *Scottish Journal of Religious
Studies* 16, no. 2 (Sept. 1995): 75–88.

Parts of chapter 5 were previously published in "The
Erotic Ascetic and the Religiohistorical Sublime," in
*Notes from a Mandala: Essays in Honor of Wendy
Doniger,* ed. Laurie Patton and David Haberman (New
York: Seven Bridges Press, 2001), and appear here by
permission.

Most of chapter 11 was previously published as "A
Tapestry of Kings: Edited Volumes and the Growth of
Knowledge in Religious Studies," *Religion* 29 (summer
1999): 243–59.

Library of Congress Cataloging-in-Publication Data

Gold, Daniel.
   Aesthetics and analysis in writing on religion :
modern fascinations / Daniel Gold.
       p.   cm.
   Includes bibliographical references (p.) and index.
   ISBN 0-520-23613-0 (cloth).—ISBN 0-520-23614-9
(paper)
     1. Religious literature—Authorship.   2. Aesthetics—
Religious aspects.   3. Religion—Methodology.   I. Title.
BL41   .G65 2003
200' .7'2—dc21   2002151316

Manufactured in the United States of America

12   11   10   09   08   07   06   05   04   03
10   9   8   7   6   5   4   3   2   1

Contents

Acknowledgments

Articulating long-contemplated ideas is always gratifying, but it is all the more so when people actually pay attention to them.

Certainly, this book would not have taken the shape that it has if I hadn't spent the 1996–97 academic year at Cornell's Society for the Humanities. The seminar that year—its topic was "disciplines"—helped me understand my project in a larger context, see the book as a whole, and begin writing. Mieke Bal, whose work spans religious studies as well as much else in the humanities, was generous with me then, as she was with others. With his customary acumen, Dominic LaCapra led weekly discussions. My thanks go to these and to all the seminar participants.

A few years later, when the end of the project seemed in sight, Frank Reynolds and Zayn Kassam both expressed interest in reading a manuscript with its final chapters missing. Frank was an old adviser with a voice whose authority lingers; Zayn was a new academic acquaintance, who I knew would be reading the manuscript and not reading me. Their suggestions and encouragement provided energy for the home stretch. Reed Malcolm, too, expressed enthusiasm for the project at that point, and—not so common for an editor—was also ready to have a look at unfinished work. His comments then surely saved considerable rewriting later. Earlier, Ivan Strenski, editor of *Religion,* where a version of chapter 11 was published, provided some helpful comments on one of that chapter's initial drafts. At the final stages, Ciriaco Arroyo offered linguistic counsel, and Elsie Myers Stainton helped with the title.

Special help at the beginning and end of the project was offered by old friends. Anna Gade, reading the first chapters, recognized before I did the priority I was giving to religionists' *fascinations*—even though I'm not so sure she really approved of the idea herself. She also, for better or worse, encouraged me to write some history alongside the theory. Blame her, if you will, for part 4. Greg Alles offered careful and extensive comments on a final draft; he was also most generous in sharing his knowledge of German sources. His help went far beyond the bounds of disciplinary collegiality, and I am very grateful for it.

Ann Grodzins Gold read the chapters as they were written, even though her schedule was usually more hectic than mine. As an anthropologist in a religion department, she has a practiced eye for religionists' collective muddles and has helped me see through some of my individual ones. Jonah and Eli seemed for the most part to take their father's preoccupations in stride: after all, both their parents have been involved in writing projects since before they were born. I thank them for living with us so gracefully.

Modern Dilemmas
in Writing on Religion

Notoriously diverse in the truths they profess and the methods they use to arrive at them, most religion scholars nevertheless seem to share a fascination with the human depth of the material they study. This makes the aesthetics of writing on religion more central to the institutional coherence of their field than many of them realize. For a number of the most influential writers on religion have consistently managed to express something of the depth that they see in the data of religious life to others inside and outside the academy. And if part of what many writers on religion do is to communicate their visions of human truths, then they have something in common with artists. The success of artful writers on religion, moreover, suggests the importance of art itself in real-life scholarly endeavor.

This book pursues a line of thought about the aesthetics of writing on religion, engaging some questions raised by its apparent centrality in the field of religious studies. Has a peculiarly expressive genre of writing on religion emerged from a particular historical moment? If so, what does this emergence suggest about the cultural significance of religiohistorical practice? Perhaps of greater interest to active practitioners is just what aesthetic moves humanistic writers on religion tend to make, in general and in specific. Inevitably, too, the art of religiohistorical writing comes up against the science of religion, an idea still alive in religious studies— at least in the German sense of *religionswissenschaft,* an organized body of knowledge about religious traditions. So how do questions of truth come into the aesthetic picture? How, further, might a body of knowledge that draws on the aesthetic vision of scholars with very diverse worldviews build on itself and grow? This book attempts to rethink religious studies in a way that takes seriously the aesthetic dimensions of an influential strand of humanistic writing on religious life.

INTERPRETIVE WRITING IN RELIGIOUS STUDIES

I have called this strand interpretive writing. It is practiced in many of the subfields of religious studies that have developed in the Western academy since the mid-twentieth century. While the study of religion is often housed in departments that were once devoted exclusively to biblical studies and theology (and were titled accordingly), it has expanded to include non-Western traditions. Although these were at first sometimes taken as part of a missiological curriculum, their study has in fact transformed scholarly ways of thinking about religion. For with more than one tradition on the horizon, not only are comparisons possible but also analytical projects on the ways in which religious traditions work: the cultural and psychological dynamics of myth and ritual; the structures of religious narratives; the sociology and politics of tradition and change. Interpretive writing looks at what is suggested by specific materials of religious life for these larger problems of religious traditions.

In analyzing the dynamics of religious traditions, interpretive writers readily borrow from established disciplines, humanistic and social-scientific alike. Subfields in religious studies have emerged with the refinement of various disciplinary approaches for studying religion. All too often, these subfields are denoted by affixing the term *religion* to a broad academic specialization; "religion and psychological studies," for example, examines both the special psychological turns of religious life and the religious possibilities of normal human development.[1] Gaining some distance from tradition through analytic approaches, scholars in these subfields often work with familiar Western traditions. The distance characteristic of analysis, however, is paradigmatically found in work on the traditions of *others,* whose unfamiliar religious ways may also seem particularly compelling. When understood to contribute to the study of religious traditions generally, scholarship on others' traditions forms part of the "history of religions"—probably the most current English equivalent of *religionswissenschaft*—and it is on interpretive writing in that field that this book will focus.

Not surprisingly, the two interpretive writers on others' religions who have been arguably the most influential in the recent past have also been among the most artful: Mircea Eliade and Clifford Geertz. Although both these writers once had ambitions in the literary world, there their similarity ends. Differing in both their presence in religious studies and their approach to religious materials, they present a radical complementarity. Eliade seems to have almost single-handedly revitalized history of religions in the 1950s and 1960s with large-scale comparative treatises that pointed effectively to felt human truths. Geertz, an anthropologist who has written frequently on religion, has stood at the field's institutional margins, offering considered descriptions of cultural and historical specifics that could reveal the everyday religious dramas of real human beings. Eliade saw religious meaning primarily in a broad vision of humankind in the universe; Geertz has understood acutely how it stemmed from specific human situations. In most interpretive writing on religion, both these types of perception come into play.

Eliade was a precocious intellectual in his native Romania, where he is remembered primarily as a writer of fiction. At the impressionable age of twenty, he went to India, staying for three years. Returning to Bucharest in 1931, he wrote (in addition to a dissertation on yoga) a successful semiautobiographical novel about a European's unsuccessful love affair with an Indian woman.[2] Eliade's academic career in Romania was disrupted by World War II, after which he remained an émigré—first in Paris and then, beginning in 1956, at the University of Chicago, where he was appointed professor of History of Religions. There he developed what he called a "total hermeneutic" that would interpret traditional religions for contemporary humanity.[3] From the late 1950s through the early 1970s both academic and lay audiences were dazzled by Eliade's large synthetic vision, which could reveal profundities in diverse traditions as well as in ordinary life. Although his books were frequently promiscuous in their mixing of religions and cultures, the enduring patterns he identified seemed to ring true. In the years after his death in 1986, Eliade's personal reputation has become clouded by revelations of his sympathies for Romanian fascism and of his ready cooperation with the Bucharest regime—although not (yet) of any specific unforgivable acts. But Eliade's academic influence had already begun to wane during his later years, as his writing seemed increasingly repetitive and his vision stale and etheric. Increasingly, students were undertaking fieldwork and writing in concrete ways that drew inspiration from Geertz.

Returning from World War II with aspirations to be a successful novelist, Geertz found that he could go to college (Antioch) on the G. I. Bill, went on to graduate school at Harvard, and has pursued a successful academic career ever since, for many years at the Center for Advanced Studies at Princeton. Geertz did fieldwork in Indonesia and then in Morocco, writing some long books that are still widely read and many oft-cited articles. He has a talent for telling an engaging story that both reveals cultural nuances and says something about larger cultural (very often religiocultural) questions. This is a crafted writing, which Geertz has compared to a fiction, in the sense of "something made"; it is fundamental to what he has called *The Interpretation of Cultures*—the title of his 1973 prizewinning collection of essays.[4]

With clear echoes of Geertz, the phrase "interpretive writing" carries some pointed associations with the recent scholarly past, so it was only with hesitation that I adopted it as a term for the central subject of my analysis. I stuck with it because the particular sense in which I use the term here does have some real continuities with Geertz's crafted ethnological "fictions," as well as with Eliade's total interpretive hermeneutics. Still, although usually crafted in Geertz's sense and hermeneutic in Eliade's, the interpretive writing I discuss in this book might best be characterized by its strategic use of perspective.

Even if it does not always do so self-consciously, interpretive writing very evidently presents something of an author's individual view. It is thus distinguished from a number of different genres in religious studies in which the author's personal voice may be strategically mute: phenomenological description, naturalist explanation, accounts written to give voice to a received theological doctrine. Interpretive writers, by contrast, try both to represent their subject more or less accurately and to sharpen their perspectives on it. Their perspectives, importantly, give their picture depth in two senses: depth of knowledge and depth of vision.

The two senses of depth produced by an interpretive perspective point to two sorts of truths. Depth of knowledge can offer truths of enlightened science. At its best it offers a profound rational understanding of a subject, perhaps even a degree of scientific truth. Depth of vision, by contrast, offers truths of romantic art. It presents an individual perspective on a scene that reveals insights into it not otherwise easily known. When one talks about interpretation in religious studies these days, it is this romantic depth of vision that comes first to mind, especially when *interpretation* is contrasted to scientific *explanation*. The two terms have come to signal a contrast between a relatively softhearted humanistic stance toward religious traditions and one that is more hard-minded and critical. This is another reason why I stuck with the term "interpretive writing." For even though I hope to show that the characteristic religio-historical aesthetic has a necessary rational edge, if forced to choose I take the position here as closer to the softhearted side.

THE ARGUMENT

Interpretive writers, I argue in part 1, tend to suffer from an uncomfortable modern dilemma. They *like* religion—in the sense that they see it as revealing vital human truths—but they *believe* in science, that is, in some version of post-Enlightenment positivism. Their ambivalent feelings draw them toward the stuff of religious life but keep them twice removed from it: not only are they fascinated by the religions of *others,* but they assimilate these through their aesthetic (as opposed to religious) sensibilities. In coming to this conclusion, I begin by working backward, outlining the origins of contemporary religious studies from an interpretive point of view. Inevitably, I suggest in chapter 1, even old stalwarts of hard-minded Enlightenment-style and softhearted romantic-style scholarship on religion harbor ambivalent feelings toward the materials of their study. Chapter 2 then examines more closely some ways these ambivalences play out in the lives of two confessedly conflicted scholars from the first half of the twentieth century: Jane Harrison and Erwin Goodenough, both of whom wrote memoirs. Coming from different sides of the religious spectrum, they each moved toward the middle: Harrison, the self-avowed secularist with a growing passion for Greek ritual; Goodenough, cherishing warm memories of boyhood Methodist enthusiasms even after losing faith in them. In neither case were their feelings toward their subject at all simple.

Part 2, "The Art of Writing on Religion," is the central section of the book. It begins, in chapter 3, by reflecting further on the relationships between perspective and depth alluded to above, bringing in a third term: *imagination.* If scholars of religion are like artists creating art objects, what are some of the imaginative processes entailed in the construction of *religiohistorical* objects—that is, of crafted pieces of writing that reveal the realities of religious subjects through the subjective visions of their authors? To examine the ways in which different types of religious materials suggest characteristic aesthetic strategies, I turn in chapter 4 to works by four important writers on religion in the last half of the twentieth century: Eliade, Geertz, Georges Dumézil, and Wendy Doniger. These examples, along with some work of Jonathan Z. Smith, provide a basis for exploring in chapter 5 what seems to me the characteristic aesthetic dynamic of interpretive writing on religion, which draws on the ambivalences explored in part 1. Interpretive writers are fascinated by the stuff of religious life, which appeals to their imaginations, but their scientific sides also make them prone to rational analysis. Since the play between imagination and reason was explored at length by Kant, this leads us to his aesthetic theory, and the characteristic aesthetic of interpretive writing elaborated here turns out to be a version of Kant's sublime.

Because the sublime demands imagination *and* reason, interpretive writing must give scientific reason something it can take as true. So part 3 examines the scientific truths of interpretive writing in light of its aesthetic ones, exploring relationships between the two truths. Chapter 6 argues that interpretive writing is limited in the degree of scientific truth it can attain and that its most appropriate range is a middle ground between isolated statements about particulars and grand generalities. Within that range, however, its statements can be as valid as those in any humanistic field. The argument is amplified in chapter 7 by examining the relevance of some of our aesthetic concepts to scientific ones: In what ways can the religiohistorical objects created by interpretive writers seem objective in a scientific sense? What parallels can be drawn between depth of religiohistorical vision and depth of scientific explanation? Because questions of truth in religious studies have been the subject of a number of recent monographs, I have restricted my discussions in part 3 to what aesthetic issues of interpretive writing bring to the debate. I make up for the brevity of part 3, however, in part 4, which explores some historical territory thus far largely uncharted.

Part 4 examines problems in the collective science of religion. How is writing that emerges in good part from individual vision woven into a fabric of public religiohistorical knowledge? The short answer is obvious: very loosely. Nevertheless, examining ways in which people have (and have not) worked together does reveal interesting patterns in that fabric's loose weave. Just how these patterns may take shape is suggested by the extended historical examples of chapters 8 through 10—taken, respectively, from Dutch phenomenology, British and German diffusionism, and classical studies in Edwardian Cambridge. These examples suggest as well the ways in which the theoretical principles of the earlier chapters may work out in ordinary religiohistorical practice. If our historical forays give some grounded complexity to our idealized formulations, they together also emphasize the limited conditions under which religionists have in fact undertaken extended close collaborations. But if instances of collective work are few, ideals of public knowledge, we see in chapter 11, are many, driven by different understandings of the significantly true and the academically possible. An afterword sketches some turns these different understandings have been taking as they encounter critical approaches at the beginning of the twenty-first century and suggests what those newly critical religiohistorical turns might mean for the future of interpretive writing.

THE FASCINATED WRITERS

This book deals with the work of many writers. The more obscure ones are treated in historical contexts in parts 1 and 4 and are introduced briefly when they appear. The five writers whose work forms the basis for the central theoretical discussions of parts 2 and 3, however, have been important figures of the present and recent past—if not well known to all readers then familiar to many. All readers nevertheless deserve to know why these writers have been singled out for special attention.

Little more needs to be said now, I think, on the centrality of Eliade and Geertz for the work on which I focus. However we value the effect of Eliade's towering role in twentieth-century history of religions, his legacy remains evident. And whatever Geertz's primary disciplinary affiliation may be, he is a master of interpretive writing on religion in culture and has reflected articulately and influentially on his practice. Eliade wields the great, universal vision; Geertz tells the small, perceptive story. Of the three other writers treated at length, two—Doniger and Dumézil—find a place in the discussion because their work, in whole or in part, combines elements of broad vision and telling specifics in ways that complement the work of Eliade, Geertz, and each other.

Wendy Doniger is a specialist in Hindu mythology, the first occupant of the Mircea Eliade chair in History of Religions at the University of Chicago. Like Eliade, she looks for larger significances in myth and is not shy of broad comparisons. Like Geertz, however, she is a teller of stories and revels in vivid, specific detail. A witty and prolific writer, she is also a bold personality, unafraid to change her name in midcareer (she made her reputation as Wendy O'Flaherty). Her widely read books, focusing largely on Indian myth, have dealt engagingly with broad issues of illusion, gender, and sexual ambivalence, thus opening her arcane material to a broad readership in religious studies and beyond. In this sense, Doniger is an interpretive writer par excellence. I focus on her first book, *Śiva, the Erotic Ascetic,* where she presents in detail all the stories surrounding a specific Hindu divinity in a way that suggests implications of truly universal import.

Georges Dumézil, who died in 1986, was an Indo-Europeanist whose reconstructions of ancient Indo-European mythologies I will consider as a whole. Thoroughly familiar with the French sociological tradition of Durkheim and Mauss, Dumézil was by training and inclination a philologist—a master of all the Indo-European languages, living and dead, and several more languages besides. A prolific writer, Dumézil spent most of his career in Paris: first in the Section des Sciences Religieuses of the École des Hautes Études at the Sorbonne, and from 1948 to 1968 as professor at the Collège de France. In 1979 he was honored by election to the Académie Française. Like Eliade, Dumézil painted on a large canvas, and comparison was crucial to his arguments. But the conclusions he drew were, like those of Geertz, often limited to a single—if in his case very large—cultural frame. In its attempt to establish a picture of ancient Indo-European society from fragments of language and myth, his work could resemble a feat of intellectual engineering. His aesthetic was correspondingly often bare and architectonic, depending less on suggestion (like that of Geertz and Doniger) than on coherent form. Questions have been raised about the significance Dumézil's broad scheme may hold for European fascists, who might have read (and may still read) *Indo-European* as *Indo-Aryan,* with nefarious implications. But whatever Dumézil's political sympathies during World War II, his academic legacy has, like Eliade's, survived the suspicions, as scholars in Europe and North America continue to follow his lead in exploring the ways in which the specifics of particular myths fit into the general Indo-European picture.

In parts 2 and 3, where discussions revolve around strategies for bringing the specific and general together in aesthetically and intellectually powerful ways, Eliade, Geertz, Doniger, and Dumézil present points on an analytic compass. Standing counter to them all is our fifth scholar, Jonathan Z. Smith, whose work is met with at points throughout these two parts and the rest of the book, too. Displaying the human depth of his material to make a larger point, Smith's writing is eminently interpretive in our sense, yet it tends to be more tightly reasoned than that of the others, presented through pithy argument in individual articles, not extended monographs. Smith is a master of the short essay, and his longer works have taken shape largely as collections of articles and as published lecture series. His analyses—which treat materials ranging from his early studies of late antiquity through the South Seas, Siberia, and Jonestown—have regularly juxtaposed traditions in original ways. In doing so, they have frequently been critical, questioning previous scholarship and inviting us to look at religious phenomena from newer, perhaps deeper, perspectives. Having taught at Dartmouth and UC Santa Barbara, Smith has long been based at the University of Chicago but has had an uneasy institutional relationship with the history of religions program there. His work, however, has had a strong impact on historians of religion there and elsewhere, consistently bringing clear rational thought to an empathy with religious subjects in a way that appeals to hard-minded and softhearted alike.

Many of the writings I discuss are from the 1960s and 1970s, a formative period in the contemporary study of religion, and reflect some of the more romantic resolutions of modern dilemmas characteristic of those decades. Despite the impact of more recent critical theory, those resolutions—which privilege depth of meaning over surface play, unified argument even amidst scattered foundations—continue, I think, to be relevant, outliving some theoretical excesses of the years since. Nevertheless, the very pervasiveness of the past decades' diverse critical currents (which can be exciting as well as excessive) has made this book possible. For when I first started thinking about religionists' fascinations, the notion of a science of religion could still look naively naturalistic, and ideas about the aesthetic nature of academic writing seemed almost too daring to enunciate. Since then, the wave of critical thinking that peaked in the 1980s has both definitively weakened our sense of natural foundations and brought to the surface the role of the aesthetic in intellectual life. Still, as with many enveloped in the study of visionary worlds, the specific theoretical currents of that wave at its peak never pulled me too far in any particular direction. And by the time I was ready to give my thinking some historical and theoretical shape, the wave had already begun to break and the tide to ebb. I experienced some effects of its surge but never really rode with it.

In the interpretive study of religions, late-twentieth-century theoretical currents have left in their wake some critical concepts that can sharpen our thought,[5] but with them also a hypercritical attitude that offers our thinking little room to develop as a discourse of its own. Indeed, some have gone so far as to see the field of religious studies itself shattering under the recently breaking wave, an event then celebrated as the disintegration of a discipline with no real object.[6] That celebration is not one I have joined. A vital field is indeed necessarily diffuse, I argue, because it must incorporate the visions of diverse scholars, but it can still cohere in its own way around the fascinating material at its core. So here I am writing about truth and beauty in the study of religion. Mine may be seen as a retrograde attitude, perhaps, but I prefer to think of it as humane: appreciative but not all-embracingly theological, analytic but not mordantly critical or numbingly scientistic. I think there remains a need to articulate a practical attitude that modulates the extremes. For the dilemmas that have given rise to interpretive writing on religion have not yet gone away, and the genre, I suspect, will be here for a good while longer.

PART ONE

Ambivalent Feelings

THE FEELINGS THAT INTERPRETIVE WRITERS on religion bear toward their subject are extremely diverse but rarely simple. The nature of their professional work seems to dictate some ambivalence. Certainly, if the stuff of religious traditions—creation myths, liturgical display, mystical journeys—did not somehow fascinate scholars, they would not study it; but without some degree of detachment in their studies, most would not also be drawn to the academy. The gamut of interpretive writers' attitudes toward their material runs from a condescending scientific curiosity—sometimes scornful, often empathetic—to a personal engagement that may ideally enhance the scholar's own religious experience. This book will focus on writers falling in the broad middle of this continuum. These are people who find that looking seriously at myths, rituals, and dynamics of institutions can lead to an understanding of important truths about the human condition. They themselves, however, take for granted some version of a modern Western worldview that is more or less secular—critically Marxist, liberally Christian, personally idiosyncratic, or perhaps not well thought through at all. Basically, these scholars *like* religion, but really—at some fundamental, taken-for-granted level— they believe in science.

Much of the most compelling work in contemporary history of religions emerges, I think, from the creative predicament of these scholars-in-the-middle. The truths that they see in their material—often deep and wide-ranging but usually appearing in naturalistic tones—are personally meaningful to them and, they feel, worth conveying to others. Their professional success then depends in good part on their ability to present their privately meaningful visions publicly to an interested academic (and sometimes lay) community, in the process integrating their private understandings into a common store of collective knowledge. The ways in which they attempt to do so constitute the main subject of this study.

Part 1 will set the scene by presenting a morphology of scholarly ambivalences about religion, situating the middle against the extremes. Chapter 1 highlights some hesitancies even in classically extreme detached and engaged stances. Chapter 2 focuses on two scholars from the first half of the twentieth century, each of whom moved from one of these extremes toward a middle ground. Reflection on what their stances share—which, not surprisingly, highlights their appreciation of religio-historical *stuff*—will suggest some of the principal lines of argument pursued through the rest of the book.

CHAPTER I

Fascinated Scientists and Empathizing Theologians

The different ambivalences toward their subject found in present-day writers on religion derive in part from their field's imperfect fusion of two historically distinct intellectual traditions. One of these is dominant in the social-scientific end of the field. It looks back to Enlightenment rationalism and maintains a spirit of scientific discovery triumphant in the late nineteenth century.[1] The other, more consciously humanistic, carries a spark from early-nineteenth-century romanticism that has enlivened historical studies and encouraged sympathetic directions in phenomenological work. In twentieth-century religious studies, these historical and phenomenological streams came together in a hermeneutical enterprise often carried on by self-aware Christians who could locate their studies within broader, usually liberal, theological frames. Convinced voices from both the Enlightenment and romantic camps have been sounded resolutely through the beginning of the twenty-first century. But less-settled voices have also been heard, often quieter and more reflective—voices replete with the hesitancies of thoughtful scholars finding their different ways toward engaged analyses. To provide some measure for understanding the ambivalent middle grounds in the history of religions, I will survey the field's historically extreme stances toward religious traditions. Yet the extremes, I will argue, are not without their hesitancies either. For whatever scholars' conscious ideals, neither a path of scientific detachment nor one of religious empathy can readily be trodden to its end. As writers move toward the logical conclusions of extreme ideals, they inevitably step back—to heave a sigh of wonder, dismay, or resignation.

SCIENTISTS FIND RELIGION PUZZLING

When scholars want to cite the most strident critic of religious traditions from the radical Enlightenment they often turn to David Hume.[2] Hume did in fact have sharp words for religious traditions, but he also found them finally perplexing and enigmatic. Writers before Hume had, for the most part, seen pagan forms of religion as degradations of a primitive monotheism—a vision that admits of a common biblical Eden and sees the possibility of a noble soul in the simple savage.[3] The worldview presented by Hume in his *Natural History of Religion* is, however, as the work's title suggests, eminently *naturalist,* locating the origin of religion in diverse human fears that produced a manifold, unconnected polytheism.[4] This psychological account of the origin of religion has little room for anything positive in the religious traditions of common people, which are contrasted to the divine truths that philosophers can comprehend. The latter present "the good, the great, the sublime, the ravishing"; the former consist of "the base, the absurd, the mean, the terrifying" (93). For Hume, "the religious principles that have prevailed in the world" are nothing "other than sick men's dreams" (94).

But these famous words of Hume, characteristically caustic about "prevailing" common religious traditions, do not tell the whole story. The contrast between the base traditions he finds about him and the sublime forms of theism he also recognizes is itself a source of wonder for him. Hume concludes that "[t]he whole is a riddle, an enigma, an inexplicable mystery. Doubt, uncertainty, suspense of judgment appear the only result of our most accurate scrutiny" (95). This uneasy doubt is not a comfortable feeling for a clear-minded philosopher, and it struck Hume deeply. Hume obviously didn't *like* religion, but it remained a source of wonder for him—mysterious, perplexing, in its very contradictions itself strangely numinous.

Standing in contrast to Hume's pondering philosophical deliberations, the scientific investigations of religion that began in the latter half of the nineteenth century gave serious attention to the data at hand. For the most part, eighteenth-century philosophers and savants concerned with religion tried to present coherent rational narratives based on the piecemeal data available to them.[5] Although Hume's psychological "natural" history marked a break from Deist devolutionary and Euhemerist accounts, in all of them the larger picture was central. If authors had no use for particular traditions they knew about, as was often the case, they could, like Hume, simply dismiss them as "absurd, mean, and terrifying." Although nineteenth-century scientists also had their theories, both the temper of the scientists and the intent of the theories demanded more detailed elaboration of proofs. Even unsavory religious traditions needed to be considered carefully, not merely dismissed. All the unruly data of religion needed to be *explained*—or at least labeled and fit into a system. With the scientific spirit glorying in the *facts,* the mystery of religious diversity that Hume saw in the polarized whole now became reflected in the particulars, presaging the lasting fascination with the stuff of religion that remains vital in religious studies today.

The late-nineteenth-century concern with particulars of tradition, however, might seem alien to a turn-of-the-twenty-first-century exegete concerned with the psychological, cultural, or critical implications of a favored individual myth. There was at that time still too much unsorted data to be able to look comfortably at particulars in isolation; these called, instead, for order among themselves. Faced with the astounding bulk of details accumulated over centuries by explorers, missionaries, and orientalists, the new scientists of religion attempted to make sense of its diversity. What were sought were keys that could unlock the secrets of how the particulars fit together. Many were suggested: Max Müller's solar mythology; several diffusion theories;[6] but the most exciting key, the most widespread—the most *scientific*—was evolution, of which the most successful anthropological proponent was E. B. Tylor.

Tylor begins *Primitive Culture,* in which he gives his most substantial treatment of religion, with a chapter on the "science of culture."[7] Two axioms underlie this science. First, there is a pervasive uniformity in culture resulting from the "uniform action of uniform causes" (1:1). A corollary of this is the existence of a basic consistency in the "character and habit of mankind": Tylor finds truth in Dr. Johnson's remark that "one set of savages is like another" (1:6). Second, "various grades of culture" should be regarded as "stages of evolution" (1:1). In applying these axioms to the study of civilization, an important first step in his scientific method is then to "dissect" culture "into details, and to classify these in their proper groups" (1:7). The result is a detailed array of human customs linked by type, not individual culture, that reveals the fundamentally uniform cultural evolution of humankind.

The detailed array of religious traditions found in the second half of

Primitive Culture presents exotic beliefs and customs in straightforward prose. "What causes volcanos?" The Australians say that demons "threw up red-hot stones"; people from Kamchatka say that mountain spirits heat up their houses and throw the brands out the chimneys; Nicaraguans seem to offer human sacrifice to a spirit of the mountain, "for one reads of chiefs going to the crater, whence a hideous old naked woman came out and gave them counsel and oracle" (2:293). All over the world, humankind in a similar state of evolution has faced similar intellectual problems in ways that may diverge but are broadly similar in type. Scientists should look at these bizarre traditions dispassionately and see them in their proper place.

Nevertheless, as vestiges of an early stage of a *common* humanity, exotic religious traditions are part of our collective heritage as human beings. They fascinate us in part because in them we may see intimations of what we once were; even as we have moved beyond them, they are with us. Somewhere, humans much like us still visit the "hideous old naked woman"—and although her image, of course, should no longer instill any foreboding in civilized human beings, it sometimes, inexplicably, still does.

A similar stance toward exotic traditions is taken by James George Frazer in *The Golden Bough,* which brings the ordered catalogue of data into the twentieth century, poeticizing it and broadening the scope of its audience. Whereas Tylor sought a scientific, evolutionist key for understanding the diverse data of religious traditions, Frazer found an ordering principle in a central myth. His monumental work begins with the story of the priest at the temple to Diana at Aricia. Consort of the goddess, the priest was known as King of the Wood; eventually, he would be challenged and killed by his successor, who first had to steal the golden bough that he guarded.[8] For Frazer to unravel the mystery of the King of the Wood meant to examine sacred marriage and dying (and rising) divinities, as well as the ideas of magic, spirits, and taboo that give these concepts meaning. Sharing some of Tylor's presuppositions about the uniformity of humankind, Frazer explored these concepts very widely beyond the Roman context of his story. More than Tylor's *Primitive Culture,* Frazer's *Golden Bough* became, by its third edition, a veritable encyclopedia of exotic religious lore.

Frazer's classical frame-story, together with his literary style, helped popularize the study of religion among a much wider educated public and presaged the deeper study of myth that would take place later in the century. But Frazer himself was no depth psychologist, and by the twelfth volume of *The Golden Bough* his central mythic thread appears as little more than a wispy leitmotif that links highly diverse data. Its role in the work is to provide a perplexing story that lets Frazer ask questions. Religious customs, for Frazer, were curiosities.

Like Tylor, Frazer saw the religions he studied as outmoded, something *historically* interesting. Even if what each of these scholars studied intrigued him because it revealed a collective human past with which he could identify, it was of no immediate personal use. The relics of the past Tylor and Frazer found in religious tradition, rather, might reveal important secrets about humankind in general. This stance toward religious materials—a fascination with the important human truths they suggest, together with a strict personal distance—is an attitude that continues to mark one end of the spectrum of religious studies.

BELIEVERS BROADEN THEIR HORIZONS

The other end of the spectrum is marked by a generous personal engagement with religious traditions, often on the basis of a considered theology. Many of the most forceful advocates of some attitude of engagement had theological training, and several were also known as creative theologians—usually liberal, most often Protestant. The history of religions, they intimated, might help us discern some ways of the divine in the world. An attempt to penetrate the diverse religious experiences of humankind, moreover, could prove a valuable experience for one's own self-development.

Foregrounding any such stance is thus an appreciation of religious experience, but in the background lurks the acknowledgment that our understanding of another's experience can never be complete. Here, then, lies the echo on the religious side of the rational scientists' fascination with religion in the face of their personal distance from it. Those scientists, although remaining personally aloof, had still demonstrated a wonder at religious tradition—either in the contradictory whole, like Hume, or in the intriguing particulars, like Tylor and Frazer. Scholars who, on the other hand, would grow personally close to the religions they studied recognized the inevitability of some personal distance, whether they liked it or not.

A theology of experience first comes to the fore in the Protestant world with Friedrich Schleiermacher. As a young man, Schleiermacher was close to Friedrich Schlegel and his circle of romantic cultural revolutionaries, but by the time of his death he was professor of theology at

Berlin and "the most distinguished theologian of Protestant Germany."[9] History of religions looks primarily to the *young* Schleiermacher, the radical romantic who at the age of twenty-nine wrote *On Religion: Speeches to Its Cultured Despisers*. Published in 1799 as a rejoinder to secular contemporaries—die-hard classical rationalists and burgeoning romantic poets alike—this work dramatically introduces two propositions that find a place in the theological agenda of most historians of religion who consciously have one. First, enunciating a view of religion in tune with romantic sensibilities, Schleiermacher claims that religion is, preeminently, feelings: these are "what is autonomous" (47) in religion. Second, arguing against Enlightenment attempts to find a single Deistic religion that all rational people could believe, he affirms religious plurality in its historical richness: "each religion was one of the particular forms [the one] eternal and infinite religion necessarily had to assume among finite and limited beings" (99). Adding an appreciation for diversity to an elevation of experience, the young Schleiermacher still speaks to many who find studying other religious traditions personally enriching.

Once the science of religion was taken up in earnest in the twentieth century, Schleiermacher's exuberant proclamations were given new substance by Rudolf Otto, who wrote an introduction to *Speeches*.[10] A professor of systematic theology at Marburg who produced philosophical and comparative studies, as well as translations from Sanskrit, Otto is best remembered in religious studies as the author of *Das Heilige*, translated into English as *The Idea of the Holy*.[11] There, like Schleiermacher in the *Speeches*, he presents the essence of religion first of all as a kind of feeling, but he also takes this experience of the "numinous" to be grounded in a sense of "the holy"—a specific a priori category construed within the neo-Kantianism of Jakob Fries.[12] As a category of its own, the holy becomes intrinsic to the experience of humankind and the wellspring of all religious phenomena. On this basis Otto can offer a short catalogue of the ways in which the numinous has manifested itself throughout the world. Although his examples are mostly from Western traditions, they also include some from the Indian sources with which he was familiar. In *Das Heilige* the holy becomes an object of study, theoretically grounded and historically revealed.[13]

A highly influential book when it was published in 1917, *Das Heilige* has continued to excite scholars personally open to the religious traditions they study. Not all of these scholars, however, have followed Otto to his theoretical conclusions. Professor William Brede Kristensen of Leiden, a contemporary of Otto's who remained professionally active well into the 1940s, saw no need for Otto's philosophically grounded idea of the holy: "We must put the questions differently than Otto does. We should not take the concept 'holiness' as our starting point, asking, for example, how the numinous is revealed in natural phenomena. On the contrary, we should ask how the believer conceives the phenomena he calls 'holy.' "[14] The scholar must then "form an accurate conception" of the believer's religious reality and "understand it from within" (23). More than any reification of the holy, it is this insistence on sympathetic understanding, on the attempt to experience something of another religious reality in a way that can be personally broadening, that will be emphasized as the defining characteristic of this side of our religious-studies spectrum. By studying religion, the student "grows himself religiously."[15]

Some important implications of what growing oneself religiously by studying religion can entail are emphatically articulated in the work of Wilfred Cantwell Smith. Smith has focused on world religions, which can provide "a living encounter . . . between people of diverse faith."[16] Unlike Kristensen, who abandoned theological training for long philological studies and then took up ancient religions, Smith's early training in theology and Islamics led him to go with the Canadian Overseas Mission Council to Lahore, Punjab, where he became acculturated to South Asian Muslim life.[17] Attached to educational institutions, he gained an acute understanding of the society in which he lived[18] and, more important for the turn of his later work, evidently valued his interactions with Muslims. In a famous essay published in 1959, Smith underscored that "the study of religion is the study of persons. . . . Faith is a quality of men's lives."[19] Studying religion, from this perspective, focuses attention on people's self-conscious beliefs, on their feelings and attitudes—not only of those studied but of the scholar as well. In this deliberate personalization of the study of religion, key words are *encounter, communication,* and, especially, *dialogue*—which may ideally become a mutual, all-encompassing, global discourse: "The culmination of this progress," writes Smith, "is when 'we all' are talking *with* each other about 'us.' "[20]

But as Smith realized in 1959, our circle of understanding is not yet so broad, collaborative, or harmonious and perhaps never will be. In all of these personally engaged writers, together with the hope for broadening understanding, there is an awareness of limits. Kristensen, formulating a primal distinction between "ancient" and "modern" religions, perceived a gap between a contemporary Western post-Enlightenment outlook and *all* other traditions—a gap that could only be partially fathomed. For Otto, his translations and comparative work notwithstanding, the experience of the holy was perceived as one of the "wholly other"; it was something daunting to encounter in one's own tradition, not to mention in another culture.

Thus, despite their desire somehow to comprehend other religious worlds deeply, these religiously committed scholars all recognized the boundaries of their own cultural horizons, the limits of their individual efforts, as well, perhaps, as the rootedness of their own personal faiths. Representing one extreme of the spectrum of stances in religious studies, their enthusiastic, but admittedly limited, inward engagement mirrors the cool but fascinated detachment of the uninvolved scientist at the other. Neither all-embracing engagement of others' religions nor absolute aloofness from them seems practically tenable in scholarly work.

CHAPTER 2

Finding Middle Grounds

In balancing analysis with engagement and detachment with empathy, interpretive writers have found distinct stances within the middle grounds of religious studies—that expansive scholarly space where head and heart come to terms with one another about the subject of religion. Scholars' own, not always positive, personal experiences of religion (in more and less conventional varieties) have coalesced uneasily with their alternative ideas of what it means to be scientific. From the beginnings of the modern study of religion at the turn of the twentieth century, anthropologists, classicists, and biblical scholars, among others, have had intellectual encounters with obscure but compelling traditions that led them to question comfortable realities. From our twenty-first-century standpoint, some of these encounters can seem surprising indeed.

SCIENCE, RELIGION, AND HUMAN MEANINGS THROUGH THE MID-TWENTIETH CENTURY

Particularly surprising were some vocal participants in extended turn-of-the-twentieth-century anthropological debates. Although these debates were conducted in the spirit of rational British science, they included some Britons who clearly recognized the importance of human capacities other than reason itself. Perhaps the most interesting of these scholars was Andrew Lang. A talented man of letters with diverse interests, Lang produced prose about religion in the same staid tone as his more exclusively anthropological contemporaries, but he recognized dimensions to his subject that many others did not.[1] Religionists today most frequently remember Lang as the first forceful advocate of the existence of "primitive high gods," a claim that early humanity, too, knew some sort of abstract, supreme divinity—often seen as a god of the sky.[2] This claim developed from Lang's enthusiastic championing of the anthropological study of myth, which led him to continued public diatribes with the philologist Max Müller.[3] Lang's contemporaries, however, knew him best not as an academic but as a literary man fascinated with folklore—a prolific and engaging author who penned, among other works, popular fairy tales for children.[4]

Concurrent with his literary, anthropological, and folkloric endeavors, however, Lang was a founder-member (and sometime president)[5] of the Society for Psychical Research, organized "for the purpose of inquiring into a mass of obscure phenomena which lie at present on the outskirts of our organised knowledge."[6] The society was a haven for upper-class aficionados of all varieties of then-fashionable theories that looked beyond a philistine Victorian materialism; the ideas of Freud and Jung were considered, as well as examples of "dowsing rods, poltergeists, and automatic writing."[7] Lang's interests seemed to be less in the narrowly psychological than in the broadly supernatural, and he integrated these with his folkloric work through the study of ghost stories, of which he collected many.[8]

This otherworldly dimension of Lang's folkloric work raised the eyebrows of his more sober-minded colleagues. In a response to criticism by Edward Clodd in the latter's presidential address to the Folk-Lore Society in 1895, Lang chided the narrow empiricism advocated by Clodd: "I am in disgrace with the Folk-Lore Society," he complained, "for maintaining . . . that some people *do* see hallucinatory pictures in glass balls, in carafes of water, in ink."[9] His own claims here were limited and pertained to human—not superhuman—phenomena. Not affirming that psychic phenomena were objectively real, he merely suggested that some might be subjectively so in a genuine way, that not all psychics were frauds, as Clodd had implied. In an article called "Protest of a Psycho-Folklorist," however, Lang admits more openness to the possible objective reality of supernatural events, in which "honorable men" may believe: "What I cannot understand is this: as long as . . . belief rests only on tradition it interests the folklorist. As soon as contemporary evidence of honorable men avers that the belief reposes on a fact, Folklore drops the subject."[10] Scholarly interest in uncanny phenomena, he intimates, should not be daunted by the possibility of their reality. Although the superhuman realities that catch his attention—ghosts and psychic phenomena—made him less religiously reverent than were theologically oriented scholars like Rudolf Otto or Wilfred Smith, Lang insisted along with them that scientists of religion should (at least) be allowed to be open to the intangible dimensions of what they study.

More ensconced than Lang in the anthropological establishment was R. R. Marett, who held the chair of social anthropology at Oxford from 1910 to 1936. Preceded in that position by E. B. Tylor, his mentor, and succeeded by the functionalist A. R. Radcliffe-Brown, Marett stands in a rather hard-nosed empiricist lineage. He himself, however, is remembered as seeing the origin of religion in *mana,* a Melanesian word that describes a sense of awe in the face of unexplained powers. Like Otto, who appreciated his work,[11] Marett is then led to understand that "man's religious sense is a constant and universal feature of his mental life."[12] And in identifying *mana* as what is crucial in religion, Marett—like Otto with "the numinous"—gives priority to feelings over speculation. "The religious sense" is to be sought "in that steadfast groundwork of specific emotion whereby man is able to feel the supernatural precisely at the point at which his thought breaks down."[13]

Although Marett did take a trip to Australia, he was trained as a philosopher and, like most anthropologists of his day, wrote more from the accounts of others than from his own field encounters. In the fashion of Tylor and Frazer, Marett often seems to present exotic examples as tantalizing curiosities, detached from their contexts and ordered through type. But among his types are basic religious feelings that he sees as transcending a Tylorean evolutionism and continuing to resonate in the religious sensibilities of his own contemporaries. Thus the book that emerged from his Gifford lectures he titled *Faith, Hope, and Charity in Primitive Religion*—an apparent oxymoron that reflects the ambivalent sentiments still found among scholars occupying the middle ground in religious studies. Marett was an early purveyor of British social anthropology who displayed a respect for "fundamental Religious Feeling" that we might rather expect in an explicit theology of experience; *mana,* his key term, he defined as the Power of Awe, or Power—which he always dignified with a capital *P.*[14]

Meanwhile, on the Continent, religiously engaged scholars, who had all felt the impact of Otto, began to look more carefully at the way "the holy" appeared in specific kinds of contexts. In Holland, Gerardus van der Leeuw, footnoting Marett, started from an idea of sacred Power to fashion an ordered phenomenology of religion.[15] Structured on the relationship between subject and object, van der Leeuw's phenomenology presented religious reality as something with which human beings have *interacted* in myriad ways. Sacred power remained sacred but was also manifestly and diversely human. Joachim Wach brought the German hermeneutic tradition of Dilthey and Troeltsch to religious traditions through sociology, which, as Gregory Alles points out, was a trendy new field when Wach took it up.[16] The holy was still something to be understood subjectively but was now seen as embedded in specific kinds of social forms. In Scandinavia, Lutheran scholars moved away from traditional salvational understandings of the Old Testament. Emphasizing careful philological work, they took a broader historical view of the Hebrew Scriptures and put forward some interesting theses about the ritual traditions behind them.[17] Among Scandinavian scholars, the most towering figure was clearly Sigmund Mowinckel, professor of Old Testament at Oslo. An acute textualist, Mowinckel was a scholar's scholar, but he had a broad peripheral vision, too. His most influential textual work was on the ritual background of the Psalms,[18] yet in addition to a great many philological studies, he also wrote a judicious theology of the Old Testament for laypersons and a theoretical treatise in the history of religions.[19] For the most part, all these continental scholars had theological credentials and explicit personal beliefs, which they understood to be both widened and honed more finely through their scholarly explorations of others' religions.

Like their more positivist fellows, these religiously oriented scholars reveal differently nuanced personal ambivalences to diverse materials of tradition. As their feelings about what they study become less straightforward, moreover, scholars from both sides of the spectrum seem to approach some common grounds. Crucial features defining these common grounds in the early and middle decades of the twentieth century can be identified by examining two cases: the classicist Jane Harrison, who scorned "theology" but was drawn toward the mysteries of Greek ritual, and the erstwhile biblical scholar Erwin Goodenough, who moved from a conservative Christian upbringing through liberal theology to become an eminent historian of symbols.

Beginning with Harrison places the emergence of the fertile middle grounds of religious studies in the brief Edwardian epoch, the window between the beginning of the twentieth century and the start of the First World War, during which Harrison's most memorable works were produced. This timing is significant, I think, because that epoch highlighted the tensions between a naturalist outlook and the fascination with religion that are still endemic to historians of religions. Until the outbreak of World War I, naive Victorian beliefs about the progress of science were still common. But by the end of the nineteenth century, they had become less emotionally compelling, making room for Fabian Socialism, Psychical Research, and, I think, an ambivalent stance in the study of religions that is still with us.[20] Goodenough then reveals a religiously respectful variant of that stance from the middle of the twentieth century.

In their days, both Harrison and Goodenough were leading scholars in their fields. And both, significantly for the present work, have left memoirs that help us see their scholarship against their individual religious lives. These memoirs, like most, tend toward the ideal, identifying an order within complex lives. But despite any skepticism we may harbor about the selective detail foregrounded by our memoirists' hindsight, we can still take seriously the general directions in which they saw their attitudes toward religion move. And for our story, these are telling. Starting from opposite poles of the compass of personal engagement in religious studies, the two nevertheless end up sharing an exultation in the particulars of religious traditions—a sense that the specific materials of religious traditions have something exciting to say about humankind, something valuable that may not be easily known through any other means.[21]

Abandoning Theology to Save Religion in the Work of Jane Harrison

Of the Edwardian scholars remembered in the study of religion, the classicist Jane Harrison is the one whose work seems to reverberate most closely with that of scholars today. In contrast to Frazer, her older classicist contemporary, who filled out a light, skeletal narrative with assorted, loosely related facts, Harrison sought coherent patterns in the bounded field of Greek religion. She did this by looking at her textual materials through social-scientific frames—among the first of her generation seriously to do so. The social-scientific movements that influenced her, moreover, singled out motives for human behavior that were not simply rational: Durkheim's stress on social cohesiveness, Freud's unconscious. She recognized powerful nonrational forces behind the patterns of religion she delineated.[22]

Harrison's feel for the power of religious forms plays against a sensibility that stands aloof from traditional religion. Two distinct models for piety were apparent in her childhood home: her father, of nonconformist background, "incapable of forming a [religious] conviction"; and her stepmother, "a fervent semirevivalist."[23] Harrison's attitude was clearly closer to her father's. Her stepmother, she tells us, admonished her charges that they must be "born again" and that "God would have our whole hearts or nothing." By this last teaching young Jane sincerely tried to abide, she says, but "the holocaust I honestly attempted was a complete failure. I was from the outset a hopeless worldling."[24] Nor did Harrison seek solace in traditional religion during her old age. In the conclusion of a memoir written in her seventies, she expresses a satisfied materialist metaphysics: "I have no hope whatever for personal immortality, no desire even for a future life. My consciousness began in a very humble fashion, with my body; with my body, very quietly, I hope it will end."[25] Exposed to her stepmother's evangelical religion early in life, Harrison followed it as a matter of course. At least in hindsight, however, she found it oppressive: common evangelical precepts about God's wrath, salvation, and hell, she later confides, are "a grim and awful thing to tell a child."[26] The profound revelations she would have in her adult life would come through intellectual, not consciously religious, pursuits.

Three books, Harrison tells us in her *Reminiscences*, had a particularly profound influence on her, marking "three stages in my thinking: Aristotle's *Ethics*, Bergson's *L'Évolution créatrice*, and Freud's *Totemism and Taboo*" (80). Each book, moreover, added an element to the overall religious orientation she did finally develop. Aristotle freed her from her family religion; Bergson gave her a new vision of an Absolute; and Freud invested that vision with deep human dimensions.

Harrison's encounter with the *Ethics*, prescribed during her first year at Cambridge, was exhilarating. She presents that encounter as a liberating experience, releasing her from misguided religious outlooks that lingered from her girlhood: "To realize the release that Aristotle brought, you must have been reared as I was in a narrow school of Evangelicalism. It was like coming out of a madhouse into a quiet college quadrangle where all was liberty and sanity, and you became a law to yourself" (80–81). The *Ethics* authorized Harrison's newfound independence. Moreover, in highlighting "the *summum bonum* . . . as an exercise of personal faculty . . . [and] the perfect life that was to include . . . as a matter of course friendship," the *Ethics* affirmed for Harrison the value not only of the individual but also of the intense personal relationships that would regularly stimulate her life and work. This was heady stuff "to one who had been taught that God claimed all" (81).

Whereas Aristotle gave Harrison a new sense of self, Bergson gave her a new sense of spiritual possibility. Bergson's concept of *durée,* which can be simply translated as "temporal flow," Harrison gloriously describes as "that life which is one indivisible and yet ceaselessly changing."[27] *Durée* would then be able to provide an exalted referent for the mythic divinities she studied. Freud, finally, taught Harrison that the mysterious forms of these divinities had definite human referents, too. The plentiful references to sex and psychoses found in much of Freud initially put her off, she writes, nor was she a fan of psychoanalytic therapy.[28] *Totem and Taboo,* however, impressed her mightily: "Here was a big constructive imagination . . . probing the mysteries of sin, of sanctity, of sacrament— a man who, because he understood, purged the human spirit of fear."[29] Clearly, a fearless, probing imagination—which Harrison cultivated in herself—was something she valued.

Not mentioned among the three great influences on her psyche—but acknowledged elsewhere—is the work of Émile Durkheim, which offers some of the most immediate background to the understandings of religious truth she would put forward publicly. These she expressed succinctly in a talk given in 1913 before the Heretics, a Cambridge society to which she belonged, founded "to promote discussion on problems of Religion, Philosophy, and Art."[30] Her topic was a small group of contemporary young French poets known as the "Unanimists" (from *una anima*—"one spirit") and what they could reveal about conversion, which Harrison then took as "the essence of religion" (22).

Harrison was drawn to the Unanimists, now largely forgotten, through the ways in which they gave voice to the spiritual sides of her two great French intellectual heroes, Bergson and Durkheim. "Life is one—but you may think of that oneness in two ways. There is the stream of life in time . . . what Professor Bergson calls *durée.* . . . Or we may think of the oneness spatially, contemporaneously" in the social groups of Durkheim (8–9). To these abstract concepts of unity, the Unanimists gave concrete expressions in poetry that offered parallels to the suggestive particulars Harrison would find elsewhere in ritual and myth. Inspired poetry, like evocative ritual, could elicit the experience of universal life.

"The stream of life in ceaseless change, yet uninterrupted unity . . . the oneness of life lived together in groups, its strength and dominance . . . the value of each individual manifestation of life, and the . . . ecstasy that comes of human sympathy" (18–19)—these were the real spiritual truths recognized by Harrison at the peak of her career. Conversion, moreover—in the "old-world . . . evangelical" sense of being born again—is nothing "but a sudden Unanimism" (19, 26). Invoking William James, Harrison sees them both as varieties of mystical experience. Thus, in the childhood religion that frightened her, she finds a kernel of truth she can accept—one that reflects a vision of human community in space and time. A year earlier, in *Themis,* she had identified a similar kernel of truth in the archaic forms of Greek religion.

Harrison wrote her two major works on Greek religion, the *Prolegomena* to its study and *Themis,* as a research fellow at her Cambridge alma mater, Newnham College.[31] She had returned in 1898 after seventeen years as a private scholar based in London. During that time she had visited Greek archeological sites and museums throughout Europe, lectured with great success on Greek art and archeology, and produced several books. Of those, the most notable was *Mythology and Monuments of Ancient Athens,* which reflected some fashions of the age: an idealistic aesthetic current in the 1880s and 1890s married to a British rationalism interested in the facts.[32] In Cambridge Harrison's perspectives changed and widened. Her *Prolegomena to the Study of Greek Religion* drew on her archeological expertise to present a view of Greek religion that gave priority to ritual. Innovative, but solid, it was well received among classicists; not so her next major work, *Themis,* which was more daring.

The new material Harrison brought to Greek religion in *Themis* was not the evidence of Greek archeology but parallels from the cultural anthropology of nonliterate peoples. In *Themis,* Harrison attempted to establish a basic initiatory and cyclical seasonal pattern as the basis of Greek—and implicitly all—religion. Her vision was not only wider but also higher than before. The introduction to *Themis* makes specific mention of Durkheim and Bergson. "Dionysos," she wrote, "with every other mystery-god, was an instinctive attempt to express what Professor Bergson calls *durée* . . . "—the "one, ceaselessly changing" life.[33] Yet despite her flights of high revelatory insight, she found basic religious patterns grounded, à la Durkheim, in social forms, a perception of religion that moves sharply away from the still-dominant rationalism of Tylor and Frazer: "primitive religion was not, as I had drifted into thinking, a tissue of errors leading to mistaken conduct; rather it was a web of practices emphasizing particular parts of life, issuing necessarily in representations."[34] Religious representations at once held expansive meanings and were embedded in human social realities.

Discussing the progression of her intellectual enthusiasms from her lectures in London to her major books, Harrison confides: "happily . . .

bit by bit art and archeology led to mythology, mythology merged in religion; there I was at home."[35] At the same time, Harrison is emphatic in her agnosticism and insists that her home in religion is a hardheaded academic one: "Please don't misunderstand me. It was not that I was spiritually lonely or 'seeking for the light'; it was that I felt religion was my subject."[36] Harrison obviously liked religion—it revealed matters of vital human significance to her that she felt comfortable writing about. She did not, however, like theology—"after-the-event explanations"[37] of experience, which she personally identified with a fearsome evangelical faith. Indeed, she claims, in a moment of spiritual exuberance, we "must . . . drop theology if we would keep religion."[38] Here she gives voice to what may be the central cultural dynamic of the twentieth-century humanistic study of religion: an attempt to recover the truths that religion offers through analyses that demand loosening—if not abandoning—traditional theological understandings. Several decades later this same dynamic would be expressed by Erwin Goodenough during the course of his work on early Christianity and Judaism. His personal point of reference, however, was always a positively valued experience of tradition.

Goodenough Remembers a Happy Faith

In moving from matter-of-course belief in traditional doctrines as a child to a basic rejection of them as an analytic scholar, the intellectual side of Goodenough's personal religious trajectory resembles Harrison's. In the affective side of those trajectories, however, there was a crucial difference: Harrison never really seemed to accept her stepmother's evangelical religion and disparaged it in her old age;[39] Goodenough was, for periods, fully engaged in religious practice and remembered his experiences warmly. Harrison, as we have seen her put it, "was from the outset a hopeless worldling," but Goodenough never quite stops being religiously engaged.

Born in Brooklyn in the last decade of the nineteenth century, Goodenough worked actively throughout the early and middle decades of the twentieth, with his first academic work published in 1923 and his last in 1968. By midcentury, he was a preeminent professional in the field of religious studies in the United States, the president of the American Society for the Study of Religion from 1955 to 1962.[40] The course of Goodenough's career, moreover, is indicative of a common secularizing turn taken by many scholars starting out religious in his era: it progressed from a theologically informed study of early Christianity to a more inclusive, academically framed examination of religious life and practice outside the immediate Christian world. Yet even as the orientation of Goodenough's personal beliefs shifted from "religion" to "science," as we have used the terms, the intense religious experiences of his Methodist boyhood stayed with him. These he describes in a late work entitled *Toward a Mature Faith*.[41] Broadly reflective as well as autobiographical, the work attempts to reconcile Goodenough's later groundings in depth psychology with the religious life of his youth.

Goodenough emphasizes that his deeply devout family environment made him understand the vitality of religious experience, an understanding that would inform all his later scholarship. The Methodism he knew firsthand included an orthodox Calvinist side (he details the strict Sabbath prohibitions at home)[42] and more rapturous aspects—exemplified in his Uncle Charlie, whom he characterizes as a mystic. He describes an experience at a camp meeting with Uncle Charlie, where, as a high school boy, Goodenough "was completely overcome, lost all power of walking, and had to be helped out by two men." Experiences like this, moreover, would leave a lasting imprint on the mature scholar. "However far I have come in later years from seeking such rapture, I have never forgotten its reality, and ever since, as I have read descriptions of ecstatic religious experiences . . . I have felt a sympathy with them. . . . These experiences are not aberrations, but the logical end of prayer and of most symbolism" (20).

Like Harrison, Goodenough describes an awakening of intellect in his college years that would eventually lead him to study history of religions. Goodenough's intellectual break with the past, however, was less radical than Harrison's and more gradual. Still intent on the ministry during his college years, he at first saw his newfound scholarly ambition as something separate from his religious career; the two would ideally be able to coexist without conflict. What had originally excited Goodenough's scholarly curiosity were college papers on the sources of Shakespeare's plays. Encouraged by his professor, he had dreamed of emotional fulfillment through the ministry while pursuing creative scholarship in literary history. "That the two drives, the drive to emotional experience and the drive to creative understanding, could have any relationship to each other, be coordinated into a single drive, had not yet entered my head" (24). The two drives do finally come together in Goodenough's historical studies of early Christianity, which thus explicitly appear as the fruit of a marriage of religious experience and analytic understanding.

During the course of Goodenough's academic life, the analytic aspects of his work became increasingly pronounced. For a year and a half, he studied at Harvard Divinity School, "where empiricism was at its noblest" (27). He then studied in Europe for nearly three years, mostly at Oxford. During this period he discovered the "scientific mind," which "is characterized by its lifelong distrust of old faiths and by its delight in getting facts which make new faiths necessary" (29–30). He realized the threat that the scientific mind could pose to traditional faith, but his own new intellectual orientations evolved incrementally, he tells us, without crisis. There was no world-shattering break for Goodenough reminiscent of Harrison's epiphany at Aristotle's *Ethics* but a gradual change in points of view: "When I had lost the old Faiths, already, like a snake, new skin had grown under them, so that I was never without the protection of an orientation" (30). Moreover, the new investigation carried out by the scientific mind could not only coexist with a feel for religion but could also become almost as intense: "Here was an atmosphere," he writes of his early postgraduate intellectual environment, "that fired my enthusiasm as nothing since Uncle Charlie's mysticism had done" (30). Goodenough found a marriage between his two drives that was both viable and intense.

This marriage found fruitful consummation in Goodenough's lifework. Returning from Europe, Goodenough found himself theologically too "far left" (31) for most Protestant seminaries but did find a job as an instructor of history at Yale. He stayed at Yale, eventually becoming a professor of history of religions and university professor with appointments in five departments.[43] Although Goodenough's work started from familiar Christian ground (his dissertation was on the theology of Justin Martyr), he became better known for his work on Hellenistic Judaism— first on Philo and later on Jewish symbols. The last became the subject of his most ambitious work, a thirteen-volume opus in the Bollingen series in which he treats vast amounts of iconographical detail in the contexts of cultural history, the dynamics of symbolism, and the psychology of religion.[44]

Despite Goodenough's wide geographical and analytical range, much of his work, he tells us at the beginning of the summary volume of his magnum opus, was driven by a question about Christianity: how could "the teaching of a Galilean carpenter . . . so quickly have become" a full-fledged "Greco-Roman religion even though it called itself the Verus Israel."[45] Looking for a historical answer, Goodenough considered archeological evidence found in ancient Jewish synagogues and graveyards— evidence that seemed initially puzzling. For much Jewish religious archi-

tecture of the Hellenistic period contradicted received ideas about orthodox Jewish iconoclasm, featuring images not only of cups and
grapes—which could be dismissed as merely decorative—but also of
human and apparently divine beings. From that and other evidence,
Goodenough could infer that the seemingly quick transformation of
Jesus' teaching into a Greco-Roman religion had in fact not been so
quick but had a prehistory, with at least some communities within
"Verus Israel" having begun to assimilate pagan forms into their religious life well before the beginning of the common era.

This conclusion, however, led to further questions, for just as widespread as pagan symbols in Jewish religious architecture were signs of
antipathy to paganism in Jewish religious writings. So just what did
Greco-Roman symbols mean for the Jews who adopted them? More
questions followed, theoretical and historical: What happens when symbols migrate from one tradition to another? Was there a lingua franca of
symbolism in Hellenistic time? Do symbols have any abiding psychological significance?[46] Starting with a problem of Christian salvation history, Goodenough was led to pursue questions that were less theologically weighty but more religiohistorically intriguing.

The expansion of Goodenough's sympathetic religiohistorical curiosity as his career unfolded seemed impelled in part by memories of a happily pious early home life, together with an awareness of just how far
from that life he had traveled. The universe of faith his family knew before the two world wars was, he admits in his memoir, "basically a world
of illusion." But speaking of the "elements of truth in anything by which
men have lived with even partial success," Goodenough observes, "I have
clung to those elements from my boyhood while I have gone into . . . a
series of different worlds."[47] The informing imprint of Goodenough's
childhood religion, further, continued to keep him distant from those
iconic forms to which he devoted his thirteen-volume magnum opus. "I
was brought up in a Protestantism," he writes, "which, for all my work
with form-symbols, has made them essentially foreign to my personal experience" (68–69).

Intellectually a man of the Enlightenment, but still cherishing influential religious experiences of his youth, Goodenough appears, pace
Schleiermacher, as a cultured *respecter* of religion. Like the eighteenth-
century men of reason who were numbered among religion's cultured despisers, Goodenough maintained "a critical attitude toward hypotheses"
(29), including religious ones; but, not particularly like them, he still
found value in the human religious imagination. Thus, about the big ques-

tions, he expressed agnosticism: "What is the meaning of life?" he asks. "I cannot say. Does it in itself have any purpose or meaning? We do not know." Nevertheless, he continues, religion remains salutary: "How may we put meaning into life? . . . For this . . . we must have faith in our imaginations and their fantasies" (93). Reading Freud, Goodenough could speak of religion as an "illusion," but he did not, as Hume and Enlightenment extremists did, take it as the dreams of *sick* men. Truly, Goodenough liked religion, but almost regretfully, he believed in science.

THE FASCINATING STUFF OF RELIGIOUS LIFE

If both Harrison and Goodenough felt the need to abandon traditional theology to restore the truth of religion, just where in tradition did they find the truth to restore? Harrison gives us a straightforward answer: it is not exactly religion that is the focus of her attention but ritual, which for her links religion and art: "When I say 'religion,' I am instantly obliged to correct myself; it is not religion, it is ritual that absorbs me. . . . Art in some sense springs out of Religion . . . and between them is a connecting link, a bridge, and that bridge is Ritual. On that bridge, emotionally, I halt."[48]

For Goodenough, the corresponding bridge was wider. He describes the objects of his life research as "the dreams, the poetic fancies, the symbols of all kinds, which have gone into making up what men have called religion." He writes of these as "things" that "I as an individual have found valuable, and I as a historian see that our ancestors found valuable."[49] This focus on the *things* of religion—rituals, icons, myths, dreams—is a striking feature of the contemporary humanistic study of religion. Often finding it difficult to engage with traditional theologies, historians of religion attempt to elicit important truths from diverse symbolic forms. If these have had value to others, we hope they may also have value for us as well.

For the symbolic materials used by people distant from us in space or time promise to reveal much beyond them. Goodenough understood symbols as "the words or forms in which our sub-verbal thoughts are embodied" (54). Thus, by penetrating the meaning of symbols we can comprehend the unsaid, the ineffable in cultures and humankind. Harrison's mature stance toward the religious "representations" she studied is given expression in her last work on Greek religion, a short, generalizing synopsis of her views she titled her *Epilegomena to the Study of Greek Religion*. Now more in touch with the teachings of Freud than

Durkheim, she writes of how those teachings make meaningful the stuff of her dreaded "theology": "Psychology sets theology in a new and kinder light. Those of us who are free-thinkers used to think of it rationalistically as a bundle of dead errors, or at best as a subject dead and dry. But conceive of it in this new light and theology becomes a subject of passionate and absorbing interest, it is the science of the images of human desire, impulse, and aspiration."[50]

Theology thus becomes transformed into a "science of images," and the underlying object of religious studies is "human desire, impulse, and aspiration." For Harrison, as a "free-thinker," the study of religion is a self-consciously secular pursuit, but the symbolic material of religious traditions nevertheless remains of "passionate and absorbing interest"— valuable for what it can tell us about the deeper motives of humankind. For Goodenough, too, theology is replaced by a sort of science of images, which he pursued with extraordinary vigor in his thirteen volumes on Jewish symbols. But Goodenough had once cared dearly for theology and is similarly respectful to the "things" of religion he later studied. Writing of these things of religion, he declares, "To me they unquestionably have the most important place of anything in human life."[51] Through the beginning of the twenty-first century, scholars have continued—with various degrees of reverence, passion, and puzzlement—to use the stuff of religious traditions to throw light on the shadows of the human psyche.

Religious Objects and Scholars' Traditions

If, in the hearts of at least some religious studies virtuosos, traditional religious observance has given way to the practice of the science of religion, what are the links between their experience of their scientific objects— the stuff of religious life they study—and that of the religious traditions they once cherished, or didn't, or never really knew? While those links sometimes seem quite strong, they are not always straightforward.

Certainly, they may be more complex for a lapsed Methodist like Goodenough than for a scholar whose personal religious commitment is alive and well. Kristensen, we recall—the theology student turned historian of religions at Leiden—thought that by understanding "traditional" artifacts "from within" a scholar may "grow himself religiously." However dimly discerned across the abyss from ancient Egypt (or wherever), continuities could still be found between the scholars' own experiences and those of people acculturated to the symbolic forms that they study.

The latter, ideally, can stretch the former. This process may lead to un-orthodox worldviews, to be sure, but ones that individual religious lib-erals regularly manage to maintain.

Goodenough's relationship to the religious materials he studied, how-ever, was more problematic. Because his religious life was more alive in his past than during his scholarly present, he did not have much vital re-ligious experience for the objects of his study to expand. Instead, those objects seemed to represent an alien other in his present experience—an other that he managed to identify with his earlier pious self. Although he admits, as we have seen, that the ancient Jewish symbols of his magnum opus were "essentially foreign to [the] personal experience" of his Methodist boyhood, he nevertheless realizes "that what other religions, or other branches of Christianity, were doing through symbol and ritual, we were doing directly in immediate expression."[52] His objects of study seem not so much to have invoked the intense religious experience of his youth but to have helped keep it present for him; this presence then helped him find profound value in the religious material that he now treated with scholarly distance.

Harrison, by contrast, with little happy religious experience to re-member at all, discovers the study of ritual life as a new love to which she is passionately driven: "these ritual dances, this ritual drama, this bridge between art and life . . . it is things like these that I was all my life blindly seeking."[53] These objects were destined for her, she seems to be-lieve, and fulfilled a deep unconscious quest that was left unsatisfied be-fore. In this sense they stand in *contrast* to her past experience of tradi-tion, which never inspired her. If most scholars of religion do not talk of their passion for their material (or of their life in general) as expansively as Harrison, many are detached from their own traditions but are inex-plicably drawn to study the traditions of others in ways similar to hers. Perhaps even most of all for people without well-formed religious un-derstandings of their own, the stuff of other religious worlds can appear somehow numinous.

Religious Sensibilities Twice Refracted

Drawn to their objects of study in different ways, scholars of religion find in them striking meanings—often larger, more revealing, or at least with more varied and interesting nuances than their own traditions (or lack of them) seem to provide. In offering these larger meanings to people who do not easily find them in the modern Western world, the history of

religions presents them twice refracted. First, it presents them through
the religions of *others*—distant either in cultural space or historical time
or both. Understanding the effects of this first refraction, especially at the
present historical moment, calls for a consideration of the particular
colonial and postcolonial predicaments in which historians of religions
have found themselves. Second, history of religions presents its objects
not directly to readers' religious imaginations—whose existence in themselves they may deny—but to their aesthetic sensibilities, which can assimilate larger meanings in theologically neutral ways. This second refraction will lead us in part 2 to a detailed examination of some aesthetic
moves found in religiohistorical writing. But let us first consider briefly
contemporary religion scholars' postcolonial dilemmas. In encountering
others' traditions somewhere in the middle grounds of empathy and
analysis, how might historians of religion approach the collective burden
of past Western colonialist sin? Although the burden cannot be avoided,
for scholars who have taken religious people seriously, the sins do not
seem mortal.

As a twentieth-century Western enterprise that attempts to encompass
the traditions of the world, the history of religions certainly maintains
something of the spirit of imperialism. It would, moreover, not be possible in its present form without profiting from its share of colonialist
booty. A great deal of the stuff that intrigues us from Asia and Africa has
arrived on Western shores through the offices of colonialist regimes that
worked from practical, self-interested motives: administrators studied
native law in order to rule more effectively; missionaries attempted to unravel primitive myths in the process of making converts to Western
faiths. Further, endemic to the work of many of these, as well as to the
work of apparently innocent folklorists and scholars, has been the image
of the colonized subject as an alien other that cries for enlightening Western ways. At least this much the extensive recent scholarship on colonialism makes clear.[54]

At the same time, however, to the extent that the study of others' religions has filled an existential void experienced by some Western intellectuals, the other presented in colonialist discourse—particularly in its
romanticized versions—has testified to our lack, not to our superiority.
Too often we have looked for depth in others' traditions just because we
couldn't always find it easily in our own. Certainly, other traditions do
not always—or even usually—reveal the same secrets to us that they do
to those within them. We are likely, moreover, to differ among ourselves
as to the real meanings of those secrets, just as do people within the tra-

ditions themselves. The inner worlds that historians of religions try to penetrate are subtle if nothing else—elusive and changing, but also, we like to think, apprehensible at deep levels of understanding. A Western project, history of religions serves Western religiocultural needs, but in doing so, it often lets non-Western voices be heard in ways more profound than they have been before. It is true that these are usually not just the same voices heard on their home ground, but, transformed in the imagination of the scholar, they may reverberate more tellingly here.[55]

Moreover, the subtle reception of others' traditions by historians of religion has fed into a body of knowledge that is a discourse not so much about the Orient as about religious traditions. As we have seen in the work of Goodenough and Harrison, that knowledge encompasses Western cultures and histories, too, in ways—particularly evident in *Themis*—not always flattering to Western self-esteem. Thus, although the history of religions has in fact drawn on different orientalist knowledges, as an intellectual project attempting to generalize about religious traditions, it is not focused on an orientalist stereotype of any one subordinated civilization. It is as political as any knowledge is, to be sure, but the imperialism that drives it is sooner that of the Enlightenment intellect—an attempt to comprehend all there is within a single purview—than any specific colonialist agenda.

Nevertheless, orientalist images have pervaded scholarship in the history of religions and linger on, outliving the old colonialist era.[56] The part that history of religions may best be equipped to play in helping redeem the West from its collective colonialist guilt is to wean it away from those images. In doing so, we are likely to end up creating a picture of humankind as a complex whole—not of stereotypes or even archetypes but of diverse identities moving in counterpoint within and between cultures. In thus helping to depict the real religious problems (and possibilities) inherent in complicated ongoing processes of cultural and economic globalization, history of religions can be politically progressive.

Leavening an aggrandizing Enlightenment vision with a more integral plurality, history of religions is still distinguished by an enlightened analytic style that is not shared by all writers who have come in touch with the religions of the East. The influx of information about the exotic traditions of new imperial domains was not assimilated by everyone with an air of scholarly detachment. Some people tried more direct experiential means: in addition to the new science of religion, the turn of the last century also saw a resurgence in occultisms—new religious syntheses that promised adherents access to ageless divinities. In ways parallel to those of scholars bringing different traditions together into studies of "comparative religion," members of new occult movements mixed and matched religious traditions—from Egypt, India, the Rosicrucian West—into some dramatic pastiche.[57] From this cultural vantage point, scholars of religion can appear as those among the educated elite who were intrigued by others' traditions but whose personal tough-mindedness (usually) kept them from active participation in the Order of the Golden Dawn or the Theosophical Society. If a number of early religionists were also members of the Society for Psychical Research, that organization at least held fast to what it took as principles of science, fostering a culture of healthy skepticism about specific psychic occurrences and of the consequent need for testing and experiment. Maintaining a scientifically oriented vision of the world, rational historians of religions tended to appropriate the numinousness they still saw in others' traditions, not, like occult revivalists (or some of their own more romantic colleagues), through some experience they might see as spiritual, but through their sense of the aesthetic.

For sympathetic secular-minded scholars, this approach to the stuff of traditions through the aesthetic did not prove to be the troubling move it could be for the theologically inclined. Since Schleiermacher, resonances between religion and aesthetics had been discerned in the German theological tradition, where by the turn of the twentieth century a common reaction was to insist on a clear distinction between the two: this was an important theological context for Otto's affirmation of the holy as a category of its own.[58] Nevertheless, Otto, for one, still seemed in spite of himself to sense religious reverberations in "the aesthetic experience of nature,"[59] and non- (or anti-)theological intellectuals like Goodenough or Harrison, when they considered the issue, had no reason to find it particularly problematic. Quite the contrary—Harrison, as we might expect, waxes enthusiastic: "A ritual dance, a ritual procession with vestments and lights and banners, move me as no sermon, no hymn, no picture, no poem has ever moved me."[60] Religious traditions for her here seem to offer the most powerful aesthetics imaginable, and she reveled in them.

In its appropriation of what is religious for others as something aesthetically comprehensible to modern, naturalistically minded humankind, religiohistorical endeavor presents its own version of the oft-noted displacement of religious experience in the secular world.[61] But the responses of historians of religions have not been fundamentally political, like Marx's, or psychological, like Freud's. Responding to their religious objects aesthetically, many scholars in their writing transform their reactions into aesthetic objects of their own creation.

In doing so, successful interpretive writers usually manage to wield an imaginative synthesis of the opposite poles seen in the field. The explicit knowledge they offer is in the Enlightenment mold: analytic, grounded in a naturalistic worldview, oriented toward some larger academic question. But the details of tradition they show us lead to a romantic vision: a wonder at the power of myth, ritual, and religious life together with a sense that these may lead to the profoundest insights about humankind. Most scholars who have made an impact in the field have articulated a naturalist argument but have also demonstrated a broad human view.

These certainly include the five writers presented in the introduction and who will figure prominently in the next part of this book. Jonathan Z. Smith—of influential contemporary scholars perhaps the one most consciously indebted to the British rationalist tradition—treats his human subjects much more sympathetically than did his nineteenth-century predecessors. His presentations of small-scale religions as traditions of problem solving, as will be seen in chapter 5, evoke feelings not of condescension toward primitives engaged in bad science but of empathy at human beings caught in very difficult situations. The scholars more celebratory of the symbolic material itself—Geertz, say, or Doniger—present it from a convinced naturalistic perspective and orient it to vital intellectual questions as they probe its human depth. Even Eliade's vision of a nexus of symbols in sacred space and time—whatever its theological groundings—has been effective just because it is framed in neutral, nontheological terms. And Dumézil's vision, although sweeping across a very broad Indo-European horizon, is always grounded in thorough philological research. The peculiar aesthetic of religiohistorical writing is built just from bringing together the two poles of the field in creative ways. An analysis of this aesthetic is developed in part 2.

PART TWO

The Art of Writing on Religion

HISTORY OF RELIGIONS' DISTINCTIVE AESTHETIC, it seems to me, is determined by the two faces of the field seen in part 1—the appreciative and the analytical. For the art found in the most successful historians of religion plays on the tension between a romantic evocation of the human imagination and a rationally enlightened, scientifically true, analysis. Although that tension can produce engaging writing in any number of humanistic fields, in religious studies it often produces a distinctive sublime edge of its own.

I begin, in chapter 3, by exploring the ways in which the historian of religion seems to work as a creative writer. Chapter 4 then looks at the analytic challenges presented by some different types of religious materials and the characteristic aesthetic strategies to which these lead. The classic examples of contemporary scholarship examined there will be further probed in chapter 5. There I reflect on the distinctive qualities of the experience evoked by exemplary religiohistorical work, on the dynamics of the "religiohistorical sublime."

CHAPTER 3

A Creative Process

What does it mean to say that interpretive writing on religion is an art? All that is entailed in the creation and appreciation of works of art has been the subject of long philosophical discussion, so thinking about the aesthetics of interpretive writing could easily lead us into extensive ruminations on classical mimesis, romantic expressionism, and contemporary speculation about the role of institutions in the creative process. We will not, however, let ourselves be so led: all three of these broad approaches to aesthetic theory will be considered, but briefly and schematically. Still, situating the process of interpretive writing even sketchily within the main historical lines of philosophical aesthetics can, I think, help us better understand what many historians of religions actually do.

A ROMANTIC WORLD, A CLASSICAL STYLE, A MODERN IDIOM

Deriving from the tension between the scientific and imaginative sides of its practitioners' sensibilities, the practice of interpretive writing on religion brings together important aspects of the neoclassical and romantic attitudes toward art. Nearly half a century ago M. H. Abrams characterized these two aesthetic temperaments through the metaphors of the mirror and the lamp, which were used by writers of each temperament respectively to envision artistic works. The mirror of the (neo)classicists reflects an external reality: according to most classical and Enlightenment theory, artists in their work give an idealized representation of something outside themselves. Romantic theorists, by contrast, emphasizing internal vision and self-expression, spoke of the work of art as a lamp that illumines reality through its own light. (Another recurring romantic metaphor was the work of art as a fountain, expressing the artist's overflowing emotions.)[1] Understood as an art, interpretive writing on religion seems to me to give a vital place to the romantic expressive voice: after all, I was led to an aesthetic conception of writing on religion by a sense that successful writers manage to "communicate a vision" of their materials. Not a restrained, if enlightened, rationalism, much less any religious orthodoxy, but a kind of creative expression is crucial, I believe, if a piece of religiohistorical writing is to move others. This expression, however, is not exactly the self-expression of the romantic poet, which was valued as a usually exuberant outpouring of a unique creative genius. The vision expressed by the scholar instead needs visibly to reflect some outside realities, somehow to represent the religious worlds of others. Religiohistorical writing is thus *also* a mirror with an external referent. Neoclassical and romantic stances therefore seem inevitably to interact with one another in practical work.

Even when offered as a mirror, then, interpretive writing still usually reflects a world filled with the symbolic stuff that has drawn romantic poets and students of religion alike. Both religionists and romantics seem, moreover, to have been attracted to symbolic forms for similar reasons: the ways in which symbols intimate unspeakably large worlds. "The infinite [can] be brought to manifestation on the surface," wrote the romantic man of letters August Schlegel at the beginning of the nineteenth century, "only symbolically, in pictures and signs."[2] Students of religion, too, are fascinated by the ways religious symbols may reflect larger realities. Harrison's Greek rituals and Goodenough's Jewish icons all give the worlds they inhabit the potential for unusual depth. At the same time, the infinite possibilities for interpretation presented by symbolic forms present problems of limitation and definition that inevitably lead back to solutions grounded in more classically precise ways of thinking.

Not the least of these is evident in the interpretive writer's frequent predilection for pattern and structure. Romantically attempting to express their visions of these symbols, yet aware of the seemingly infinite possibilities these suggest, interpretive writers often elicit crucial meanings less from nuances of detail than from recurring *configurations* of symbol and myth. This recourse to ideal forms is well within the spirit of a neoclassical rationalism: in Enlightenment theory, the work of art as a mirror was taken not only as a representation of reality but as a representation that reflected "that Rule and Order, and Harmony, which we find in the visible Creation."[3] If the romantic side of the interpretive writer looks for depth, the neoclassical looks for rule and order, for pattern and type. The latter especially, then, often serve as standard-bearers for a kind of scientific writing about religion[4]—writing that may be further enhanced by a classical literary style: balanced and rational, following a mimetic ideal.

In this way interpretive writers paint a lucid picture that highlights their material's significant forms, its distinctive features seen from a particular perspective.[5] These can then be subsequently regarded from a distance—if not always with much aesthetic appreciation, then at least with the eye of our science. Thus, the vision of Greek ritual outlined by Harrison in *Ancient Art and Ritual,* her culminating (although not her best) work on the subject, revealed some intriguing detail but was for the most part generalizing and schematic. It presented an angle on the rituals she loved that she thought would give her readers a broad-stroked comprehension of what she found fascinating in them.[6] If, as romantic artists, we attempt in our writing to evoke some of the power we see in the stuff of religious life, as scientists we represent that stuff in an ordered array, having considered it from a perspective that lends it some general import.

Alongside its orientation toward mimesis, (neo)classical theory was also concerned with rhetoric: the created work was useless if it did not affect its audience.[7] Artists followed prescribed rules so that their works might affect others; art was thus inevitably bound up with life. By the beginning of the twenty-first century, this pragmatic connection between art and life has been extended to encompass not only the effect of the artist on his or her audience but also the ways in which institutions shape the actions and consciousnesses of them both.[8] For writing on religion, these include not only the world historical stage of colonialism, capitalism, and market economies but also the more specific market factors of the academy: tenure committees with their own ideas about canons of scholarship; forward-looking publishers trying to anticipate the next intellectual wave; and not least, I hope, colleagues beset with the prose of students and specialists, wishing they'd be able to read something engaging for a change.

It is by providing the last of these constituents with an engrossing read, I think, that interpretive writers are likely to find their greatest success. Language and area specialists may suspect religionists' philological and cultural expertise: Harrison did not find a steady academic position early in her career because she was not perceived as a "sound scholar" who had studied classical languages since childhood.[9] What is interesting about interpretive scholars' ideas, further, is more often a novel application than originality per se. Like Harrison, many interpretive writers take enlightening ideas from other disciplines to the romantic world of religion—just as often riding the last intellectual wave as cresting on the new. Less than philological acuity or brand-new ideas, successful interpretive scholars have been able to sell a distinctive presentation of what they see—an engaging and insightful vision into the ways of religious humanity.

In reflecting on their presentations of others' religious visions to enlightened academics, religionists of very different stripes have revivified a central term of romantic thought: *imagination,* taken in its Coleridgean heyday to invoke the wellsprings of artistic endeavor and thus suggesting positive ideas of creativity and freedom.[10] Using the term in reference to religious people dignifies the ways in which those people exercise human capacities to aspire to higher ideals, meet new challenges, live well, and dream. It gives interpretive writers a way to show their respect for the religious life of others without necessarily affirming the validity of others' objects of devotion.

At the same time, scholars of religion also speak of the role of imagination in their own work. In the introduction to his *Imagining Religion,* Jonathan Z. Smith suggests that religion itself as an object of study has been "imagine[d]" by Western scholars of the last few centuries. Although much in world cultures can be and has been characterized as religious "by one criterion or another . . . *there is no data for religion*" in any explicit sense. Religion, rather, "is created for the scholar's analytic purposes by his imaginative acts of comparison and generalization."[11] Describing the study of religion as an analytic endeavor, Smith also underscores, with his invocation of the scholar's imagination, the creative processes it entails.

Parallel, then, to the "religious imagination" of which interpretive writers sometimes speak, perhaps there is something like the "religiohistorical imagination"—a derivative faculty that is wont to perform rational acts on peculiarly fascinating human materials.[12] This propensity seems to be something endemic to modern intellectuals caught between the allure of the "data for religion" they find and their predisposition to analyze them. It develops as we reimagine others' imaginings in terms of our own insights and determinisms, hoping to express our visions in ways that people in our own communities will find intellectually compelling.

CONSTRUCTING RELIGIOHISTORICAL OBJECTS

The creative processes elicited by the religiohistorical imagination—as well as the genre of created objects that result—can themselves be graphically imagined. Smith's dictum that the data of religion are where we find them, although in his practice married to a highly enlightened rational project, at the same time suggests an expressivist truth also congenial to a romantic temperament: religion, for interpretive writers, is what elicits a religiohistorical response; it is what inspires them to create a religiohistorical object—that sculpted representation of the data that, through its sharp and poignant reflection of reality, we hope will move our colleagues and a wider public. Discussing romantic conceptions of artistic creation, the philosopher Charles Taylor adopts the artist's voice: "I am taking something, a vision, a sense of things, which was inchoate and only partly formed, and giving it a specific sense of shape."[13] To reflect on what is entailed in this process of religiohistorical creation, I will begin with an image appropriate, I think, to a field that takes a scientific temper and an artistic vision to materials often difficult to fathom—an image adapted from science fiction.

UFOs on the Horizon

The vague and fleeting intuition with which a writer on religions often begins first appears to me, at least, as an unidentified flying object hovering about my materials: a UFO, for short. As the glimmering origin of a piece of religiohistorical writing, this intuition appears as neither a mirror nor a lamp but has something of the properties of both. Emerging on the horizon where the writer's vision seems to penetrate other worlds, a UFO reflects those worlds but shines through the lights the writer sees in it; it seems to have origins in an alien reality, but maybe it is just a mirage emerging from the writer's wishful thinking. If a UFO in the distance is indeed a mirage, it will likely disappear when it is approached through further research. If it still seems real, it may eventually inspire the writer who focuses on it to create a publicly perceptible religiohistorical object—a construct made of, say, Greek myths or Jewish symbols. Paradoxically, however, the more clearly visible this created object appears to others, the more evidently constructed it is likely to appear on close examination—*reflecting* a genuine reality, perhaps, but from a particular point of view. The finished religiohistorical object is thus conceived as an art object in the romantic mold: suggesting something important about its model, conveying something about the writer's vision, and beginning as an intuition. Out of the many fleeting, sometimes bizarre, hunches that first appear to us as UFOs, the finished object takes shape from one that leads to a sustainable truth.[14]

The emergence of a finished religiohistorical object from a barely discernible UFO can be a slow process. In their initial stages, UFOs seem to be communicating messages from other cultural or historical worlds or truths of the great universal psyche. Lurking somewhere between imagination and reality, they remain suspicious and are usually unverifiable. Even though hardly visible, they can nevertheless seem important, so we may pull out lenses of different sorts to focus on the UFOs from various angles: culture-theory telescopes, textual microscopes, postmodern kaleidoscopes.[15] If and when a UFO comes more clearly into view, we may get excited and begin to talk about it.

It is the act of reporting on these unidentified flying objects—trying to point them out to others, to convince those around us of their existence—that may be the most crucial event in changing our own understanding of their reality. Once publicly described, they become *less* unidentified; as their identity becomes established, they are less liable to fly away. Out of fleeting UFOs dimly seen by us as individuals, we create identified religiohistorical objects capable of moving others. This image of UFOs gradually coming into focus and taking concrete shape through the act of their identification presents the process of writing on religion as a transformation of our initial, fleeting, private intuitions about alien realities into weighty public objects. It takes place through a dynamic of private vision and public articulation, of imitation and construction, of listening to alien voices and giving them an expression that resonates in our own world.

Objectification, Perspective, Focus, and Depth

Deriving from the culture of the middle of the twentieth century and applicable to writing practiced into the twenty-first, my UFO metaphor—with its prioritizing of the "object"—carries an agenda that seems distinctively more modern than postmodern. And in fact, the attention to plural voices in the scholar and the studied that come to the fore in postmodern—and especially postcolonial—discourse are not here necessarily brought to the fore. Writers excited less by the different surfaces of their material than by UFOs launched *from* it—and who are then impelled to construct objects that hold together on their own—do not always seem so sensitive to *all* the subjective dimensions that their materials may elicit. For these writers, attention to plural voices in themselves or those whom they portray may seem less important than creating an aesthetically moving work.

But in the best of writers, a singular voice indicates a rational limitation of infinite symbolic possibilities, not an objectivization of others' subjectivities. Although interpretive writing may sometimes depict people schematically and abstractly—as scientific objects—in itself it ideally constitutes an aesthetic object capable of reflecting aspects of their subjectivities vividly and deeply. The potential to shine is inherent, I think, in the subjective religious lives of many people everywhere, but these religious lives often reflect visibly into our world only when presented through some sharp angles of focus. Those angles, in turn, are given shape by a writer's own subjective perspective. In interpretive writing, the subjectivities of others shine through the subjectivity of the writer.

The interpretive writer's subjective perspective is not necessarily personal and intimate—as is, ideally, that of a romantic artist. Yet it is in an important sense unique—framed by a writer's idiosyncratic predilections, obsessions, and prejudices, as well as by his or her particular experiences of social and educational institutions. It is the product of a writer's individual life history. At the same time, individual lives are lived in larger historical arenas: both the idiosyncratic and the institutional factors shaping our perspectives are informed by a zeitgeist's immediate enthusiasms and a culture's long-lived understandings. If, as most of us like to think, our personal outlook is somehow distinctively our own, it is, in many of its essentials, also common, in greater or lesser degrees, to wide spheres of humanity encircling us. Moreover, the outlook of religion scholars is regularly refracted through that peculiar modern academic ambivalence about religion discussed in part 1. Thus, even though our initial vision of a UFO may be private, in the sense that we haven't been able to formulate it yet in ways that others can see, the perspective we eventually bring to it is liable to resonate in important ways with our readers.

Constructing a public religiohistorical object inspired by our initial private sighting of a UFO entails bringing that perception into clear focus. A distant UFO, launched as our vision makes contact with our data, begins as a shimmering reflection of an alien world, one that is not only rather pale but also a little fuzzy. To serve as a framework for our construction, it needs to be in focus. Although my discussion of perspective called on romantic concepts of individual self and collective *geist,* considering focus brings to mind some neoclassical norms of clarity and proportion, of foregrounding ideal exemplars.[16] As will be discussed in chapter 4, ways of focusing are many and depend in good part on the lay of the land surveyed. Scrutinizing an ethnological landscape, for example, our vision may focus on a specific set of cultural meanings, with key concepts clustering around a few central symbols. Are we doing a comparison between different civilizations? Then the distinct religiocultural complexes we encounter may throw each other into relief, mutually determining the outlines they will each reveal. Alternatively, we may cast our gaze about widely, descrying categories rooted in the natural universe, the human mind, or some dynamic of interaction between the two; working from an abstract frame, we present a panorama. In all cases what seems crucial in focus is a clarity of outline that reveals points where apparently diverse materials converge. This concept of focus can then help us formulate a more precise meaning for the notion of depth that has been repeatedly invoked as crucial for successful interpretive work.

Depth of vision in interpretive writing seems to be a product of sharp focus and wide perspective. Ultimately, the religiohistorical objects we construct are made up of the detailed myths, histories, and human dramas that are the stuff of religious life. Wide perspectives give the human details we identify some space to resonate; they let the stories we tell about other worlds intimate truths about our own. A sharp focus brings suggestive truths together in what appears as a scientifically believable fact; they let our human details make a case. A religiohistorical object "communicates the depth" that its creator sees in his or her material when it elicits a response from an audience that is at once affectively resonating and intellectually graspable; it brings large, less-than-conscious, expanses of a reader's emotional resources into play with intellectual truths he or she understands. Even especially fuzzy UFOs, then, can be worth pursuing, for the radical depth of focus we need to bring to them may in the end elicit particularly broad perspectives. Drawing on outward analytic perspectives and inward emotional subjectivities, this sense of depth ideally found in interpretive writing—although long implicitly valued by many—has not always been explicitly respected in religious studies scholarship.

In particular, this privileging of depth in writing stands in contrast to earlier ideals of phenomenological description still found among religionists. Husserl, in his philosophical phenomenology used terms such as *epoche* (from the Greek, meaning "suspension") and *bracketing* (*Ein-*

klammerung) to refer to processes through which investigators could free themselves from every presupposition—including that of "the natural world"—in examining their objects. In going "back to the things themselves," Husserl aimed to describe phenomena "uninterpreted according to any opinions or theories or metaphysical points of view." [17] Such perspectiveless description is, in our terms, necessarily flat, without any of the depth found in compelling interpretive writing. Fortunately, most historians of religion who have talked about bracketing use the term in ways more relaxed than Husserl did, rarely really attempting to approach his—to us, flat—ideal. As a specific practical concept, an idea of bracketing one's presuppositions is probably most crucial to scholars with explicit confessional beliefs who attempt consciously to disengage from them when contemplating other traditions. In other contexts, it usually seems like a somewhat negative way of referring to the attempts at open-minded, empathetic understanding in which most scholars in the human sciences in one way or another engage.[18]

Very frequently, pieces of loosely phenomenological empathetic description are crucial elements in interpretive writing, but compelling interpretive work binds these pieces together through sharp arguments. Certainly, if we have no empathetic understanding of our materials, the constructs we create from them are likely to be unsubtle at best and may offer badly distorted reflections of the reality they should represent. When put together well, however, a construct will present not only an adequate representation of those materials but also a broadly conceived argument about them. Looming above a flat horizon, it reflects both sides of it: "them" and "us," "data" and "analysis." Our constructs appear real to the extent that they bridge those two sides with vitality and credibility. Indeed, paradoxically, the better constructed they are, the more they seem to correspond to a reality—not just the reality "of the things themselves" but a deeper reality, too, one intimating our understandings about a cultural world, the human psyche, and/or the workings of religious traditions. In part 3, I will turn to the kinds of truth potentially reflected by religiohistorical objects, but first we need to examine more closely the ways in which they are constructed.

CHAPTER 4

Other Scholars' UFOs

Bringing evocative materials together in rationally cogent ways, interpretive writers try to make arguments that are both emotionally and intellectually compelling. Their arguments must stand, however, in a world of diverse cultural and religious sensibilities and, more crucial for our discussion here, of increasingly fragmented intellectual life. The UFOs with which interpretive writers begin—intuitions glimmering on the horizon—may gain considerable weight from carefully constructed arguments, but fissured intellectual grounds still offer religiohistorical constructs no sure place to rest. The arguments that bind these together are thus of necessity *internally* coherent. Nevertheless, decisive dynamics of a construct's internal coherence derive from factors outside it. Because a construct is made up from examples culled out of materials at hand, it is shaped by the particular lay of the land against which its author's intuitive UFO first appeared. This chapter, then, examines the types of internal coherence found in interpretive writers' arguments, categorizing them according to the dimensions of the terrain that provides the material of their construction. It reads as a sort of manual of religiohistorical engineering.

DIMENSIONS OF COHERENCE

Attention to the internal coherence of our arguments necessitates some consideration of logical norms that differ from those unreflectively held by many of us bred in an age of material science, norms that take for granted the existence of a firm foundation. A foundation approach to truth elaborates a metaphor of architectural design: valid knowledge, like a well-engineered building, must be constructed carefully from the ground up. In a foundation argument, an authoritative statement must find a basis in some unquestioned fact; it is built up step-by-step from an accepted basis in truth. What is important is that the steps and the grounds both be firm.[1]

This approach to crafting arguments continues, as a practical ideal at least, in many physical sciences and may still have an appeal to humanists of scientistic bent. It has never had much real currency in most humanistic pursuits, however, and is today often explicitly disparaged.[2] Although civil engineers continue to pay close attention to the foundations of the buildings they design, historians of religion, like most humanists, now craft their arguments in a largely postfoundational world. There, causal links are rarely clear, and grounds tend to shift according to who is standing on them: scholarship at the beginning of the twenty-first century has made us only too well aware of possibly insidious political motivations behind even the most apparently noble theorizing, including that of some revered religionists.[3] But even with a generous view of our colleagues' motives, it is often difficult to find much common ground in religious studies. Scholars examine different materials, employ alternative analytic frameworks, and have their own—sometimes highly idiosyncratic—(ir)religious and/or metaphysical perspectives. There is little authoritative truth there, either empirical or theoretical. Like most other humanists, we have long been forced to make the pieces of our arguments depend not on any authoritative foundation but on one another. We thus invoke an alternative principle of validity in knowledge, one informing much idealist epistemology and most practical logic—that of coherence.[4]

Strategies for making arguments through coherence necessarily differ from those for making arguments through foundation. Instead of trying to identify specific causes, we look for other kinds of relationships among our data—often the "patterns" and "structures" endemic to religionists—of which some are more explicitly coherent than others. Instead of leading our arguments back to a foundation, we try to show that they encompass all the relevant data. We thus get two kinds of criteria for judging these self-coherent arguments: on the one hand, the explicitness of the coherence, its tightness, the evident cohesiveness with which apparently circumstantial evidence comes together; on the other, the comprehensiveness with which it covers its field—it should be able to account for everything it needs to explain. Usually, we find that tight coherence and comprehensiveness of argument are not easily compatible and that we must make trade-offs between the two.

These inevitable trade-offs will be illustrated in examples by four of the important contemporary writers on religion whose achievements I sketched out in the introduction. The historian of religion Mircea Eliade and the anthropologist Clifford Geertz, we recall, together frame the interpretive writing of this study, typifying in their works its prime complementary genres—Eliade, the sage with the broad view, writing comparative treatises at once magisterial and affecting; Geertz, the master of the suggestive detail, finding important meanings in everyday human dramas. Georges Dumézil and Wendy Doniger then put different dimensions of broad view and suggestive detail into play in their very different styles of interpreting myth. Dumézil, an Indo-Europeanist, usually keeps the grand panorama in sight but is precise in his treatment of necessarily spare philological examples. Doniger, an Indologist, is focused in her materials but generous in her evocative examples and happy with the ambiguities of Hindu myth. In their own ways, all four scholars have managed to engage their readers mightily in their materials. The different strategies these scholars have used toward this end depend in part on the different types of horizons on which their UFOs first appeared—on the lays of the land they saw when they were inspired to create their work. As types, the four different horizons seen by our writers are determined by two variables: *visions* of local or universal import and *fields* of compact or extensive materials.

Visions are primarily *local* or *universal* according to the breadth of their implications. A local vision reveals the particularity of religions in a specific area or within a specific community; a universal one suggests something more about religious traditions in general or about human religious perception. A vision—the sighting of a UFO—is not the same thing as a claim, an articulated statement, and not all universal visions lead to explicit universal claims. Sometimes, of course, they do, as will be seen in Eliade's work. Just as often, however, a universal vision stands behind a more modest claim about a particular culture but leaves this claim open to very wide implications; this, I will suggest, is the case with Doniger's early, much-acclaimed study of Shiva.[5]

Whichever type of vision lies behind them, our intuited UFOs appear against a horizon—a field offering materials out of which a religiohistorical object may be constructed. These fields can be either *compact* or *extensive*. A compact field consists of a single, if often complex, religiocultural terrain—Geertz's ethnological examples, say, or Doniger's

Hindu India—moreover, as with the sets of scriptural texts on which Doniger often works, it is also sometimes conceivably finite. An extensive field, by contrast, presents variety in religiocultural context. It brings together different religious worlds, as with the different Indo-European societies that Dumézil's comparative studies survey; it is, moreover, as in much of Eliade's work, often clearly infinite.

These two ideal axes of our typology—visions of local or universal import; fields of compact or extensive materials—describe the first sighting of the UFO, the moment of our inspiration. That inspiration, if valid, derives from our own grasp of others' reality at extremes of consciousness, both ours and theirs: UFOs begin to appear at the limits of our own imaginative horizon and promise an insight into the ways others deal with their own limitedness. Now problems with limits—human mortality, the dissolution of individual finitude in community, helplessness at one's fate—are at the heart of much religious life and thus of much writing on religion. And related issues of limits, as will be seen in chapter 5, also figure crucially in classic theorizing on the sublime. The four possible combinations of the variables in our typology, then, in configuring the limits of the religiohistorical objects we eventually create, frame types of which each presents its own characteristic sublime edge. But to display that edge, our objects must first be firmly constructed.

PATTERNS OF LOCAL ORDER: THICK AND ROBUST

In examining the ways in which the logical coherence of our four examples shapes each as an aesthetic whole, I will start with writers grounded in the concrete, those looking with a particularistic eye for patterns of local order. Here, a frequent approach in religious studies is to surround the UFO hovering around our materials from many sides at once. Because we think we have seen down to the crux of a particular situation, we recognize our insight as something more than *only* psychological, say, or cultural, or sociological. Our insight may, however, be reflected from all these points of view, which we proceed to outline in their interrelationship. Our object then becomes identified as a complex of particular cultural, psychological, and sociological factors.

If my characterization of the identified object in religious studies as the concrete embodiment of insights is viable anywhere, it is no doubt viable here, in this many-faceted crystallization of local patterns. For both writers discussed in this section employ methods that have been described in language of weight and body. The first, Clifford Geertz, characterizes his compact and many-layered descriptions of cultural events as *thick.* The second, Georges Dumézil, proposes various, more extensive and abstract, delineations of ancient Indo-European society that come together in a model of the sort that some natural scientists speak of as *robust,* that is, one deriving from a well-defined structure that can support different analytic perspectives at once.[6]

Thick Description: Cultural Analysis as Fiction

Thick description, as many readers already know, refers to a deep and radical contextualization of meaning that can make what at first sight seem familiar activities appear almost as alien as extraterrestrial phenomena. In what is probably his most famous example of thick description, Geertz discusses a cockfight in Bali.[7] At first glance, we might want to place this on our phenomenological map somewhere between horse racing and craps—personal wagering on the outcome of an animal contest. But Geertz shows us that this phenomenon really is something *other* than these, that it won't fit neatly on any universal, decontextualized list. He does this by showing us all the meanings of the cockfight: the psychological attachment of the Balinese for his "cock," which makes the same pun in Balinese as it does in English; the meaning of animality in Balinese culture; the political and kinship factors involved in betting on the match; even the economics of the wager. But in showing us how these phenomena really are different from the gambling and wagering we are familiar with, Geertz also makes them *comprehensible* to us. Geertz's aliens are aliens with whom we can communicate.

Because his thick descriptions attempt to reflect the reality of a complex human situation through selected significant detail, Geertz can compare them to "fictions" in the sense that they are "something made," "something fashioned," not in the sense that they are "false [or] unfactual."[8] Now our principal criteria for judging literary fictions are usually not neatness and elegance: if a work of fiction is too elegant, we tend to think it contrived; if it is too neat, we find it difficult to believe. An effective piece of fiction usually presents a whole that we grasp as *profoundly* coherent but not simply or explicitly so. In the same way, a "fiction" in Geertz's academic sense is believable not because it neatly elucidates links of coherence but because it comprehends a complex, concrete situation as a meaningful totality. In the trade-offs between explicitness of relationships and comprehensiveness of scope in coherence arguments, the accent here falls heavily on the latter. We see that *all* the aspects of the situation really do relate closely to one another, even if we may not see precisely how.

How does the aesthetic reception of this type of argument work? Although we find a literary fiction believable in part because it is not simple, we are likely to find it compelling because it draws us into engaging human scenes. Thick description seems to work aesthetically in much the same way, by drawing on the power of engrossing human situations. Geertz makes his aliens at once comprehensible and engaging by letting us understand their many motivations—economic, sociological, political. We can identify with them as people—jealous, generous, afflicted, or triumphant. Like literary fiction, thick description presents us with another world that seems not only to be believable but also to be one in which we can ourselves become involved. Writers of the two genres, however, have contrasting challenges: novelists have to work on the believability of their interesting inventions; thick describers, however, have to build up engrossing webs of significance around their facts.

In harnessing the affective power of veracity, moreover, a thick describer faces some literary constraints that a novelist doesn't. The coherence of a novelist's world can usually be presented through a neater narrative line, without the recurrent reflections and abstractions of academic writing. The characters may be more exciting than the ordinary folk of ethnography, although religious studies has its exciting figures, too, not to mention exotic settings. But while academic writing limits the fluidity of imagination, it heightens its effects by linking imagined realities to the factually true. Because we believe that a complex, human thick description really is grounded in the concretely real, it is that much more compelling. And, conversely, because we are made to see that the distant religiocultural worlds described contain vital complex people, some details of the worlds in which they live may seem worth making an effort to understand.

Abstract Models, Exact and Robust

Whereas Geertz describes comprehensible aliens he can talk to, Dumézil points us toward a UFO that landed thousands of years ago, in a bygone millennium—one that has, nevertheless, left traces to be tracked down. So, while Geertz builds his objects out of layers of meaning derivable from an immediate ethnographical present, Dumézil culls vast amounts of mythological material in order to make an objective argument about the prehistoric past.[9] In particular, he wants to reveal the dimensions of a specific tripartite structure in Indo-European society, where he sees priests, rulers, and commoners having some definite mutual relationships. Geertz, for his descriptions of complex and very human webs of meaning, borrowed the term "thick description" from semiotic studies.[10] But to examine the ways in which Dumézil develops his more abstract and idealized structures we can look to more exact sciences.

There are two important ways in which models from the natural sciences become increasingly overdetermined or, as some scientists say, gain robustness. First, several middle-sized systems of knowledge can help confirm a larger system that encompasses them: for example, when all the different subspecies of physics help support general physical theory. Second, several different analytic techniques appear separately to confirm a specific, if difficult, hypothesis. Here, when treating complex problems with a number of differently simplified models, as the population biologist Richard Levins says, "[O]ur truth is the intersection of independent lies."[11]

Dumézil's reconstruction of ancient Indo-European mythology is at once general enough and specific enough for him to take both these principles of robustness to an argument in religious studies. First, he shows the systematic variations of the tripartite structure in the various separate Indo-European cultures; second, he confirms the broad dimensions of that structure through different techniques of sociological, mythological, and linguistic analysis.

Dumézil certainly does marshal considerable data to support his claim, but in this instance, exhaustive comprehensiveness is neither expected nor necessary: non-Indo-European sources have influenced some of the specific cultural systems; materials are not everywhere extant. A reasonable totality will do. More crucial to his argument is the consistency within the systems he does outline. Thus, his theory of tripartite structure in ancient Indo-European society becomes increasingly robust to the extent that each of the different cultural and analytic systems to which he points has its *own* integrity. Dumézil's outlines of the later Indo-European cultural complexes need to reveal the specific characteristics of each specific culture as well as the common pattern, and each of his different analytic techniques must make sense in its own terms. For Dumézil's detective work to be convincing, then, it is less important that he offer a totally comprehensive reconstruction of the past than that the separate puzzles he solves both reveal a larger picture and demonstrate internal coherence on their own.

This building of robust arguments, reinforced tightly from a number of angles, can lead to something like what the architect Le Corbusier has called the engineer's aesthetic, a modernism in which form follows function.[12] Indeed, Dumézil's construction has a number of qualities that suggest parallels with a modern architectural design: the massiveness of the project, the geometrical abstractness of its form, the ways in which its different dimensions present some uniform, solid lines. What are the aesthetic qualities we value in modern (if not particularly in postmodern) architecture? In the largest sense, perhaps, the construction should suit the terrain—in this case, perhaps, the mass of data on which it rests. And if the terrain is tricky, we admire the skill with which the form is adapted to what is there. Looking more carefully, we want to see that the different pieces of the construction are derived from the right materials and that they all fit neatly into place. They need to be held together securely as well as elegantly. With its broad material base and the apparently trustworthy links forged between its pieces, Dumézil's coherent edifice can, like a piece of architecture, seem indeed to have firm foundations.

Moreover, if we live for a while with Dumézil's opus, overarching and extensive, it may begin to orient our space, to give us a sense of a big picture, however distorted we may later find it to be. It does this not by arresting our attention with its individual pieces but by presenting us with a seemingly sturdy, integrated whole. Indeed, however much it may orient our inward awareness of our world, in its pieces it remains lifeless and external. This stands in contrast to a Geertzian fiction, where the separate vignettes pull us in, where much of the power of the writing derives from its representation of the humanity of individual persons. Dumézil's writings do not give us much empathy with his individual subjects, who lived long ago and left only obscure signs of what they were like. The power of his vision derives instead from its vast collectivity, its representation as the mythic and social structure at the root of large expanses of world civilization. The gravity of Dumézil's argument needs firm structures to support it; and, conversely, to the extent that those structures do give it accessible, well-formed shape, they contribute to the weight we give it ourselves.

UNIVERSAL STRUCTURES
IN MICROCOSM AND MACROCOSM

When the striking thing we see in our examples is not the local religio-cultural contours they suggest, but their very broad human implications, our strategies shift, becoming less disciplinarily variegated. No longer circling around a religiohistorical core (of Bali, say, or the Indo-Europeans) from diverse angles of approach, we instead bring a particular broad vision of our materials into sharp focus. Our examples are now tilted to reveal a specific wide angle. Thus "the episodes and words of the myths" used by Doniger to portray her composite structuralist image of Shiva "are necessarily *slanted*" (my italics).[13] Analyzing our examples from a single perspective, we can more easily be *both* tightly coherent *and* comprehensive. To suggest a universal vision compellingly within a compact microcosm, both tight coherence and comprehensiveness of analysis need to be presented with some rigor; in a more extensive macrocosm, this rigor is almost necessarily relaxed.

The Significance of Contradictions in Mythic Thought: A Complete Example

Although Doniger is careful to limit the claims she actually makes in *Śiva, the Erotic Ascetic* to the Hindu world, the work stems, I think, from a vision that is universal. These universal dimensions are intimated at the outset from Doniger's explicit debt to Lévi-Strauss's comprehensive structuralist ideas about the role of myth in overcoming logical contradiction.[14] Like a mythic character in a classical structural analysis, the Hindu deity Shiva, as Doniger portrays him, toys with the logical constraints of everyday life: he is both erotic and ascetic. Doniger argues, however, that Shiva brings these opposites together in a way that differs from those of the mythic beings in the nonliterate societies treated in classical structuralist anthropology. There, according to Lévi-Strauss, myths *mediate* contradictions. Shiva, however, *contains* both radical opposites—certainly a Hindu quality but one that may also suggest the representation of divine beings in other, perhaps more familiar, literate civilizations. (Think, for example, of Mary—both virgin and mother—or Jesus, spiritually powerful but "meek and mild.")

In hindsight, the Hindu world appears an opportune place to have glimpsed new religious significances of structuralist contradictions; for it brings religious attitudes common in the small-scale traditions studied by Lévi-Strauss to a civilizational complexity crucial, I think, for the new significances Doniger reveals. In the nonliterate traditions Lévi-Strauss analyzed, he focused on the meaning of myth in the social order he could see. Doniger, by contrast, shows us wide-ranging religiocultural resonances in the Shiva mythology that only emerge from the evident resources of a vast literate civilization. Thus, with a multitude of divinities, as in a small-scale society, Hindu tradition suggests itself to structuralist analysis; yet because this tradition is of civilizational scope, it can reveal in the structuralist contradictions of its most overarching divinities, at least, some extremely complex religious resonances. Intentionally or not, it seems, Doniger has shown how a structuralist insight born of small-scale anthropological study can grow to account for the psychological power of divine representations in complex societies.[15] Hindu divinities, to be sure, may combine contradictions more exuberantly than most, but perhaps their excessiveness in this respect just offers a vivid illustration of the general type.

Using a method adapted from Lévi-Strauss, Doniger demonstrates persuasively that the contradictions found in the mythology of Shiva work differently than do those to which the master himself typically points. And the different dynamics of those contradictions suggest ways in which complex religious images can play in human psyches the world over. Still, the universal dimensions of Doniger's work remain implicit— as such dimensions must with most broad visions focused in a particular example. They are suggested by the origins of her method, its evident potential, and the success of its immediate application. Doniger's limits on her immediate claims, moreover, allow her to present a very successful argument, indeed; for within the Hindu world, Doniger seems most comprehensive. Despite her introductory caveat about the slant of her examples, her work gives the impression, at least, of telling the total story of Shiva, using all the relevant texts. Perhaps more crucial than the comprehensiveness of her scope, however, is the rigor of her analysis. Doniger delineates an extensive set of motifs in the texts and shows that they do recur in contradictory ways with astonishing persistence. To drive the point home, she uses a marginal notation to key all of her narratives to an elaborate chart showing the motifs in opposition to one another. Very graphically, then, we see Shiva constructed from his contradictory elements.

In this way, Doniger, like Geertz, creates a comprehensible alien—but of a different sort. Geertz, in consciously translating the meaning of a cultural event, makes the Balinese peasant understandable to us in his or her foreignness. Indeed, the alien peasant is comprehensible to us just because of the very smoothness of the translation. Doniger's comprehensible alien is sooner Shiva himself, who—dealing in radical cultural oppositions—seems less amenable to smooth translation. Shiva, portrayed in detail, is likely to remain alien in his Hinduness. We comprehend Shiva's essential nature more abstractly: he is a representation of divinity containing contradictions, as many such do—in Christian traditions as well as others.

In making her alien universal, not familiar, Doniger makes him compelling through a different aesthetic from Geertz's. Effectively realizing some apparently universal existential truth demands not only an abstract intellectual understanding but also some recognition of its reality for oneself. And throughout her work, Doniger supplies both strands. Her highly abstract motif notations do indeed keep us intellectually dazzled, but these are keyed to vivid stories of sex and sublimation—human realities that most people face. As with Geertz, there is power in the pieces here—in the individual stories themselves, which can fascinate and engage. But as with Dumézil, the gravity of the work lies in the totality. What is compelling here is that the stories and the analysis all together point to a larger vision beyond them.

To appreciate that larger vision, the readers of Dumézil and Doniger face different demands. Dumézil presents readers with an extensive external construction already put together, which readers must summon patience to survey. To appreciate the larger vision Doniger suggests, readers must bring the pieces she assembles together themselves, confronting both affectively and abstractly what appear to be universal human potencies. Because visions of universal scope, like Doniger's here, demand a certain amount of personal assent, it may be with these that the aesthetic and analytic sides of the writing must reinforce each other most fully. In Doniger's book, the intellectual rigor of the argument through specific, alien materials elicits the inward emotive confrontation; conversely, that personal confrontation gives Doniger's compact argument some universal weight.

The Religious Imagination and the Natural Universe: "Patterns of Comparative Religion"

Eliade's vision of universals in religious studies is of a much wider range than Doniger's. He moves beyond the meanings of mythic beings in culture to that of religious humanity in nature. In *Patterns in Comparative Religion*, Eliade examines the human religious imagination as it comprehends the elements of its environment.[16] For Eliade, each natural phenomenon—the sky, the moon, water, vegetation—is a hierophany offering its own reflection of the sacred. Eliade's global treatment yields broad characterizations of different *forms* of the sacred and their interrelationships. Thus, according to Eliade, the sky, because it is high and distant, is linked with high gods and transcendence. The sun, an unchanging focus of light in the sky, often represents enduring power and is likely to find a place in imperial symbolism, as with Louis XIV, the French sun-king. The moon, waxing and waning, may signify change, menstrual cycles, and women.

Eliade's interpretation is reasonably comprehensive, drawing on sources from diverse cultural areas and religious traditions. At the same time, his logic of the relationships among natural symbols is more or less coherent. And because Eliade treats the fundamental natural phenomena systematically, his logic can be taken as exhaustive in its sphere. But the symbolic logic of *Patterns in Comparative Religion* is definitely not of the mathematical variety—on which Doniger's sometimes seems to verge. Given the sweeping nature of Eliade's enterprise and the diversity of his materials, too rigorously systematic a treatment would hardly be credible.

In a sense situated between Dumézil's coolly crafted engineering and Doniger's evocative analysis, Eliade's panorama is one of calm, modulated grandeur. If the elements of Eliade's logic of symbols, loosed from specific human worlds, seem abstract and externalized, like those of Dumézil's constructions, they come together through a logic that, like Doniger's, seems more internally sensed. At once broad and deep, poetic and—in its way—believable, Eliade's vision of the universe has impressed not only many historians of religion but also a wider academic and popular audience.

Where Eliade can most easily be faulted as a writer is in his treatment of particular examples. For in Eliade's very comprehensive landscape, individual UFOs sometimes seem to have an extremely brief life span. No sooner do they appear than they are identified. Neatly identified, they then cease to take shape in unexpected ways. Eliade knew where to look for his religiohistorical objects and what they would look like where he found them. In fact, one feels that nearly anywhere he looked he could find *something* religious. His patterns of comparative religion then appear to have been used beyond their originally intended function. At first they seem to describe the boundaries at which strictly separate sacred and profane worlds intersect. But then—just because they appear all-inclusive—they are eventually able to transform *anything* profane into something sacred.

And, it appears, the other way around. In appreciating Eliade, the *en-*

tirety of his vision seems to be the moving thing. One gets the sense that the whole universe was once his UFO, which he eventually reconstructed in an identifiable way that continues to move new readers. But in the construction, the separate pieces became fixed. Identified as they are with the whole, they lose their own independence. And then *they* cease to move: to grow themselves and then to move us.

Packing the freshly specific into a stale general mold is an aesthetic danger in all religiohistorical writing that brings a large view into play, whether through the universal scope of its vision or the extensive field of its materials. And more than in the other writers examined, this danger is realized in Eliade's oeuvre: the (relatively) compact field of Doniger's Shiva mythology keeps presenting new contradictions between emotionally riveting images; and Dumézil's local Indo-European vision still has its particular intellectual puzzles to unravel. In Eliade's work, however—which offers both a universal vision *and* an extensive field—the sacredness of the whole too often really does profane the pieces.

CHAPTER 5

The Religiohistorical
Sublime

The excitement elicited by interpretive writers in their readers is, it seems
to me, of a distinctive aesthetic genre, generated largely by a characteristic dynamic between the intellectual structures and imaginative resonances of individual works. Yet the failure of Eliade's intellectually static
extended oeuvre to maintain that excitement over time also suggests that
individual works do not exercise their appeal through that dynamic
alone. Religiohistorical art also seems to need an encompassing science
of religion that remains vigorous and fresh. This chapter will explore
some reasons for the characteristic aesthetic appeal of interpretive writing on religion, examining the dynamics of individual works as well as
the roles played by the fresh perspectives offered by a collective science
of religions. My approach to both these dimensions of religiohistorical
aesthetics, as well as to some of the links between them, has been suggested by the work of the Oxford art historian Paul Crowther on the
sublime.[1]

A fashionable topic not so long ago, the sublime was originally a category of classical poetics. It was rediscovered in eighteenth-century literary studies, appeared again in mid-twentieth-century criticism, and
has been an important category in the poststructural theories that are
still with us. Crowther revises some eighteenth-century Enlightenment
doctrines, revealing interrelationships between those of Edmund
Burke—who emphasizes shock, and by extension novelty and change—
and those of Immanuel Kant, whose treatment is still central to most

contemporary reflection on the sublime.[2] Although the Burkean tradition can offer insight into the aesthetic role of a dynamic field of religious studies, the Kantian is more crucial for understanding the aesthetic power typically presented by individual works of interpretive writing.

Kant's analysis can, of course, support a variety of readings, but contemporary critics writing on the sublime still note with exasperation the many different ways the term has been used. Prefixed by *postmodern, religious, romantic, American,* and *Indian*—among other qualifiers—the sublime has been taken to describe diverse types of aesthetic phenomena and affective states.[3] Like most other authors adding a qualifier to the sublime, I am here simply trying to describe an aesthetic actually found in a particular genre of writing. Calling that aesthetic "the religiohistorical sublime" is meant to offer playful deference to recent critical usage, while testifying to a more serious reading of Kant. After exploring some religiohistorical implications of the Kantian sublime and what these might suggest about the works of the four writers discussed in the last chapter, I will turn to what Burkean insights imply about the value of a vital science of religion for the aesthetics of religiohistorical writing.

REASON AND IMAGINATION
IN RELIGIOHISTORICAL WRITING

The sublime, according to Kant, in contrast to the beautiful—which "concerns the form" of a necessarily "bounded" object—presents *"unboundedness."*[4] Effective interpretive writing on religion, I will argue, offers readers some graspable sense of "unboundedness" by portraying others' religious worlds through a distinctive aesthetic dynamic of the type described by Kant. The evocation of unboundedness is regularly possible in writing on religion because religion itself characteristically concerns significant life boundaries, their ruptures, and dissolutions: people's recognition of their own mortality and that of those close to them; the dynamics through which individuals lose their limited sense of self in larger religious groups; most generally, the ways in which human beings come to terms with their own finitude in the face of forces that they cannot control.

Interpretive writers on religion, as seen in part 1, are eminently caught between a modern worldview and a fascination with human depths that seem missing in it. Like those moderns of many stripes disengaged from traditional religions but lately drawn to the sublime, interpretive writers have been struck by the ways in which particular objects in the world can present that sense of the boundless historically offered by religious traditions. But the objects in the world to which interpretive writers' ambivalent feelings about religion have led them are religious traditions themselves, now taken as human phenomena. Instead of seeing these traditions as revealing a transcendent meaning in any traditional sense, they often find in them a profound play of human limits. Kant's aesthetics can help us understand how this play of limits, when presented effectively, can affect a reader's own sense of finitude.[5]

Playing with Limits

The endurance and wide applicability of Kant's aesthetics are due in good part to their description of "the logical and phenomenological outlines of a very fundamental experience."[6] As everywhere in his critical philosophy, Kant speaks to basic issues of individual perception and response. Aesthetic response, for Kant, is located in the interrelationship between two kinds of human psychological faculties: imagination, which appeals to our senses; and the faculties of the intellect, which include understanding *(Verstand)* and reason *(Vernunft)*. Aesthetic experience arises when these two broad kinds of faculties—imaginative and intellectual—find themselves in free-flowing engagement around some perceived object. Beauty derives from the play of imagination with "understanding," which for Kant entails here not discursive thought but concepts of form—the shapes in a painting, say, that together may freely combine into differently nuanced images. The sublime, by contrast, derives from a play of the imagination with reason itself, which deals in ideas and logical reckoning.[7]

It is the mutual engagement of logical argument and imaginative vision that, I think, gives most interpretive writing on religion its characteristic appeal. Together, the two may produce in the reader the gasp that occurs when reason, playing (often hard and long) with ambiguous religious images, finally grasps what may be a coherent meaning behind them. The crux of the sublime for Kant, however, is not in that gasp of recognition but in a moment of profound bewilderment that may precede it—in a tempest just before the calm. And religiohistorical objects, typically created from paradoxical elements, often evoke that moment of bewilderment in a very powerful way.

Crucial to any high aesthetic response, according to Kant, is that the engagement between the imaginative and intellectual faculties really be free, without predetermined ends. In the case of the sublime, that freedom is shattering. Imagination and reason enter into a dynamic that seems to go beyond the limits of either: reason cannot conceive all that imagination suggests; imagination cannot present to itself all that reason says is possible.[8] But the intensity of the engagement is also stimulating: pushed to their limits and beyond, reason is at once exhilarated and exhausted, imagination stretched and then suddenly relaxed. It is in the moment occurring when our cognitive powers are thus pressed beyond their capacities that Kant locates the characteristic experience of the sublime. This is, to be sure, a temporary experience. Eventually we recover, "coming to our (imaginative) senses" and "finding our (rational) wits"— perhaps also uttering a gasp of new understanding as we do so. Providing a momentary peak, the experience of the sublime can appear as a kind of revelation that makes things seem different from before.[9]

As the loss of an accustomed sense of self followed by a realization of continuing existence, the experience of the sublime is comparable to a religious experience. Engaged together, reason and imagination have played with the limits of an individual's perception, still leaving him or her whole, but perhaps a little changed. This results in the feelings characteristically evoked by the sublime: wonder, awe, seriousness, respect— not the more characteristically delightful feelings evoked by the beautiful. "The beautiful charms us," wrote Kant in his first published work on aesthetics, but "the sublime moves us."[10] For Kant, what most often triggered a sublime response were not aesthetic constructions but objects in nature: the mighty mountain, the powerful waterfall. But well-constructed religiohistorical objects—however charming they may also be— may move us in similar ways. Indeed, the aesthetics they can present offer parallels to the two main modes of the sublime that Kant describes: the mathematical and the dynamic.

The mathematical sublime works through sheer unfathomable extent. Here, the intellect tells us that the mountain, the sea, or the Milky Way is very, very large. But if we attempt to fathom just how large, we may find that the object is beyond any rational measure we can meaningfully imagine: it simply doesn't make sense to think of the ocean's vastness as a multiple of the area of our familiar local pond. Thus even "shapeless mountain masses" and "the gloomy . . . sea"—when contemplated in a way that "finds all the might of the imagination still inadequate to reason's ideas" (26:256, 113)—can evoke a sense of the sublime. Indeed, the sublimity of nature is found in all "of its appearances whose intuition

carries with it the idea of their infinity" (26:255, 112). In religiohistorical writing, it is unfathomable *human* extents that can send the mind
reeling. Thus, the mathematical sublime seems evoked less by Eliade or
Dumézil's measured visions across broad fields than by those of Doniger
and Geertz, reflecting compact human materials. We see how Doniger's
structuralist oppositions in fact seem to fit the rich Shiva mythology
nicely, but even as they multiply and multiply, they can never quite contain it all. Geertz's thick description shows us Balinese culture from increasingly many sides at once, probing ever more deeply with no con-
ceivable end. Reading these writers, we may get the sense their reasoned
presentation really could go on and on and on: always another opposition to be found, another layer of meaning to unravel. Their works have
made the standards of measure they introduce natural to us and compelling, but we also see that those standards can never fully encompass
the worlds they map.

In contrast to the mathematical sublime, which can have an intellectual headiness about it, Kant's "dynamic" sublime—characterized by
"its might over the mind" (29:268, 128)—appears more emotionally
threatening. It shows us more clearly the double edge created by the dialectic of the sublime. In contrast to beauty—where imagination and understanding play in harmony—in the sublime, imagination and reason
come into tension, if not into conflict (27:258, 115). Instead of simply
liking the aesthetic object, we are ambivalent toward it.[11] Objects in nature inspiring feelings of the dynamic sublime thus often seem fearsome,
if not downright menacing: "bold, overhanging . . . threatening rocks,
thunderclouds piling up in the sky . . . volcanoes . . . hurricanes . . . the
boundless ocean . . . the high waterfall of a mighty river" (28:261, 120).
Evoking nature's infinite power, such objects compel us "to subjectively
think nature itself in its totality" (29:268, 128), which we soon find we
cannot really do. When the mighty waterfall evokes the fearsome power
of nature in its entirety, all that we could possibly comprehend simply
overwhelms our imaginations.

Many deeply suggestive materials from religious traditions, I think, can
affect us in a similar way, evoking the power not of physical nature but of
a naturally linked common humanity. Once we start thinking seriously
about the diverse human implications of Shiva mythology (even without a
structuralist lens) or of the ramifications of a tripartite Indo-European social structure, it's easy to feel that we'll never really comprehend it in its entirety. It follows that writers working in an extensive field—with diverse
materials from many cultures—are particularly liable to evoke this sense of

being overwhelmed by an ideal totality, especially if those writers also have a universal vision. Thus, Eliade's *Patterns* is liable gradually to overwhelm new readers with all the associations a natural phenomenon can have: we may see a coherence behind those associations but no real end. Revealing a graspable sense of the countless human significances given to nature, not a vision of nature's limitless raw force, Eliade presents a natural totality less frightening than Kant's but just as overwhelming. Eventually intimating *some* symbolic links among practically all phenomena of nature, Eliade suggests how any of them can somehow reveal the divine. The sum of possibilities that might then present themselves could be truly unimaginable.

Refracting Religious Imaginings

When used by historians of religion to speak about human religious capacities in a secular but respectful fashion, the term *imagination* carries a somewhat different sense than it did for Kant. Kant's imagination (*Einbildung*) was an element of eighteenth-century faculty psychology, a basic human capacity for image making, association, and memory; it pertained to the way we put our sense impressions together and retain them.[12] The more contemporary concept of imagination found in religious studies is postromantic, suggesting "the creative imagination"—artistic, expressive, and affectively full. Yet, although differently nuanced, the contemporary religiohistorical and eighteenth-century Kantian notions of the imagination are continuous in the importance they give to the play of association. That play is crucial, we have just seen, to the workings of Kant's aesthetic: the mighty waterfall evokes the sublime because it elicits associations of the overwhelming totality of nature. Modern interpretive writers, for their part, often point to the very broad suggestiveness of religious symbols as intrinsic to their characteristic effectiveness: even on occasions when a symbol does have a clearly defined meaning, wider imaginative associations are also likely to be at work in the minds of religious subjects.[13] The eighteenth-century Kantian and the modern-religiohistorical senses of imagination differ primarily here in the *value* given to the human capacity to play creatively with images— which, in an avowedly secular, postromantic age, gains a heightened significance as it tries to stand in for the magic of divine inspiration.

Much the same human capacity of associative play is also at work in the fascination religious images have for the academics who study them—that is, in the *religiohistorical* imagination. But the associations brought to religious data by writers on the scientific and the pious sides of the scholarly spectrum derive, understandably, from different scholarly traditions. Religionists oriented toward "science" might, for example, be drawn to the wide-ranging and frequently loaded psychological implications to be found in all sorts of tantalizing religious images. The unnaturally surreal worlds of myth, often replete with sex and violence, can, for some of us, powerfully suggest human fears and conflicts or dilemmas of moral trespass.[14] Those of a more pious bent, on the other hand, have often been more impressed by the ways in which the materials of religious traditions can also offer an intimation of an infinite reality that they revere. What Eliade talks about as an "eruption of the sacred" is described by William Brede Kristensen in tones that seem more personally respectful; at the same time, Kristensen's language is distinctly suggestive of Kant's mathematical sublime (which he may well have been consciously recalling). He refers to internal factors of "awareness" not only as "absolute" and "infinite" but also as freely "spontaneous" and "incalculable": "From the viewpoint of Phenomenology, the sense of sanctity appears in all the instances in which the phenomena arouse the awareness of spontaneous factors which are infinite and absolute. Another world invades the world we know and this other world is an incalculable world which makes all the calculations of ordinary life quite insignificant."[15]

More historically oriented scholars, in addition to sighing at the abstract language of Kristensen's statement, may be less than excited by its sentiment. A phenomenologist more religiously convinced than many interpretive writers, Kristensen here presents a reverence toward "another world" crucial to his own experience of a mathematical sublime but likely to stifle a parallel experience in readers of interpretive works. For a powerful evocation of the sublime in interpretive writing derives not just from a writer's pious appreciation of a religious object, a contemplation of it from a reverent distance, but from a simultaneous attempt rationally to *fathom* it: to discern from it something humanly important, to calculate at least some aspect of the potentially incalculable significance it may hold. The aesthetic power of interpretive writing depends as much on reason as on any contemplative imagination.

Using reason and imagination together to comprehend the crucial significances of another religious world, interpretive writers create their own aesthetic objects that ideally evoke the religiohistorical sublime in readers. A reader's sense of the religiohistorical sublime, of course, is not the same experience as that evoked by religious materials on those who traditionally revere them. But, then again, it could never be. Not only do religious materials regularly lead individuals in tradition to *different* experiences, but very few of these, for most of us, are attainable with any intensity. The objects constructed by interpretive writers, by contrast, offer an experience in which secular moderns can participate with enthusiasm. For interpretive writers do not, as some phenomenologists ideally might, simply try to open the religious imagination of sensitive readers to necessarily attenuated reverberations of others' religious objects. Instead they use reason to present imaginatively evocative materials in ways that can be moving to their rational contemporaries. They offer a traditional religious vision once removed, to be sure, but one that has an impact on people who would in no way experience the traditional vision firsthand. At its best, then, interpretive writing does more than give us some reasonably faithful reflection of a religious object in its particularity. By providing intellectual perspective as well as imaginative sensibility, it also conveys a deep comprehension of that object's sway over its adherents; it transforms the latter's religious force into a potent aesthetic.

This transformation takes place in different ways, peculiar to different types of materials and authorial sensibilities; indeed, there is a sense that each piece of interpretive writing, as an aesthetic object, is unique. To be sure, not all works regularly take readers to that moment of imaginative overload where Kant located the crux of sublime experience; but, then again, religious materials don't generally take most people who revere them to the extreme of experience either. But, as do many theological treatises and metaphysical maps for people involved in traditions, much interpretive writing does in fact manage to bring reason and imagination together into extended and vigorous play—if not always to dizzying heights, very often with some sense of overpowering depth. Just as religious traditions remain broadly compelling through some conjunction of vivid representation and believable narrative, not the occasional mystical flash, what is crucial for aesthetically effective writing, I believe, is less the transitory sublime moment than the sustained maintenance of *both* imaginative pull *and* rational acuity.[16] When no suggestive imagination is evoked, we will not respond to a religiohistorical object as profound; without rational sharpness, we will not see it as clearly true. In the first case, we are liable to an arid accounting, with a subject not just dead and on the table but detached from its dreams and history, too; in the second, we are left with an airy presentation, "mere" phenomenology at its worst. Writing on religion is aesthetically powerful, I think, to the extent that imaginative and rational factors are both fully present, vital, and integral in their own terms.[17] And if the two really are separately coherent, they are in fact likely to come together in a way that is *not* predetermined, to play together freely in a way that can potentially elicit a Kantian sublime. For the two poles together to do this, however, the reader must also be able meaningfully to engage them.

Spaces of Engagement

How, then, do readers engage reason and imagination around a religio-historical object? Or, to pose the question from a writer's point of view, how might his or her created object lead readers to bring reason and imagination together within their own psyches? Given that religiohistorical objects, as outlined in chapter 4, have some different characteristic shapes, we might expect that this internal engagement correspondingly takes place along some distinctly different lines—along different tracks in the reader's psyche. We might then try to discern the psychological domains in readers where the particular dimensions by which religiohistorical objects have been typified make their impact. Those dimensions, we recall, are two, producing four variables: religiohistorical objects could be built from extensive or compact *fields* of materials, which could in turn present universal or local authorial *visions*. Psychologically—to introduce our parallel categories all at once—these two dimensions seem to correspond to continua, respectively, of emotional and intellectual engagement and of awareness of self and other. How so? Let us briefly examine the reasoning behind these correspondences, previewing the examples that will be developed as the discussion unfolds.

Considering the compactness of a field of materials leads us to a place somewhere on a continuum between emotion and intellect because readers tend to meet a piece of writing closer to the visceral ground as its materials become more down to earth and culturally specific. Since compact materials are likely to feature characters that are full-featured and stimulating, writing can become more graphic, personalized, and affectively powerful. Thus, the examples from Geertz and Doniger discussed in chapter 4 were created from compact fields: the first presents real people, the second a complex cultural image; both have the potential to create a visceral response in readers. The work in extensive fields done by Dumézil and Eliade, by contrast, is of necessity more abstract and hence, in comparison, cool.

Considering the universality of authors' visions directs us to a point somewhere on a continuum of self and other simply because readers can often find some personal implications for themselves, too, in visions that seem convincingly universal. Thus, for most of us, the local visions of Dumézil and Geertz, however charming the latter's writing may be, remain primarily writing on the other. Eliade's *Patterns,* by contrast, and sometimes Doniger's erotic and ascetic Shiva, have seemed universal to many readers in ways that they can relate immediately to their own internal lives.

A diagram may be helpful:

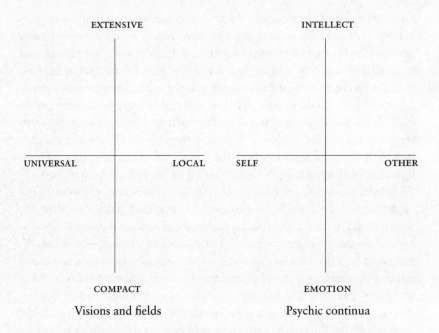

EXTENSIVE   INTELLECT

UNIVERSAL   LOCAL   SELF   OTHER

COMPACT   EMOTION

Visions and fields   Psychic continua

Certainly, these correspondences may not be the only way to trace the impact of the particular dimensions of religiohistorical objects on readers' psyches, but they seem to make sense for the writers treated here. Exploring them may help us see better just how interpretive writing communicates the depth an author sees in the stuff of religious life. For religiohistorical objects, we recall from chapter 3's tale of UFOs, begin with intuitions at the ends of a writer's horizons—which, psychologically considered, correspond to the internal space where his or her cognitive sensibilities temporarily reach an extreme. The dimensions of the objects writers eventually create, developing from these intuitive origins, may lead readers to similar places in themselves. Together, they point to different possibilities for the play of limits crucial to the religiohistorical sublime, different directions in which a successful aesthetic can push our sensibilities to their limits. From this perspective, our four examples present themselves to us in a different light than they did in chapter 4 and will be considered in a different order.

Monumental Works in Extensive Fields   What, first, are the implications of an extensive field? Remember that a field refers to a range of materials used in the construction of a work, and an extensive field means one that is wide-ranging, not focused in a single culture or body of texts. Our examples here were Dumézil, who ordered diverse Indo-European materials, and Eliade, who collated materials from around the world. Grouping these two scholars together by a shared aesthetic of extent might make us wary of it: haven't Dumézil's historical reconstruction of an Aryan past and Eliade's antihistorical evocation of pattern and recurrence both been taken by some as arising from less than noble, politically oriented, motives? In fact, there does seem to be a relationship in principle between an aesthetics of extent and a moral turn that in writing on religion can easily become dubious—a relationship that Kantian analysis can help us understand. But first we must turn to the aesthetic itself.

THE AESTHETICS OF EXTENT Visions in an extensive field are inevitably to some degree abstract, less sparked by concrete detail than glimpsed in ideal outline. To comprehend materials from diverse areas in an intellectually coherent way, these broad visions regularly draw on general types: Dumézil's tripartite scheme, say, or Eliade's "Patterns." In extensive fields, a religiohistorical object's overarching structure is shaped not by felt cultural nuances that emerge from authorial interactions with live people or rich texts but by some kind of thought-out logical model brought down from intellectual heights.

As readers encounter these broadly conceived objects, the emotional tenor of their imagination rises to meet a logically delineated scheme. When imagination engages reason at this more abstract, intellectual register, the sense of sublime that is likely to be evoked has an important overtone of monumental grandeur. Dumézil and Eliade move us, if at all, in good part through the vast, sculpted arrays they present, the ways in which they give coherent shape to a nearly overwhelming amount of materials. But although they both partake in a grandeur that comes from a coherent vastness, Eliade's universal vision can be, for most of us, more personally involving than Dumézil's local one.

Although Dumézil's scope is broad, his vision of Indo-European myth and society remains, in our sense, local and leads him to specific claims. (Our sense of *local* here—that is, as the opposite of *universal*—includes

all specific historical claims.) Although Dumézil himself may indeed have
had an unhealthy attachment to an Aryan heritage, his arguments, like
most local arguments, are ostensibly about an other—and in this case an
other long past. He not only creates a grand edifice, but he also keeps us
detached from it, not least through the staid tone of his writing. The
other that Dumézil presents is not one with which most readers will identify personally. Perhaps more than the work of any of the other writers,
Dumézil's edifice may appear to most readers as one of Kant's images of
nature: the mighty mountain or waterfall—or, perhaps better here, the
long, deep canyon, with smaller branches taking shapes of their own.
Wondering at the sheer extent of its connectedness, we may feel dwarfed.
But for those of us who don't identify strongly with the ancient Aryans—
as some of Dumézil's readers, alas, do—his work does not evoke much
that we relate to as our own. As with an overwhelming object of nature,
our reason and imagination are brought to engagement through something perceived as fundamentally outside the self.

We can be reached personally, however, through a universal claim. If
effectively presented, an assertion about the religious life of humanity in
general is likely also to reverberate in us, too. This, I believe, is part of
the power of Eliade's work. Like Dumézil, Eliade in *Patterns* works on a
level of abstraction that engages reason and imagination in a detached,
unemotional way. But the images of nature that he describes are not just
out there, external to readers; instead, they constitute a symbolic language of wide resonance. Yet even though readers may personally respond to Eliade's archetypes as something humanly meaningful, their engagement with them tends to remain relatively cool—cooler, say, than the
archetypes of Jung, with which they are sometimes confused.[18]

Although the different emotional responses to Jungian and Eliadean
archetypes stem primarily from the distance between Jung's pointed psychological concerns and Eliade's more idealized vision of the sacred, they
also derive from differences in the systematicity of the archetypes' presentation. Jung's archetypes, even though drawn from a field as extensive
as Eliade's, are usually approached one at a time.[19] Providing a central
focus for a study of mythic patterns in life, they engage reason and imagination at the more vivid emotional register typically elicited by interpretive writers through the evocation of mythic details and historical
personalities in a *compact* frame. For in history of religions, the intimately suggestive tenor possible in a Jungian unraveling of mythic symbols finds its most likely echoes in small-scale stories about people's
struggles with demons, gods, and fate. Eliade's large-scale archetypes, by

contrast, appear as ideal forms illustrated by some arresting examples but unendowed with gripping mythic flesh. The disembodied quality of Eliade's archetypes then allows him to present them together in *Patterns* as an extensive, coherent system that itself calls forth an abstract intellectual response. In providing readers an orientation to some universal other, then, Jungian and Eliadean archetypes work differently. Jung's archetypes, by investing mundane if sometimes deep human feelings with broader significance, seem designed to raise a reader's sense of personal, intimate self toward an identification with something beyond his or her finite person. Eliade's symbols of nature, by contrast, are presented as a vision of the other outside that nevertheless has broad implications for the way we all see the world. It offers readers patterns felt less emotionally than intuitively.

CONTRADICTIONS AND DISTORTIONS Given the broad—if some-times distant—resonances that Eliade's presentations regularly elicit in many lay readers, why have scholars in the field begun to tire of him? From an intellectual point of view, we sometimes say that many of Eliade's individual judgments are simply wrong: they are not apt interpretations. But the other side of this intellectual critique is an aesthetic problem that seems tied to Kant's insistence that the play of intellect and imagination evoked by sublime (or beautiful) objects be *free*. Literarily, this problem might be described as a lack of narrative suspense. We already know the end of our journey and maybe much of the route, too. Identified too closely with a larger totality, our specific datum tells us too much too soon. Since we know it cannot surprise with free movement, we are no longer prepared to be moved. As the patterns of our landscape become overfamiliar, they leave little scope for the free play of association crucial to aesthetic response.

Extensive, monumental projects thus inevitably face an aesthetic contradiction. Our awareness of their overwhelming dimensions contributes to their impact on us, exciting our imaginations, but as our reason pursues their nuts and bolts at length, we often find a repetitive consistency in construction that can seem deadening. It is true that this consistency reflects a coherence in argument necessary for a work's credibility, but too much of the same kind of coherence over too wide an area tends to become not only intellectually facile but also aesthetically lifeless. No longer evoking an aesthetic response, it traces out a norm.

This inherent drift toward the normative in an aesthetics of extent can help make the monuments of Dumézil and Eliade seem indeed like suspicious constructions. Viewed in their breadth, the works of these two scholars sometimes seem to reflect less a free play of imagination and reason than a set of judgments made "when the imagination is compelled to proceed according to a determinate law, [when] its products are determined by concepts" (Kant, *Critique of Judgment,* 22:241, 91). In Kant's terms, such subordination of imagination to reason indicates "a liking not for the beautiful"—or we might add, for the *true*—"but for the good" (ibid.). And in interpretive writing this liking for some version of the good is liable to slip into a fixed normative vision that can betray both scientific truth and humane politics.

Should we, then, see the works of Dumézil and Eliade as impelled by politically suspect norms? Neither case seems clear-cut. The implications of Dumézil's active scholarship during the rise of Nazism in Europe need not be belabored, especially since it was the work of a "self-proclaimed 'man of the right.' "[20] Still, as serious scholarship stemming from a specific local vision that elevates the writer's sense of self along with his or her heritage, Dumézil's work bears comparison with much in contemporary ethnic studies—even though that same comparison might reveal it as reflecting a socially insidious "white pride." Eliade's devaluation of history in his vast universal vision is of less obvious import; but—much like the critic Paul de Man's work in literary deconstruction[21]—it has been taken as an intellectual cover for the author's possible historical wartime sins, here seen as insignificant against a vision of eternal recurrence.[22] From this perspective, the works of Eliade and Dumézil offer neither scientific truth nor aesthetic evocation but (im)moral vision, presenting hierarchies of values that favor each author's predilections and/or excuse his shortcomings. To what extent this was actually the case with either of these two prolific writers, I do not know, but it is easy to see how their interpretive scholarship could have become skewed. When concepts are no longer in free interaction with imagination, but control it instead, we can readily move from aesthetic play and scientific discovery to a fixed normative stance that is necessarily limited, often expedient, and sometimes dangerous.

Human Worlds in Compact Frames   This creep toward prescriptive norm is less common in compact frames. Materials in a compact frame—a thick description, say, or a textual exegesis—are denser than those in an extended one and meet us closer to the ground: imagination engages reason at a register that is typically less abstract, more personal, and more emotional. These emotive elements help keep imagination alive, and fresh human angles keep adding dimensions that seem significant. As we interact with dense human materials, our imaginations may continue to transform not only the rational concepts we have taken to them but also those that have emerged in their analysis. Thus, even when working on a smaller, confined scale, conclusions may never be fully complete. With Geertz, focused on an immediate religiocultural scene, we are left with "turtles all the way down"—the fabled retort of the informant replying to a question about the foundation of the world (which, he said, rests on a platform that rests on the back of a turtle, which rests on the back of another turtle, ad infinitum).[23] Broader generalizations remain suggestive, perhaps, but are rarely stated with emphasis, as may be inferred from Doniger's analysis of Shiva. Whereas an extensive frame demands explicit concepts to make sense of a diverse array, a compact frame often presents the imagination with a coherence simultaneously so intuitively felt and complex that our rational conceptualization of it may never become fully finished. When compact frames are used in interpretive writing, the enigmatic humanity of our subject comes to the fore.

When appearing in an argument stemming from a local vision—one that sees into the dynamics of a specific tradition—this humanity normally takes shape as a particular other. That other, especially in Geertz's work, is often presented as "like us" but is clearly also *not* us—in the sense that usually what is at stake is a description of cultural values not our own.[24] Described in interactions with kinsfolk and community, this other is also characteristically human in an everyday, unelevated way—*homo*, to be sure, but not necessarily *religiosus*. If reason and imagination reach an excited engagement, it is likely to be through a very down-to-earth drama. To make theoretical points, as well as to describe religiocultural patterns, then, Geertz regularly serves up stories of people whose obviously human limits lead to ironic, sometimes poignant, predicaments: in "Ritual and Social Change," he questions the sociological truism that ritual fosters social cohesion by telling an affecting tale of the sectarian controversies surrounding the funeral rites of a young boy;[25] in *Islam Observed,* he makes a strikingly broad religiocultural panorama vividly imaginable through stories of two Sufis from opposite ends of the Islamic world. Even though his sweep is broad in *Islam Observed,* his aesthetics remains that of compact frames, now juxtaposed: his observations about Islamic traditions stem from textured stories about people. And no matter how broad their sweep—even, as here, across Asia—particular claims about others' worlds remain claims about others.

A universal vision emerging from a compact frame, by contrast, although still usually presented as a story about others, may also have the power to resonate directly with our own human sensibilities, religious or otherwise. For if it seems truly universal, it concerns us too. The human elements we now see in a compact frame are then less those simply of other people in other worlds than of Humanity with a capital *H.* Our *homo,* moreover, usually does have something of the *religiosus*—if only because the universals we identify normally reflect something of the inward aspects of religious life in which universal vision tends to roam. When suggesting a universal vision, then, compact materials usually sound chords more subtle than those resounding from sympathetic description generally. For they now point to a dynamic evident over a broad class of historically unrelated religious phenomena to which readers may respond in more than ordinary ways. This, I think, is what Doniger's study of Shiva does, suggesting something of the powerfully ambiguous nature of great divinities found in many complex traditions. It deals with issues both profound and general enough to be broadly resonating, but it deals with them in a world of embodied detail that can also draw an affective human response. In pointing to very broad implications of materials that are also imaginatively compelling, Doniger shows the potential of writing that is both universal and compact to elicit a sense of the sublime in a very powerful way.

Certainly, not all the writing of any of our four writers regularly evokes a strong sense of sublime excess. Geertz's aesthetic, with its artfully arranged, well-told vignettes, often seems more akin to Kant's beautiful: harmonious and charming. Reading Dumézil's detailed and sometimes turgid prose may neither charm nor exalt—even as it may sometimes dazzle us when we see an unexpected cultural detail fitting neatly into his construction. Still, whether bringing readers' reason and imagination to a state of romantic, unrestrained excess or engaging them deliberately in more classically restrained analysis, interpretive writers succeed, I think, when a free imagination gives life to reasoned argument.

The presence of imagination alongside reason, to be sure, is cited as crucial not only in aesthetics but also in much scientific discovery.[26] In natural science, however, the two together present a dynamic that normally brings to the fore a rational method of everyday investigation. Comparable rational methods are frequently employed in extended investigations by those many religionists who, like Dumézil, see themselves first of all as scientists, not artists. For to a reason oriented toward nature, making a situation seem real enough to take seriously often entails a prolonged perusal of somewhat tedious facts and extended arguments. When the methodical rigor of science is obviously employed in humanistic scholarship, new insights into the human data are likely to appear as dramatic scientific breakthroughs. The excitement of dramatic discovery then suggests a somewhat different, but related, sense of the sublime—one that reveals the role of a collective science of religion in the aesthetics of religiohistorical writing.

SHOCKING REVELATIONS AND EXCITING NEW KNOWLEDGE

Although Kant's sublime remains crucial for individual interpretive works, his near-contemporary Edmund Burke also had some valuable insights into aesthetics, and these present interesting institutional ramifications for the study of religion. Burke's sublime is an experience felt more physically than Kant's, offering a parallel to it that is sensed at a more down-to-earth level. In certain cases, then, the two could conceivably be evoked at the same time, to very potent effect. Attention to this "existential sublime," as Crowther calls it, will thus take us into some positive and negative *extremes* of scholarship on religion as science: exciting moments of discovery and sensational exposés of exotic worlds.

The "existential" in Crowther's characterization of Burke's sublime seems to refer first of all to an existential *contradiction:* for Burke, a sense of the sublime originates out of our perception of *danger* from a place of *safety*. In such circumstances our vitality is quickened, as it is when we feel threatened, but our rational selves are not alarmed. Thus, in Burke's view the sight of a raging waterfall from a distance inspires less a sense of the overwhelming power of creation, as it does for Kant, than an apprehension of being crushed by the waterfall—together with a simultaneous awareness of being physically intact. Instead of imagination overwhelmed by a concept of totality we get a stimulation of the senses from a poise that remains secure. From a Kantian perspective Burke's view suggests reason and imagination not in an intense dynamic but in a peculiar disjunction: we can *imagine* disaster, but reason, tied to our everyday physical sensibilities, gives us assurance otherwise. Although reason might possibly be cogitating on the deep significances of imagination's object (which could potentially produce a simultaneous Kantian effect), it needn't be and usually isn't. However else reason is occupied, all it really needs to do is maintain a sane self-possession in the body, where images of danger stimulate vital energies. The Burkean sublime enlivens our experience by providing excitement without anxiety, offering the potential for cheap thrills.[27]

Crowther's analysis of the Burkean sublime stresses the felt need for sensory and emotional excitement in the somewhat boring and repetitive industrial world order that was just taking shape when Burke wrote; it points to the value of shock itself to a mundane consciousness.[28] With an industrial world order still substantially in place, Crowther continues, this Burkean insight is evidenced at a popular level today in the pervasive place of violence in media: people seek vicarious stimulation because modern lives are tame. In higher culture, it is evidenced in the role of the avant-garde, much of the appeal of which is just in its novelty and shocking effects. In the history of religions, the analogue to the popular violent TV show seems to be the depiction of the gruesome, weird, and wonderful in less-responsible writing about other peoples' religions. The analogue to the working of the avant-garde seems to be the way in which new discovery in the science of religion may come with an energizing shock. At its most vulgar extreme, the depiction of the weird and wonderful in history of religions is marked, as will be seen, by a *lack* of the Kantian play of reason and imagination, while that play is inevitably *also* present in striking advances in religiohistorical knowledge. Yet whether or not these two religiohistorical dimensions of the Burkean sublime entail the Kantian as well, they are both experienced as a jolting novelty: in the one case a shallow exoticism, in the other a scientific iconoclasm that may be akin to genius.

Sensational, Sublime, or Fantastic?

Although the interpretive writing on which I focus is aimed largely at intellectual (if not necessarily scholarly) audiences, some of it also has wider, less-exalted ambitions and may be prone to a few of the less-savory aspects of popular writing on other cultures. Apparently gratuitous descriptions of bizarre instances of human behavior, moreover, were frequent in the travelers' accounts and missionary reports on which early armchair students of religion relied, tending to color their work. Tylor's example, cited in chapter 1, of Nicaraguan chiefs getting counsel from an old naked woman emerging out of a volcanic crater, came from a twenty-volume mid-nineteenth-century encyclopedic collection of early travel reports on the Americas.[29] The original is quite graphic: the author, a Spanish scholar and adventurer named Gonzalo Fernández de Oviedo, was told by a Nicaraguan chief that the naked woman "was old and wrinkled, that her breasts hung down to her belly; that her hair was thin and bristly; that she had long and pointed teeth like a dog, [and] a color darker than Indians usually have, with sunken, blazing eyes" (133). Moreover, "the day before or after this consultation, she was given a sacrifice of one or two men, some women, and some children of both sexes" (132). Although postcolonialist scholars may emphasize the ways in which reports of scandalous barbarisms among subjugated peoples could help justify a colonialist project, what made the reports sell was more likely their ability to excite people's imaginations: the senses of complacent Europeans could certainly be vitalized by hearing of exotic customs—violent, sexually suggestive, and sometimes scarcely believable. This is especially so, as with the Nicaraguan example, when the stories are told with a straight face: even though they seemed to flaunt common sense, perhaps they really happened. Then, as now, the wondrous, shocking, and unbelievable find a ready market.[30]

Like readers of travelers' reports—and *National Enquirer* articles—serious students of religion, as we have seen, are also regularly fascinated by the bizarre customs of others. What, then, differentiates the religiohistorical sublime of interpretive writing from the cheap thrills of the popular exotic? The answer, I think, is to be found in the place of reason. What is crucial in the Kantian religiohistorical aesthetic, I have stressed, is the engagement of imagination with reasoned reflection.[31] The popular exotic merely titillates the imagination but doesn't seriously engage it with analytic thought. Scandalous examples are presented, but they aren't seriously explained: "strange but true!" Even when cataloguers like Tylor and Frazer appropriate such examples, they tend merely to plug them into their typological schemes without explaining them individually. Trimmed of detail and amassed together as support, the examples may now bemuse us collectively. As cataloguings of the bizarre, a good deal of the early science of religion thus seems to evoke a Burkean sublime of the less-elevated sort: from a safe "scientific" distance, we get to conjure up hideous old women and human sacrifice, but we don't have to think too hard about the rational implications of our particular bizarre examples.

When the stories presented to us are bizarre to the point of unbelievability, the result seems to be neither a Burkean nor a Kantian sublime but an aesthetic closer to what Tzvetan Todorov calls "the fantastic."[32] Todorov defines fantastic narratives as those in which *apparently* supernatural events intrude into the everyday world. The *apparently* here is important, for Todorov locates the fantastic *between* the "uncanny," where all that seems mysterious can be reduced to a totally rational explanation, and the "marvelous," where supernatural beings really do appear in this world. By presenting ambivalent perspectives, the fantastic keeps us in doubt as to whether the apparently supernatural occurrences really are so. Thus, Fernández de Oviedo, in alluding to the veracity of his Nicaraguan story, in fact hedges his bets: first he suggests that the old woman might have been some genuine malevolent spirit with which the chiefs had a relationship (133); but later he refers to the story as "superstition" (134). Like Fernández de Oviedo's story, a successful tale of the fantastic never reaches a resolution, and because reason is finally not quite sure of what the imaginative representation is, it can't really manage to penetrate it. The two poles of reason and imagination tantalize each another but don't come together decisively enough for a judgment to be made.

Interpretive writing, by contrast, ideally brings the two poles together with some decisiveness. In doing so it may spur us to a state of sublime excess, but as we recover our wits we are led to a definite perspective, although not always a definitive statement about religious life. We are not left asking ourselves whether there might indeed have been some ugly old woman living near the Nicaraguan crater, as we might when reading Tylor's paraphrase, if not Fernández de Oviedo's original. Interpretive writing instead leads us to a level of truth at which reason and imagination *can* effectively engage. In this case, for example, we might shift our focus to the meaning of the imaginative representation itself, whatever its reality in the physical world. Bereft of any definite historical background, of course, an interpretation of Fernández de Oviedo's old woman is likely to be unsatisfyingly light: we might see her as a guardian spirit of the mountain, say, who can be pleased with fiery sacrifice. Adding some grounded historical reasoning about our imaginative representation might make for more vital speculation: perhaps the chief stressed the hideous appearance of the old woman to the conquistadores in order to add some terror to his own mien; in that case, does the story of the sacrifice—together with the chief's collective closeness to the goddess—imply a veiled threat? Although the extent of detail supplied by Fernández de Oviedo won't get us too far in this line of speculation, the vigorous investigation of individually bizarre examples may well end in a significant increase in religiohistorical knowledge; moreover, when the bizarre is not just viscerally stimulating but also intellectually incongruous, it may come with a jolt to our existing scholarly paradigms.

The Shock of the Bizarre and the Expansion of Knowledge

Perhaps the most intellectually important iconoclast in the history of religions over the last decades has been Jonathan Z. Smith, who has in several articles worked with the concept of "situational incongruity."[33] Smith's situational incongruity differs from the incongruity we might see in a narrative of the fantastic, where a marvelously imagined world intrudes into *our own* sense of everyday reality. The situational incongruity invoked by Smith derives instead from a disjunction *within* an imagined religious world: we sense that something in a particular religious text doesn't quite fit. And if *we* sense an incongruous element, isn't it reasonable to believe that people in religious communities might have recognized it too? Rationally understanding the incongruity in an imagined world can then reveal a genuine historical problem faced by a religious community.

In a 1976 article,[34] Smith looks at situational incongruities in two texts that had been taken as foundational in separate traditions of religiohistorical scholarship: the description of the Babylonian New Year's festival, seen as a rite of renewal, death, and regeneration by the British Myth and Ritual school; and the Melanesian myth of Hainuwele, taken as a story of human, as distinct from divine, origins in later German diffusionist thought.[35] In the case of the Babylonian New Year's rite, a situational incongruity strikes us through the formulas of ritual humiliation enjoined for the king. Although the ritual humiliation itself might be readily assimilated to patterns of dying and renewal, its specific language here can make us think twice. Specifically, why is the king directed to say that he "did not destroy Babylon" and "command its overthrow" (91)? In an ancient renewal festival of a long-established community these statements would seem uncalled for, somehow out of place. Similarly incongruous in the story of Hainuwele, presented as an ancient myth, are the twentieth-century objects excreted by our heroine before her untimely murder: "Chinese porcelain dishes, metal knives, copper boxes, golden earrings, and great brass gongs" (97). The incongruous elements in both stories, according to Smith, can be explained through the rites' primary pertinence not to an ancient past but to a disastrous present, a world order subject to a new imperialism. Thus, while it seems odd to require a native king not to destroy his own city, it seems less so of a foreign conqueror. And the brass gongs and such produced by Hainuwele were, in fact, objects of trade, suddenly necessary when islanders had to pay a cash tax to colonial powers. So the incongruous elements we felt in both stories also represented something troubling to the mythmakers. The new myths reveal people drawing on their old resources to help come to terms with a painfully unfamiliar situation.

In attempting to meet perplexing challenges by reasoning creatively with established canons, Smith's mythmakers recall the rational primitives of nineteenth-century British scholars; they are here, however, invested with a grown-up humanity crucial to the article's aesthetic effect. The impact of Smith's article, I think, derives not just from any iconoclastic jolt it might present to those familiar with old religiohistorical theories but also from a reasoned analysis that entails the sympathetic imagination of human drama—a combination that, as we have repeatedly seen, is aesthetically potent. Smith presents his mythmakers as dealing in "matters of science" (101), explicitly invoking the idea of religion as primitive science espoused by Tylor and Frazer. As found in the work of those scholars, this concept tends to portray "primitives" of the past and present as simpleminded children, whose failed attempts at true scientific knowledge we can condescendingly survey. Smith, by contrast, presents his subjects as historical adults and shows us the difficult political situations they faced. They are human beings to whom we can relate. Our imaginations are not just titillated by the exotic but can resonate with the problems of real people in trying conditions.

Despite Smith's outspokenly rationalist stance, his method here draws explicitly on the possibility of intuitive sympathy with his religious subjects: he hopes that his reader "will both trust his sense of incongruity and allow himself to suppose that the same element appeared incongruous to the originators of the text." Moreover, our impulse to rational investigation will come only after we are first intuitively "*seized* [my italics] by an element of incongruity in each text" (90). Our imaginations awakened, we attempt to follow the complex mythic and historical reasoning of our subjects: even if they, as we, cannot normally solve historical problems through myths, they can at least use myth to try to make sense of their painful circumstances.

The aesthetic power of this interaction between reason and imagination in historical situations is only enhanced by the iconoclastic frame of Smith's argument. In appearing to undermine old analyses as he presents a creative new one of his own, Smith provides an extra intellectual shock: the thrill we may get at seeing old intellectual edifices shamelessly—if not violently—destroyed. Over and above the rational engagement with human drama encountered in much writing on religion, we may get here a decisive jolt to some intellectual moorings, although, for most of us, not to cherished beliefs. In possibly being stimulated by Smith's strikingly new stance, but probably not deeply outraged by it, we may be experiencing something of the Burkean, "existential" sublime.

This impact of the strikingly new seems to be a link between art and science crucial in the humanities. For although sometimes stimulating from a Burkean perspective, a move beyond old norms that simultaneously suggests new ones also seems to be the kind of achievement that Kant might call an act of genius.[36] As a capacity to work in new ways, genius, for Kant, "is a talent for art, not for science." For in a science "we must start from distinctly known rules that determine the procedure we must use in it" (*Critique of Judgment,* 49:317, 186). Genius, by contrast, entails the undetermined play of intellectual and imaginative qualities characteristic of aesthetic endeavor—creative leaps occurring when the free imagination "suppl[ies], in an unstudied way, a wealth of undeveloped material for the understanding which . . . quicken[s] the cognitive powers" (49:317, 185).

In the human sciences genius seems to occur when our contemplation of our predecessors' theory and practice comes up against immediate realities in a way that sparks exciting new thought. In working creatively, we are thus all like the mythmakers Smith presents as dealing with "matters of science," rethinking past traditions in light of present concerns—even if the problems we treat are for most of us less existentially acute and so more easily soluble. In the case of the young Eliade, working alone in Romania, creative genius seemed to spew forth into scholarship as he reflected on new Indian experiences in the light of his broad background in European humanities. In more compact social-scientific fields, creativity may appear as an internal development of a progressing scholarly tradition; thus Geertz developed theories to fit new field practice out of a stream of established Weberian social science.

Although the human sciences, at least, thus seem to need the imaginative life found in aesthetic play to progress as fields of knowledge, the existential jolt provided by an exciting new approach is also part of their aesthetic appeal. When a human science is static, its attraction wanes. We were finally bored with Eliade not only because we knew how all his individual stories would turn out but also because we were tired of the dominant Eliadean paradigm itself. We wanted something new—which is just why we might have been excited by Eliade on first encounter. In the aesthetics of scholarship, then, creative endeavor appears as a historical phenomenon, defining itself against established tradition even as it inevitably emerges from it.

This historical dimension even to the aesthetic impact of our work speaks for continuity as well as change.[37] To position ourselves against tradition, we must speak in its terms—if only to deny them and move decisively beyond. At the same time, for the rational pole of the religiohistorical sublime to pull its weight against imagination, we must believe what we read as true—a belief that usually derives in good part from received religiohistorical knowledge. Shaped by continuing discoveries—for the most part more historical and ethnographical than interpretively creative—that knowledge is itself constantly in flux. What sorts of possible truths can it offer? What are its characteristics and its limits? Part 3 will examine the ways in which religiohistorical knowledge lets us grasp its truths as effectively valid—if not for all things and not forever.

PART THREE

Two Truths

THE AESTHETIC OF THE SUBLIME described in part 2 entails an engagement with two sorts of truth. To engage our scientific reason, interpretive writing must move toward an interesting proposition graspable by our everyday no-nonsense minds. But the dialectic of the sublime occurs only when the implications of that proposition play out within imaginative worlds that are never quite fully determined. Successful interpretive writing on religion thus inevitably presents its readers with, first, explicit statements about traditions that we can discuss with colleagues, expand, and refine; and, second, insights into the human imagination that draw us in and fascinate us but that are intuitively sensed and not easily expressed.[1]

These two sorts of truth in interpretive writing recall the two famous truths of classical Indian philosophies—truths that, particularly in Buddhist variants, are inextricably embedded in one another: one of an everyday, very ordinary, world; the other of an inexpressible, supramundane reality.[2] Transposed into a secular aesthetics, the two truths of interpretive writing are less extreme: ordinary statements about the everyday world that are still abstract enough to be intellectually stimulating; and subtly expressed insights that penetrate human imagination but not ultimate reality. Yet, like the two truths of Buddhism, these two—the rational statement of science and the imaginative insight of art—are also inextricably linked. Part 3, focusing on the scientific truths of interpretive writing, will explore their relationship with those sensed by the imagination. Chapter 6 will discuss what the undeterminably full imagination invoked by the aesthetic of the sublime implies for the limits of the scientific truths presentable in interpretive writing. Chapter 7 will then suggest what the characteristic aesthetic of interpretive writing implies for those truths' quality and power.

In attempting a level of interesting abstraction, the scientific truths of interpretive writers often differ substantially from those emerging from the detailed investigations of philologists, text editors, and ethnographers. If the concerns of the latter scholars are with an accurate representation of particulars, those of interpretive writers are with making statements about those particulars—statements that contribute to a continuing discourse on religious traditions. The status of these statements as knowledge has provoked a good deal of writing in recent years: considered reflections on the relations between hermeneutics and critical theory and pointed dialogues about the roles of reduction and theology in the study of religion.[3] Although some of these discussions are necessarily touched on here, I will not rehearse them but will instead concentrate on examining what can happen to questions of truth in religious studies when the aesthetics of interpretive writing is taken seriously.

CHAPTER 6

Relating Stories about
Religious Traditions

To explore the scientific truths of interpretive writing, I will draw on a
set of primary metaphors that differ from those used in the last section
on the aesthetics of the writing per se. The language of vision used there
will now yield to one of story. Instead of describing how writers "see
depth" in their materials and express it in created objects, I will examine the ways in which they try to convince readers of their stories' truth.
Although a language of vision will still creep up on us now and then—
for our aesthetic truths impinge on our scientific ones[1]—discussing stories shifts our attention to the element of believability that makes the aesthetic work. Thus, although many of the same examples found in the last
chapter will also be used here, their significance now changes. Those examples described aesthetic constructs that were taken as reflections of religiohistorical vision—subject to the limitations of their type, to be sure,
but still, in their artifice, ideally perfect. Now, treating problems of truth
and knowledge in religious studies, we are more aware of the imperfec-
tions inherent in scholarly discourse, of the difficulty of making statements about religious traditions. Sometimes all we seem to have in our
discourse are stories upon stories, more and less true: some confirming
one another, others mutually contradictory; some meeting one another
obliquely, others ignoring one another entirely. The ways in which these
stories come together in a fabric of collective knowledge about traditions
will be discussed in the last chapter of the book as a less-than-conclusive

conclusion. Here I will examine some ways in which interpretive writers combine stories within a single piece of work.

Most interpretive writers, in fact, seem to tell two kinds of stories at once—each serving truths both scientific and aesthetic. There are one or more stories about some specific materials: we can call them *small* stories. These help to tell a *large* story—usually just one—about some problem of religious life or tradition. Small stories are full of particulars. As data, these particulars can present apparently hard facts for the no-nonsense positivists in us, crucial elements for our scientific truths. But as the stuff of religious traditions, the same particulars may simultaneously reveal dramatic images or events that captivate the imagination; they are thus also integral to any aesthetic truth apparent in the writing. Large stories, sometimes only intimated, present a complementary dynamic, adding intellectual significance to the facts and refracting broadly the human drama they suggest. They thus offer a general narrative within which a scientific statement can be made, a framework for theoretical abstraction. But at the same time, they present a perspective from which the aesthetic depth of the material can be viewed, a frame for artistic vision. Although attention to particulars of small stories is endemic to history (as opposed to, say, philosophy) of religion, a hint, at least, of a large story is also a defining trait of a characteristically interpretive writing.

The stories characteristically told by interpretive writers are also (surprise!) *interpretations*. That is, they are internally coherent accounts of religious meanings reported by actors and inferred from contexts. As such, they are sometimes taken in contrast to *explanations*. Explanations, finding their model in the physical sciences, may sometimes simply ignore what religious actors say they think and feel, deducing behavior instead from external factors. To do this, they are likely to invoke the direct, one-way relationships we speak of in ordinary language as "causes." Thus presented, interpretation and explanation appear as ideal types characteristic of humanistic and naturalistic methods.[2]

In practice, however, it is not always easy to distinguish between interpretation and explanation in any field, and not least in religious studies. They often appear rather as poles on a narrative continuum, with naturalistic attitudes and accompanying rhetorical usages hardening interpretive perspectives into causal explanation somewhere along the way. To what extent (or even whether) interpreters and explainers in the human sciences actually do follow fundamentally different methods has been seriously questioned from both sides. Thirty years ago Karl Popper, discussing "historical explanation," argued that human scientists, offering hypotheses based on their reasoning about actors' motives and understandings, are following the same rational procedure as natural scientists hypothesizing about physical phenomena.[3] More recently, Gavin Flood, in a move with which I have much sympathy, has simply subsumed explanation into his fundamentally interpretive model of religious studies.[4] From a perspective like this, explanation becomes a kind of interpretation that introduces at least a rhetoric, and more definitively a logic, of causes.

Despite their continuities, however, at their extremes interpretive and explanatory presentations can appear very different, and in the following discussions I will preserve explanation as a separate category. For a logic of causes can lead both to special problems in religiohistorical knowledge and to a very powerful aesthetic in writing on religion. It thus seems worth examining the ways in which explanatory writing on religion reverberates against a more interpretive norm.

LARGE EXPLANATION, TOTALITY, AND COMMUNITY

Together, the two sets of categories—interpretation and explanation, large and small—suggest four types of writing about religious traditions, each highlighting a possible binary combination. Yet in the discussions of part 2 only three of these possible combinations turned up. Writing on religion yields plenty of works that highlight (1) small interpretive stories, those of the sort told by Geertz. These small interpretations typically present the religious meanings found in a particular tradition but also attempt to suggest something larger about how religious traditions tend to work. Sometimes, as seen at the end of the last chapter in J. Z. Smith's comparative work, small stories also give an important role to direct causes—historical, political, economic—thus becoming (2) small explanations in our sense. There are also (3) a few important interpretations told from the large perspective, like Eliade's *Patterns of Comparative Religions,* a work that deals seriously with religious meanings but gets its data from many, briefly presented, small accounts; subordinated to a large story, these are sometimes homogenized in the process. But we have not yet seen a large explanation that presents a counterpart to a large interpretation like Eliade's. There is a reason for this: large explanations are the exception because they are very difficult to assimilate even into the widely inclusive discourse of religious studies.

To discuss large explanations, I will turn to Marvin Harris, who wrote a number of books popular in the 1970s and 1980s that attempted to demonstrate the natural origins of the puzzling human behavior frequently found in religious traditions. Strange customs, according to Harris, are often ecologically adaptive and can be explained through reference to the natural ecology within which they emerged. I examine Harris—even though his influence has waned—for two reasons. Most important, Harris offers an extreme case, one with which even normally irenic religionists can find little way to compromise. Harris's aesthetic, in addition, which works through an engaging presentation of exotic materials, can seem deceptively similar to that of many good interpretive writers, and it will be instructive to reflect on its differences. As a self-described "cultural materialist,"[5] Harris would no doubt have emphatically resisted being taken together with the interpretive writers treated here so far. And rightly so: he is presented here as the one who doesn't fit, the large explainer from outside religious studies who treats religion in ways that most within the field cannot digest.

Nevertheless, like interpretive writers at the top of their form, Harris is eminently readable. If his books are usually not as nuanced as, say, Geertz's, they are on the whole more popularly accessible. They seem to be meant to be page-turners. For as Harris states baldly in the first of his popular books on the ecology of culture, *Cows, Pigs, Wars, and Witches,* he has "deliberately chosen bizarre and controversial cases that seem like insoluble riddles."[6] These, as we have seen, are just the types of cases that have traditionally fascinated historians of religion. Like many interpretive writers, Harris is wont to tantalize readers with the strange and incongruous.

Harris differs substantially from interpretive writers, however, in his *attitude* toward striking religious cases. The unraveling of his riddles demands little sympathy with what actors experience as religious—with their sense of something beyond the ordinary—but is instead grounded in a conviction of everyday human misery: "Ignorance, fear, and conflicts are the basic elements of everyday consciousness. From these elements, art and politics fashion that collective dreamwork whose function it is to prevent people from understanding what their social life is all about" (6). This unhappy, hard-nosed vision of humanity leads Harris to two important conclusions about the study of religious phenomena. First, considering the meaning of beliefs and practices to those who hold and perform them is not essential: "we don't expect dreamers to explain their dreams; no more should we expect lifestyle participants to explain their lifestyles" (ibid.). Second, "even the most bizarre-seeming beliefs and practices turn out on closer inspection to be based on ordinary, banal, one might say 'vulgar' conditions, needs, and activities." Harris explains: "a banal or vulgar solution rests on the ground and is built up out of guts, sex, energy, wind, rain, and other palpable and ordinary phenomena" (5). With these assumptions, Harris attempts to explain "lifestyles which others claimed were totally inscrutable" through "definite and readily intelligible causes" (4).

Harris's ambivalence toward religion, then, like that of Hume in his *Natural History,* is less than benign: a fascination for the bizarre that tempers an apparent personal repugnance. This is an ambivalence substantially different from that of the moderate majority of interpretive writers. These, we recall from part 1, characteristically believe in science but like religion because it says something deep about humanity. Harris, by contrast, doesn't seem to like religion very much and finds it merely echoing nature.

Harris's most famous example of the ecology of culture is undoubtedly his explanation of the sacredness of the cow in India. It begins *Cows, Pigs, Wars, and Witches* and also figures prominently in a later book devoted to food customs.[7] Harris's solution to the "Riddle of the Sacred Cow" demands our acceptance of some strong theoretical propositions. To his general assertion that sanctified custom is really "dreamwork" masking material (often ecological) imperatives he adds a corollary: enduring culturoecological complexes are adapted not to maximum efficiency during normal times but to the survival of crises. Given these two hypotheses, Harris's explanation follows with easy logic. The tough Indian Zebu cow fits into the Indian ecosystem fundamentally as draft animal, not source of food. The Hindu ban on cow slaughter prevents the farmer from submitting to the temptation of slaughtering and eating his cows during periods of famine; for if he lost his draft animals, he really wouldn't be able to survive. Instead of the waste and inefficiency seen by carnivorous Western analysts, then, Harris sees the ban on cow slaughter as a natural element in a self-preserving system of ecology.

The solution to one of Harris's riddles, then, suggests another: it's like "potato chips," he says, you can't eat just one (vi). From the ban on cow slaughter in India we move to the prohibition on pork in Semitic religions. Harris has a ready answer: pig raising is ecologically wasteful in the dry Near Eastern environment, but the concentrated fat and protein in pork is very tempting. Religious strictures against pork emerge in culture so that the desert environment can more easily sustain itself. What, then, about the cycle of pig breeding, pig slaughter, and ceremonial war

among the Maring of New Guinea? Here, pig raising makes good ecological sense—until too many pigs compete with humans for scarce resources. Thereupon begins a season of controlled destruction. And so on,
moving through primitive political systems to some down-to-earth
causes for bizarre Western religiocultural phenomena, including European witchcraft and American counterculture.

As a large story, Harris's book has a number of similarities with Eliade's *Patterns*. Both authors are generalists without apology. Each, moreover, has had a vision of something he thought was important, something
he believed was directly relevant to a crucial contemporary situation—
in the one case ecological crisis, in the other existential void. Their exhaustive thinking on important questions leads them both to take positions that can seem dogmatic, if not rigid. Each, to make his case,
assembles numerous, disparate examples. The aesthetic of their two
books then derives from the ways in which diverse examples are woven
together into a coherent narrative, and the books' persuasive force
emerges from those examples' cumulative effect.[8] Harris's story differs
from Eliade's, however, as an explanation does from an interpretation,
with implications both for the design of its narrative and the acceptabil-
ity of its truth.

If, literarily, Eliade can sometimes seem deep, then Harris can frequently seem clever, which is often more popularly appealing. Even
though many readers may eventually find Eliade's recurrent themes pre-
dictable and tire of them, their initial encounters are often with a perspective on humanity that they find profound. A comparable human
depth is generally missing in Harris, who, instead, weaves some thoroughly ingenious plots into what he sees as a weighty explanatory narrative. Both authors know where they are going, but Harris's routes continue to surprise. The surprises Harris offers, moreover, do not derive
from the reverberation of material cause against religious imagination,
as seen in Jonathan Z. Smith's article discussed in the last chapter, but
from the deft concatenation of the exclusively external causes that he
finds. His is sooner the aesthetic of the mystery writer than that of the
mystery monger—as Harris might characterize the "obscurantist" interpretive anthropologists he derides.[9]

For examining problems of truth in interpretive writing, however,
more crucial than the two writers' alternative literary analogues are the
different degrees of exclusive allegiance each demands. Although Eliade's
view can be just as fixed as Harris's, it can be taken by other scholars as
simply a view, one interesting perspective among others. Because reli-

gious meanings very frequently seem complex and difficult to encompass, writing that attempts to evoke readers' resonances with them lends itself to a perspectival attitude toward truth. Thus, even though interpretive writers, attempting to evoke the depth of their materials, may reasonably think they have found valid perspectives, they can also find truth in some other perspectives, too—if in these, perhaps, a less compelling vision. Thus, on the meaning of the sun as center of power, for example, there can legitimately be different complementary views: Eliade's general understanding, noted in chapter 4, and one or more readings particular to a specific religiocultural world (that of the Incas, say, with their sun symbolism conjoined to specific imperial ways). If not always without tension or with equal degrees of insight, the same religious situation can often be reasonably interpreted through more than one story.

Treating Harris's large story in such a cavalier fashion is not so easy. The whole point of his search for explanations is just that all religious riddles can be explained through "definite and readily intelligible causes." If these are not always ecological, they are always external, having little to say about what a religious actor thinks or feels. Harris's story presents us with a yes or no proposition: if it is right, others are wrong—or else truly insignificant. This ideal of explanation that is (provisionally) correct or incorrect, derived from the natural sciences, is also found in versions of several social-scientific disciplines on which interpretive writers draw. How, one might ask, do interpretive writers manage to finesse this potentially contradictory interdisciplinary borrowing? What is their secret?

Religion scholars' little secret is that when they take social-scientific theory to their religious materials, they almost always weaken it. In effect, they transform the theory into a perspective, an approach. Syllabi in history-of-religions methods courses make the point nicely: a great many spend at least part of the term running through a series of "approaches," especially those of classical sociology and psychology: Durkheim, Weber, Freud, Jung. Class time is spent in discussing the "insights" each of these perspectives brings to religious materials. When discourses in disciplines are presented as perspectives only, the sharper edges of the theories they advocate get smoothed over. Groundings posited in innate psychological complexes or regular social "facts" disappear at the ends of our horizon. Interpretive writers thus acquire a habit of turning explanatory frameworks into interpretive ones. Although this softening of theory may sometimes lead to sloppy analysis, it is to some extent inevitable in writing that depends on an aesthetic that seeks an engagement with "science" but wants to keep the religious imagination alive, too. The trick is in doing it responsibly: understanding what kind of ostensible explanations can readily be treated as interpretations and the perils that lurk in treating them as such.

Let us imagine a continuum of large stories about religion: bold, explanatory ones on one side and innocuous, interpretive ones on the other. We might see Harris, with his natural ecological causes, close to the explanatory pole. Freud, looking to complexes that are innate but human, would appear further toward the middle, and Jung further still—the biological origin of Jungian archetypes sometimes looking like the afterthought of a man of science. With Eliade's archetypes we have definitely moved over to the interpretive side of our continuum but, because his morphological patterns give some coherent content to his perspective, not all the way to its end. Closer to the interpretive pole is a phenomenologist like van der Leeuw, whose vision is presented as a long, ordered list of religiohistorical categories—more of an enumeration than a narrative.

On the explanatory side, stories are characterized in various degrees by a close coherence—one that ideally derives from unidirectional causes, which in turn rest on firm grounds. Moving toward the interpretive pole we find self-coherent perspectives of decreasing closeness and complexity. When interpretive writers turn to social-scientific explanations, they are usually excited by the closely coherent patterns they see but tend to gloss over the significance of the groundings given to them in their own disciplines. They can then pull out the patterns that intrigue them and integrate them into their own interpretations. This kind of maneuver is more successfully done in some types of cases than in others.

In general, the closer to the explanatory pole a large story is, the more difficult it is to read it as an interpretation. With the whole bound by necessary causes, the entire large story must be taken seriously for a piece of it to make any sense at all. Try extracting the solution to one of Harris's riddles from his large explanatory story. His explanation of the ban on cow slaughter only makes sense given his presupposition that culture is driven by nature working to maintain ecological systems, whatever human actors understand. This is, in fact, a lot to accept, implying a view of the way the world works that is not easily falsifiable. The force of Harris's accumulated examples can carry the reader with him for a while, but questions may well arise along the way, and maintaining enthusiasm over increasingly ad hoc applications draws on the doctrinaire stubbornness of the true believer.

Although classical psychological theories can also have true believers, it is easier to loosen significant pieces of them from their theoretical roots. This loosening is possible because the logical progression of the theories of Harris and of the great psychological thinkers moved from opposite directions. The psychological thinkers, beginning with complex practical problems of human feeling and behavior, developed some more or less coherent ideas that are theoretically interesting and therapeutically useful. Only then did they go on to find some ultimate grounding for them that satisfied their sense of medical science. Harris's explanations logically depend on his ecological presuppositions; the practical value of Freud's analyses does not depend on his speculations in *Totem and Taboo*. Thus, whereas the true believer can extend the network of Freudian ideas to the beginnings of human history, less-committed admirers can encounter those ideas at their more immediate human core and incorporate them into one or another interpretive perspective.

Nevertheless, because a large explanatory story like Freud's still has its own coherence, any significant part of it carries some implicit theoretical baggage. Its unstated theoretical implications may complement a religiohistorical interpretation nicely but may also sometimes seem out of place. Conceptual incongruities can easily occur when interpretations combine pieces of different large stories. They are most likely to take place, moreover, when those stories are from the same general discipline, where alternative theoretical baggage tends to occupy the same explanatory space. Thus, a religiohistorical interpretation may easily highlight either a Freudian complex or a Jungian archetype, but one that gives them both attention may just as easily seem analytically discordant. For even when ultimate causal grounds are clouded over, implicit causal directions remain: backward to recollection of (Freudian) trauma, say, or forward to integration of (Jungian) archetypes. Interpretations significantly incorporating large explanations consequently tend to take on something of their causal spin. Thus, although parts of two different explanations may sometimes both be engaged successfully, care must be taken that their directional gears mesh. Large explanatory theories, although often readily weakened, can easily grate when they are brought together.

Of course, even though a large story closer to the interpretive pole tends to offer parts more easily integrated into *another* writer's vision, the person who originated it may have believed it as much as he or she believed anything. Jane Harrison's theory of ritual, influential in its pieces for a generation of English writers, was enthusiastically proclaimed by the writer herself as a historically grounded whole. For Harrison, her theory was an encompassing explanation of crucial religious phenomena; for later scholars, it presented some new ideas from which they could spin their own interpretive webs.[10] The same, of course, could also be said of greats like Durkheim and Eliade. If these writers didn't really believe their theories when they presented them, it is unlikely that those theories would be as insightful and long lasting as they have been. The degree of a large story's malleability is a consideration for the new interpreter, not for the original writer. But given the community of scholars in religious studies, I think it remains an important consideration.

As Thomas Kuhn told us almost fifty years ago, large explanatory stories—his "paradigms"—can have crucial roles in many scientific communities. Taken for granted by almost everyone during periods of "normal science," they form the background for everyday work. Their implications pursued with dogged tenacity, they can lead to exciting discoveries. When they start leading to too many dead ends, new paradigms, espoused with the enthusiasm of the freshly converted, can lead to radical changes in how the world is viewed. Notwithstanding the numerous commentaries on this scenario over the last half century,[11] it is still highly suggestive of the relationship between the way scientists work as a group and what they ultimately believe about the world they explore. Despite the lack of any all-encompassing unified field theory, most scientists, in one way or another, work seriously with large stories in their own fields most of the time.

Among interpretive writers, however, the opposite seems to be the case. Caught in modern dilemmas, interpretive writers face internal conflicts that may leave them hesitant about the big picture behind the religious worlds they explore. Large explanations—materialist or theological—demand too much assent. A metaphysical perplexity may lead some to creative visions of the material at hand, but many may still not be so sure of what they finally *believe* about it. What stood out about Harrison and Goodenough in chapter 2 was precisely these scholars' change in perspective, their unorthodoxy, their refusal to hold with any nicely codified belief. If individual writers on religion don't abide large, neat, and lasting stories about the true nature of their subject, they can hardly be expected to adhere to one as a group. There is no normal science of interpretive writing because many of those drawn to interpret religious phenomena are profoundly unsure of those phenomena's significance.

In this context, even when firm belief is not based openly on a theological creed, it has a distinct theological tinge: doesn't Harris's hand of

nature sometimes seem to move in mysterious ways? Although an exciting, if unfalsifiable, determinism may arouse some enthusiasm for a
while, it rarely achieves consensus beyond a small group. Nevertheless,
large totalizing explanations may stimulate the interpreter's intellectual
imagination; they can be good stories. And central ideas from explanations that treat human sensibilities in an interesting way often acquire a
life of their own among interpretive writers.

For people who take their large explanations seriously, of course, a
loosening of ideas from their systematic roots and the interpretive softening of theory can appear as a kind of heresy. "Eclecticism" ranks just
behind "obscurantism" among the sins against which Harris rails most
fiercely in his *Cultural Materialism,* which argues for his kind of anthropology against all others.[12] Similarly, Donald Wiebe writes strongly
against the "infect(ion)" of religious studies by implicit theological agendas that would "preclude causal explanation," criticizing the field for a
"failure of nerve."[13]

These writers make a valid point, I think, in claiming that much writing on religion does not attempt strong causal arguments. But that, I
would argue, is because so much of it is driven less by a committed intellectual stand (theological or otherwise) than by an aesthetic vision—
one that seeks to frame some specific religious materials in ways that
bring reason into play with imagination but not necessarily to make a
final pronouncement. Indeed, as we saw in the case of Eliade in the last
chapter, when a large story becomes too clearly enunciated, that play easily loses its requisite spontaneity. Moreover, if, as artists, interpretive
writers want to make their characteristic aesthetic work for a wide audience, they may want to aim for general rational believability instead of
extreme intellectual audacity. These points are made not to justify what
has been seen as a less than rigorous practice of argument but to look at
that practice from an aesthetic point of view. Interpretive writers can be
daring, even nervy, but what they often demonstrate is the nerve and daring of art.

THE MIDDLE OF RELIGIOHISTORICAL KNOWLEDGE

If what scholars of religion really share is a fascination with the materials of religious life, their common discourse will be pointed discussion
about them. Analytically, this is a middle ground, one between concrete
data and totalizing theory: a realm of incomplete typologies, particular
comparisons, and suggestive generalizations.[14] What sorts of intellectual

propositions are possible in this realm? And how do they derive from the stories told by interpretive writers?

Arguably the first prerequisite for discourse about a diverse body of material, religious or otherwise, is a commonly understood vocabulary. This is a truism that early scholars of religion understood very well, if not to a fault. Of the first large stories in the science of religion, some of the most memorable appear as exercises in academic categorization, from the evolutionary typologies of Tylor to the detailed phenomenologies of van der Leeuw and others. Tylor's categories, contributing to an evolutionary narrative, derived from a large explanatory story. Van der Leeuw's, however, as noted above, are close to the extreme interpretive pole. His work thus nicely reveals some limitations of the large interpretive frames often found in writing on religion.

As a large interpretation, van der Leeuw's *Religion in Essence and Manifestation* is more than just a presentation of types, but not too much more. The work does have something of a structure: categories are grouped according to whether they represent the object of religion (taken by van der Leeuw to be power of different sorts), the subject of religion (persons and groups), or subject and object in their interrelationship (practices and experiences). But the work's 110 short chapters focus the discussion on particular categories—for example, the Mighty Dead, the King, Purification—on which the author ruminates, drawing on his knowledge of the religions of the world. As an aesthetically imagined overview, van der Leeuw's categories together appear as an abstractly ordered mosaic, less integrally coherent than Eliade's set of complex archetypes and more evidently personal and subjective.

To familiar concepts from ordinary language van der Leeuw attaches religiohistorical significance that we may not thoroughly understand and to which we may not completely assent. Nevertheless, his descriptions give his categories enough body and life that we may be able to employ them in conversations with others. The phenomenological typologies of old could thus at least bring a level of intersubjective intelligibility into religiohistorical conversation.[15] But they did not in themselves offer much intellectual rigor or excitement. With such work among the most characteristic achievements of comparative religion in the first half of the twentieth century, Geertz could, with good reason, write in the late 1960s about the "pigeonhole disease" from which the field suffered.[16] Enumerating categories from on high was no substitute for suggesting hypotheses about data.

When used to make statements about materials, however, general categories may become more interesting, taking on new life as they find un-expected meaning within the contingencies of particular religious worlds. Now they may reveal unanticipated relationships among multiple realities of human life: cultural, social, political, psychological. In doing so, moreover, they are also liable to elicit the tension between reason and imagination characteristic of the aesthetic of interpretive writing. For seen in detailed context, evocative myths, rituals, or doctrines may spark our reflection about the ways the worlds in which people live seem to shape (or to be shaped by) their most deeply rooted ideas and feelings. This reflection—sometimes lingering, sometimes a little fevered, occasionally stymied by sublime excess—might be powerfully provoked by an apparent explanatory cause, but it is likely to be stifled by a neatly totalizing explanation. Aesthetically and intellectually, then, engaging writing on religion emerges when scholars mix large, open-ended, more or less interpretive stories with smaller, specific ones.

In thus bringing together large and small, writers start from different directions. Sometimes they work from the top, exploring the implications of a general concept in a specific context (as does Doniger with structuralism in the mythology of Shiva). Sometimes they start more empirically from the bottom, seeing how far what seems significant in one historical situation finds parallels in others (as does Jonathan Z. Smith, moving between the ancient Near East and Melanesia in his work discussed at the end of chapter 5). A few important writers, like Dumézil, are concerned with particular religiocultural complexes but may take them to high degrees of abstraction.[17] Numerous others, like Geertz, raise some very broad questions from a single specific event. Many are the paths by which interpretive writers find themselves making those interesting, but less than emphatic, statements characteristic of the middle of religiohistorical knowledge.

Doniger's *Śiva, the Erotic Ascetic* shows us how radical explanatory theory, once tamed, can become suggestive in new ways. Although Doniger adapts a Lévi-Straussian structuralist method to some complex Hindu mythology, she does not take it to Lévi-Strauss's extremes. As seen in chapter 4, she argues that the mythology of Shiva, instead of simply (or complexly) mediating contradictions, as Lévi-Strauss would see the function of myth, contains them in their contradictoriness. Shiva, as a supreme divinity, doesn't really present a resolution to a cultural polarity of asceticism and eroticism but instead manifests both qualities to the utmost. This analysis of Shiva appears as a qualification of a strong explanatory position: myth regularly works with contradiction, as Lévi-

Strauss has shown us, but not always in the *way* he has shown us. In presenting her thesis as a statement about the representation of divine beings in Hindu India, Doniger makes a generalization that is broad (not just confined to Shiva) but still limited (not asserted for divine beings elsewhere). Still, although not asserted beyond Hindu tradition, Doniger's hypothesis can prove intriguing to scholars of religion fascinated with Lévi-Strauss's *Mythologiques* but uneasy with the finality he gives to binary thinking: perhaps embodied representations of supreme divinity in other traditions, too, bring together profound existential contradictions highlighted in their own cultures, even if they may do so with less mythic fullness than those in India. Doniger's book deals in universals and specifics but in suggestive, not absolute, terms: it weakens a potentially totalizing theory through a single complex example but then invites reflection on that example's global implications.

Dumézil's claims about tripartite mythic worlds among Indo-European peoples, by contrast, derive not from a universal theory of binary thinking but from Durkheimian ideas about religions' representing societies—ideas that have frequently led the anthropologically inclined to culturally specific analyses. From this perspective, Dumézil's claims are of the sort that might be made by a hypothetical ethnologist of prehistory: they present ideal religiocultural categories written very large, but still meaningful only within a particular cultural complex. Dumézil is insistent that he always begins with "the facts" and that "the system is always inherent in the material."[18] The introductions to his works sometimes dwell on that system's long and painstaking process of discovery.[19] Making genetic comparisons within the Indo-European family, he points to inherited similarities and identifies characteristics of different branches of the family tree. Although some may find Dumézil's *method* exemplary, his system, "inherent" in his specific Indo-European materials, does not speak suggestively beyond them. His work nevertheless comes into our ground of midlevel discourse through the very extent of those materials and their significance to Western civilizations. Just because Dumézil's studies treat a cultural complex that looms so large and wide, they can intersect with the work of many others.

Geertz's small-scale studies, on the other hand, move into the religiohistorical middle by being crafted as apt and suggestive models that prompt reflection on large questions of religion and culture. He is thus prone to fashion his ethnologies around neat, but broadly resonating, exemplars (for example, the "theater state" in Bali)[20] and to make comparisons that highlight diverging cultural styles. Known for "circl(ing) steadily within" a single cultural form in his thick descriptions, he can also "move between forms in search of broader unities or informing contrasts,"[21] as he does in *Islam Observed*—a work originally presented as the Terry Foundation Lectures in Religion and Science at Yale and offered self-consciously as a work in "the comparative study of religion."[22] Examining two distinct regional variants of Islam—one in Indonesia, the other in Morocco—Geertz interprets the images of a classical hero and preeminent modern leader in each. Effectively evoking a sense of the diverging characters of Indonesian and Moroccan Islam (and hence of the scope of Islamic tradition), Geertz's dual comparison—over cultural space and historical epoch—also lets him discuss two ranges of largish religiohistorical questions: those of unity within diverse world religions and those of tradition and modernity.

Combining interesting speculation with crafted examples, Geertz's work enters into the middle of religiohistorical discourse from both sides. Because his theoretical perspective is loose enough that his large concepts, which seem insightful, also seem to carry little baggage, they are easily adopted by students of religion. At the same time, Geertz's particular cultural examples are stylized (and stylish) enough that they can enter into a common parlance as nicely formed illustrations of an idea worth examining elsewhere. But with Geertz's work presenting a continuing interpenetration of big ideas and specific examples, his fusings of large and small seem fluid and discursive. As in "Ritual and Social Change," which presents a counterexample to truisms about the socially conservative force of ritual,[23] he is more likely to question common wisdom than to offer any new, specific hypotheses about the way religious traditions work. For these, we had better look not to an interpretive anthropologist but to a historian of religion of a more scientific temper. So let us now return to Jonathan Z. Smith and his "A Pearl of Great Price and a Cargo of Yams."

That article, examined in chapter 5 for its successful evocation in readers of both empathy for religious subjects and shock at scientific discovery, is also notable for the way it adopts scientific method. Making a comparison between ancient Babylon and early-twentieth-century Melanesia, we recall, it argues that the impact of imperialist power in both areas may have led the overpowered peoples to experiment with ritual in order to address their unhappy plight. In proposing this hypothesis, Smith expands the bounds of an already established religiohistorical category: cargo cults, the early-twentieth-century South Pacific movements that employed the ritual logic of indigenous traditions in an attempt to get a share of newly prized Western trade goods (known as "cargo").[24] He calls his Babylonian and Melanesian examples "cargo situations." Like Geertz, Smith brings together small stories and a larger concept, but his small description is less complex and his concept is not so large. Instead of using specific examples for an incomplete reflection on perpetually abiding issues, Smith is looking for a midlevel regularity: how far can we take the "cargo" pattern? Like the methods of many empirically oriented natural and social scientists, his is probing and experimental. His cargo situations, moreover, imply *causes*. They are the results of a specific, unidirectional relationship: the impact of an alien politic on a native society.

Taking causes seriously, Smith's analysis is clearly "explanatory" in our sense, but it does not depend on an overarching deterministic explanation. His explanation remains a small one. Although Smith gives more priority to politics and economics than many interpretive writers, like most of them he leaves ultimate causes in the distance. And as an interpretive writer, he gives us rational analysis that reveals human imagination and inventiveness. In a small frame, then, and when juxtaposed against religious imagination, causal explanation can be both intellectually powerful and aesthetically very effective.

Doniger's particular structuralist thesis, Dumézil's tripartite Indo-European schemata, Geertz's stylized examples and broad discussions, Smith's small explanatory hypothesis—each seems interestingly applicable to some range of religious traditions. Each scholar makes some specific claims about those traditions (well, maybe not Geertz) and suggests some implications beyond them. None, however, attempts a universal explanation. All of the analyses are in different ways restricted or hesitant, if not limited to a particular broad civilization, then offered only for a possible type of recurring situation.

Thus the middle-level realm that seems the natural haunt of interpretive writers—one between isolated case studies and doctrinaire theory, between unique descriptions and categorical typologies—produces statements that are themselves midlevel, moderate in two senses: significant over some medium-sized range of traditions and true only with a fair degree of probability.[25] These are the kinds of truths about the dynamics of tradition that interpretive writers are likely to assert, the propositions of any science of religion that might develop from their work. In what ways can we talk about these statements' validity? In what ways is interpretive knowledge also objective?

CHAPTER 7

Aesthetic Objects and Objective Knowledge

The dilemmas presented to writers on religion by questions of truth, validity, and objectivity can sometimes seem extreme. Dealing with diverse religious and scholarly worlds, interpretive writers may find it hard to escape the conclusion that specific religious beliefs are in an important sense relative. Seeing those beliefs in their respective contexts, moreover, interpreters may also be all too aware of the ways these can become entangled in social structures and political programs. Religious belief, it would seem, like much knowledge, is constructed from experience and economic interest, accident and exploitation; epistemes vary by history and culture. At the same time, though, interpretive writers, fascinated by their material, continue to see some human value in what they study. They are not, on the whole, ready to dismiss the fruits of others' traditions and their own collective scholarship as simply (pace Geertz) class interests and cryptotheology all the way down.[1]

Because the path of absolute relativism has been popular—indeed fashionable—at the turn of the twenty-first century, the surprise may be that more interpretive writers have *not* followed it more closely to its end. But their hesitation makes sense when we consider the poles of their basic modern dilemma. In both science and religion—toward which interpretive writers have been in different ways pulled—truth is taken very seriously indeed. A predisposition toward some sense of real truths in the midst of obviously relative worldviews may thus, I think, easily be characteristic of an interpretive writer.[2] Discussing the virtues of philosophical realism,

Thomas Nagel suggests its literally pivotal role in helping us try to "climb out of our own minds."[3] To the extent that interpretive writing has been a way for scholars to try to get beyond themselves personally, it may involve a sense of the real in its science as well as in its religion.

Still, if an attempt to get beyond oneself by writing on religion appears as a quasi-religious effort, it is also a naturalized and (usually) *liberal* one—requiring truths that are significant but less than absolute. One viable attitude toward these statements' possible truth might best be described as fallibilist: we see them as representing a reality out there but aren't quite sure if we've got it exactly right; we are open to revision and expect there to be some. This kind of fallibilism may suit the temperament of scholars prone to take problems of both science and religion seriously but who also regularly encounter the relativities and contingencies of belief. It also has an important practical similarity with some current social constructivist, neo-Nietzschean stances. One of the main intellectual virtues of a radically critical philosophical constructivism is to make us actively question our own and others' presuppositions; but an attentive fallibilism can do this too, and its hopefulness may, for scientists of religion, be more energizing.[4]

The problem for interpretive writers here can become complicated, however, by the ways in which the apparent importance of any philosophically realist claims found in their scientific statements depend on an *aesthetic* constructivism in their writing. The significance of interpretive statements as truth seems to derive in part from the crafted religiohistorical constructs of which they form a part: their objectivity depends on the firmness of those constructs, and the aesthetic depth of these enhances those statements' profundity. The aesthetic objects discussed in part 2 thus reappear here as vehicles of a sort of scientific objectivity, while aesthetic depth reappears as depth of thought. What can these two multivalenced concepts—objectivity and depth—tell us about the ways in which the aesthetic dimensions of interpretive writing inform the qualities of its scientific truths? In examining these two concepts I will adopt a stance sympathetic to what I read as the characteristically fallibilist temperament of religionists, but most of what I have to say should also make sense from a constructivist point of view.

OBJECTIVITIES AND SUBJECTIVITIES

In realist philosophies, objectivity generally has an ontological significance, denoting a reality distinct from the subject, but in common usage the term *objectivity* is also employed in three other senses important for religious studies. The least consequential of these we can call descriptive objectivity. When we talk about a description as objective, we usually mean that it is unadorned and bare, bereft of any personal opinion: "just the facts, ma'am, and nothing but the facts." Ethnographic and, more pertinently, phenomenological studies of religion sometimes invoke the virtue of this bare, descriptive objectivity: objective truth as a presentation of the Things Themselves. Some versions of this first, "just the facts" objectivity—assuming, pace Husserl, that there really are things out there to be described—do in fact seem to entail an "objectively" realist ontology.[5] However, this kind of bare objectivity may not always be of much use to interpretive scholars trying to write in a way that is deep as well as true. As it happens, the norms of objectivity on which they are more likely to rely are, in fact, less ontologically demanding.

Those two other norms of objectivity can be characterized as "procedural" and "dialogic."[6] Procedural objectivity is frequently invoked in natural science: if all the steps of an experiment are performed according to prescribed methods, its results carry a scientific authority they otherwise would not.[7] In the human sciences, procedural methods are usually much less codified. Nevertheless, some authority normally comes with at least the appearance of having done one's homework: research carried out, references cited, appropriate fieldwork undertaken. In both natural and human sciences, moreover, it seems to be more than just authority that is at stake: following customary academic procedures usually does help researchers "establish the facts" to current standards of accuracy. If procedural objectivity is crucial in determining the validity of data, integrity of interpretation can be enhanced by dialogic objectivity. Here, *objectivity* means impartiality in a legal sense, a freedom from bias that comes from seeing different sides of the situation. In religious studies, this entails not only understanding different academic angles but—usually more important—an empathetic understanding of religious subjects, the presentation of a situation from different human points of view. This is an objectivity that comes from sensitive perception, sustained conversation, and occasionally sharp dispute.[8] And as some legal cases and much Geertzian anthropology reveal, this kind of dialogic objectivity can present a very complex picture of the matter at hand.

Now, procedural and especially dialogic objectivity are normally taken as qualities not only of scholarly work but also of scholars. It is scholars themselves who are careful about method and evenhanded in their accounts. As qualities of people, not things in themselves, these two senses of objectivity can become criteria for judging the *integrity* with which our aesthetically informed religiohistorical objects are crafted—criteria readily comprehensible within constructivist assumptions about mind and world. Thus, in whatever sense our religiohistorical constructs are (or are not) taken to represent a reality, a methodological soundness gives them a sense of solidity, and an equitable dialogic acumen provides serious complexity. If it is objectivity as a trait of scholars that thus makes their constructs trustworthy and compelling,[9] then interpretive writing becomes objective (at least in part) through interpretive writers' subjectivities. These subjectivities, in turn, become crucial to some persistent problems of religiohistorical creation and judgment.

A Romantic Objectification

Marrying a sense of objectivity to a creative structuring of religious materials can easily lead to a concept of objectification. An uglier word than *objectivity*—which still carries the hope of levelheaded neutrality—*objectification* raises the specter of classical Enlightenment projects that posit humans in the natural world as simply objects for the knowing subject.[10] In submitting religion to rational analysis, interpretive writers undeniably participate in a classical project of this kind, but by writing in ways that present something of the religiohistorical sublime, they are also drawing on an imagination more characteristic of romantic sensibilities. Ideally, their objectifications are also aesthetic objects imbued with human subjectivities—both their own and those of religious actors. These subjectivities, moreover, become integral to interpretive writers' rational arguments.

Whether we like it or not, classically reasoned arguments inevitably find a place in most intellectual work. In the preface to a book that focuses on the *difficulties* of classical reasoning, Barbara Herrnstein Smith still notes that "problematic features of classic formulations and arguments (for example, their essentializing reifications and self-affirming circularities) seem to reflect cognitive tendencies that are, in certain respects, valuable or indeed indispensable."[11] Perhaps we need not worry too much if the self-affirming patterns of coherence of our religiohistorical constructs sometimes appear as stable reifications. These may be inescapable—sometimes even healthy—characteristics of much human cognition.

Interpretive writers, however, deal in reason and imagination both. To a classically cognitive backbone they add flesh and muscle from the suggestive stuff of religious life, which—while sometimes unsettling individual arguments—can make a construct as a whole seem not only more aesthetically objectified but also more dialogically objective. For the material of religion adds valuable density to skeletal arguments in part through its very ambiguities. In keeping us open to alternative suggestion, these help elicit the dialogic reimagining that makes for judicious representation: with different facets of a situation in mind, it is easier to be advocates for different sides at once. Our objectifications become truer—that is, closer to the elusive balance mark, more trustworthy—to the extent that they present the sensibilities of diverse religious actors as well as those of each particular writer. Thus fleshed out, they present recurrent themes from different angles—ambiguating them, perhaps, but reinforcing their importance, too. The cognitive solidity of constructed religiohistorical objects hence derives in part from the human sensitivity with which they are made.

Consensus and Fascination

That same sensitivity, when employed with aesthetic finesse, can also add to the weight of religiohistorical objects in academic communities, vitalizing the dynamic through which scholars arrive at intersubjective consensus. No doubt scholarly consensus around a work enhances its author's reputation, but consensus may also be taken as a measure of truth itself. While for a pragmatist like Rorty, a temporary, if broad, consensus is the only truth we have,[12] scholarly consensus has also been taken as a mark of a truth more realistically conceived. The perspectivalism of Charles Peirce, despite his well-known pragmatic views, seems sometimes to present scholarly convergence as moving toward a real end: "Different minds may set out with the most antagonistic views, but the progress of investigation carries them by a force outside of themselves to the same conclusion. This activity of thought by which we are carried, not where we wish but to a fore-ordained goal, is like the operation of destiny."[13] As a pragmatist, Peirce saw meaning in results,[14] so truth here is the end of investigative process. Yet Peirce's image of necessarily intersecting approaches might also suggest something about the way the world is: to the extent that scholars' views converge, we may be approaching a real truth. Of course, sometimes scholars' views never converge, particularly on big issues. But convergence may be likelier on the middle-range statements of interpretive writing—more modest general-

izations that often employ concepts only weakly attached to an encompassing worldview. Needing less than total assent, they are statements on
which reasonable convergence is a viable possibility.

Inasmuch as the emergence of scholarly consensus can be taken as a
measure of truth, it carries more weight to the extent that it begins with
genuine divergence, with people who tend *not* to see things in the same
way. Unfortunately, though, scholars with consistently diverging views
sometimes don't trouble to read one another's works at length. They will
be more likely to give those works sustained attention, however, if these
manage to display the *aesthetic* common ground of interpretive writing:
a compelling presentation of the materials of religious tradition. The
imaginative pull of the materials may then lead readers to see things from
the author's point of view, at least while they are reading. If, after due
consideration, a work does not substantially alter a reader's diverging
perspective, it may still have widened his or her horizon. And it may indeed turn out that on important middle-level statements, differently oriented minds can, in fact, meet. Although the aesthetic strength of a piece
of interpretive writing alone will not build rational consensus around the
scientific truths it proposes, it can certainly enhance the possibility that
a consensus will emerge.

Postcolonial Ironies of Consent

How can writing that is a self-consciously personal interpretation yield
statements that support a general rational consensus? On this question
the philosopher Nicholas Rescher makes a point that seems particularly
germane. Objective views, he tells us, like all views, are necessarily personal, but we need to distinguish "between those aspects of personal
views that are (or should be) compelling for rational people in general
and those that are shaped by . . . particular biases, preferences, and loyalties."[15] Even though our personal views of the way things are may be
idiosyncratically our own, *certain aspects* of them probably do support
objective truths. Like Peirce, Rescher is aware of the presence of "antagonistic minds" in intellectual life. Preaching to the converted does not
get us far along the road to objective truth: "To strive for objectivity is
to seek to put things in such a way that not just kindred spirits but virtually *anyone* can see the sense of it. It is not so much a matter of being
impersonal as impartial."[16] But Rescher's impartiality here is not the sympathetic openness of an evenhanded dialogist. Rather, like a strong
metaphysical realism, Rescher's impartiality deals in absolutes: since

"virtually *anyone*" should see our objective sense of things, it implies that norms of rationality are universal. In this post-Kantian epistemic objectivity, however, the weight of the absolute shifts from the real structure of the universe to the reason of the knowing subject. Instead of trying to describe "the way things are," it attempts to determine "the way rational people (should) see things."

In anthropology and religious studies the possibility of this epistemic objectivity has led to some ironic postcolonial complications. On the one hand, influential constructivists, acutely sensitive to problems of knowledge and power, have argued for the radical historical rootedness of all knowledge. There are no all-inclusive norms of rationality, they say; contingent political and economic interests condition human thinking down to its very core. Understandably, versions of such radical epistemic relativity have been espoused by those suffering from norms of Western patriarchy: women, gays and lesbians, ethnic minorities, and (some) colonized peoples. On the other hand, some of the postcolonized themselves, arguing against romantic exoticizing of the other, do in fact see some form of universal utilitarian reason: natives are human like everybody else and don't normally act in ways that *anyone* should find irrational.[17]

Interpretive writers contemplating problems of broad consensus can be tempted in either of these directions, depending on just whose consensus we seek. The stance followed in the main argument of the book, emphasizing general consensus among Western scholars and wide coverage of traditions studied, is in fact in line with a moderate version of a (constructivist) epistemic relativity. People drawn to interpretive writing are for the most part pretty well informed by a historically grounded Western rationality (which also makes them open to a Kantian aesthetic). They are, moreover, sometimes fascinated by the diverse religious worlds of others just because these do, at first, seem irrational to them. Products of a single broad intellectual culture in which they continue to work, they can be happy among themselves. Where is the necessity of invoking universal norms of reason? But, pulled in the other direction, we could also expand the breadth of our consensus to our intellectual counterparts in the religious communities we study, invoking universal norms of liberal utilitarian reason in a more sympathetic way. As Wilfred Cantwell Smith first suggested in the 1950s, we could invite members of the community we have written about to judge our work too. Let us have a truly global discussion; let us judge us.[18] Smith, then—once sent by a missions council to colonial India—appears as a precursor to an important postcolonial voice. The moral earnestness of an earlier era of scholarship still seems relevant today.

Nevertheless, even granted universal norms of reason, the idea of an expanded discussion—Smith's dialogue between members of traditions—presents difficulties for interpretive writers. These difficulties arise principally because most members of a religious community are concerned with aspects of its representation that differ from those dear to Western comparativists. Community members are sensitive to the tone of a piece of scholarly writing, to be sure, but they are also sensitive to accurate representation of the facts of tradition as they know them. A perceived error with important implications for a large theological story may lead to explosive encounters; those of little theological import—say some details in a ritual—may just be the cause for mild vexation or a condescending shaking of the head. Perhaps the results of variant traditions or of a scholar's honest (or careless) mistake, these ground-level misrepresentations are what tend to be noticed by anthropological "informants"—often together with what *wasn't* included in a description. Generalists in religion, likely to be blissfully unaware of such errors and omissions, will also be more forgiving of them if these don't seem germane to a work's interpretive point; what is more crucial to them is any suggestive generalization the work offers. Certainly, both ground-level statement and middle-level generalization can be taken as representations of reality, but they seem to represent it at different *depths*.

DEPTH OF VISION, DEPTH OF KNOWLEDGE

It is difficult to speak of realism, fallibilism, and a progressive scientific truth at the beginning of the twenty-first century without mentioning the most forceful proponent of "objective knowledge" in the twentieth, Karl Popper. Although Popper's observations on historiographical method, cited here and in other religious studies discussions,[19] seem appropriate for interpretive writing, the better part of his critical rationalism, with its emphasis on falsification and testability, seems much more appropriate for natural science. Still, Popper's discussion of "the problem of depth" in explanatory theories presents some enlightening continuities between the intuitive side of natural science and the aesthetic aspects of interpretive writing.

In attempting to discern which of two competing scientific theories is deeper, Popper is at an uncustomary analytical loss. "I believe," says Popper, "that this word 'deeper' defies any attempt at exhaustive logical analysis, but that it is nevertheless a guide to our intuitions."[20] As might be expected, however, Popper does have some ideas on how a concept of depth thus functions as an intuitive guide. "Two ingredients seem to be required," he writes, for theoretical depth: "a *rich content,* and a certain *coherence* or compactness (or 'organicity') of the state of affairs described. It is this latter ingredient which, although it is intuitively fairly clear, is so difficult to analyze" (my italics). Thus, Newton's dynamics is deeper than either "Galileo's terrestrial [or] Kepler's celestial physics" because it contains them both—and so has richer content than either—and, in explaining them, corrects them both, proving to be a system more coherent both within itself and with the external "state of affairs."

This element of coherence or "organicity" that Popper finds difficult to specify resembles one that humanists face regularly in constructing their analyses. Although religiohistorical coherence is admittedly a somewhat different species than its analogue in natural science—tending, for one thing, to lack the latter's compactness—it has the same general function of subsuming parts into an integral whole. In interpretive writing, as seen in chapter 3, this sense of the whole comes from a particular angle of vision, a coherence from a certain point of view. There, depth of vision in writing on religion was characterized aesthetically as a product of two elements: sharp focus and broad perspective. In the analysis of imagination and reason then presented, these two elements let widely resonating human details intersect to make an arguable case. Taken within the discussions of this chapter, however, these same two elements seem to present dimensions of Popper's coherence and content, respectively. The relevance of sharp focus to increased coherence is not so difficult to grasp: as focus sharpens, it becomes more penetrating, able to grasp central relationships, and may even lead to that compactness of analysis often missing in interpretive writing. The correspondence between a statement's content and a perspective's breadth, however, is both more complicated and more instructive.

For Popper, the content of a statement is the class of all its logical consequences.[21] In general, then, for a statement to have a content that is at least somewhat rich, it has to be relevant to a range of data, not just to a very particular situation. To encompass a range of data in interpretive writing, a writer's perspective needs to be at least moderately broad. Demands for rich content, then, lead from ground-level description up to midlevel generalization. But Popper's concept of content might also *keep* interpretive writers there, inhibiting them from soaring to some of their characteristic heights. For Popper also makes a clear distinction between

statements with many true consequences and those that are true but logical tautologies.[22] Keeping this distinction in mind, the phenomenological pigeonholing that is common in sweepingly broad interpretive visions
like van der Leeuw's makes for a statement with very little content. To
the extent that its truths are definitional only, they are tautologous. So if
we have been struck by a shallowness in much traditional phenomenology of religion, Popper can help us understand why. To have a degree of
depth, in Popper's terms, statements about religious traditions should
not only be coherent but should also demonstrate some complexity that
is not, on the surface, logically obvious.

Relatively deep statements about religious traditions make up at once
the contribution of interpretive writing to any science of religion and the
fulcrum of its own characteristic aesthetic of the sublime. Lying at the
core of our religiohistorical constructions, they often present themselves
as patterns, models, or structures. Examining a type of tradition, or a
family of traditions, or a recurrent situation, they purport to tell us something new and interesting about religious life. They suggest a proposition
that has some content—one that, in realist terms, may tell us something
about the way the world is. Moreover, to the extent that the knowledge
they offer seems *deeply* real—more fundamentally coherent and consequential—the more fully will our reason be engaged with the suggestive
materials from which this knowledge emerges. And if, engrossing our
reason, what we have to say also has logical consequences that really are
unexpected, it can lead to an additional shock that may, for a while, seem
world shattering. The deeper the knowledge, the deeper the experience
of the sublime.

Even for philosophical realists, though, encompassing any science of
religions within Popperian understandings has severe limits. Popper
would lead us on to theoretical analyses ever higher and deeper. Religiohistorical statements, by contrast, tend to stay in the middle and spread
out, implicating and suggesting one another. Not always quite coherent
with one another on a middle ground, they often just lead to further
questions: Popperian conjectures perhaps, but without his complementary refutations. To resolve their questions, interpretive writers
cannot move to the analytical heights—and corresponding theoretical
depth—Popper advocates. There are genuine constraints on the height of
the statements they can reasonably make, for once they get beyond a
middle ground, they can only be visionary interpreters, not scientific explainers. Their personal visions help them arrive at interesting statements
about traditions, but any sense of those statements' objectivity seems de-

rived not from their links to a particular overarching theory but from thorough, evenhanded scholarship that presents an argument overdetermined enough to find scholarly consensus.[23]

In offering middle-level religiohistorical patterns that significantly organize ground-level data, religiohistorical statements often do make sense from different analytic perspectives. But they usually do so because they are by nature interpretive views with rounded edges, not unidirectional causal explanations with logical consequences that conflict sharply with one another. Indeed, in tending to transform causal explanations into interpretative perspectives by smoothing over their hard corners, interpretive writers effectively deny much Popperian content to the crowning hypotheses of originally strong theories: the logical consequences of these theories' basic presuppositions are not always taken very seriously. Thus, less than in any scientific statement it presents, interpretive writing's potential for depth is more readily available through its aesthetic impact, which draws on imaginative factors that are inherently less precise—less in need of smoothing over and more properly ambiguous.

In practice, the value of our middle-level statements to a collective science of religions turns out to be not so much that they are part of increasing layers of theoretical explanation but that they are extractable from their contexts—sometimes presenting patterns that may well be replicable, often just posing pertinent questions. Objective inasmuch as other people can see them too, they have increasing scientific value to the extent that other writers can take them to their own materials. As Doniger did with Lévi-Strauss on myth, writers with visions of their own will employ others' theories according to their own lights, making their own adjustments, not necessarily invoking all of a theory's original presuppositions. Thus, despite the attention given in this chapter to contrasting constructivist and realist stances in religious studies, when we are actually engaged in a collective science of religion, we often find ourselves slipping into the language of pragmatism: a work is "useful" and an understanding "helpful"; an analysis "bears fruit." If as critical analysts we tend toward constructivism, and our aesthetic of the sublime is heightened by a sense that we are dealing in realities, in sharing one another's research we are normally pragmatists: we use it if it works. This pragmatic aspect of religiohistorical sharing will become paramount in part 4, which examines some ways in which scholars of religion have worked together publicly and privately.

PART FOUR

Working Together

SCIENCE SUGGESTS A COLLECTIVE ACTIVITY, but interpretive writers—whose feelings about religion are individually ambivalent—develop pronounced personal perspectives of their own. Thus arises a characteristic dilemma of public and private in the study of religion. Aesthetic depth in writing on religion comes from finding a focus for broad personal perspectives, and although that focus typically finds public articulation as a clear, if guarded, statement, the private perspective from which it derives may be unified in less than articulate ways.[1] Arising from individual visions, interpretive statements often seem isolated from one another—coexisting in a middle-range realm of religiohistorical knowledge but not in strong mutual relationship. The fabric of public religiohistorical knowledge thus often seems loosely woven to the extreme. How, then, do individual writers on religion see themselves participating in a collective academic endeavor? And how have they, in fact, worked together in practice?

Part 4 examines some of the pragmatics entailed by the necessary interplay of private vision and public knowledge in the academic study of religion. Its first three chapters, detailing some specific instances of scholars working with or against one another, move through a dialectic of practice. Those chapters are capped by a "transcendent fourth," which suggests some different *ideas* of collectivity held in the field.

The dialectic of the first three chapters works out some institutional ramifications of the categories of interpretation and explanation introduced abstractly in part 3. Chapter 8 explores individualistic extremes of interpretation, examining the ways in which the expansive visions of successive Dutch phenomenologists play against their immediate predecessors. Chapter 9, tracing the fate of some British and German diffusionist theories in the early twentieth century, reveals how explanatory hypotheses really can provide common grounds for working groups, even if these dissolve and become forgotten as their hypotheses prove false. Chapter 10 returns us to a figure who is still remembered and with whom we are already familiar: Jane Harrison. In chapter 2 we examined Harrison's telling ambivalences toward religion; here we will investigate her collaboration with close academic colleagues in a group known as the Cambridge Ritualists. The intellectual relationships among the major

Ritualists, more personalized and less tight theoretically than those grounded in diffusionist explanations, suggest some ways in which characteristically interpretive writers are able fruitfully to interact.

These examples were chosen as extreme cases, able to reveal not only the possible fruits of different dynamics of scholarly practice but also some of their characteristic problems: grandiose interpretations, obsessiveness in programmatic explanation, and intellectual friendships that become too intimate. There were other criteria, too. The Dutch phenomenologists were chosen because they seemed important enough in the history of religious studies that they had to be accounted for, the German diffusionists because they were little known in the English-speaking world and seemed interesting enough to expose to a wider audience. In all cases the examples selected were the ones I thought could help me best make my points given the disciplinary history with which I am familiar.

After these examples (and counterexamples) of genuine collective work, chapter 11 turns to more deliberately constructed, generally less-interactive, groups: the collections of scholars assembled by anthology editors. Through the designs of their collections, editors suggest possibilities about the ways through which knowledge in religious studies builds on itself and grows—possibilities, alas, that too often remain unfulfilled. The ways in which the complementary designs of four edited volumes do and do not manage to fulfill the visions of intellectual coherence behind them finally reveal some characteristic textures in the fabric of evolving religiohistorical knowledge.

The detailed pursuit of historical examples in part 4 provides scope for exploring the everyday complexities of the concepts developed in the earlier parts of the book. Framed in terms of the notions of interpretation and explanation developed in part 3, the historical discussions here also reveal the variously ambivalent feelings of scholars toward religious material seen in part 1. Not only do the different collective endeavors themselves reflect different stances toward science and religion, but the tension between those stances may also be experienced by each member of a group in his or her own distinctive way. The aesthetic dimensions evident in the artful writing of part 2 are less evident in our discussions here. Not all of the scholars here treated can legitimately be characterized as interpretive writers in our aesthetic sense, and those that can be were not always such successful ones. Moreover, in examining the intertwinings among works and lives within different scholarly groups, I pay more attention to the lives in groups than to the works in detail. Nevertheless, we will still come across examples that show interesting variations on the aesthetic dynamics of part 2, and the occasional glaring absence of them can in itself be suggestive. As in most religiohistorical practice, I think, seeing the significance of our analytic concepts for the lives and work of real people makes them at once less precise and more meaningful.

CHAPTER 8

Interpreting Anew
and Alone

Vision and Succession in Dutch Phenomenology

Among the different English renderings of *Religionswissenschaft*—
which include "the science of religions" and "comparative religions,"
alongside "history of religions"—one sometimes also encounters the
phrase "phenomenology of religion."[1] Highlighting the "phenomena" of
traditions can lead scholars, in one direction, to try to describe the stuff
of religious tradition as it exists in its own right, leaving their own vision
as far as possible outside the picture. In this sense, phenomenology tries
not to be interpretive. But highlighting the phenomena of religion can
also lead scholars in another direction, toward abstractions about the
materials of traditions, toward identifying basic types of phenomena. In
this sense, phenomenology is an inherently interpretive exercise: Eliade's
work is sometimes characterized as a phenomenology, even though he
did not normally refer to it as such himself. The writer who most fa-
mously embraced the term "phenomenology of religion" for his own
scholarship was the Dutchman Gerardus van der Leeuw, and the term is
sometimes used specifically to characterize his and related work by
Dutch pioneers in religious studies. In the interplay between privately intuited vision and publicly articulated statement out of which religiohistorical knowledge grows, these early Dutch phenomenologists sometimes struck a radical posture. Indeed, especially as exemplified by van
der Leeuw, they often seemed to present their private syntheses *as* public truth.

On its surface (and at deeper levels, too) classical Dutch phenomenology of religion bears little resemblance to Husserl's philosophical movement of phenomenology, which developed contemporaneously with it in Germany and later in France.[2] But the religionists' use of the term *phenomenology* has its own pedigree. As George Alfred James points out, this term has been used in different senses in two distinct communities of discourse: not only in the German and French philosophical tradition but also in nineteenth-century British empirical science.[3] In German philosophy, the term has been used in different ways to probe the relationship between subjective and objective realities—from the internal dynamics within Hegel's manifesting *Geist* to Husserl's phenomenological method of getting at the "the things themselves." The British usage, by contrast, is much more pedestrian, referring first of all to descriptive ordering as the first phase of empirical inquiry. It is primarily in this sense that the term has been used by religionists: the classical phenomenologists of religion offered ordered presentations of the totality of religious objects they saw. Some, however, including van der Leeuw—perhaps seduced by the ambiguity of the term—have explored the subjective dynamics among their categories or adapted Husserlian method to what is primarily an exercise in systematic arrangement.[4]

If the phenomenologists' science was one of ordered description, it was of description presented to their remarkable religious intuitions, which were guided by different senses of order. The diverse, widely encompassing, phenomenological sciences that emerged could thus appear both highly personalized and grounded in a sense of spiritual self-confidence. Like Eliade, the classical phenomenologists tended to be "great men" with great visions.

Standing out primarily as individual interpreters guided by their own lights, the Dutch phenomenologists also sometimes seem to respond to predecessors in tradition. These responses tend to show little direct influence save that of general style and vocabulary. More often, the response appears as a reaction; the tradition of scholarship looms as a backdrop against which men of vision can distinguish themselves. In this sense, the kind of scholarly interaction that we find among these phenomenologists presents a caricature of the patterns of interpretive work in the humanities. Valued in contemporary humanistic interpretation, newness and originality are even more highly prized in twentieth-century art. The grand interpreters in the science of religion, creating aesthetic syntheses, sometimes demonstrate the virtues (and vices) of originality to a very high degree.

The phenomenology of religion had its heyday in Holland during the end of the nineteenth and first half of the twentieth centuries. In addition to fostering the work of van der Leeuw, Holland was also the home of two founders of the science of religion—P. D. Chantepie de la Saussaye and C. P. Tiele. My focus will be on the chair in phenomenology of religion at Leiden. Although never held by van der Leeuw—perhaps the greatest of "great men"—it housed the greatest *number* of early influential scholars in the field: first Tiele, then William Brede Kristensen and Hendrik Kraemer. The personal ambivalences that all three had toward the materials they studied derived from a tension between a scientific outlook and a personal attachment to a Christian confession. A self-consciously Christian stance, it is true, might lead to doctrinaire understandings of other traditions, but it could also foster sympathy for and sensitivity to others' religious lives. Both these tendencies reach a crescendo in Kraemer, the last and most controversial of the three. They are also both apparent in Tiele, the first of them, but less vociferously. Indeed, in Tiele the tension between potentially conflicting Christian and scientific persuasions seemed least problematic, finding a straightforward, theologically comfortable, resolution.

TIELE'S LIBERAL TRIUMPHALISM

Active in the latter decades of the nineteenth century, C. P. Tiele embraced the evolutionary paradigms reigning in science at the time, particularly the Tylorean anthropology of religions, but he was simultaneously a churchman trained in theology and sensitive to the ways of religious life. The conflict between a unilineal Tylorean vision of the evolution of religion and Tiele's own sense of personal piety was mediated in part by attention to historical contexts—also "scientific" in a ground-level empiricist (rather than a midlevel generalizing) sense. Different historical contexts could allow elements of higher religions more *advanced* meanings than similar elements found in apparently earlier traditions. As higher religions evolved from the lower, they became more profoundly *complex,* embodying increasing dimensions of unity and diversity and thus tending ever more toward the universal.[5] In his final systematic work, the two-volume *Elements of Religion,* Tiele treated the evolutionary and the pietistic aspects of religion separately. The first volume, which he calls "morphological," looks at "laws of development" in tradition, which were in fact rather loose; the second, called "ontological," tries to establish the common essence of the historically attested phenomena. Tiele still has a concept of evolution, if in an attenuated form, but he also conceptualizes "religion" as having a basic unity.

Tiele's vision of the basic unity of religion owes an obvious debt to Schleiermacher's theology of experience, discussed in chapter 1.[6] In its essence, according to Tiele, religion "lives in the heart," and its origins are "traceable to emotions."[7] But in addition to emotion, religion also contains "conceptions" and "sentiment"—the latter a quality that "impels to action" (2:18). The three are essential in any religion: "morbid symptoms" and "narrow-mindedness" (2:23) in religious life arise from a lack of balance among them.

With religion essentially one, but its forms many and evolving, the way is open for a vision of a wide-ranging Protestant triumphalism. As civilization progressed ever onward through the nineteenth century, reasoned Tiele in the spirit of his age, people all over the world should embrace it in its advance, and with it increasingly civilized forms of religion. People resist change because "they do not see that the form of religion in which they have been brought up . . . is but one of the forms of religion, and that religion itself is entirely independent of such forms" and that "their form of religion, which they identify with religion itself, no longer accords with the present stage of civilization, but with an older stage" (1:222–23). The religion of the present stage of civilization is, by this reasoning, the best and should be adopted by all enlightened persons. A student of Near Eastern traditions with extensive philological training, Tiele represented the traditions in which he specialized (and, in his general works, contemporary world religions, too) as accurately as anyone in his generation.[8] But the whole into which he brought them all together obviously reflected a particular vision of a convinced man of faith in an age of scientific progress.

KRISTENSEN'S SYMPATHETIC SCIENCE

William Brede Kristensen, like Tiele, was a specialist in ancient Near Eastern traditions, but he contemplated his materials within a vision of the whole that emerged from a poise toward the religionist's modern dilemmas that was more romantic than Tiele's. Both scholars recognized a religious impulse for scholarly work, but in Kristensen that impulse was oriented not toward understanding the evolutionary place of his confession but toward fostering an inner growth. At the same time, the rational, scientific outlook that was for Tiele an end product of human evolution could for Kristensen also be an obstruction to the sympathetic understanding of ancient traditions.[9] The two scholars' different ambivalences toward the traditions they studied were reflected in the changing title of the chair they successively occupied. Tiele was professor of the History and Philosophy of Religion, a title that in fact reflects the twofold approach seen in his *Elements:* a historically oriented morphology and a philosophically styled ontology. He did not seriously develop a category he called "phenomenology." When Kristensen succeeded to the chair in 1901, however, its title changed to a professorship in Phenomenology of Religion,[10] a category Kristensen took very seriously indeed.

In the introduction to his major theoretical work, Kristensen justifies his use of the term "phenomenology of religion" instead of the more familiar "comparative religion," which, as he presents it, seems to describe important aspects of Tiele's morphological enterprise. The comparative religion of preceding decades, writes Kristensen, gave "a general view of the different degrees of religious development and indicat[ed] the place of each religion in this line of development"[11]—often to apologetic ends. The phenomenology of religion offers another kind of comparison, a different sort of "over-all view" of "numerous and widely divergent data"; instead of ranking whole traditions from high to low, it attempts to determine "religious content and . . . values" of the divergent data by classifying them according to type.[12] The bulk of *The Meaning of Religion* thus comprises short topical sections ("Sacred Times," for example) arranged according to a number of broad categories—cosmological, anthropological, and cultic—the first of which especially, in its expansive morphological sweep, recalls Eliade's *Patterns in Comparative Religion.*

On the face of it, this embrace of broad typology seems at odds with the image of Kristensen that I presented in chapter 1—the empathetic scholar concerned with understanding the meanings of religious data in particular contexts. Kristensen, however, saw little conflict between typology and empathetic study, finding the two complementary—indeed fulfilling each other. A careful scholar in his own field, Kristensen was well aware of the fragmentary nature of the evidence for the ancient Near Eastern religions that particularly interested him. If he could attempt to bridge the inevitable gaps in his knowledge of, say, some ancient Babylonian sacrifice with what he knew of sacrifice as a general, multi-dimensional phenomenon, then he might understand it better. He still insisted that "every religion ought to be understood from its own standpoint," but he acknowledged at the same time that "only approximate knowledge is possible" (6). It made sense, then, in coming to grips with obscure particulars, to take what help one could from categorial understandings; at the same time, any knowledge of particular cases might help us better comprehend the general patterns of human religious life. This hermeneutic of category and instantiation has continued to inform much of what is most commonly known as phenomenology of religions, with many scholars interpreting particular instances as examples of a larger type and a few enunciating large visions of ordered types. Of the latter, two spent time at Leiden during Kristensen's long tenure there: P. D. Chantepie de la Saussaye and Gerardus van der Leeuw.

A CONSOLIDATOR AND A REVOLUTIONARY

Chantepie de la Saussaye, Kristensen's older contemporary, had come to Leiden two years before him, in 1899, as a professor of Theological Encyclopedia, Doctrine of God, and Ethics; he stayed until his retirement in 1916, working largely on the philosophical and theological topics reflected in his title.[13] He had come from the University of Amsterdam, where he in fact completed the bulk of his religiohistorical work, which included, monumentally, the first modern global survey of religions: the *Manual of the Science of Religion,* first published in German in 1887–89.[14] The survey began with an extensive phenomenology, with chapters on "holy places," "gods," and "religious writings," to name just a few. It then moved on to a short ethnological section—treating the religions of small-scale societies areally—and a longer historical section on world religions. Thus, both the older historicodevelopmental approach pursued by Tiele and the phenomenological style that would flower later with Kristensen and his successors were presented as integral elements of a unified science of religion. Chantepie de la Saussaye insisted that this science was something distinct from theology, and the example of his career testified to his simultaneous conviction that the two could legitimately be practiced by the same person. With van der Leeuw, by contrast, phenomenology blossoms exuberantly through overt grounding in philosophical and theological concerns.

Van der Leeuw studied at Leiden from 1908 to 1913. Majoring in history of religions in the department of theology, he had Kristensen as his main professor, but he also studied with Chantepie.[15] By all accounts, van der Leeuw indeed presented the image of the "great man"—with broad interests and an expansive personality. As a professor at Gronigen, he expounded to his students outside class; after World War II, he served his country briefly as minister of culture.[16] The phenomenology of religion that he produced is similarly broad and expansive. Deriving its

structure from concepts foregrounded in German philosophical phenomenology—subject, object, and their "reciprocal operation"—it finds
its primary idea of the sacred—power—in the emotive *mana,* identified
earlier as basic by the anthropologist Marett.[17] The hundred-odd categories to which these concepts give rise in *Religion in Essence and Manifestation* offer a vast ordered array of religious phenomena, presented
with considerable erudition.

   Religion in Essence and Manifestation—as well as the other early
Dutch phenomenologies—offers something of an aesthetic of extent, the
schematic, emotionally cool approach examined in chapter 5 in the work
of Eliade and Dumézil. Eliade, we recall, employed this aesthetic in a universal way that could reverberate in his readers; Dumézil restricted himself to Indo-European cultures, if on a grand scale. Although the early
phenomenologists surveyed traditions widely, their orientations appear
more restrictedly Christian than inclusively universal, and in their detached presentations of diverse materials they often seem to have more
in common aesthetically with Dumézil than with Eliade. Religious subjects, for them, generally appeared as the other under their gaze, not part
of an encompassing humanity that included the reader and writer. Thus,
the total effect of their aesthetics of extent is more often, like Dumézil's,
to cause us to gasp at the enormity of it all than it is, like Eliade's, to suggest truths that we may see reverberating in ourselves. If their phenomenologies often included a treatment of major world religions, it was as
a series of local visions, not a universal one. Thus, even though the cumulative effect of their works might be overwhelming, it has not been
one that, for most readers, hits home. And many readers, I think, have
not even approached the phenomenologists' works as wholes in ways
that might in fact overwhelm them. Instead, they have mined them in
their pieces as handbooks—and as such they are out of date and today
largely unread.

   The exception here is the phenomenology of van der Leeuw, which
has been repeatedly reprinted[18]—maintaining an audience, I think, just
because it can appear as a compelling whole. Indeed, as the unfolding of
an elaborate intuitive play deriving from basic binary categories, *Religion in Essence and Manifestation* recalls the heady dynamic of
Doniger's structuralist analysis of Shiva. Van der Leeuw's types begin
from a logical base and grow and grow but still, we may suspect, might
never quite cover the field. In presenting a potential completeness that is
never quite fulfilled, *Religion in Essence and Manifestation* (or at least
its table of contents) thus might well elicit in some readers a sense of the

religiohistorical sublime: mathematical in its increasing multiplicity, as well as dynamic in its encompassing breadth. In its concluding chapters, moreover, it gives explicit justification for its own inventiveness.

Portraying himself as a revolutionary, van der Leeuw in fact situated himself toward the traditions of scholarship he encountered in a very different way than did Chantepie de la Saussaye. The latter, attempting to establish an independent science of religion, carefully surveyed scholarly opinion on the questions of his day in the introduction to his *Manual*. He examined both the problem of origins current among anthropologists and the phenomenologists' penchant for the "division of religions"— that is, how to classify religious traditions according to type—giving detailed outlines of the schemes of Hegel, the German thinker Eduard von Hartmann, and Tiele.[19] Chantepie wanted to identify some ground for his science and build from it. Van der Leeuw, by contrast, wanted to activate an already established field in an exciting new direction. His advocacy of the need for perpetual revolution in the field seems almost Maoist in its absoluteness, if not in its practical scope: "The phenomenology of religion is dynamic," he tells us in the concluding paragraph of *Religion in Essence and Manifestation:* "as soon as it ceases to move it ceases to operate"; it has "infinite need of correction [in] its innermost being."[20] In coming up with his new categories, van der Leeuw thus felt free to play with fresh currents from Continental thought. In presenting their contents, however, he cited widely from established scholarship to create a broad, synthetic picture very obviously shaped by his own particular humanistic vision but nevertheless worthy of continuing academic attention. Van der Leeuw's incitement to perpetual change, of course, probably had more rhetoric than substance: would he really be upset that *Religion in Essence and Manifestation* still survives as a minor classic? But it does suggest the value artistic personalities might find in an interpretive originality that plays against familiar ways of their predecessors.

HENDRIK KRAEMER, SCHOLAR AND MISSIONARY

Hendrik Kraemer's strong personality led him in a different direction— one that may seem seriously dubious to many of us in the secular academy, for it was grounded in a reassertion of Christian fundamentals. Certainly, one can question the results of van der Leeuw and most of his phenomenological predecessors, but few—until the rise of recent postcolonial qualms—have questioned their motives. By leavening their theologically grounded worldviews with extensive factual knowledge of other traditions, one charitably supposes, they would expand their own religious horizons, making these more flexible and subtle; in the process, moreover, they would ideally open their Western contemporaries to new understandings of religious life. The case of Hendrik Kraemer, however, was much more problematic. About the same time that van der Leeuw was becoming impressed with the value of philosophical phenomenology, Kraemer became inspired by the stalwart theological spirit of Karl Barth. This he actively injected into a theory of Christian missions that inevitably informed his study of the religions of the world.[21]

Kraemer's work, then, presents a sharp contrast to that of Kristensen, his predecessor at Leiden. Succeeding Kristensen in 1937, Kraemer served in the following year as a leading participant in a World Missionary Conference at Tambaram, Madras, remembered for its heated discussions about the relationship of Christianity to "the religions." In addition to giving a plenary address, Kraemer wrote a background document for the conference: *The Christian Message in a Non-Christian World*. Outspoken yet scholarly, this volume remains the work for which he is best known.[22]

The attempt made by Kraemer in *The Christian Message* to balance distinguished scholarly credentials vis-à-vis the "non-Christian" religions with an unambiguously Christian perspective toward them has marked his career, surrounding him with controversy from its outset. As a new alumnus of the Dutch Bible Society intent on missionary work in the Dutch East Indies, Kraemer came to Leiden in 1911 to study philology with the great orientalist Snouck Hurgronje; he also took a course with Kristensen and came into contact with Chantepie de la Saussaye.[23] After defending a thesis on Javanese mysticism in January 1921, he proposed further research to the Bible Society but in a part of central Java where their mission did not operate. There was considerable opposition to this proposal on the part of important authorities in the Society but enough support for Kraemer to carry out his plans: his official instruction was to "study . . . the spiritual life of the Javanese people" as an "ancillary service to the mission."[24] Thus, not only as a missionary among scholars—where his outspokenly Christian views ran counter to the more "scientific" academic current—but also as a scholar among missionaries, Kraemer raised questions. After serving as professor of Phenomenology of Religion from 1937 until 1948—he was Kristensen's own choice as successor[25]—he became the first president of the Ecumenical Institute at the Chateau de Bossy, Switzerland, retiring in 1955.[26] In this last "ecumenical" phase of his career Kraemer stressed issues of communication and dialogue among religions, in this respect resembling Wilfred Cantwell Smith, who also moved from a missionary career to an academic one.[27] Paying less attention to questions of diversity *within* traditions than Smith did, and thus skirting a number of vital religiohistorical issues, Kraemer today is remembered with reverence sooner within missiological circles than among historians of religions.[28]

Kraemer's stance toward "non-Christian religions"—sharply articulated in *The Christian Message* in 1938—was expressed in more moderate tones in later works written during his ecumenical phase in the 1950s and 1960s, but it did not fundamentally change.[29] Kraemer initially presented this stance in deliberate contrast to the reigning scholarly norm. Commenting in the first pages of *The Christian Message* on the relativism and secularism of the present age, Kraemer cites a sentence from the classicist Gilbert Murray, a colleague of Jane Harrison's and one of the Cambridge Ritualists to whom we will turn in chapter 10: "Religion essentially deals with the uncharted region of human experience"—which Kraemer reads as the realm of magic and ritual.[30] This idea of religion, cited as an example of a "universal notion" among secular thinkers, is, I think, one that many students of religion could live with—as a truism if not as a definition. According to Kraemer, however, it is "erroneous—from the standpoint of true religion," for although a human being is "a religious 'animal' by nature, he is at the same time deeply irreligious, if we take the word religion with the seriousness we have learnt from Christ."[31] True religion is thus specifically Christian and—with its belittling of ritual—implicitly Protestant. "The Church," he admonishes his audience at the beginning of *The Christian Message,* "is emphatically reminded that it, alone of all human institutions in the world, is founded on divine commission."[32] In his 1960 *World Cultures and World Religions,* he continues to be straightforward about his approach, maintaining that it is as fair as any: "This book is written from a definitely Christian standpoint and therefore ultimately will make an endeavor to offer Christian interpretation. . . . I hope to show that to write and interpret from a distinctly Christian background, with a fair knowledge of the facts, about this fascinating meeting of cultures and religions is as biased or unbiased an effort as any humanist attempt pretends to be."[33]

Non- (or post-)Christian readers who have little use for Kraemer's theoretical pronouncements are likely to be surprised at the knowledge and sensitivity he brings to his presentations of "non-Christian" religions. Indeed, Kraemer's particular missiological perspective affects both the empathy and vision he brings to his scholarly work. He argued early in his career that in contrast to ordinary students of religion, whose "intuitive" identification with their subject is sparked by mere scientific curiosity, the missionary student, moved by "love to those he had to serve," would try to understand their religious conditions from within.[34] Later, he would expand this approach to sophisticated theological teachings. In his 1956 exposition of the modern Hindu philosopher Sarvepalli Radhakrishnan, Kraemer offers a clear and detailed analysis, taking Radhakrishnan's view of Hinduism seriously as religious doctrine—doctrine, however, that he believes is false. Standing against the Schleiermachian thrust evident in most theological history of religions (and which Radhakrishnan shares), Kraemer identifies the main problem in Radhakrishnan's interpretation of Hinduism as its positing of religious authority in experience alone, with even the Vedic scriptures taken as the "experience" of the sages who gave utterance to them. In Radhakrishnan's Hinduism, argues Kraemer, "the word 'revelation' is thus emptied of all its genuine significance,"[35] and for Kraemer, revelation along with experience was central. Kraemer's emphasis on biblical revelation as the core of Christianity leads him to look for core beliefs in other traditions, too; he wanted to identify what was central in religious traditions and to see how these situate human religious sensibilities in the world. In looking at traditions as organic wholes, he recalls less his predecessor, Kristensen, than Kristensen's predecessor, Tiele, and like Tiele—but more outspokenly—he sees an evolutionary Christian triumphalism at work in the universe.[36]

VISION, SUCCESSION, AND THE PROBLEMS OF GREAT MEN

Kraemer's outspokenness has, at least, the virtue of underlining the close relationship between his theological and phenomenological writings. This stands in contrast to his phenomenological compatriots, who tended to present their phenomenologies as separate from their theologies. Yet those theologies were often well developed and inevitably shaped their phenomenological work, if not always obviously providing apologetic warrants for it. Jacques Waardenburg of Utrecht, an heir to and chronicler of the Dutch tradition in religious studies, suggests that "on the whole, 'classical' phenomenology of religion has had an apologetic function and a solipsistic tendency."[37] Kraemer's work brought the "apologetic function" latent in much phenomenological work out into the open, but his thrust toward confrontation and dialogue is hardly solipsistic. Among the classical phenomenologists, the "solipsistic tendency" seems most pronounced in van der Leeuw, whose outlook seems the most all-inclusive and self-contained among others in a series of grand visions of the religious life of humankind.[38]

As with most large-scale interpreters, the professional success of the classical phenomenologists depended less on any exciting new discovery than on the presentation of a vision that was novel and engaging. In this respect they appear much more like poets than scientists and in their attitude toward their predecessors display some of the Oedipal feelings described by Harold Bloom in the *Anxiety of Influence*.[39] Thus, Kristensen and Kraemer both wrote short biographical pieces about their immediate predecessors at Leiden—reverential, of course, but also underscoring their differences with them: Kristensen's moving away from Tiele's evolutionary approach; Kraemer's differing with Kristensen, much as he did with Radhakrishnan, in the authority they both accorded experience to the exclusion of revelation.[40] The actual theoretical resonances we thus see in the line at Leiden, then—the organicism and evolutionism in Tiele and Kraemer—in fact skip a generation.

The dynamic in collective research presented by the classical phenomenologists—as by many humanists of large vision—is more imperialistic than collaborative. Even when they did original philological work of their own, they stand out as phenomenologists through their syntheses of the research of others. They thus draw broadly on their contemporaries in the wider realm of religious studies (including branches of anthropology and what we would today call area studies), helping to give that diffuse field an identity. At the same time, to their immediate phenomenological predecessors—with whose work they were certainly familiar—they present a studied difference. What is passed down through the academic generations was less a body of knowledge, or even an approach to conceptualizing problems, but a precedent, a style of studying religion deemed as legitimate—one on a grand scale that fostered the expression of lofty insight. More aesthetic than scientific, it was liable to grow increasingly inward and idiosyncratic as it was developed by great men in their determinedly distinctive ways. With its virtue almost solely in its vision, it led to works that were in fact inimitable. If the great men found disciples, they had no method to leave them, and they didn't have much to collaborate about among themselves, either. Theirs was not an approach destined to spawn group projects.

CHAPTER 9

Explaining Together

The Excitement of Diffusionist Ideas

Emerging in a fragmented discipline that fosters individual insights, group projects in religious studies have been much more the exception than the rule. Usually small-scale and short-lived, they depend on some potent combination of institutional circumstances, personal styles, and unifying ideas. As bases for public knowledge, central ideas in group projects tend to be presented in an explanatory style: they are offered as explicit formulas that anyone should be able to apply. Yet the formulas that have seemed to inspire the most projects have been grounded less in a strong causal logic than in a grand historical narrative. Indeed, what seem to have been the most enduring group projects on religion throughout the twentieth century were dedicated to tracing patterns of religio-cultural diffusion, an endeavor that in Indo-European studies continues into the twenty-first with the continuing vitality of scholars inspired by Dumézil.[1]

In contrast to interpretive phenomenological visions, diffusionist explanations provided concrete programs of collective research. In the study of early cultures and civilizations at the turn of the twentieth century, "diffusion" vied with "evolution" as a concept that could explain the similarities found in the lifeways of diverse peoples. Evolutionary theories, positing an essential unity in the development of humankind, presumed that the same discoveries would naturally be made independently in different societies at similar stages of cultural progress: do not all human beings have the same capacities, and is not all human culture ultimately one? Propagated by Tylor from the 1870s, and carried on by Frazer into the 1910s, evolutionary theories were, at the turn of the century, the generally accepted academic explanation. Diffusion theories then appeared in the first few decades of the twentieth century as new and exciting ideas, positing diversity—if not hierarchy—among human cultures. A historical perspective now meant not tracing the gradual progress of human culture but attempting to understand the migrations and mutual interactions of different peoples. Important human knowledge—of the stars, say, or of useful metals—was discovered once for all, spreading as advanced cultures penetrated less-advanced ones. Even during the years of excitement, the migration of cultures could become a subject of sober study for many ethnologists, particularly Americanists looking at the prehistoric movement of populations across the Bering Strait. Today, moreover, most students of prehistory see both independent discovery and diffusion of culture as complementary, each having a place in the explanation of separate, complex situations.[2] But as ideas of cultural diffusion began to gain recognition at the beginning of the century, they were sometimes championed by people who took them to radical extremes.

Radical diffusionist projects were often promoted by just one or two people taken up with a daring new idea about the origin and spread of cultures. Typically, that idea drew the scorn of most established scholars and the attention of some less-established ones, who might then become inspired to contribute to the project. Although the theories that emerged could eventually cover more and more ground, they still remained less all-embracing world pictures—like those of the Dutch phenomenologists—than the obsessively pursued implications of a particular historical hypothesis. As historical narratives, they hover between small explanations written on a large canvas and a large explanatory story with some specific historical roots. When they were careful, diffusionists might stress the specific historical nature of their major hypotheses, which could thus be theoretically falsifiable. Yet their theories—referring to events in the distant past—were not in fact easy to falsify conclusively, although enough counterevidence and the attraction of even newer ideas could eventually leave more radical projects bereft of much support. The history of diffusion theories thus appears as one of the exciting ideas pursued and then eventually abandoned by all but the most stalwart. Championed by outspoken proponents able to arouse an initial exhilaration among a group of colleagues, these ideas have led to collaborative work that eventually petered out.

Often engaged with work in anthropology or archeology, or at least
with difficult philologies, diffusionists saw themselves as scientists—
more so than most writers we have examined. Nevertheless, as seen in
chapter 1, scholars drawn to work with religious materials—even if of
extremely scientific temperament—still tend to be somehow personally
fascinated by them; and the drive with which diffusionists pursued their
theories suggests a very strong fascination indeed. Yet the fascination
that religious materials hold for the scientist pursuing a theory tends to
be of another quality than the fascination they hold for the interpreter
of myth and symbol. What allures here is less the pull of deep human realities than the potential solution to very important questions about
human life on earth.

In the three diffusionist cases to be examined—the first from Near Eastern studies, the second and third from historical ethnology—the data of
religious traditions raised intriguing questions that motivated scholars to
pursue their different visions. The German Panbabylonians, riveted by the
force of complex esoteric ideas they discovered in ancient Mesopotamian
civilization, found in them the unique origin of cultural patterns spread
ever more widely throughout the world. The chief British pan-Egyptianist,
Grafton Elliot Smith, had by contrast a vision that was more concrete. An
anatomist whose first academic position was in Cairo, he was struck by
the burial practices of ancient Egypt and what these implied about the advances of its civilization, which he saw as moving across the globe through
colonial enterprise. The wide-ranging historical ethnography of Father
Wilhelm Schmidt and his Vienna school, finally, was impelled by a frankly
theological vision: if the "anthropologically earliest" culture could be determined, it might offer evidence of a primal revelation, presenting a historical counterpart to biblical teaching. The hypotheses put forward by
the diffusionists may seem far-fetched to us now, as they did to many
scholars in their own day, but as public ideas that were exciting and definite, they could also provide groups with a basis for active collaboration.

ASSYRIOLOGISTS WITH IMAGINATION

At the turn of the twentieth century, the excitement sparked by newly
available texts from the ancient Near East engaged a number of scholars
but none more than Hugo Winckler, Alfred Jeremias, and, to a lesser extent, Eduard Stucken, who together stand out for their extreme and systematic program. The three were the principal members of a group usually referred to as the "Panbabylonians," sometimes in contrast to (or

conflated with) the "Neobabylonians," like Franz Delitzsch, who were interested in exploring the broader ramifications of similar texts in more restrained, if still controversial, ways.[3] Themselves fascinated by the idea of a single pervasive ancient wisdom, the Panbabylonians can continue to fascinate us through their imaginative zeal for finding coherence and system. Central to the prehistoric religion identified by the Panbabylonians were teachings of "the center of the world" and the "world mountain" which, as Jonathan Z. Smith points out, was a major source for Eliade's teaching and continues to reverberate today.[4]

In an entry on Panbabylonians in the second edition of *Die Religion in Geschichte und Gegenwart,* Jeremias gives a brief statement of their position. "The Sumero-Babylonian cultural world," he writes,

> set forth a world-teaching according to which all forms of political and social organization were regulated, all laws proclaimed, all property administered and protected, and all sciences and arts traced back to a primordial wisdom revealed from heaven. In its cosmogony and doctrine of rotational cycles, this ancient oriental world-teaching sketches a picture of space and time that can be read from the starry heavens. . . . Panchromatic film would offer proof that *this astral worldview has given its stamp to all cultures and religions of the world* and that the biblical world especially also owes its language of symbols *(Symbolsprache)* to this worldview.[5]

Thus, the social, political, and intellectual world of the ancient Near East—its "religion"—was, according to the Panbabylonians, a coherent whole. It was constructed from a science of the stars, and it spread all over the world.

In looking to the heavens for the root of religion, the Panbabylonians had company. Stucken, Winckler, and Jeremias were all founding members of the Society for the Promotion of Comparative Mythology, which advocated the so-called astral mythology that was championed by Ernst Siecke.[6] Reacting against Tylor's then widespread anthropological teaching that all myth and religion evolved from animistic beliefs, this movement of philologists offered a new version of a theory—popular among earlier, more literarily oriented savants—that myths were at root explanations of natural phenomena.[7] In identifying the heavenly bodies with their complex cycles as the fundamental phenomena explained in myth, the astral mythologists gave their theory a more precise, intricate, and thus apparently more "scientific" form.

The Panbabylonians, then, can appear as a particular group of astral mythologists, one that saw the worldwide diffusion of a particular civilizational order that was rooted in a science of astronomical cycles,

which in turn found expression in star myths. To Panbabylonian enthu-
siasts, diffusion was the only reasonable explanation for the similarities
among myths and civilizational patterns that they identified throughout
the world. Because the esoteric science behind the civilizational patterns
was elaborate and its corresponding mythology profound, both civilization and myth must have emerged together from the collective understanding of the wise; the relationship between the two was not to be
found in simple correlations that might be discovered independently by
different peoples. In examining the diffusion of Mesopotamian myth into
the lands of the Bible, of course, the Panbabylonians were not alone. But
they are distinguished from general astral mythologists and Neobabylonians through their specific program, which attempted to describe an ancient, unified "spiritual culture." In developing this program, the three
principal members had their distinct roles.

Eduard Stucken, Scholar-Litterateur

The first to publish a major Panbabylonian work was Eduard Stucken,
part 1 of whose *Astralmythen der Hebräer, Babylonier, und Aegypter*
appeared in 1896.[8] Remaining productive throughout his long life,
Stucken was at once the most creative of the three and the least devoted
to the Panbabylonian project. His first love, in fact, was literature, and
he turned to scholarship only when his early promise as a neoromantic
writer did not strike a responsive public chord: "since naturalism had
conquered the German stage in the [eighteen] nineties," he wrote, "I
threw myself into the arms of science and studied Assyrian and Egyptian."[9] At university in Berlin, he was encouraged in his academic pursuits by his uncle, the eminent folklorist Adolph Bastian, to whom he
dedicated *Astralmythen.* But the academic world wasn't really ready for
Stucken either. Although he had prepared *Astralmythen* as a dissertation,
his professor declared himself incapable of judging it. Stucken then abandoned his doctorate, even though he would long remain a productive
scholar.[10]

    Presaging the dual career of Mircea Eliade, Stucken moved back and
forth between literature and myth scholarship throughout his life, with
each pursuit affecting the other.[11] Unlike Eliade, however, Stucken finally
became best known as a writer of literature, finding international acclaim in his fifties with *Die Weissen Götter,* published in 1917—a long
saga of the Spanish conquest of Mexico translated into English as *The
Great White Gods;* earlier, he had been most prolific as a dramatist. With

something of the self-image of the great man in him (like Eliade), Stucken also had the great man's contrariness toward elders seen in the Leiden lineage of phenomenologists: even though he dedicated *Astralmythen* to Bastian, as a diffusionist he explicitly rejected the strongly evolutionist ideas for which his uncle was famous.[12]

Initially influential to the Panbabylonian program, Stucken was too eclectic in his interests to be tied to it. Hugo Winckler, writing in 1900, would affirm that "the understanding of the map of the heavens as the key to mythology belongs to Stucken."[13] And from 1897 to 1907, Stucken would write four more volumes of *Astralmythen,* each examining the figure of a major personage from the Hebrew Bible against his astral interpretation of earlier Mesopotamian myth. His method was to parse the Mesopotamian stories into motifs and then cite biblical passages that corresponded to them, often letting the parallel excerpts speak for themselves. Thus the myth of Ishtar's descent into the netherworlds, for Stucken, is one of two main sources for the biblical legends of Abraham. It presents motifs that recur several times in Genesis, "even if scattered and faded and represented by diverse characters" (1:11). According to Stucken, these motifs appear in the stories of Sarah, Rebecca, and Tamar, with different emphases in each (1:1–16). The story of Sarah, for example, long barren before finally giving birth, features the motif of sterility—a motif also central in the Ishtar myth, for "the sinking of [Ishtar] the 'she-star' *(der 'sternin')* into heaven's underworlds" leads to "the unfruitfulness of all living beings" (1:11).[14] Particularly in the last two volumes of *Astralmythen,* on Esau and Moses—published ten years later than the first—Stucken connected the biblical narrative to star lore through a wide-ranging tour of world mythologies. By the end of *Astralmythen,* Mesopotamian origins no longer seem to be the point.

Eventually, Stucken became particularly interested in the Pacific and the Americas (he had immersed himself in Mexican lore when writing *Die Weissen Götter*). He still saw ancient history through a diffusionist lens, but by 1927 some dubious linguistic parallels he had uncovered among Polynesia, the Americas, and Sumeria made him question one of the Panbabylonians' basic principles: perhaps the origin of culture was not the Near East after all but somewhere in the South Seas—Indonesia, perhaps, Siam, or maybe even the lost Atlantis. Still, a Panbabylonian view was also a possibility: "Just as the Phoenicians and the Arabs after them, perhaps the people living on the Euphrates and Nile, too, were able to make amazingly long sea voyages even in the most ancient times."[15] The conviction, however, was no longer there. Still, throughout his many enthusiasms, Stucken remained a friend and ally to the Pan-babylonians. Becoming a father for the first and only time on his sixti-eth birthday, he asked Alfred Jeremias—the last old stalwart of the group—to be godfather.[16]

Hugo Winckler, Tragic Genius

It was Winckler who provided the drive and systematicity that brought coherence to the Panbabylonian project. An extremely productive scholar still respected as a historian of the ancient Near East, Winckler shifted his scholarly course in the middle of his career.[17] The turning point was during the very last years of the nineteenth century, between the two volumes of his *Geschichte Israels*. Through the first volume, published in 1895, Winckler remained an empirical, if somewhat un-orthodox, researcher. A year later, however, the first volume of Stucken's *Astralmythen* appeared. Stucken's initial presentation of the astral key to Near Eastern mythology captivated Winckler's imagination and led him to a unifying vision of his own. This he introduced in 1900 at the end of the second volume of *Geschichte Israels*—on Israelite legends—in a chapter called "The System."[18] The system was "created [by] the *ancient oriental world view*"; its basic forms of thought shaped what the writ-ers of the Hebrew Bible produced just as "the research of a modern nat-ural scientist is conditioned by the basic principles of his science."[19] Since this worldview "is alive through the end of the middle-ages," Stucken's collection of suggestive parallels became, with Winckler, a well-worked-out "scientific" blueprint for understanding the civilizations of the world.

Winckler's enthusiastic espousal of Panbabylonianism was no help to him in his career. His unusual ideas aside, many of his scholarly col-leagues recognized him as an energetic and original researcher and as a fine translator and editor.[20] Still, he had to wait until he was forty-one to be appointed to an associate professorship in Berlin, a post from which he never advanced.[21] He died nine years later, in 1913. In an obituary in *Orientalistische Literaturzeitung,* a periodical that Winckler had co-founded with his friend Felix Peiser, the latter lamented the shabby way the university treated its "outsiders and trailblazers of genius."[22]

Winckler's academic career also was not helped by his notoriously dif-ficult personality. His "rough exterior" and his "stiff, forbidding *(schwer zugänglich)* nature" were traced in a memorial address by his friend Je-remias to his childhood—which suffered from the premature death of his mother.[23] As a lecturer, Jeremias continued, Winckler regularly put off students at the beginning of the semester so that "only the best would remain" (6). His polemics, although "never personal," were "sharp and cutting." And he did not respond seriously to questions of methodology: to accusations about his historical work, he would retort, "The Ancient Orient is my method" (ibid.). In any event, even before his Panbabylonian enthusiasms, Winckler managed to antagonize many in the older generation of ancient historians with his early work on Babylonia and Assyria, at the same time alienating established liberal theologians with his research on the Hebrew Bible.[24] His academic friends thought he was a genius, notes the Semitist Carl Niebuhr, while his circle of enemies mistrusted everything he did. "The powerful individuality that drove him," Niebuhr continues, "never protected him enough, and therein lies the tragedy of his worldly fate."[25]

Although Winckler's detractors might rightly find his historical work unmethodical, this is not a fair critique of his presentations of his Panbabylonian hypotheses, which were methodical to an extreme. His absorption in them led critics to speak of his "fantasy,"[26] and even his friends were astounded: "Association with him," wrote Jeremias, "could make you believe in reincarnation: sometimes he seemed just like an Assyrian king who had witnessed everything, or who was exploring his people's treasures of knowledge."[27] Winckler presented his Panbabylonian manifesto in short programmatic works that put forth his radical views in a coherent way. The full title of one of the clearest gives a good idea of the claims it makes: "The Babylonians' Concept of Heaven and Earth [Himmels- und Weltenbild] as the Basis of the Worldview and Mythology of all Peoples."[28]

In "Himmels- und Weltenbild" Winckler's Panbabylonian assumptions are argued clearly, if not always convincingly. It is true, Winckler concedes, that we don't know just how the ancient Babylonian teachings spread throughout the world, but then there is much about ancient history we don't know (7). And once we admit that the worldview of all premodern civilized people has been touched by the Babylonian, he adds, then we need only distinguish between the old Babylonian view and our own contemporary one (9). Together, these two statements may not seem easy to take seriously, but the second draws, in fact, on attitudes shared by more moderate thinkers of the era. Indeed, in positing a basic divide between a modern worldview and all the rest, Winckler presents a perspective similar to that we saw in chapter 1 as held by W. Brede Kristensen, another scholar of the ancient Near East, who arrived at his

views about the same time. Despite the pointed contrast between Winckler's excited ideation and Kristensen's cautious phenomenology, their
materials reveal to both of them a romantic vision of a unified world to
which they are necessarily alien and which they try to recapture through
their own versions of the science of religions. In their different ways, they
responded to a similar academic zeitgeist.

Perhaps most distinctive of Winckler's particular version of Panbabylonianism was the importance he gave to its "number theory," which
comes down to us in the Pythagorean teaching, itself "a child of the orient" (13). Based in a sexagesimal system, "number . . . here works as the
outpouring of divine or heavenly power" (20) that finds cosmic expression in planetary cycles and human expression in the cults and festival
cycles to which these give rise. Thus, Winckler eventually gets down to
concrete myth and ritual forms but finds their ultimate significance in an
abstract mathematical scheme.

Alfred Jeremias, Scholar, Pastor, and Friend

It was up to Alfred Jeremias to see the heavens not, in his own words, as
an "account book"—like Winckler—but as a "picture book."[29] "As
Winckler's system gradually transformed in [Jeremias's] hand, an *astral
symbolism* increasingly took shape." [30] This move from Winckler's fever-
ish intellection to a more emotionally encompassing vision of pictures
and symbols in Jeremias's lavishly illustrated *Handbuch der altorientalischen Geisteskultur* is indicative of the latter's broad (to say the least!)
Christian worldview.[31] Winckler, Jeremias tells us, was conscious of himself as a "heathen" whose interest in world history, even in his childhood,
stopped at the year 1 B.C.[32] Jeremias himself, however, spent most of his
working life as a Lutheran pastor in Leipzig. Having studied Assyriology
together with his theology, Jeremias throughout his career managed to
keep up his academic pursuits alongside his pastoral ones. Thus, his best-
known work, *Das Alte Testament im Lichte des alten Orients,* attempted
to bring Panbabylonian insights to the study of the Hebrew Bible. First
published in 1904, with a fourth edition as late as 1930, it has been translated into English and can still be found in many academic libraries. Jeremias's *Handbuch,* presenting his vision at greater length, was expanded
from *Das Alte Testament*'s introductory chapter, which remains the most
easily accessible cogent summation of Panbabylonian assumptions.

The explanation of the biblical creation story as explained in chapter
4 of *Das Alte Testament* reveals both Jeremias's methodological deter-

mination and his theological turn. Listing a number of important points of the creation narrative, Jeremias deals with them one by one, usually making reference to antecedent sources treated in the earlier chapters of the book.[33] Thus, to explain the biblical "let there be light," several stories of ancient Near Eastern gods of light are given, all of which reflect the centrality of the heavenly orbs in their courses (68–69). Significantly, however, when Jeremias can't find a parallel to an important point, he underlines the theological *differences* between the biblical world and the earlier one. Thus, the universe comes into being in the Bible not as the result of the brooding of the spirit on the face of the deep, as "one would expect in a purely mythological representation," but through the "word" of God. Here, Jeremias points out, "religious thought breaks through." We see a God "independent from the world and elevated from it" (67). This was, according to Jeremias, no accident. "The editor of Genesis 1 is a religious reformer. He knows the ancient oriental world-picture *(Weltbild)*" (77). But even as "he fills the old form with new contents," he has little regard for mythological concepts and speculation. Nevertheless, "the editor knows that the world of the stars plays an important role" (77–78). Doesn't he begin by telling us that "In the beginning God created heaven and earth" and conclude with an affirmation that these are filled with his "hosts"—a clear reference, as he has earlier shown, to the stars?[34] Thus Jeremias manages to marry his Panbabylonian beliefs to his Christian theology—which, at least in its antievolutionism, was a conservative one for its day.[35] The union of Jeremias's theological and Assyriological beliefs may strike us as strained, but, then again, he was a pastor who, characterizing his friend Winckler as an old Babylonian king, also toyed with the idea of reincarnation.

Three Men's Fascinations, Three Aesthetic Styles

As a man of religion at heart, Jeremias had a fascination for his subject that differed in quality from the corresponding fascinations of his two principal Panbabylonian colleagues: Stucken, the scholar-litterateur; and Winckler, the philological scientist. The different dynamic of engagement each had with his material then led to characteristic aesthetic styles in their work. Although the versions of the Panbabylonian story they presented varied only slightly, they told it to greatly varying effect.

Stucken, as we have seen, although obviously intrigued by astral mythology as a key to important truths, as a literary man had other interests, too. The five volumes of his *Astralmythen,* written separately

over eleven years, thus represent separate bursts of enthusiasm and reveal a meandering eye, prone to dally in world mythologies. Like the
phenomenologists we examined in the last chapter, Stucken painted on
an extensive canvas but not, like them, in broad strokes. A playwright
and novelist, he moved between cultures less by general "phenomenological" category than by correspondences in concrete thematic detail,
working creatively and ingeniously: thus, as we saw above, Ishtar corre-
sponds to Sarah through the first's descent and the second's barrenness—
understandable parallels, perhaps, but not immediately obvious. In progressing through thematic correspondence, Stucken's method recalls
that of Lévi-Strauss, whose concretely intuitive structuralism we saw in
chapter 4 as an inspiration for Doniger. Stucken's five-volume *Astralmythen* can thus present a parallel to Lévi-Strauss's four-volume
Mythologiques, where readers are guided through the native cultures of
the Americas by a trail of concrete mythic associations.[36] Both multivolume works, moreover, face similar aesthetic limitations. Achieving part
of their cumulative affects through their sheer bulk, both may dazzle
readers mightily, leading them to cogitate long expanses of stimulating
mythic materials; but they are both also sufficiently dense in their arcane
analyses that they demand dedication from readers to persevere. Readers have to believe that the premises behind the works have real validity
and are important enough to be worth following to some conclusions.
As works of art, both are primarily for aficionados to appreciate.

A good deal of Winckler's work, on the other hand, was considerably
more accessible than Stucken's. He started from a schematic outline that
might recall an Eliade, a Dumézil, or a Dutch phenomenologist; and his
aesthetic, like theirs, had a similar coolness about it. But this coolness derived from Winckler's own intense rationality—which when focused on
the data in his system could then itself become quite fevered. His was
thus not really, like theirs, an emotionally distant aesthetic of extent, encompassing different cultures from on high. Focusing instead on
Mesopotamia, Winckler was able, with his scientist's acumen, to make
a neat case of the sort more often seen in compact, well-defined cultural
frames. And in "Himmels- und Weltenbild," written for a nonspecialist
audience, he was able to present his case very neatly indeed. In contrast
to Stucken's *Astralmythen,* readers could engage with "Himmels- und
Weltenbild" without having first assented to its major presuppositions:
even if they were skeptical of its truth, they could still be pulled in by its
cogency. Winckler here thus presents a parallel to Marvin Harris, whose
very cogent telling of an often unbelievably large ecological story was

seen in chapter 6. Although the readers of both might on reflection often find they can't accept the authors' premises, those same readers might at least be impressed while engaged in their reading. And like Harris and Eliade—but not Dumézil, with his specific Indo-European claims—Winckler imbued his truths with a profound universal significance. People swayed by "Himmels- und Weltenbild" might then be moved deeply, letting Winckler's cogent cerebrality play with their own rooted senses of world order.

Jeremias, with his religious outlook, seemed to have thus been moved by Panbabylonian understandings, but his enthusiasm for them was tempered by his Christian conviction. His pastor's disposition, moreover, apparently gave him a broad view of human life. In his *Handbuch,* he used images from ancient Near Eastern art to thicken Winckler's schematic outlines, thus giving a balance to the play of reason and imagination more characteristic of the main lines of interpretive writing. If Winckler, the excited scientist, reached his readers first of all through their reason, Jeremias, the mature pastor, spoke to the whole person. Their scholarly approaches could thus present a nice aesthetic complementarity. In their scholarly partnership, however, the two could appear as an odd couple indeed.

The Panbabylonian Alliance

Eventually to become close allies in their work, Jeremias and Winckler started off as academic enemies. Winckler, true to form, had attacked Jeremias in print; Jeremias responded in kind. But a chance encounter on the street brought them together, and they parted late at night as friends. This was during the period when Winckler was moving from his empirical to his Panbabylonian phase, "just at the time when his lack of success had most deeply embittered him."[37] The next day Winckler confessed that he had been on the verge of burning the fateful second volume of *Geschichte Israels,* where he had first sketched out his all-encompassing ideas. From then on the two experienced sorrow and joy together, "more sorrow than joy." Despite their very different views of life and ultimate reality, they supported each other closely. Winckler never offended Jeremias in his religious convictions, and "when others did so in his presence, he found sharply dismissive words." Banding together in battle to promote their new understanding, the two edited a series of polemical Panbabylonian tracts with a very polemical name: "In Combat for the Ancient Orient: Writings of Defense and Dispute."[38]

Even earlier, Panbabylonian works had found a ready audience through Winckler's indefatigable entrepreneurial efforts, which had led to the establishment of vehicles for scholarship even before his Panbabylonian ideas were conceived. In 1886, soon after receiving his doctorate, Winckler and his friend the Assyriologist Felix Peiser founded a scholarly society, the Akademisch-Orientalische Verein zu Berlin. Not a lasting success, it was rejuvenated in 1896 through the efforts of Winckler into an enduring body: the Vorderasiatische Gesellschaft.[39] This society sponsored two important publication series: its own "communications" (*Mitteilungen*), which often consisted of hefty academic monographs; and a more popular series called *Der Alte Orient*, dedicated to making Assyriological discoveries known to the larger cultured world. In addition, about the same time Winckler was organizing his Society, Peiser—the son of Berlin publisher Wolf Peiser—started a monthly journal, the *Orientalistische Literaturzeitung* (1898–) at his father's press, with Winckler as cofounder. None of these serials was limited to a narrow Panbabylonian agenda, and all three long outlived the movement's heyday.[40] But they provided an immediate vehicle for some of the earlier Panbabylonian writings and gave them some respectability. Thus, Winckler's "Himmels- und Weltenbild" was published as the third volume of *Der Alte Orient*.

After Winckler's death, Jeremias would continue to expand the program and to defend it. In 1918 he published a treatise on the general history of religions that recalls the Dutch phenomenologies, beginning with an elaboration of a set of basic concepts that is followed by descriptions of the world religions. Jeremias's unifying idea, of course, is the underlying Panbabylonian symbolism: a single religious system stands behind all the religions of the world.[41] Keeping with his program, Jeremias published a second, greatly expanded, edition of his *Handbuch der altorientalischen Geisteskultur* in 1929. Here he tried to make Panbabylonian sense of all the Assyriological discoveries that had taken place since the first edition thirteen years earlier, going further than Winckler ever had.[42] Until his last days, Jeremias defended the system not only against more traditionally minded critics but also against a more sinister threat: Neobabylonian diffusionists of a different persuasion.

Particular venom was reserved for Peter Jensen, a Semitist at Marburg and renowned Gilgamesh expert who saw the central role of that epic in myths of kingship throughout the Near East. An old rival of Winckler's, Jensen bitterly criticized his "Himmels- und Weltenbild"—probably summarizing it too rashly but perhaps astutely suggesting that in that work Winckler was a better poet than Assyriologist.[43] Jeremias, further, was no doubt offended by Jensen's frankly disrespectful approach to traditional pieties. Although Jesus, in Jeremias's view, may have inherited something of an old Babylonian worldview, he definitely was *not* just Gilgamesh in another form, as asserted by Jensen, who proclaimed at the end of a monumental one-thousand-page study that "Jesus . . . is nothing but an Israelite Gilgamesh."[44] Certainly, in tracing divine kingship to Gilgamesh, whom he saw as a solar deity, Jensen could be (and has been) taken broadly as a Panbabylonian.[45] But he found his ultimate source not in the encompassing ancient world-system based in astral mythology but in the single Gilgamesh myth—which made him no Panbabylonian as far as Winckler and Jeremias were concerned. The Panbabylonian name was theirs, Jeremias insisted, and referred to people who followed the main lines of *their* program, certainly not to their opponents.[46]

With their own self-proclaimed identity, the Panbabylonians reveal some regular characteristics of scholars working together to promote a radical new idea. A small devoted core, Winckler and Jeremias, is given support by some others—especially Stucken but also Peiser, Niebuhr, and others.[47] These were less invested in the project but sympathetic to its key figures and sometimes contributed to it in important ways: Peiser, for example, was more than just a friendly editor—he rushed to Winckler's defense in print immediately after Jensen's bitter critique of "Himmels- und Weltenbild."[48] It also seems no coincidence that the three major figures of the group were institutionally marginal: Stucken was a scholar-litterateur with no doctorate; Winckler was a difficult personality and was academically insecure for most of his career; and Jeremias spent most of his working life as a pastor, not receiving a university chair until he was fifty-eight.[49] Working without the restraints of the academic establishment, the three were able to develop their new ideas freely. At the same time, they no doubt vigorously promoted these ideas in part to gain the recognition that they believed was undeservedly denied them. The core members of the group, further, were very dogged in their views. In rebutting their many critics, Winckler and Jeremias reveal a defensiveness in their persistence that may have come from their sense of being brothers-in-arms against entrenched scholars. But they also had a growing solidity of conviction. Like scientific paradigms and religious doctrines, the Panbabylonians' hypotheses were large but malleable explanations; as such they were conducive to endless systematic application that seemed to support them further. As the logical circle broadened, its central hypotheses grew more stable in the minds of their propounders.

Jeremias, in particular, continued to pursue his Panbabylonian agenda to
the very end, long after its initial academic commotion had ceased to
draw much attention. These three traits of the Panbabylonian project—
a fully invested core with outside support, marginality to mainline institutions, and intellectual tenacity—all find their different counterparts in
the two radical diffusionary episodes of early-twentieth-century ethnology to which we shall soon turn.

Nevertheless, despite similarities in its institutional dynamic, the Panbabylonian project differed in its place on the continuum between interpretation and explanation from the two ethnological projects. Like the
Panbabylonians, the central figures in the two ethnological movements—
Grafton Elliot Smith and Father Wilhelm Schmidt—were intellectually
obsessed institutional outsiders. But they had something in common with
each other that they did not share with the Panbabylonians. The first a
natural scientist, the second a Catholic priest, they both had a predilection for explanation from absolutes that was gained in fields outside
those in which their theories of diffusion were to play out. The Panbabylonians' convictions, by contrast, emerged largely from within their
own field of study, a historical discipline with narratives more consciously constructed and tentative. Despite the Panbabylonians' explanatory exuberances, the story they told could finally mellow into an
interpretive one that left lasting insights.

Less than crucial for their larger story, the Panbabylonians' strong explanatory mode initially derived not only from Winckler's mathematical
formulations and personal style but also from external institutional exigencies. Biblical theology seemed to be encroaching dangerously on nascent Assyriology, so for Assyriologists to locate an exciting, encompassing truth in their own materials might enhance the independent value of
the fledgling field in the academy.[50] But in fact the Panbabylonians seem
to have much in common with many people outside, and a few inside,
the academy (where they are sometimes called perennialists) who are interested in esoteric lore and identify in the texts they read a version of a
pervasive ancient wisdom.[51] For nonspecialists, this notion often remains
a vague idea that gives meaning to what may appear as striking parallels
among astrological systems and Gnostic understandings in any number
of old traditions. The Panbabylonians, however, in their scientific excitement, gave it a specific form and historicity.[52] They countered theological studies by offering an encompassing vision of their own—in its
way also theological, to be sure, but still fluid and in the making.

Presenting their story—in the manner of Western theology—as at least in part a historical explanation, the Panbabylonians, in telling it, nevertheless drew heavily on powers of imaginative coherence common to humanistic interpretation. Indeed, in his old age, Jeremias moved into an avowedly interpretive mode: "The much-misunderstood 'Panbabylonianism,' " wrote Jeremias in 1927, "means nothing more than this: The Sumerian spiritual culture [*Geisteskultur*] had a creative meaning for the uniformity of human civilization [*Einheitlichkeit der Menschheitsbildung*]."[53] There is a broad pattern in world cosmologies that reverberates from Sumer, he seems to tell his readers, but you can understand for yourself just what this reverberation means. By the end of the day, then, the Panbabylonians can be seen as humanists giving large interpretations of religious materials, as humanists are wont to do. Thus, even after their factual errors have come to light, a good deal of their vision of a sacred, centered cosmos remains with us, through Eliade and beyond.[54] Much less remains of the two radical diffusionist projects in early-twentieth-century ethnology. Predisposed to look for ultimate causes, their core figures did not give explanations of the sort that could easily soften into elegant interpretations. When accumulated evidence did not support their findings, there was little left to salvage.

HELIOLITHIC DIFFUSION: NATURAL SCIENTISTS CONVERTED

In their theories, cultural style, and dynamic of collaboration, the two radical ethnological projects present a clear-cut contrast to one another. In Britain, Elliot Smith's theory of the global diffusion from Egypt of a single archaic civilization was propounded forcefully by a few well-placed scholars who stirred up lively controversy in the academy. In Austria (and later Switzerland), members of Schmidt's Catholic missionary order, drawing on the help of their many brothers in the field, tried to demonstrate the existence of an original monotheism by adapting methods already developed by German historical ethnologists. Like the Panbabylonians, the radical British diffusionists were a relatively small group captivated by a new, all-encompassing idea: the world was first civilized, they said, by people whose culture originated in Egypt; since these people were thought to worship the sun (*helios* in Greek) and build large stone monuments (megaliths), their culture was termed heliolithic.[55] During the 1910s and into the 1920s the idea of heliolithic diffusion drew some support and caused some controversy, but by the end of the 1920s all the excitement was over. The Vienna-based search for primitive monotheism through the study of existing "culture-circles" lasted longer—indeed, through most of the first half of the century—and was theoretically more subtle, pursued through a complicated method that could make sense of large masses of ethnological data. The German-speaking scholars then presented their proofs for intricate patterns of migration in encyclopedic tomes of comparative ethnography; the British diffusionists, by contrast, took limited archeological evidence as the basis for forceful, often sweeping, arguments.

Together, the British diffusionists presented some impressive credentials, scientific and otherwise. When Elliott Smith published his first book on heliolithic diffusion in 1911,[56] he was already famous as an anatomist; today, he is still noted for his contributions to the theory of human evolution.[57] W. H. R. Rivers, whom Smith credits as bringing him into anthropology, had by 1911 become a major figure in that field, the president of the anthropological section of the British Association for the Advancement of Science; but Rivers was a physician who had come to anthropology through earlier research in neurology and perceptual psychology, fields that he never fully abandoned and to which he would return in later life. W. J. Perry, the only member of the group without formal training in natural science, was a student of Rivers in anthropology whose career was nurtured by Elliot Smith. Combining approaches from both his mentors, he brought the exposition of heliolithic cultural diffusion to a fulfillment that, although scientifically dubious, was aesthetically engaging.

The relationship among these three presents an interesting—if not exact—parallel to that among the three major Panbabylonians. Elliot Smith, like Winckler, was a dynamic organizer and outspoken propounder of a new theory. He was eventually joined by Perry as a close collaborator, and the two, like Winckler and Jeremias, were known as the core of the group. But whereas Jeremias was something of a father confessor to Winckler as well as a colleague, Perry—younger than Elliott Smith—was at first his disciple and protégé. Nevertheless, like Jeremias, Perry provided a valuable complement to his predecessor's work, approaching the subject somewhat differently and giving the project continuing momentum. Rivers, for his part, like Stucken, made a significant contribution and added a valued voice of support but was less than fully invested in the collective diffusionist project. For, also like Stucken, Rivers was a multifaceted personality with a number of disciplinary interests and some other diffusionary ideas of his own.

The radical British diffusionists, however, differed markedly from their Panbabylonian counterparts in their relationship to the academy. Not, like the Panbabylonians, standing at the academic fringes of a field in which they had worked all their lives, the British diffusionists spoke from established academic authority—even if, in the case of Elliot Smith, this authority came from outside the field in which his diffusionist theory would take shape. Remaining marginal to the mainline anthropological establishment in their radical claims, the three major diffusionist scholars were all nevertheless academically well placed—none more so than Elliott Smith himself, from 1919 to 1936 head of the Institute of Anatomy and Embryology at University College in London.

An Anatomist with an Imagination

An Australian by birth, Elliot Smith arrived in Cambridge at the age of twenty-five. This was in 1896, just after Cambridge had agreed to admit qualified graduates from other universities. Elliot Smith thus appears as one of the first colonial scholars to make a mark in the British academy. Excelling very soon, Elliot Smith became a research fellow in 1899 and was appointed the next year to the new chair of Anatomy at Cairo. This turned out to be a fateful appointment, for Cairo captivated his imagination. It was "intensely fascinating," he wrote in 1901, "the gayest and most cosmopolitan city on the face of the earth." Indeed, all of Egypt—with its pyramids and mastabas and many visible antiquities—impressed him mightily. Living in Egypt through 1909, he came to view it as verily the cradle of civilization.[58]

About six thousand years ago, Smith and his colleagues would eventually contend, the people in the Nile valley developed a complex of basic cultural forms—including agriculture, social organization, and organized religion—that were nowhere in evidence earlier, either separately or together. The ideological underpinnings of this first civilization derived from what Elliot Smith took as the basic religious striving found even in precivilized peoples: the prolongation of human life. Did not the use of red ochre in prehistoric graves testify to the fact? Life, according to Elliot Smith, was identified with blood and by extension with other red things; leaving such life-giving things at the gravesite would ensure continued existence. Egyptian religion offered an elaboration of these early burial practices, he continued, but focused them on the king. Seen to have power over the waters, the king was a divine protector of the nation, and his existence in the afterlife should be prolonged for the common good. To this end, his body was preserved through mummification;

just as important for the development of the heliolithic theory, it was also surrounded by objects that would sustain it in the other world. Of life-giving objects there were many even in prehistoric times: cowries were sculpted into female torsos, suggesting fertility; in Egypt, gold—which bore the color of the sun—was paramount. Indeed, however mundane the value of gold and cowries would become, these objects were originally treated as precious because they were deemed to be what the British diffusionists dignified as "givers of life."

The diffusion of early civilization was thus motivated by a worldwide quest for life-giving substances. If not colonizing other populations outrightly, the ancient Egyptians at least spread their civilization through extended contact, leaving cultural centers in their wake in Asia and the Americas. In Peru as well as India, all higher culture can be traced, either directly or through secondary transmission, to that original archaic civilization that had developed in Egypt. The original cultural forms were, of course, altered as they traveled; and the civilization itself regularly degenerated, sometimes mixing with the ways of precivilized humanity to such an extent as to be barely recognizable.[59]

Although Elliot Smith and Perry, like the Panbabylonians, saw the diffusion of culture from a single Near Eastern origin, theirs was no systematic vision of an idealized, ordered world. The cultural traits of early civilization—at least for Elliot Smith—were seen as individual and arbitrarily brought together: all the more proof of a common historical origin when found in different places.[60] In itself, for example, gold is simply a "soft metal of slight intrinsic value" that even in Elliot Smith's day "uncultured peoples in Australia, New Guinea, Africa and elsewhere . . . do not bother to pick up."[61] The value given to it in later civilized societies can be explained by its role as a giver of life for early civilized humanity. The diffusion of civilization was thus driven by a practical, thoroughly reasonable, motive: the pursuit of life-giving wealth. Culture was not disseminated, as the Panbabylonians would suggest, through the pervasive spread of an idealized worldview in ways not fully fathomed but through the completely understandable imperial striving of a technically advanced people.

Indeed, as Misia Landau points out, Elliot Smith's vision was more than just that of an Australian among the British elite, taking imperialist motives for granted; it was also that of an empirically oriented anatomist. Central to the first civilized religious thought was not the systematic understanding of the heavens identified by the Panbabylonians but a particular applied science of the human body: the art of the embalmer, who "mus[ed] deeply on the problems of life and death." All civilization was the elaboration of the embalmer's art. Since the mummy "would be reanimated as a living being," around it "were created not only many of the essential arts and crafts (architecture, stone- and wood-working, sculpture and painting, the drama, dancing and music) . . . but also the deepest aspirations of the human spirit."[62] Civilization emerged from the reflections of an anatomical genius in an imperialistic world, an ancient counterpart to what was probably Elliot Smith's image of himself.

As the brainchild of an anatomist, the pan-Egyptian theory was eminently scientific—not through any meticulous method but in the material base from which it started and the causal chain grounded in that base. Truly, it provided an *explanation*. It could give people who took explanatory scientific thinking for granted a vehicle for contemplating intriguing discoveries of the hoary past in perfectly reasonable ways. And because it reflected a vision of universal significance—one of the genesis of all civilization—the theory was not only fascinating at its Egyptian core but could also seem profoundly important. To those early-twentieth-century Britons whose religiohistorical dilemmas came replete with a commonsense utilitarianism, pan-Egyptianism could provide a resolution. If its origins seem accidental—what would have happened had Elliot Smith found his first appointment in Boston, say, or Calcutta?—its acceptance by some and consideration by more seems indicative of the temper of its times.

Starting in 1911, Elliot Smith advanced his arguments in a series of books and papers. These took shape in part as specific answers to critics, of which he had no dearth.[63] Elliot Smith was most convinced of his thesis by the existence throughout the world of two items of culture that he identified strongly with Egyptian burial customs: mummification practices and megalithic monuments—the latter understandably differing from their Egyptian prototypes when built abroad by "colonists . . . using native laborers."[64] He had no doubt, for example, that certain technological features of mummified bodies from the Torres Strait (between New Guinea and Australia) that he examined in Brisbane were first invented in Egypt after the ninth century B.C.E. and must have somehow come directly or indirectly from there. When anthropological colleagues thought otherwise, he wrote a detailed tract on the subject that set forth the evidence he had so far to support his claim.[65] Elliot Smith also wrote works for a broader audience. One of his old students, the Australian anthropologist A. P. Elkin, tells us that "he was a compulsive spreader of knowledge and ideas—in newspaper articles and journals, and through publication of abstracts of his addresses which seemed innumerable."[66] His monumental *Human History,* written after scholarly interest in his diffusion theory had waned, attempted to combine both the physical and cultural aspects of his work on early humanity into a lucid narrative for the general reader, a complete history of the origins of humankind as we know it.

An Elder Statesman Lends Support

Elliot Smith was initiated into anthropology and encouraged in articulating his unorthodox views by W. H. R. Rivers, who had developed his own ideas of diffusion beforehand. The two became acquainted at Cambridge, where Rivers, a physician, had first come in 1893 as a researcher in neurology and psychology. In 1897, he progressed from this "insecure and marginal"[67] position to a regular appointment as the university's first lecturer in Physiological and Experimental Psychology. Rivers's anthropological career began the following year when he joined the Cambridge Anthropological Expedition to the Torres Strait. There Rivers worked on problems of visual perception, his previous psychological specialty, conducting, as Elliot Smith tells us, "the first systematic fieldwork in the experimental psychology of primitive people."[68] In 1900 and 1901 Rivers did research on the same topic in Egypt, where, renewing his acquaintance with Elliot Smith, he "quite unwittingly" drew the latter "into anthropology."[69] Rivers embarked on his first independent project in ethnology proper in 1902, among the Todas, a tribal people in the Nilgiri Hills of South India; in 1908 he went back to Melanesia for his next (and last) major field research.

In his field research, Rivers made a conscious "attempt to apply rigorous methods in the investigation of sociology and religion."[70] These were not the in-depth methods of a later generation of "participant observers"—indeed, Rivers stayed in the field for relatively short periods and always used interpreters.[71] Rather, they were the efforts of someone with a technical background to ascertain objective facts. In addition to the "direct corroboration of independent accounts," Rivers also looked for "indirect corroboration." In Rivers's hands, this approach, which looks for facts that are *over*determined, employs principles of "robustness" seen in our discussion of Dumézil in chapter 4—principles introduced there through the work of Richard Levins, like Rivers a biological scientist. Rivers gives two examples of his robust method. First, because Toda life presents "an intricate web of closely related practices," eliciting information about one aspect of culture inevitably leads to knowledge that corroborates findings in another. Second, and "more important," the ethnologist was to obtain "the same information first in an abstract form and then by . . . a number of concrete instances."[72] This second application in particular brings to mind one of the actual applications of robustness discussed in chapter 4, where different historical variants assembled by Dumézil point to a hypothetical Indo-European abstraction. And like Dumézil in his field, Rivers saw himself introducing new standards into anthropological research—although Rivers not only took pains to corroborate his facts but also tried to keep them separate from his analyses.[73] Indeed, his student John Layard tells us that Rivers once declared that the inscription on his tombstone should read: "he made ethnology a science."[74]

Rivers's science eventually took a diffusionist turn, but in interpreting the limited domains of his own field research, Rivers was not as extreme as Elliot Smith or Perry. He was less a "radical diffusionist" looking for explanation on a world scale than a historical ethnologist explaining particular cultural configurations through the origins of their specific elements. In his attempts at local totality, however, his historical explanations can sometimes appear excessively ad hoc—especially in his monumental *History of Melanesian Society*. He could nevertheless be most outspoken in expressing his diffusionist views. Thus, even though his radicalism was less full-blown than that of his diffusionist colleagues, he was still their intellectual and institutional ally.

Rivers's "interest in the contact and blending of peoples" seems to have been sparked by his research among the Todas.[75] Because the complex of customs he found there did not fit any of the evolutionary paradigms with which he was familiar, in the last chapter of *The Todas* he suggested some hypotheses about a migration from the Malabar Coast that might account for some of them. He knew the limits of his data, however, and admitted that these hypotheses were "open to the charge of being highly conjectural."[76] His explanations are more intricate and given with less reservation in his *History of Melanesian Society*, based on a six-month survey of the islands on the Percy Sladen Trust Expedition of 1908.

In a 1911 presidential address at the anthropological section of the British Association, Rivers credited the Percy Sladen survey with having precipitated a profound shift in his views, a momentous change of conviction that the eminent historian of anthropology George Stocking characterizes as a "conversion."[77] Rivers, now having seen the light, confessed to his audience: "I was led by facts to see how much, in the past, I had myself ignored considerations arising from racial admixture and the blending of cultures" (125). Rivers continued by revealing how far from his naturalist background he had come as a social scientist. To identify the historical elements of a composite culture, he urged, follow the social structure: it is that which is "fundamentally important and [not] easily changed except as the result of the intimate blending of peoples" (134). In the massive two-volume *History,* published in 1914, Rivers would then use the varying social forms of the different Melanesian peoples to chart their histories. His analysis there was complex and not entirely convincing. The American anthropologist Robert Lowie, himself generally partial to diffusionist views, in reviewing the work tells us that he "cannot avoid feeling that some other student who shared Dr. Rivers's knowledge of this area might construct an argument no less consistent, elaborate, and plausible, yet widely diverging from that here presented."[78] Rivers intended this intricate historical analysis of Melanesian society to be his masterpiece and legacy to ethnology, but of his anthropological writings it is still the groundbreaking "scientific" ethnography of the Todas that is most widely read.

In the 1911 presidential address chronicling his conversion to diffusionism, Rivers did not mention Elliot Smith or Perry. Instead he focused on "the chief characters of the leading schools of different countries" and suggested that mainstream British anthropology learn from the "German School" of historical ethnology, mentioning Wilhelm Schmidt by name. In fact, Rivers was initially skeptical of Elliot Smith's hypothesis in its extreme form. He was, however, convinced by the latter's analysis of the Torres Strait mummies and had no qualms about telling the world. In a 1915 meeting of the British Association, Rivers announced that he "no longer hesitate[d] to believe" that the "megalithic" civilization "developed in Egypt and spread thence to . . . many parts of the world."[79] He had a few reservations about the "whole list of practices and beliefs" attributed by Elliot Smith to that "special wave of migration," but he accepted Elliot Smith's eighth century B.C.E. date of heliolithic diffusion, and his tone was highly enthusiastic: "the contribution of Professor Elliot Smith" to the meeting was "[g]reat and far-reaching [in] its consequences"; moreover, "it has a worthy companion in the paper of Mr. Perry,"[80] who would incorporate Rivers's emphasis on social structure in his own diffusionist work. Rivers, then, was thus ready and able to give Smith and Perry powerful support.

By the time Rivers offered his outright endorsement of heliolithic diffusion in 1915, the most active phase of his career in anthropology was
drawing to a close. *The History of Melanesian Society* had been published the previous year, and World War I had broken out in Europe.
With his great anthropological opus completed and meeting less than
universally enthusiastic acclaim, Rivers's energies would be drawn in
new directions by the exigencies of the war. Always keeping up his professional commitments in psychology, Rivers now found a calling in min-
istering to shell-shocked war veterans. In 1916 he accepted a commission
as captain in the Royal Army Medical Corps and served as psychiatrist
in army hospitals. On return to Cambridge in 1919, Rivers was made
Praelector of Natural Science Studies at Saint John's College, an office
that he welcomed as a chance for increased interpersonal relationships
with the students. At the same time, the position provided him freedom
to pursue his many interests, in which ethnology now appears subsidiary
to a complex of issues in psychology.[81]

Rivers's contemporaries report an opening and widening of his personality during this period, particularly during his years in the army.
Clearly, Rivers was a formidable figure in those days—and probably before, as well. The celebrated war poet and memoirist Siegfried Sassoon,
who first met Rivers as a patient, paints a reverential picture of him as a
wise army psychiatrist in one of his semiautobiographical novels, the first
part of which is called simply "Rivers."[82] Maintaining ties to Rivers until
the latter's premature death in 1922, Sassoon speaks of him as "the most
brilliant, intellectually many-sided man I ever met."[83]

An Acolyte Provides the Causal Link

Although Rivers and Elliot Smith gave the hypothesis of heliolithic diffusion the weight of their general academic authority, the systematic development of its implications fell in good part to the industry of William
James Perry. Although Perry got his academic start as a protégé of Elliot
Smith, he had studied anthropology at Cambridge as a student of
Rivers's. Perry's work reflects his anthropological training and gives
more weight to social realities than Elliot Smith's. Thus, beginning from
an ambitious hypothesis first enunciated by an anatomist with reference
to mummification practices, skull types, and racial categories,[84] Perry
eventually derives a generalized historical sequence of cultural patterns.
His most important theoretical contribution to the project was to identify the motive that impelled cultural pioneers to travel over long dis-

tances: Perry was the first to seize on the idea of the search for precious metals as the driving force behind cultural expansion. This thesis was presented in a 1915 paper that correlated the sites of ancient mines with those of megalithic ruins all over the world.[85] Elliot Smith, appreciating the value of a demonstrable causal link for his unfolding prehistory,[86] took the underemployed graduate under his professional wing.

Perry had been teaching school in Yorkshire when he wrote his paper on the distribution of ancient mines, but he was already at that time involved in a "general investigation with . . . Professor Elliot Smith."[87] The professor, then at the University of Manchester, sponsored Perry's paper at the Manchester Literary and Philosophical Society, added some comments, and saw that it was printed in the Society's *Memoirs*. In 1918, Elliot Smith was able to arrange the publication of Perry's first book, *The Megalithic Culture of Indonesia,* at the university's press,[88] and the next year he managed to secure for him a readership in Comparative Religion at Manchester. Elliot Smith soon moved to London as head of the Department of Anatomy, but in 1924—the year after the publication of Perry's best-known book, *The Children of the Sun*—he was able to bring Perry into his London department as reader in Cultural Anthropology.

Perry was always careful to frame his own work in terms of his two senior mentors, but as he became established, he also came to identify a definite place of his own in the collaboration. The preface to *The Megalithic Culture of Indonesia,* written under the guidance of Rivers (9), begins with a portentous reference to the latter's 1911 presidential address, when Rivers, according to Perry, directed "the stream of ethnological research into new channels" (vii). The book's introductory chapter then summarizes the then evolving hypothesis about heliolithic diffusion in the Pacific in the work of Rivers and Elliot Smith; his own work in the rest of the book, he tells us, would contribute to the project by giving a systematic "examination of each type of stone structure" (9). An invocation of the same elders is found at the beginning of *The Children of the Sun,* but Perry, now an established scholar, is careful to define his own terrain: "In such a great movement of thought as that opened up by these two pioneers, it is imperative that each worker, while constantly bearing in mind the studies of his colleagues . . . should mark out for himself a line of study to pursue."[89] Perry's line of study, in this and later works, would bear fruit in broad-stroked recreations of early civilization in its different aspects: systematic in execution, aiming for totality of coverage, and grounded in all the evidence he could muster—which sometimes wasn't very much or very trustworthy.

Perry seemed to have squelched his predilection for the panoramic view only in his first book, where he aimed "to set forth the Indonesian evidence impartially" and so "deliberately suppressed" most of "the wider issues."[90] *The Children of the Sun* would redress the balance with a vengeance: "The investigation of this book," wrote Perry, "is, strictly speaking, a continuation of that carried on in *The Megalithic Culture of Indonesia,* but its scope is much wider" (4). Wider indeed. In this work Perry attempted no less than to give a unified account of the "rise and spread of early civilization," which was diffused across the earth by "the Children of the Sun." The 551-page book accounted for many of the then current topics in mythology and social structure—"Sky Gods as Life-Givers," "The Great Mother and Human Sacrifice," "Mother Right," "The Totemic Clan System," "Exogamy"—explaining them all in a coherent, if no longer believable, way. Still, Perry had a talent for synthesis, organization, and clear statement, and *The Children of the Sun* found a wide readership, if considerable criticism from anthropological quarters.[91] In its systematic presentation of a sweeping narrative from a few premises that might at least temporarily engage the nonspecialist, the book has the sort of aesthetic charm regularly employed by Marvin Harris (and employed more cerebrally and compactly by Winckler in "Himmels- und Weltenbild"). Generalizing from its specific pieces of data, the book does not fascinate through detail; but as an ordered, "scientific" presentation of the human epic, the whole it presents is momentous—displaying something of the grandeur that comes with an aesthetic of extent. After the intellectual excitement of pan-Egyptianism had begun to die down, the movement remained in the public eye a while longer through Perry's literary craftsmanship.

Pan-Egyptianism, a Minor Movement

First published in 1923, *The Children of the Sun* has been deemed by Stocking "the culminating work of British neo-diffusionism."[92] The creative heyday of the movement was in the previous decade, which saw activity not only from the three major scholars but also from some lesser lights, mostly fostered by Elliot Smith at Manchester. In his closing remarks on Perry's early "Relationship of Megalithic Monuments," Elliot Smith refers to the work on the distribution of shells that he hopes is forthcoming from "Mr. Robert Standen and Mr. Wilfrid Jackson." Substantial work was, in fact, produced by the latter, who became "honorable librarian of the Conchological Society of Great Britain and Ireland"

and had a paying job at the Manchester museum. Much of Jackson's out-put—eventually brought together as a book[93]—was first published in the *Memoirs of the Manchester Literary and Philosophical Society*. Indeed that journal seems for a time to have served in part as the prime pub-lishing vehicle for the fledgling movement: of the fifteen articles pub-lished in the 1915–16 volume, eight were in diffusionist anthropology—two by Perry and six by Jackson.

The 1920s, however, soon saw Rivers's death—a particular blow to Perry, who mourns the death passionately in his preface to *Children of the Sun*. Perry's subsequent works, as well as those of Elliot Smith, merely repeat and elaborate on the now-established story of heliolithic diffusion; there was not much more substantial that could be added to it. The British diffusionists would attract a few new acolytes during the 1920s, including most notably Warren Dawson, who would continue in Egyptology and later edit a memorial volume to Elliot Smith;[94] but by then only a few stalwarts were left. In British anthropological circles, the heliolithic hypothesis had always been more an issue of controversy than a generally accepted tenet; by the end of the decade—as functionalist views came to take center stage in British anthropology—even the con-troversy surrounding it died down.

Like the Panbabylonians, the radical British diffusionists not only held firm convictions individually but also supported one another as a group. Perry, although professionally indebted to Elliot Smith, was personally close to Rivers. By 1915 (the year of Perry's first major paper), the two were addressing letters to each other as "My Dear Uncle" and "My Dear Nephew": Stocking notes that in the Melanesian societies they both stud-ied, the uncle-nephew relationship is a particularly close one—sometimes even giving rights of inheritance.[95] Perhaps, then, it was as a presumptive intellectual heir to Rivers that Perry edited the latter's *Social Organiza-tion* after his death. Elliot Smith, for his part, gave Rivers posthumous tribute in prefaces to his collected papers.[96] To most other scholars Elliot Smith was exceptionally generous with praise and credit, not just rele-gating citations to footnotes but mentioning names in the text. This could be heady stuff for junior scholars, for he "sometimes wrote 'as my friend, Mr. or Dr. so-and-so, has shown.' That, indeed was honor."[97] But Elliot Smith's generalized honorable treatment could also be misleading, for when it was given to mature scholars who in fact had differences with him, it could leave the impression that they were more in his camp than in fact they were.

In supporting each other as true believers, Rivers and Smith in particular—both of whom came to their radical hypothesis in midcareer—shared something of the passion of the converted. As Stocking noted, Rivers presented his coming to diffusionist views as a "conversion." More snidely, Glyn Daniel, a prehistorian sharply critical of Elliot Smith, presents a quote from the latter's 1928 Huxley Memorial Lecture, entitled "Conversion in Science": "The set attitude of mind of a scholar," noted Elliot Smith, "may become almost indistinguishable from a delusion."[98] Elliot Smith, then, had obviously reflected on the ways in which scientific convictions could resemble the less than rational fixations of madmen and religious zealots. Even if he never spoke publicly of his own experiences in these matters, they were no doubt something that he had considered: he was a man with both insight and a "set attitude of mind" that many have considered excessive. Indeed, with their momentous midcareer conversions and small, voluntary groups, the British diffusionists—as well as the Panbabylonians—present a style of coming to and acting on belief characteristic of a fervent Protestant. By contrast, Father Schmidt's widespread institutional networks and elaborate scholastic attempts at giving intellectual demonstrations of his faith appear eminently Catholic.

THE VIENNA SCHOOL: RELIGIOUS ETHNOLOGISTS CONVINCED

Schmidt's self-consciously religious outlook had important implications for the scholarly claims he made, the structure of his arguments, and his motivation for presenting them when and how he did. Schmidt's assertion that the earliest humanity knew a monotheistic divinity is, for him, a natural corollary of Christian doctrines of primal revelation to Adam. From the outset of Schmidt's career, a concept of primal monotheism underlay his thinking about indigenous peoples and formed the central working hypothesis behind *Der Ursprung der Gottesidee* (The Origin of the Idea of God)—the twelve-volume work for which he is best known.[99] The tremendous academic industry Schmidt devoted to demonstrating his thesis, moreover, seems to have stemmed in good part from apologetic fervor. That demonstration, further, displays an understanding of how truth is reached that reveals Schmidt's training in turn-of-the-century neoscholastic philosophy: his great work is argued from basic premises, systematically presented, and tries to be all inclusive. But Schmidt's neo-Thomist norms of validity were now to be taken into a new age. In particular, his entrepreneurial work as an ethnologist drew encouragement (and financial support) from a movement to promote "Catholic Science"—an ambivalent concept current in a reactive early-twentieth-century orthodoxy that looked to tradition but did not want to abandon modern ways. Inspired by his faith, shaped by his intellectual heritage, and propelled by current socioreligious imperatives, Schmidt's science was indeed Catholic in a number of senses.

Schmidt's work was also nurtured by Catholic institutional structures. A member of a missionary order, the Society of the Divine Word, Schmidt operated throughout his career within hierarchical institutional networks both deep and wide. His closest collaborators in his ethnological project were fellow members of his order, with whom he often lived and prayed. From far-flung missionary posts, members of his own and others orders provided him with data for his analytical scheme. Schmidt's order supported his work with funds, personnel, and some bending of the normal ecclesiastical rules. But rules there were, and definite lines of authority of which Schmidt was able to take advantage and with which he sometimes came into conflict. For at the authoritative center of his order's ethnological work stood, for most of his career, Schmidt himself.

The Academic Entrepreneur in the Missionary Society

Schmidt's entry into the Society of the Divine Word unfolds as the story of a poor boy advanced by a friendly local priest through his own immediate contacts. Born into a working-class family in Hörde,[100] Westphalia, Schmidt lost his father when he was two. He remained close to his mother throughout her life, but with her remarriage two years later, Schmidt seems to have been influenced less by his stepfather than by his parish priests, particularly one Father Heinrich Wigger. At the end of 1882, Father Wigger had recently returned from a spiritual retreat across the Dutch border at Steyl, where Arnold Janssen, also from Westphalia, had founded a new missionary order seven years earlier. Wigger's suggestion to Schmidt, then fourteen, of a possible missionary vocation seems to have met with an enthusiastic response; for in late December that year, Wigger wrote to Janssen to accept "this my favorite, take care of him, and send him into 'the whole world,' that he may be Hörde's first witness, even martyr."[101] Financial help from Schmidt's stepfather would not be possible, but the local parish could provide clothes and books. Schmidt was accepted and started at Steyl the next summer, remaining there until his ordination nine years later. To the end of his life, Schmidt would live and work with his fellows in the order.

Schmidt's early academic work and ethnological projects were fostered by Father Janssen, the Society's superior general, who had come to know him well during his years at Steyl. In 1892, after his ordination at the age of twenty-four, Schmidt was assigned to teach at a new seminary the Society had started in Silesia, but just a year later he was sent to the university in Berlin. There he studied philosophy and languages—Near Eastern ones, as well as Czech and Polish—and, as he wrote in his old age, "learned what modern scientific work in the German spirit is about."[102] In those days, however, the Society's priests were not always allowed to finish degrees: they had more important business, and they should not get too proud. Thus, Schmidt was originally sent to Berlin for two semesters and was allowed to stay for one more—but no longer. When his three semesters were up, he reported to Father Janssen on his course of studies, including a note on "the scientific study of comparative religions." Unfortunately, he wrote, this field was "an arsenal from which the enemies of the church take their arguments . . . to 'prove' . . . [the] natural" origin of religion; but "the proper study of this science places the supernatural character of our religion . . . in a much brighter light." This study, moreover, was appropriate to "a mission society . . . because it comes into direct contact . . . with so many different religions."[103] Much of Schmidt's later career was devoted to developing the proper scientific study of religion as he saw it, aided by and contributing to missionaries' work.

From Berlin, Schmidt was sent to St. Gabriel's in Mödling, outside Vienna, then the Society's main seminary. Schmidt liked Austria, a Catholic country, and became a naturalized citizen in 1902. Coming to St. Gabriel's in 1895, he would keep it as his home base for the next forty-two years. During Schmidt's first years in Vienna, his academic work focused on the languages of Melanesia and the South Seas (the Society had established missions in German New Guinea). Now with something of an academic reputation, Schmidt was ready to begin his first major venture in academic entrepreneurship: the journal *Anthropos,* which he conceived as a publication in which missionaries could publish serious ethnographic reports. By 1901 he had permission from Father Janssen to pursue his idea, but he was not able to organize the publication of the journal until 1906. The superior general supported *Anthropos* from its inception, with resources both financial and human, and the journal continues today under the Society's auspices.

On the whole, the institutional relationship between Schmidt's ethnological project and the religious work of the Society was nicely symbiotic. Schmidt got needed support: "Priests in the Society joined Father Schmidt in his work or were assigned to him," writes Father Fritz Borne-mann, one of Schmidt's later colleagues, who would then become his so-ciety's archivist. At the same time, "the 'Anthropos Fathers' . . . con-tributed noticeably to the large St. Gabriel's community" in two ways. First, continues Bornemann, they gave it "a genuine missionary atmos-phere, . . . foster[ing] respect for races and peoples, cultures and reli-gions." Second, the same author adds in another study, they formed a cir-cle that "devoted itself to scientific exactitude and objectivity." Many seminarians came into contact with the *Anthropos* fathers during the course of their philosophical and theological work, and "even those who later discontinued these specialized studies had gotten a small taste of sci-entific life."[104] Although no doubt a contribution to seminarians' train-ing, the explicit relationship between Schmidt's ethnological scholarship and religious life have been less clearly beneficial for his academic work.

A "Catholic Science"

During his lifetime, Schmidt's work was criticized as being implicitly vi-tiated by its author's religious preconceptions, which he outlined straightforwardly in a frankly apologetic work translated into English as *Primitive Revelation.* First published in German in 1911 as part of a the-ological compendium, it predates most of Schmidt's major work on the *Origin of the Idea of God:* Schmidt's ideas about primitive revelation were definitely a starting point, not a conclusion.[105] As described in Gen-esis 1–3, Schmidt tells us in the first of *Primitive Revelation*'s four long chapters, God revealed Himself to early humanity, to whom He gave in-struction in the basics of moral life. That primitive humanity was capa-ble of receiving this revelation is quite clear from modern science (chap. 2), and an examination of the data shows that it actually occurred (chap. 3). After the Fall, however, most people lost touch with the one supreme being and started worshiping the gods of polytheism, which flourished in corrupt societies (chap. 4). Nevertheless, two classes of peoples pre-served "the old veneration of the Supreme sky-god, and the purer habits of life that were intimately linked with it." One comprised hunters and gatherers "pushed aside as the great mass of people developed and . . . [were] driven into secluded solitudes." The other consisted of wandering desert pastoral peoples who value "the purity of their blood" and thus "hold with particular tenacity to age-long traditions." From the latter, God chose Israel as a "vessel" for "a new and precious revelation," but the former groups can still be found.[106] In investigating isolated and out-of-the-way hunting-and-gathering peoples, this story implies, we find testimony of the primal revelation—if somewhat impoverished and dimmed over the generations; in missionizing to them, further, we restore to them what is truly their own.

Schmidt understandably had little patience with those who dismissed his ethnological work because of the religious frame in which he conceived it. His uncharacteristically terse reply was twofold. First, "absolute freedom from preconceived ideas" was impossible for anyone. Second, neither believers nor unbelievers should let "their views of the universe . . . influence their setting forth of the historical facts." For people with religious convictions, moreover, the implications of the latter statement can be momentous: "Missionaries should be careful to describe the facts as they know them accurately and exactly. . . . If missionaries describe the facts falsely, they falsify the ways of God." The same religious worldview in which Schmidt knowingly interpreted his data also contributed to a punctiliousness in his dealing with it.[107]

Schmidt's admonitions to missionaries about accurate description is from his unpublished memoirs of 1940, but they reflect the views—and anxieties—of his initial conception of *Anthropos*. In his published "Invitation" to missionaries of 1905 to join in the work of *Anthropos*, Schmidt gives "some general principles" on how to prepare articles. He stresses (the italics are his) the need for *"the basic and detailed treatment of an object."* As far as length goes, the most important consideration is that "the object be treated *as completely and exhaustively as possible."* The "actual strengths of missionaries" are that they observe authentic events in their daily work, so "in most cases" they shouldn't try to compare or theorize. As scientists, missionaries should do what they can do best: describe the facts as they see them.[108]

This exhortation to accurate representation of fact sooner reflects the mindset of scientists and believers throughout the twentieth century than that of most anthropologists and historians of religions at the beginning of the twenty-first. Sometimes all too acutely self-conscious of our ambivalent personal and political relationships to our material, we are today usually aware of the artifice in the stories we tell and at least a little mindful of our narrative strategies. Schmidt, on the other hand, at least in his ethnological work, does not seem to have had this attitude at all: he seemed quite sure of himself in his writing and to have cared little for its aesthetic impact. But Schmidt's lack of attention to the aesthetic depths of his data is to be expected. A fascination with the human depths of their material, as seen in part 1, is the penchant of scholars occupying places in the middle of the spectrum between hard-core believer and hard-nosed scientist. Schmidt, by contrast, could simultaneously identify with both of these extreme positions, and had no use for the visionary middle—a factor no doubt contributing to his neglect by contemporary readers of interpretive writing. Not really fascinated by the stuff of religious traditions, he just gathered it in quantity and analyzed it with higher religious and scientific aims in mind. If the (lack of) aesthetic dynamic in Schmidt's work seems discordant with that in most of the other works treated so far, it is in good part because Schmidt's engagement with modern ambivalences of science and religion was radically unlike that of most of the other authors. Writing neither as nor for a humanist intrigued by religion, Schmidt wrote, instead, as a believer who also saw himself as a scientist.

As such Schmidt gave voice to a concern of orthodox Catholic thinking at the turn of the twentieth century. Neoscholastic orthodoxy was being challenged by Catholic modernists attempting to bring church teachings in line with the science of the day. To do this, the modernists looked to post-Kantian philosophies and historical methods of biblical criticism, which Rome found threatening. Although Vatican authorities finally took strong measures against the modernists, many among the more orthodox did not want simply to give up on science: the church should come to grips with the new ways of research but on its own terms. In 1876, the "Görres Society for the Fostering of Science in Catholic Germany" had been founded to promote "work in different fields of science from the Catholic point of view." In 1892, a similar organization was founded in Austria, the Leo Society, devoted to "the furtherance of science and art on Christian foundations." When looking for financial support to begin *Anthropos* in the first years of the twentieth century, Schmidt successfully appealed to both of these societies, and their names were on its masthead until 1920. Father Janssen also seemed to like the idea of furthering a science that was in harmony with his religion (before starting his new order, he had been a teacher of mathematics for twelve years). With the initial success of *Anthropos,* Janssen, as Schmidt's religious superior, advised him to remember that he was working "for the furtherance of Catholic Science" as well as "for the benefit of the Society [of the Divine Word]." Janssen concluded his congratulatory letter: "we also work for the opponents of the Church that they may understand that Catholic missionaries do not despise science but promote science so far as circumstances permit." In this way, then, the practice of science would make Schmidt a better Catholic; happily, he could believe in modern science and traditional religion, too.[109]

Working as a scientist, Schmidt brought together particular elements of the ethnology of his day into a coherent, religiously informed argument. From the Scots writer Andrew Lang, whose idiosyncratic versatility was described in chapter 2, Schmidt adopted the idea of the primitive high god, a lord of the sky among native peoples. (The possible existence of such a being was championed by Lang in the latter phase of his anthropological work, about the time he was becoming actively involved with the Society for Psychical Research.) Schmidt no doubt surmised that a sky god, as a formless presence in the heavens, was the guise in which earliest humanity identified God.[110]

To understand the religious life of the earliest culture, one must somehow reconstruct its outlines. To this end, Schmidt adapted Fritz Graebner's concept of culture circles, discrete complexes of culture that were subject to historical diffusion. Although many culture circles eventually developed, according to Schmidt, they all derived from three primary ones, which were in turn seen as transformations of a single *Urkultur* that was in modern times attested in several variants, including the central (primarily Pygmies of Africa and Southeast Asia) and southern (comprising Fuegians, Tasmanians, and South Australians). These were the cultures that, through careful analysis, it had been possible to establish as the "ethnologically oldest" of those still existing. Remarkably, when examined, they fostered a humanity that was, as Jonathan Z. Smith might say, remarkably "like us": with an inferior material culture, to be sure, but monogamous, monotheistic, and capable of reason.[111]

What was the reason for the basic religious similarity between our cultures and the oldest cultures, given the religious diversity otherwise found within other peoples and civilizations? For Schmidt, the answer was clear—a primitive revelation that presaged the revelation cherished by his church. Although he never went so far as to assert that he could actually prove its occurrence scientifically, he obviously believed that a careful, scientific analysis of the evidence—including what the oldest peoples themselves say about the origins of their traditions—would demonstrate unequivocally that a primal revelation is the best explanation for the data at hand.[112]

For the development of Schmidt's thesis, the concept of a culture circle was more important than it was for Graebner's work, and it was much more complexly developed. For Graebner, a culture circle was geographically continuous, much like the "culture area" of North American ethnology.[113] A "helping concept" *(Hilfsbegriff)*, it could describe a homogenous culture but was more useful in describing the incompletely assimilated diffusion of one culture into the area of another, as, say, the Indic culture into Southeast Asia (sometimes known as "greater India"). For Schmidt, by contrast, a culture circle could be discontinuous. Thus, the examples of the central *Urkultur* Schmidt identified could be found in Asia as well as Africa, examples of the southern in Tasmania and Tierra del Fuego. Schmidt also talked about different kinds of culture circles: "independent" ones, with all necessary cultural elements, and "nonindependent" ones, which needed to borrow some; culture circles could further be viewed existentially, as actually existing, or methodologically, as ideal types. Schmidt's adeptness at thinking in culture circles let his systematic work be inclusive while still appearing consistent. With the culture-circle teaching—*Kulturkreislehre* in German—Schmidt had a method he could use to investigate his hypothesis about an early high god. Although the possibility of such a divinity was originally suggested to Schmidt by Lang, he considered Lang's work methodologically lax; using his own refined method of culture circles he would be able to demonstrate the existence of primitive monotheism in a way that Lang never thought possible.[114]

Self-contained, carefully argued, and presented on a grand scale, Schmidt's work clearly reflects his training in the neoscholastic orthodoxy current in his seminary days. Truth was eternal, consistent, and able to be rationally conceived. Not only does Schmidt's style of argument seem inspired by neoscholasticism, but his conception of human nature is distinctly Thomist: people are understood as individuals with free wills and reasonable minds. Given this conception of humankind, Schmidt sees the evidence of early religion pointing to a historically occurring primal revelation by the supreme divinity. Pristine early humanity was able to receive this revelation because it was able to come to the idea of God as Saint Thomas did and we do, through the inevitable search of reason for higher and higher causes.[115]

The personal inspiration behind Schmidt's work is more conventional and schooled than that of Elliot Smith, which seems to have been almost accidental, induced by his impressions of Egypt. Both, however, felt the need to explain their convictions with sweeping, totalizing stories—Elliot Smith's presented in broad strokes, Schmidt's in numbingly copious detail. Elliot Smith, aware of the gap between the human and natural sciences in which he worked, attempted to merge them along biological lines, with everything moving in a monogenetic evolution.[116] Schmidt's

science was more humane in its spirit—preserving the religious dignity
of an ultimately historical primal humanity. In its form, however, it was
more exact, rule oriented, and precise.

Throughout his career, Schmidt thought that the admittedly religious
origin of his thesis was beside the point if his science could demonstrate
it objectively. The amplitude of his facts and the rigor of his method
would win the day. And between the two world wars Schmidt did, in
fact, command wide attention and considerable respect among many in
his field. In 1937, the American Robert Lowie, who could be much less
than generous to the British diffusionists, praised Schmidt's erudition,
considered his claims about the existence of primitive high gods to be
supported by the evidence, and admired "his sense of cultural totality"
that could produce pictures of particular peoples that are "at once vivid
and sound."[117]

But for Schmidt, faith wedded to consistency eventually proved overly
tenacious. His method, in fact, contained a number of unquestioned assumptions that did not always prove viable: the very existence of culture
circles as he understood them, for example, and that culture was inherently slow to change. Not ready to revise his basic assumptions, Schmidt
was unable to alter his system sufficiently to accommodate recalcitrant
data. Schmidt's science failed less because it was Catholic, inspired by a
hypothesis consistent with a faith commitment, than because it was rigid,
not ready to undergo revision to meet increasingly discrepant evidence—
a situation eventually apparent to his close Catholic colleagues.[118]

Collaborative Work in Vienna and Beyond

During the peak of his career, between the world wars, Schmidt was the
center of collective projects both narrowly and broadly considered. The
more narrow was *Der Ursprung der Gottesidee* itself. Bearing Schmidt's
name as sole author, it is certainly the creation of his zealous industry and
his, so to speak, scientific imagination; it is, further, mostly in his own
German prose. At the same time, however, it was in good part a compilation, collating large stretches of others' ethnographical description according to the system of culture circles that Schmidt had established.
Much of this description was presented as summaries of specific sections
of particular books, and a good deal was quoted from other works directly, usually in a new German translation by Schmidt. Schmidt's twin
"scientific" penchants for systematic arrangement and unadulterated
ethnography thus resulted in what his biographer Ernst Brandewie terms

"an early version of the Human Relations Area Files" for German-speaking ethnography, a resource that would have value whatever the truth of the thesis behind it.[119] Schmidt's fondness for pure ethnographical research (performed by others) would also motivate his larger collective endeavor, the Anthropos enterprise—the journal, and later institute—from which his great work drew a good deal of its most crucial data.

Viennese Institutions   First appearing in 1906, the journal *Anthropos* was a major success. Its initial issues consisted largely of contributions from Catholic missionary societies, but by 1909 it included contributions from both Protestant missionaries and mainstream scholars like Graebner, Lang, the Indianist W. Crooke, and the American anthropologist A. L. Kroeber. The number of lengthy contributions submitted was soon so large that an *Anthropos* library was started, with both an ethnological series and a linguistic one: the first with sixteen volumes appearing from 1909 to 1940, the second with fourteen volumes from 1914 to 1938. By 1912, the American anthropologist A. H. Goldenweiser would call *Anthropos* "the most cosmopolitan of modern ethnological periodicals."[120] At the core of this cosmopolitan enterprise, however, were a steady stream of Society fathers at St. Gabriel's, many coming and going for brief periods, a few staying for long stretches and taking on major responsibilities alongside Schmidt. Of the latter the most important institutionally would be Wilhelm Koppers; but also spending time at St. Gabriel's during this period were two very important researchers from whom Schmidt would acquire data crucial for his analysis: Fathers Martin Gusinde, who worked with the Fuegians, and Paul Schebesta, who studied African Pygmies. Indeed, during the decades between the two world wars the journal was especially known for featuring articles on the "ethnologically earliest" cultures like these, the dearest to the hearts of these missionary scholars that made *Anthropos* work.

Schmidt himself personally edited the *Anthropos* journal until 1922, when Koppers took charge. Management policy changed in 1932, when the journal was entrusted to the newly formed Anthropos Institute. Organization was now formalized, with Schmidt as the director, Koppers the deputy director, and Gusinde and Schebesta as area editors for the journal.[121] With its large library at St. Gabriel's, the Anthropos Institute could serve as a place of study for missionary scholars returning from the field to pursue the academic side of their work. In the meantime, both Schmidt and Koppers found teaching positions at the University of Vienna, where, in 1929, Koppers founded an anthropological institute of his own. This would be a training ground for a second generation of "Vienna ethnologists," of whom only a minority were members of the Society of the Divine Word. Although members of the newer generation characteristically maintained something of the historical perspective advocated by Schmidt, they would increasingly take issue with his larger framework.

While Schmidt was busy with his diverse anthropological endeavors in Vienna, he was also an active priest—sometimes doing pastoral work—and maintained his political interests, which twice got him into trouble during the tumultuous times experienced in central Europe in the first half of the twentieth century. Schmidt's social and political roles during critical periods surrounding the world wars remain—like those of many—morally ambiguous. For a time the father-confessor to Karl, the last Austrian emperor, he seems to have done great work for the troops on the Eastern Front during the First World War but also to have gotten ensnared in courtly rivalries in ways that to some appeared unseemly.[122] Despite his love for Austria, Schmidt harbored pan-German sentiments and a parochial social outlook that made him unquestionably anti-Semitic long before the Nazi party ever existed.[123] Yet even though Schmidt was no particular friend to the Jews during the Second World War, he was no great friend of the Nazis either. For one thing, they didn't share the same racial views, which, for Schmidt—consistent with his brand of Christian anthropology—were based on an ultimate "Unity of the Human Race."[124] Thus, the original German publisher of his book on race refused to print a new edition even though it had been commissioned to take advantage of the soaring interest in the topic after 1933: the new manuscript did not suit the press director's National Socialist outlook. The 1935 edition of *Rasse und Volk*—which purports to give a scientific discussion of race in the face of the popular enthusiasm about it—was eventually published in Austria and distributed in Germany, where it was officially proscribed by the Nazis in 1936.[125] As a believing Christian, further, Schmidt opposed the "new German heathenism" *(neudeutsches Heidentum)* that he associated with the Nazis.[126] Schmidt also kept up contact with some opposition political figures. Primarily for the last reason it seems, he was, for the Nazis, a suspect figure.

The German annexation of Austria was announced on March 11, 1938, and came into effect on March 13. On March 12, Nazi paramilitary police came to St. Gabriel's, ransacking Schmidt's room. The next day, returning from Mass, Schmidt found the door to his room torn off and several members of the Gestapo standing inside; a file of his letters was taken away.¹²⁷ By then Schmidt was seventy, a respected scholar and influential Austrian Catholic—too troublesomely outspoken to just leave alone but also too prominent (and outwardly pious) simply to arrest right away. Schmidt, however, had gotten the message. He had the protection of Pope Pius XI (among his other posts, Schmidt was director of the Lateran Museum) and on April 4 managed to leave for Rome. By November, he had settled in Froideville, a small village near Fribourg, Switzerland—site of a Catholic university—where he reestablished the Anthropos Institute; by December, most of the institute's library in Vienna had been packed up and sent there.¹²⁸ Schmidt would remain based at Froideville the rest of his life—attempting, unsuccessfully, to exert his authority till the end.

Colleagues as Students and Religious Brethren   Although Schmidt did in fact manage to maintain his central position in the Anthropos establishment into his waning years, his fellow ethnologists in the order also had their own projects. And with their own programs of missions and ethnological work, Fathers Koppers, Gusinde, and Schebesta, as might be expected, sometimes had serious differences with their teacher, as they did among themselves. The Society of the Divine Word provided a lasting institutional framework for the research of them all, but with the close support came family tensions, too.

Nor was the relationship between the Anthropos fathers as a group and the Society as a whole always harmonious. Pursuing their own projects, sometimes at odd hours, the Anthropos fathers had ways of working that did not always integrate nicely with the patterns of religious life at St. Gabriel's. They also had different budgetary priorities: journals and books to buy as well as to publish, travel to academic conferences. Schmidt in particular never stinted on academic expenses when money was available. With a strong will and indefatigable drive, Schmidt himself, as leader of the group, was notoriously difficult for his immediate religious superiors. Well connected in the Society and the larger church hierarchy, Schmidt often preferred to deal with higher-ups when possible. From subordinates, however, Schmidt expected loyalty as well as effort.¹²⁹

Of Schmidt's major anthropological disciples, Wilhelm Koppers seems to have had the most ambivalent relationship with the master. Publicly recognized as Schmidt's intellectual heir, the "second head" of the Vienna School of ethnology,¹³⁰ he long kept quiet about questions he had about Schmidt's teachings; yet by the middle of his career, he was

fostering a new group of scholars with other ideas and with whom he became increasingly allied. In 1913, Koppers was appointed as Schmidt's
assistant, the first to stay after several came and went. Writing forty-five
years later, Koppers recalls that he was then, "so to speak, 'born into'
[hineingeboren] the atmosphere of the culture-circle teaching." In 1914
he began attending seminars in ethnology and Indology at the University
of Vienna and would get a Ph.D. three years later. By 1915, Schmidt invited Koppers to collaborate on his current project, a general ethnological work called Völker und Kulturen: Koppers would write on early
forms of politics and economy, his area of specialization. Although he
admits that the invitation was "certainly an honor" at the time, it would
lead to a rift between master and student many years later.[131]

In the 1920s Schmidt and Koppers both gave lectures at the University of Vienna; when a new chair (and later, institute) of ethnology was
created there in 1928, it was offered to Koppers, who—no longer also
teaching at St. Gabriel's—had come to take university work more seriously than did Schmidt, with his many other academic activities. At the
same time, Koppers continued as editor of Anthropos until the forma-
tion of the Anthropos Institute three years later, and even then he continued to publish articles and reviews in the journal. As Schmidt's
coworker, Koppers was overshadowed by the great man, and as long as
Schmidt was in Vienna, Koppers's ethnological institute at the university
could look like just another of Schmidt's outposts: through the 1930s
there was just one "Vienna school" of ethnology, and Schmidt was its acknowledged head.

Still, Koppers's new responsibilities at the university spurred his independent intellectual development. It led him, he writes, "dutifully to
read ever more widely in the methods of historical ethnology," which
made him "sensitive to the pertinent questions." By 1931 he had re-
viewed another author's applications of the culture-circle teaching in a
critique that he thought might also rankle Schmidt. By 1937, however,
he began to have serious doubts about whether one of the three culture-
circles Schmidt identified as "primary"—and which they had jointly
termed such in Völker und Kulturen—was really so. Koppers's doubts
were about the antiquity of the pastoral circle, out of which Israel
emerged, so Schmidt would have particular reasons not to want to
change his mind. For many years, Koppers kept silent: he had "too much
for which to thank Schmidt in his own scientific development," and
Schmidt's "advancing age" too had its "rights." Finally, in 1952, at an
international conference in Philadelphia, Koppers spoke up in unpre-

pared remarks, which were recorded and published. In the same year Schmidt, who had earlier been negotiating with Koppers on a new edition of *Völker und Kulturen,* omitted Koppers's name as coauthor in the manuscript he had prepared.[132]

By then, however, intellectual differences had already become apparent between Koppers's ethnological institute at the University of Vienna and Schmidt at the Anthropos Institute in Froideville. Koppers, too, had left Austria in 1938, managing to find finances for a research trip to India, where he studied the Bhils, a tribal people. On his return to Europe, he went to Froideville. After the war, however, he chose to go back to Vienna, where he oversaw the blossoming of a "new Vienna school" at the institute he continued to head. The members of the new Vienna school consisted largely of students who had originally studied with Koppers at the university and whose careers he fostered. On the whole, they maintained a historical approach to ethnology but to complement their perspectives turned increasingly to prehistory, which Schmidt himself disdained. As Schmidt's particular theories of culture circles came into conflict with the archeological evidence—not to mention other ethnological studies—they were progressively abandoned. The early history of humankind now seemed too complex to be deciphered by any neat system.[133]

In 1956, Josef Haekel, Koppers's successor at the Vienna institute, published an incisive critique of Schmidt's theories as the lead article of the institute's twenty-five-year-anniversary volume. He maintained the validity of many of the descriptive characteristics attributed by Schmidt to the ethnologically oldest cultures (the term *Urkultur* was now definitively abandoned), including the existence of a high god. He decisively discarded, however, Schmidt's concept of static, closely integrated culture circles dispersed over space. That term was now used "at most in the sense that one might speak of a Hellenistic or Islamic culture-circle"—in fact a usage approaching Graebner's original one. Schmidt's *Kulturkreislehre* had been a " 'pioneering stage' of historic ethnology."[134]

Koppers—as Schmidt's close coworker, editor of *Anthropos,* and professor of ethnology—had occasion to interact with many of the missionary ethnologists of the Society of the Divine Word. A more practically minded person than Schmidt, and apparently a good administrator,[135] he nevertheless had a strained relationship with one of the most important of the earlier missionary scholars, Martin Gusinde, whose detailed ethnographies of vanishing Fuegian cultures still command respect.[136] Their dispute derived from a perceived case of academic injustice.

A classmate of Koppers's at St. Gabriel's, Gusinde was originally interested in biological sciences and in 1912 was sent to teach at the school the Society had established in Santiago, Chile. During his first years there, he spent his spare time studying the local flora and fauna (discovering a new species of tree) and at the nearby ethnological museum, where he eventually became a section head.[137] In 1918 he grew more adventurous, taking his first trip to Tierra del Fuego. He went without the Society's financial support, receiving a government travel grant through the museum, together with some further help from Santiago patrons. On his first trip, Gusinde did some work for the museum, acquiring forty skulls and three skeletons. After his second trip the next year, financed by the Chilean government, Gusinde wrote to Father Schmidt. Since the Fuegians were, for Schmidt, one of the ethnologically earliest peoples, the great man responded enthusiastically: he soon planned to visit the United States to seek funds for *Anthropos,* he replied; perhaps he could also visit Gusinde in Chile and even accompany him to Tierra del Fuego. Gusinde was honored, but Schmidt changed his mind and sent Koppers instead. In the South American summer of 1921–22, Koppers set out to the field with Gusinde.[138]

One of Gusinde's strengths as an ethnographer was his ability to win the trust of the people, and on the previous trip he had managed to participate in a Yamana initiation ceremony and was treated as a member of the tribe. On this trip, he was able to arrange a similar ceremony for Koppers as well. They both took notes. In the meantime, Schmidt had gone over the heads of the Society's provincial authorities and local school principal to get Gusinde released from teaching duties. After a fourth, more relaxed trip to Tierra del Fuego (the others had all been confined to school vacations), in 1924 Gusinde returned to Europe, where he met up again with Koppers at Steyl. They went to England together—the British Museum, Oxford, Cambridge—and to international Americanist conferences in the Hague and Göteborg, where Gusinde gave major papers.[139]

Somehow, however, a number of people thought that Koppers was the main Fuegian researcher and Gusinde had merely accompanied him. This, Gusinde believed, resulted from treachery on Koppers's part, although it may have just been a misunderstanding to which Gusinde overreacted. The previous year Koppers had decided to publish a popular book on the Fuegians. Although publishing so soon was apparently contrary to an earlier agreement between them, Gusinde had consented, on the condition that they both be listed as authors. With this understanding, Gusinde had sent Koppers reports from his last field trip. When the book appeared in 1924, however, Gusinde was upset. Koppers alone was listed as the author; only the subtitle noted that he had traveled "with M. Gusinde." Given that Koppers was applying for a university lecture- ship during the weeks the book appeared, Gusinde might have forgiven him. But he didn't, and the lasting strain in their relationship would have serious consequences for Gusinde's academic career.[140]

Gusinde quickly got a degree in ethnology from the University of Vi- enna. During his third semester there, in 1925, he was surprised with the offer of membership in the venerable Royal Academy of Natural Scien- tists in Halle for his work on the Fuegians. A skillful speaker whose in- vited lectures had proved popular in Catholic academic circles, he had already begun to be recognized. In 1928 he applied for a lectureship in American ethnology at Vienna, having been assured by influential faculty members that his application would be accepted. Koppers and Schmidt, however, did not like the idea and convinced Gusinde to withdraw his application. Schmidt said that he would be retiring in two years and Gusinde could have his place. But Schmidt did not retire when he said he would, and Gusinde was not to find an academic position until 1948, when he settled at the Catholic University in Washington at the age of sixty-three. In addition to tensions with Koppers, Gusinde suffered from Schmidt's intellectual distrust: "He lacks training in humanities," Borne- mann has Schmidt saying of Gusinde, "he is sooner a natural scien- tist."[141] Perhaps more important, Schmidt did not think Gusinde took the culture circles seriously. At the same time, however, Schmidt thought that the subject of Gusinde's research was important and continued to foster his work in practical ways at his disposal. Although Gusinde's member- ship in Schmidt's network of missionary scholars may have hampered his rise through the academic ranks, it also provided him with continuing opportunities for writing and field research.

One of the projects Gusinde undertook through Society connections was in conjunction with Paul Schebesta. Schebesta had been sent to Mozambique as a missionary in 1912 but soon took up ethnological studies, for which he had been prepared by Schmidt's seminars at St. Gabriel's. He was interned as an enemy alien and sent to Portugal dur- ing World War I and then—like Gusinde interested in the ethnologically early cultures favored by Schmidt—managed to keep active in ethnolog- ical work, beginning with a stint at the Anthropos office at St. Gabriel's from 1920 to 1924. He had an opportunity to study Negritos in Malaya from 1924 to 1926, returned to Vienna (where he earned a Ph.D.), and

then left to research Pygmies in the Congo in 1929. The Central African
Pygmies—who had pride of place in Schmidt's scheme of "ethnologically
early" peoples—became Schebesta's principal area of research, and he returned three more times over the next twenty-five years. It was on his second trip, in 1935, that Gusinde accompanied him, to help with research
in physical anthropology. We don't quite know what happened to their
partnership, but after eight months "each was working for himself."
They came back separately to Vienna five months later.[142]

Schebesta could live happily in both Vienna and the jungle—he saw
himself as a great friend of the Pygmies—but he didn't like Froideville at
all: the house was too small and the site too isolated. After a brief visit
there on his return from the Philippines in 1939 (he was a Czech citizen
and could then still travel freely), Schebesta managed to return to Vienna
and stay there throughout and after the war—even though Froideville
was now the official home of the Anthropos fathers. A writer, in addition to ethnographies, of popular books with mildly sensational titles
(e.g., *My Pygmy and Negro Hosts*),[143] Schebesta seems to have been open
intellectually, as well as personally. Colin Turnbull, who also wrote on
Central African peoples, noted Schebesta's "utmost readiness to listen to
new ideas and consider new facts." Certainly, he did not agree with
Schmidt on important points of the latter's teachings.[144]

Schebesta, Gusinde, and Koppers were all born within six months of
each other. Although they were in seminary at St. Gabriel's together, they
do not appear to have been close acquaintances as young men, each pursuing a different course of study. Maturing as missionary ethnologists,
they developed their own styles of interacting in the field and in the academy—Schebesta gregarious, Gusinde precise, Koppers politic. Sometimes
cooperating, sometimes in tension, they necessarily remained connected
through the personal and scholarly networks provided by their religious
order. Intellectually less creative than Schmidt, their common teacher,
they all had much more concrete field experience than he (Schmidt had
once visited East Asia, where his order had long maintained missions).[145]
Their separate experiences seem to have led them to question Schmidt's
work—which none accepted in its systematic wholeness—yet at the same
time they affirmed its religious underpinnings. All choosing to study
"ethnologically early" cultures, they found people whom they saw,
rightly or wrongly, as understanding themselves to be individuals, having basic moral norms, and believing in a high god. Even though they did
not share all Schmidt's scholarly views, they shared his faith and the basic
academic implications he drew from it about early humankind.[146]

The writings of all three of Schmidt's main ethnological disciples, however, tend to read differently from their teacher's. The younger scholars worked on a smaller scale than did Schmidt and were less immediately concerned with the grand diffusionary story to which he would remain attached to the end of his life. Schmidt, we noted, as scientist and believer, never seemed much concerned about giving his extensive data an artful interpretation: their value lay elsewhere. His disciples, on the other hand, sometimes did succeed in being artful with the stuff of their more compact worlds. They were immersed in those worlds and could succeed in drawing their readers into them. In their field experiences they sometimes worked with people whom they appeared to like, and their writing could have a personal immediacy lacking in their mentor's distant voice. If, in the field, they often carried out Schmidt's injunction to missionaries simply to report what they saw and heard— Gusinde is remembered as a folklorist—they could still describe what they reported in ways that make their subjects interesting and hold their readers' attention. Indeed, Schebesta's popular books, despite their titles, regularly rise above a shallow exoticism to offer something of the sensitive interpretation that Turnbull admired. Like Schmidt, all three disciples knew themselves as scientists and believers, but they didn't take those personae to their mentor's steadfast extremes. More flexible than he, they were able to bring their religious sensibilities and analytical perspectives together in ways of their own that could make their work perceptive and engaging. They practiced a Catholic science but could sometimes read like interpretive writers, too.

As the "new Vienna school" came into its own after the war, Schmidt, in Froideville, grew increasingly isolated. Now an old man (his eightieth birthday was celebrated in 1948), he was still alert and energetic, but his authority was gradually curtailed. Accustomed to assuming multiple responsibilities, by 1950 he was no longer professor at the university, rector of the Froideville religious house, editor of *Anthropos,* or director of the Anthropos Institute—all positions he had assumed for long periods in Switzerland. Still living in Froideville, but seeing the Anthropos establishment there run by people who did not share all his ideas and whom he saw as his intellectual inferiors, he could not retire gracefully. He complained bitterly to visitors he met and wrote long, pointed letters to influential persons. In 1953, after different attempts to keep him quiet, the new authorities at the religious house finally decided to censor his correspondence and physically restrict his outside contacts, including visits from his longtime secretary. In 1954, when he was eighty-six, Schmidt managed to extricate himself from this difficult situation at Froideville and took a room in nearby Fribourg, where he died a few months later. Imperiously and devotedly, Schmidt had fathered a generation of ethnologists, both religious and lay; but he then suffered the fate of fathers whose continued attempts at control lead children to rebel.[147]

With his grand, theologically oriented understanding of the development of religion in the world, as well as his meticulousness about description, Schmidt, more than the other diffusionists, resembled a Dutch phenomenologist. But Schmidt's great opus is not, like van der Leeuw's, an impressionistic interpretation based in a personal vision. Informed instead by Schmidt's neoscholastic education, *Der Ursprung der Gottesidee* is sooner an encyclopedic *summa anthropologica,* taking Christian revelation for granted and systematically organizing the ethnological knowledge of the day in a way consistent with it. For Schmidt, as for scholastic thinkers generally, it was inconceivable that religious doctrine should conflict with rational science.

For the data of his science, though, Schmidt was highly dependent on others. His avid institutional efforts greatly increased the store of ethnological data available to him, in part through training and encouraging missionary ethnologists whose beliefs and interests were similar to his own. Often unusual characters themselves, they came to conclusions that finally did not fit into Schmidt's overarching scheme. Like the successors to the chair in phenomenology at Leiden, his students distanced themselves from their mentor. But the process was now more painful, since the major participants necessarily remained in close proximity, both physical and psychical—bound together in a religious order that sustained them, gave them new opportunities, but also made them deal with one another as persons in ways that scholars are not usually forced to do. If the personal relationships among the members of the Vienna school were thus often more complex than those among the other diffusionists, they meet their match, as we will soon see, in the intricate emotional ties of the Cambridge Ritualists—which, while they lasted, were extraordinarily intense.

CHAPTER 10

Interpreting Together

The Cambridge Ritualists' Affair of the Intellect

From the long-standing extended academic networks of a German-speaking religious order, we turn to some affectionate intellectual enthusiasms that blossomed for a time in Cambridge, England, before the First World War. For somewhat more than ten years, Jane Harrison, Gilbert Murray, and Francis Cornford—known as the Cambridge Ritualists—interacted creatively with one another in ways that were extremely fertile. The scope of their intellectual interplay also included others in classical studies—especially Arthur Bernard Cook, who is sometimes mentioned as the fourth Cambridge Ritualist—but the bonds of affection between Harrison, Murray, and Cornford were particularly intense. These affective ties contributed to an intellectual dynamic among the three that differed from those seen in diffusionist collaborations.

Diffusionist groups found common cause in their theoretical agendas, which were presented as broad explanations. If particular individuals elaborated their own hypotheses and took their investigations in new directions, they were still united in trying to pursue the ramifications of a specific historical premise. To work on their common agenda, adherents of a particular theory just had to manage to get along—they didn't have to be particularly fond of one another. There were in-group loyalties within all the diffusionist circles, to be sure, nurtured in part by outside opposition, and some real friendships among the Panbabylonians, but Schmidt and his colleagues didn't always seem to like one another very much. Binding the latter, instead, were institutional links, deeply held

belief, and personal familiarity of sometimes very long standing—a religious order's family ties, which sometimes chafed. The story of
Schmidt and his brothers in faith thus sometimes reads like an extended
family saga.

The story of the Cambridge Ritualists, by contrast, might be characterized as an affair of the intellect: tempestuous and slightly scandalous. Not only Harrison, but Cornford and Murray, too, had original
personalities and creative minds. The three came together in intellectual
interplay for a while, inspired and encouraged one another in complementary directions, and then went their separate ways. Their ideas—
which entailed bringing anthropological insights to classical texts—
were daring for their day, sometimes even outrageous in the conservative
world of their contemporary classical scholarship.[1] Adding to the aura
of scandal were complex erotic undercurrents in the feelings of Harrison
for the two men (flowing much less strongly, it seems, in the opposite direction), which were evident to some observers then as they are now.
These added tensions to interpersonal dynamics but also no doubt
helped sustain the group's fertility. What emerged among the three intellectually was less a shared explanatory theory of the sort seen among
diffusionists than a shared interpretive temperament—nurtured together
but sustaining separate projects.

Because documented examples of intellectual cooperation in the humanities are relatively rare and the Ritualists were interesting personalities, their interrelationship has been given renewed attention in the last
decades.[2] Robert Ackerman's careful work on the Ritualists presents
acute insights into their intellectual background, writings, and important
elements of their interaction. His description of them as "a more or less
coherent group with a unified program,"[3] however, has been challenged
by Mary Beard and especially by Annabel Robinson, who writes about
"Deconstructing the 'Cambridge Ritualists.' " Both of these writers emphasize the evident lack of a common agenda among the three and the
genuine differences in their works. Although I agree with them, I think
that Ackerman also saw something important. There was an unusual coherence about the Ritualists as a group, even though they didn't really
present what most people might call "a unified program" of scholarship.
That term more readily suggests a unified *science,* a compact discipline
in the philosopher Stephen Toulmin's sense,[4] but I think it is also possible to partake in sustained intellectual interaction without having scientific norms in mind. What we see among the Ritualists is a kind of intellectual cooperation natural among aesthetically oriented interpreters,

not scientifically oriented explainers. For our story, then, the Ritualists become particularly important.

THE RITUALISTS' TRIANGLE

Between 1903 and 1912 Harrison, Murray, and Cornford each published two major works—nothing particularly remarkable for productive scholars, except for the fact that all can still reward readers today.[5] True, in most cases the Ritualists' specific scholarly conclusions have been superseded, but their goals went beyond the particulars of classical scholarship. Affected by the rise of irrationalist theories (chapter 1 has shown us how Harrison was impressed by Durkheim and Bergson), all three tried in their own ways to convey what was behind the evident meaning of their texts. Memorializing Harrison, Murray writes: "she was always in pursuit . . . of some discovery which was not a mere fact, but which radiated truth all about it."[6] In attempting to convey the religious depth of cultural forms, the three really do appear as direct precursors of the interpretive writers I discussed in parts 2 and 3. As individuals, however, they were more than anybody's precursors, and the peculiarities of their personalities contributed to the fertility of their intellectual interaction. Just who were they when they came together?

An Older Woman

By the time Harrison returned to Cambridge as a research fellow at Newnham College in 1898 she was forty-eight.[7] Two years earlier she had failed for the second time to be appointed Yates Professor of Greek at London, losing to one Ernest A. Gardner. W. Flinders Petrie, writing for the appointment committee, explains: "It was generally felt that although Miss Harrison's abilities might be equal to Mr. Gardner's, she had not enjoyed the same opportunities for a thorough scholarly grounding." In fact, Harrison did not receive the early training in Greek that British public school boys could get. Although the appointment committee appreciated her lecturing skills and her imaginative insights, it did not see her, in the expression of the day, as a truly "sound scholar." "The balance of intuition may be on Miss Harrison's side," continued Petrie, "while the balance of knowledge may be on Mr. Gardner's side."[8] Even more then than now, it was the sound scholars who were hired to university positions.

Harrison took seriously the accusation that her Greek was not quite up to the highest mark. Whether she had internalized others' views, or whether she knew her limits and was being prudent, Harrison, throughout her career as a classicist, worked closely with men whose philological acumen was unquestioned. Her relationships with a few of these were merely cordial: A. W. Verrall was an older early mentor, and Cook seems to have been "just a friend." But with others of them she seems to have been emotionally involved. In London, Harrison was intellectually close to D. S. MacColl, an art scholar who is said to have proposed to her. In Cambridge, she met Murray, Cornford, and, before them, R. A. Neil—to whom she was reported to have been engaged before he suddenly died. All these men were younger than she was, Neil by just two years but the rest by quite a bit more: MacColl was nine years her junior, Murray fifteen, and Cornford twenty-five.

It is not hard to see how those with an animus against Harrison—and members of the conservative establishment generally—could be contemptuous of this unorthodox pattern of relationships. Eugenie Strong (née Sellers), for example, was a onetime younger confidant of Harrison's in London who fell out with her bitterly and eventually became an established Roman archeologist herself. Her unpublished memoirs describe a type of Victorian New Woman that "far from renouncing [the] power of fascination applied it . . . where she could on callow youths chiefly and younger women." Mary Beard, following some hints from Strong's biographer, concludes that the unkind reference here is to Harrison.[9] Harrison's friends, of course, saw things differently: Murray suggests that she surrounded herself with younger people because they were "less likely to have fixed views and established orthodoxies" and would thus be more receptive to her new ideas. "They cheered her."[10]

Harrison's later ideas *were* new in classical circles and could unsettle conventional thinkers, who never really trusted her. "With all her fame and influence," continues Murray, "she never became an accepted orthodox authority."[11] Socially, as well as intellectually, Harrison was always at least a little on the outside. People at Cambridge remember her habit of smoking (not common then among women), her unacademically fashionable dress, and some specific instances of eccentric behavior.[12] In teaching, too, Harrison was fond of the dramatic flourish. Her lectures, always well orchestrated, employed the latest in audiovisual aids: glass slides on which images of Greek art were carefully painted, projected with a "magic lantern." At one memorable talk she had two friends swing bull-roarers at the back of the darkened stage so that her audience might understand "what Aeschylus meant by 'bull-voices roaring from somewhere out of the unseen.' "[13] Harrison knew how to make an impression.

In her discussions with colleagues at Cambridge, Harrison was lively and generous. That these colleagues were largely younger men conforms not only to the earlier pattern noticed by Strong but also to the exigencies of her immediate situation. Given the limited role of women in academia at the turn of the twentieth century, any intellectual friends and confidants Harrison had could be expected to be disproportionately male. And by the time she reached her fruitful years in Cambridge, she was older than most of them anyway. No one doubts that Harrison's relationships with some of her colleagues became emotional as well as intellectual. But the ways in which Eros actually entered into her feelings for them is much less clear.

Harrison's sexuality does not seem to have been simple, and the recent feminist scholars that have looked to her as a model have included lesbian feminists. For even though presented as having twice been close to marriage, Harrison in fact remained single and had two lasting relationships with women: in the 1880s with Eugenie Sellers (later the Romanist Mrs. Strong), a younger contemporary; and in the last decades of her life with Hope Mirrlees, a former student.[14] Harrison's ties with Sellers seem to have been quite close. They went around London and traveled abroad together, actively promoted each other's work, and were roommates for a while. At the time they were a known pair. A friend writing a chatty letter to Sellers refers to Harrison as her G. A. ("Grand Amour")—a refrain echoed derisively years later by Mirrlees, who noted: "Jane said she was nearly driven mad with her G. P. ['Grand Passion']." As terms from late Victorian women's argot, G. A. and G. P. might have been used ironically to refer just to a devoted affection to a friend, but they might also, as Beard points out, suggest a knowing nod to something more.[15] The relationship between Harrison and Sellers must, in any event, have been most intense, for its ending is remembered as very stormy: Gladys Thomson, Sellers/Strong's loyal biographer, calls it a "disaster," a "catastrophe"; Mirrlees talks about a "bust-up."[16] Mirrlees, of course, had her own ideas about the relationship, for by the middle of her own association with Harrison, it was already the 1920s, with constructions of sexuality closer to our own. Mirrlees, a minor but well-connected writer, would later be known in literary circles as a lesbian, her first novel detailing the obsession of a younger woman for an older one.[17] "Jane Harrison wrote like a dyke and lived like a dyke," writes the feminist classicist Tina Passman, "as any lesbian could see."[18]

Perhaps. But Harrison's recurrent emotional and intellectual involvements with men throughout her mature life complicate this characterization, and the Oxford classicist Hugh Lloyd-Jones reminds us of the possibility that Harrison's attachments might have been "not passions of a sexual kind . . . but emotional intimacies [that] could cause jealousy and distress."[19] Harrison grew up, remember, in a puritanical home within a straitlaced Victorian culture where the thought of sex outside marriage could be deeply disturbing. By the time she moved to Paris with Mirrlees, moreover, she was already seventy-two (although they had lived together "on and off," says Mirrlees, for seven years before).[20] D. S. Mirsky, who was close to Harrison in Paris, observed that despite her "radical intellect," she remained a "Victorian lady."[21] It is thus quite possible that like many, if not most, middle-class Victorian spinsters, Harrison gave her sexual feelings little if any physical expression. But she expressed plenty of emotional affection for both men and women, and this didn't always make her life any easier.

A Friend to Rely On

Gilbert Murray provided Harrison with a steadying intellectual relationship during her Cambridge years. Murray himself was a person of many interests. A "sound scholar" of the highest order, Murray also saw himself as a literary man. Having once tried his hand at writing original dramas, he was much more successful with his pre-Raphaelite verse translations of ancient theater—the majority of which were based on his own editions of the Greek (he was an authority on Euripides).[22] Theatrical productions based on Murray's translations brought him into contact with theater people and playwrights—including George Bernard Shaw, who remained a longtime friend. An ardent liberal throughout his life, Murray once thought of a political career and was an active supporter of the League of Nations. And not least consequential for our story, Murray also seemed to be possessed of telepathic powers and was twice president of the Society for Psychical Research.

Born to the colonial elite in Sydney, Murray left Australia with his mother for Britain at the age of eleven. His father had inherited estates, increased them, and received a knighthood; but he lost his wealth, became increasingly depressed, and died when Murray was seven. When his mother went to London to be with her mother and sisters, Murray attended the very respectable Merchant Taylors' School as a day student on scholarship. Excelling in his studies, he received a further scholarship to St. John's College at Oxford, where he continued to do very well. Murray's early success was crowned by his election as professor of Greek at Glasgow at the age of twenty-three—no mean achievement for a lad from the disadvantaged gentry. Having made his way up from straightened circumstances through his academic diligence, Murray found a new place among moneyed aristocracy through his marriage.[23]

The family into which Murray married was no ordinary one. George Howard, the eleventh earl of Carlisle, and even more his wife, Rosalind, were Whig aristocrats—devoted to liberal, sometimes radical, causes. Murray's mother-in-law, known as Lady Carlisle, was an energetic, take-charge person whose temperament served her better in public life than on the domestic front. Eventually, she became president of the British Women's Temperance Association and of the Women's Liberal Federation but finally couldn't live together with her artist husband, whose political views had grown more conservative over the issue of Home Rule for Ireland.[24] First attracted to Murray as a fellow teetotaler, Lady Carlisle became his ally in his somewhat difficult courtship of her daughter Mary. This was lucky for Murray, for Mary seemed to have inherited her mother's independent-mindedness. The Oxford classicist Hugh Lloyd-Jones, a self-confessed conservative, calls Mary "alarming" and her mother "terrifying."[25] Murray, on his visits to this sometimes uneasy household, seems to have been a tempering presence, remembered by Mary's younger sister as "a witty, friendly, and always greatly welcomed playmate."[26]

The dynamics in Murray's extended family struck the imagination of his friend Bernard Shaw enough to provide a model for his play *Major Barbara*. Mary is the prototype for the intensely dedicated Salvation Army officer Barbara—but the play begins with a scene introducing Barbara's domineering mother. Murray then turns into Barbara's suitor, Adolphus Cusins, a Greek scholar who calls himself a "collector of religions"—an expression used about Murray by his friends.[27] Murray himself was of mixed minds about his portrayal, but Shaw's description of Cusins, although certainly a caricature, captures some of the personal contradictions noted by Murray's biographer:[28] "Cusins is a spectacled student, slight, thin haired, and sweet voiced"—a general physical description of the young, balding Murray—"[h]is sense of humor is intellectual and subtle, and is complicated by an appalling temper. . . . He is a most determined, tenacious, intolerant person who by mere force of character presents himself as—and indeed actually is—considerate, gentle, explanatory, even mild and apologetic, capable possibly of murder, but not cruelty or coarseness."[29] In all, this description of the mild-mannered but firm-willed scholar—born in Australia and sometimes addressed ironically as Euripides—can easily be read as Shaw's fond, if mocking, characterization of his friend.

Shaw's description of Cusins/Murray also revealed the damage liable to be inflicted by Murray's contradictory nature: "The lifelong struggle of a benevolent temperament and a high conscience against impulses of inhuman ridicule and fierce impatience has set up a chronic strain which has visibly wrecked his constitution." Murray, in fact, frequently suffered from illness, much of it probably psychosomatic (he lived to be ninety-one). Indeed, the stress of life as a young professor in Glasgow was too much for Murray, and in 1899, after nine years, he resigned his position on grounds of ill health. Murray still kept active as a private scholar, however, working on text editions and translations, while managing his finances with the help of Lady Carlisle. In 1905, he was able to return to Oxford as a fellow of New College, and in 1908 he was elected Regius Professor at Oxford.

Murray's life at Oxford was busy and full, with five children and an active social circle that included political activists and theater people. His successor as Regius Professor, E. R. Dodds, writes of his visits to the Murray home as a student: "Lunch at the Murrays' was an unpredictable experience. Anything might happen: one might encounter a cabinet minister or a famous actress, or one's neighbor might prove to be the Murrays' gardener in his Sunday best (for Lady Mary Murray's parties were conscientiously classless)."[30] The sort of somewhat unconventional environment fostered in the Murray household was also one in which Harrison could thrive, and she appreciated her visits to the Murrays in Oxford. These visits, however, were infrequent enough to be special occasions: Sandra Peacock, Harrison's psychobiographer, suggests that Harrison saw the Murrays as a surrogate family and was as ambivalent about their household as she was about her own natal home.[31] Murray himself, of course, had more than enough going on in his life without Harrison: most of the time he seemed to play a proportionately bigger role in her world than she did in his.

Murray met Harrison in 1900 in Switzerland. She was then working out the new ideas that she would spring on classical studies in 1903 with her *Prolegomena*; he had recently become freed from academic responsibility, was ready for some fresh thought, and had time to listen. He wrote to his wife: "I like her very much indeed . . . she strikes me as having a generous mind, which is rare among scholars."[32] Never based in Cambridge, Murray's face-to-face interaction with Harrison was limited. They corresponded frequently, however, and found occasion to travel together—sometimes, at first, to Mary Murray's chagrin.[33] And Harrison's intentions on these trips could indeed appear less strictly research oriented than Murray's. In March 1903 Murray was staying comfortably at the villa of the Bernard Berensons outside Florence, when Harrison arrived, as per arrangement, to take him to Naples. Mrs. Berenson wrote to her sister: "[P]oor Gilbert is to be torn from his haven for an 'amorous adventure' of which he is, and will remain, perfectly unconscious."[34] But Mary Murray needn't have worried: her husband's observations to Lady Carlisle in May of the same year help give credence to Tina Passman's intuitions about Harrison's alternative lifestyle. Harrison was, wrote Murray, "much more like a man, a middle-aged bachelor accustomed to Club life, than a woman. She insisted on a good substantial dinner, good wine and plenty of tobacco . . . and, receiving these, she talked at her ease, like a brilliant man of letters."[35] Although Mary Murray's jealousies toward Murray's actress friends may have had some justification, Harrison, for Murray, seems to have been much more a dazzling colleague than an attractive woman.[36] And even if Murray's description was just a reassurance to his mother-in-law, Harrison herself never seemed to harbor unrealistic expectations about his availability. About Cornford, however, Harrison did come to foster some disastrous illusions.

The Younger Man

In its outlines, Cornford's life seems more conventional than either Murray's or Harrison's. The son of an Anglican clergyman who moved from parish to parish during Cornford's youth,[37] Cornford came to Cambridge as an undergraduate, did well, and settled in. Rising through the academic ranks slowly, he experienced his share of insecurities and disappointments along the way.[38] In Cornford's more mature years, he was known as a dynamic lecturer but a quiet person, given to embarrassing silences and able to slip discretely out of parties.[39] But he was, like Murray, an active liberal—a Fabian Socialist who campaigned against British imperialism[40]—and in his younger days was also known for his satirical wit. He wrote light pieces for the weekly *Cambridge Review* and in 1908 published what must be the most long-lived lampoon of academic politics ever, *Microcosmographia Academica*—where he advises, for example, that "Political influence may be acquired in exactly the same way as the gout. . . . The method is to sit tight and drink port wine."[41] Although Cornford first published the volume anonymously, he later came to be proud of it, listing it in its proper chronological order in *Who's Who*.[42] The book was not, he cautions with mock solemnity in the introduction, directed at everyone but only at those "neither less than twenty-five years old, nor more than thirty and . . . ambitious withal" (91)—a fair description of his own position when he came into Harrison's orbit.

After graduating Trinity College brilliantly in 1897, Cornford had decided to continue on in Cambridge. His family resources were limited, however, and he was getting by on a small salary as editor of the *Cambridge Review* and a stipend (known locally as an "exhibition") from his old college. Having been told he would soon have to support his mother, he was contemplating becoming a schoolteacher[43]—not a particularly inviting prospect for someone who had recently scored firsts on both parts of the classical tripos. The next year Cornford did manage to secure a fellowship at Trinity and would join the teaching staff three years later. But his position at Cambridge was still very marginal in the years after he first heard Harrison lecture, soon after her arrival there. Her new ideas appealed to him as a critic of the status quo and might just help him distinguish himself academically.

Cornford was also taken with her person. "I have a vision of her figure on the darkened stage of the lecture-room," he later wrote, "a tall figure in black drapery, with touches of her favourite green, and a string of blue Egyptian beads, like a priestess' rosary."[44] He wrote her a letter about a point raised in the lecture and was invited to tea to discuss it. At that tea, Harrison might well have been struck by Cornford's appearance, too: in 1905 a Cambridge diarist describes his "fine sturdy pale face and crimped black hair—like a king or Prophet."[45] Pictures from the period reveal him as tall and good-looking, someone who carried himself with a "rather Spanish dignity."[46] The tea and talk would continue, with different degrees of intellectual and emotional intensity, until 1914.

Harrison's relationship with Cornford began as an intellectual affair between a provocative and very knowledgeable woman almost fifty and a bright man nearly twenty-five years her junior who responded to her ideas; it ended on much the same footing. In between, however, things became emotionally complicated, for the two enjoyed each other's company, and their mutual affection grew. After R. A. Neil's sudden death from appendicitis in 1901, Harrison came increasingly to rely on Cornford for emotional and intellectual support. "I never consciously fell in love," she reflected later, "but bit by bit I came to depend entirely on him."[47] They went on long bicycle rides in Cambridge together and traveled in England and abroad. It was Harrison who became smitten, but the emotional relationship was not entirely one-sided. Even if Cornford did not finally reciprocate Harrison's attachment in kind, he must have appreciated her attention: a brainy and imaginative person—but also, according to several accounts, sometimes silent for too long—he doesn't always seem to have been so easy to have been around himself. "I taught Mr. Cornford Hebrew & Phoenician that he might keep *me* straight," Harrison wrote jokingly to Murray while traveling with Cornford in 1905, "& now he is ten times madder than I am—sometimes I must have a long talk with a sane person."[48] After his marriage to another woman in 1909, Cornford would try to explain his relationship with Harrison to his new wife: "she and I were both rather lonely people, we foregathered and made friends and we have been a good deal together. Now she is feeling that someone else will be more than all friends to me henceforth. . . . [S]he can't help feeling a little lonely."[49]

This was a tremendous understatement. Cornford's courtship and marriage to Frances Darwin—a granddaughter of Charles Darwin—caused Harrison to fall into a severe depression, which manifested itself in physical symptoms over several years. Harrison felt betrayed: Cornford had written her a letter that made her "feel that things were on a different footing & that he would never marry & that our sort of unmarried-married life would be for always."[50] Harrison's psychic state was all the more complicated because the woman Cornford married was also the daughter of one of Harrison's oldest college friends, who had died four years earlier. Harrison had known her from childhood and had been instrumental in introducing her to Cornford. Many acquaintances, seeing Harrison in loco parentis to the couple, sent her messages of congratulations on the match, but in fact she had been devastated.[51]

Frances was then a young woman of artistic temperament who would develop into a poet of modest renown, an intimate of the legendary Rupert Brooke. But Frances was subject to long depressions, the first of which was triggered by the death of her mother when she was seventeen and lasted until shortly before she met Cornford.[52] Having recently returned to her father in Cambridge, she took up the study of Greek with her "Aunt Jane," who offered to introduce her to the witty, but then still anonymous, author of *Microcosmographia Academica,* by which Frances had recently been impressed. (Later, remembering her appreciation of the satire, she observed: "I was not brought up in academic circles for nothing.")[53] Ostensibly, Harrison brought Frances and Francis together as two of her closest young friends, but one can only speculate on the reasons why she paired an attractive man on whom she had become emotionally dependent with a young woman who she knew was taken with his mind. Frances herself reflected, not without some bitterness: "I was her newest human discovery and plaything and she was delighted that it should entertain him as well."[54]

Harrison didn't really reach a new emotional and physical equilibrium until 1912, when her animosity against Frances dissolved in an experience of mystical transcendence. Her feelings about religion itself, as we might expect from chapter 1, remained ambivalent. "I can't describe it," she wrote to Murray from Switzerland, where she had gone for a rest-cure, "the 'New Birth' is the best. . . . [I]t was what they mean by communion with God." Her doctor was astonished at her physical recovery, but there was "something not physical too for all the hate against Frances was gone . . . a whole crust of egotism [has] melted away, and . . . I have got hold of something bigger than me that I am part of. . . . I will never call it God—that name is defaced, but it is wonderful."[55] Despite Harrison's rejection of conventional religious terms, she had undergone a powerful experience that she sensed as religious, something both "wonderful" and physically and psychically therapeutic. But it was preceded by three years of emotional purgatory.

Cornford, for his part, tried to be sensitive to Harrison's feelings in the wake of his marriage ("About Aunt Jane we shall have to be thoughtful," he cautioned Frances soon after their wedding). But he had never understood the quality of her emotions for him or their depth. Many years later Cornford expressed puzzlement to Frances as to why Harrison acted toward him as a rejected lover might. Did it never occur to him that she might actually be in love with him? asked Frances. "She meant a great deal to me," was Cornford's apparently straightforward reply, "but she was old enough to be my mother."[56] Harrison, alas, was only young at heart and was blind to Cornford's own emotional immaturity at the time. "I often thought . . . she did not know what I was really like," he later reflected. "Did she ever know what any of her friends were really like, or did she rather see them as symbols and assign them parts in the drama of her life?"[57]

Cornford still continued to value his intellectual interplay with Harrison after his marriage, however, and this would now have to suffice for Harrison, too. Emotionally, they grew more distant, but their friendly scholarly interaction continued for five more years. Murray, long safely married, kept up fruitful academic conversations with both Harrison and

Cornford through their difficult times. The intellectual relationship among the three was strong enough to weather the storms in the affections that animated it.

AFFECTIONATE INTERPLAY

In an obituary for Cornford, who died in 1943, Murray tells how he first met him in Harrison's rooms, "listening intently to the lively discussions, meditative, admiring, and critical, seldom arguing but always—so one felt—taking ideas away with him to think over and re-examine." Remembering his younger days leads Murray to dwell longer here on Harrison than might appear seemly in an obituary for someone else: even thirty years after their active collaboration, Murray still cannot help but recall Cornford in light of Harrison's impact on them both. Her "influence on her younger contemporaries was immense. . . . She was in pursuit of what the Greeks, or their primitive ancestors, really thought; and seemed at times to have a subconscious hope that, by finding that, one might make some approach to discovering what was really true."[58] Profoundly suggestive discussion about the *real* meaning of Greek religion was at the heart of what Harrison offered younger scholars, and it excited them in ways they remembered many years later. But, like Cornford, they all took away different ideas and developed them from their own perspectives. Not everyone, moreover, played the same role in the discussions.

Personalized Collaborations

Although Harrison inspired other scholars, she also drew from them in different ways. Practically, she relied on the "sound scholarship" of younger and older colleagues alike. Harrison's original contributions to her field during her Cambridge years lay in the verve with which she incorporated anthropological and archeological insights at a time when the field itself consisted mostly of text scholars. In order to get her views taken seriously, she liked to support them with philological arguments, which were not her strong point. Her friends, however, were ready to help. Hope Mirrlees writes, "Often her latest theory depended or at any rate would be helped by some Greek word's having a certain derivation. And she would take the derivation to Mr. Neil to ask if it were a possible one and he would answer with a twinkle, 'I *think* I can arrange it for you!' "[59] In service of Harrison's imagination, sympathetic colleagues were ready to explore the bounds of the etymologically possible.

After Neil's death, A. B. Cook became her prime philological authority. Cook, the author of an encyclopedic, multivolume treatise on Zeus, was, according to Harrison's student and biographer, Jessie Stewart, "perhaps the most erudite and fertile of her helpers"; but he was, of all of them, perhaps also the least sympathetic to her ideas.[60] His acknowledgment to her in the first volume of Zeus is gracious but guarded: he was indebted to Harrison's "wide range and synthetic powers" for "valuable suggestions" but was all "the more anxious to acknowledge this debt because on matters of the deepest import we do not see eye to eye."[61] Cook was an evangelical Christian, finding time to teach Sunday school in a busy Cambridge life,[62] and never quite fit in with the less than orthodox members of Harrison's inner circle. But he was still a friend and frequent visitor and would figure prominently in their mutual intellectual life.

In addition to drawing on the sound scholarship of her public-school-educated men friends, Harrison—if at first not quite consciously—also realized the value of working out ideas with them. In a paper titled "Scientiae Sacra Fames," read before the London Sociological Society sometime before 1915, Harrison reflects on gender relationships, recalling some words of a writer whose name she can't recall. "Woman," the writer said, "is more *resonant* than man, more *subject to induction from the social current*. Man is better insulated, more independent, more individualized."[63] Later she takes this insight, which she understands as "broadly true" to an after-the-fact analysis of her intellectual relationships. What did she "get from a Man's mind" that she didn't "from a woman friend"? It wasn't new ideas, she emphasizes:

> Your thoughts are—for what they are worth—self-begotten by some
> process of parthenogenesis. But there comes . . . a moment . . . when you
> want to disentangle them from yourself and your emotions, when they are
> sending out . . . a welter of feelers in all directions, setting up connec
> tions . . . profusely and recklessly. . . . Then you want the mind of a man
> with its great power of insulation. That is why a man's mind is so resting.[64]

At the same time, the two polarized properties of the mind are not strictly dependent on biological gender, and Harrison continues in a vein more amenable to today's notions of gender equality: "Some men's minds, most artists and poets, I imagine, are as restless, as suggestive and suggestible, as ramificatory, as any woman's; what I mean is, simply, the male element in the mind, is its power of insulation." Both mental elements—sensitive female and insular male—are necessary for fertile intellectual work, she recognizes. What better way for them to come together than through amicable discussion in mixed company?

In the years before his marriage, it was Cornford who helped provide that male element for Harrison, serving, to use her term, as her mental "resting place." Apt in this role, he listened to her and responded, but didn't argue, letting her give shape to her own ideas. Harrison, for her part, seemed adept at complementing both the "sensitive" and "insulated" mental elements of her younger colleagues as appropriate. "Perhaps the secret of Miss Harrison's influence over the young," writes Murray, "was in part the generosity of sympathy with which she discussed and criticized and helped forward their immature suggestions."[65] Sympathizing with them and with the direction of their thought in her feminine way, she also firmly helped them isolate its kernel.

Cornford's role as elemental male grounding point for Harrison's intuitive expansion, by contrast, was much more passive than Harrison's sensitive direction of her students. "Where I was expected to furnish a touchstone of sober criticism," he wrote in a 1928 sketch about Harrison soon after her death, "I was too often captivated by the play of her imagination and afraid to cavil at intuitions of genius backed by a knowledge far greater than my own."[66] It did no good to entreat her about the importance of solid facts, he continued. More important for Harrison than any active contribution from Cornford here seems to have been the perceived stability of his mental presence. He wrote to Murray in the same year: "I often thought she treated me (25 years her junior) as if I were older than herself & made me feel she was the younger of the two."[67] The physically and emotionally young Cornford helped the mentally and spiritually young Harrison give birth to her ideas; for a critique of them she turned to Murray.

True to his character, Murray was forthright with Harrison in person and in writing. Living in different cities, the two corresponded often, with Harrison, at least, regularly discussing her work in progress. Murray's responses were destroyed by Harrison with the rest of her correspondence when she left Cambridge; her letters to him, however, have been carefully preserved and show that he did not refrain from speaking his mind. "Very tardily I admit that one of yr criticisms was just," she once wrote, implying that the criticisms were several. The fault that she admitted was in fact not a light one for a scholar: "I see I have not stated fairly the views of my opponents."[68] Later in their friendship, Murray told his wife of a face-to-face meeting where Harrison read him a sketch of her plan for *Themis:* "I regret to say that my criticisms were so unsympathetic that they nearly made her ill. I thought she was going to have a palpitation at dinner."[69] And Murray was forthright with Harrison on more than matters of scholarship; he also let her know his opinion on the fashionable style of dress to which she was drawn. "A perfect storm" was left behind, wrote Murray to his wife, when a colleague, going off to work, commented on the provocative nature of the current fashion. "The word provocative, which I did not originate but defended, upset Miss H. altogether."[70] She must have taken it as a personal affront, but that did not faze Murray. Twelve years older than Cornford and much more established as a scholar, Murray, uncowed by formidable women, had no reason not to speak his mind.

In addition to the subtle mental complementarities within the group, there were also more mundane ones. If Harrison's Greek was suspect, she was more comfortable in modern languages than Cornford or Murray, who disliked reading German.[71] More than those sound scholars, at any rate, it was Harrison who was abreast with advances in traditional German classical studies and au courant with the latest heavyweights in French theory: Bergson and Durkheim. And Harrison's sympathetic dynamism, even as it drew out insular male minds, could also bring them together in ways that Harrison, recovering from an operation, could refer to simply as a helpful diversion: "I had A. B. C. [A. B. Cook] and F. M. C. [Cornford] to do proofs yesterday," Harrison wrote Jessie Stewart. "They were most amusing in conjunction."[72] But even though Harrison was central for the Ritualists, lasting friendships also formed among the men, with Murray and Cornford corresponding until the end of the latter's life.

It was only in one instance, the production of *Themis,* that Murray and Cornford consciously collaborated with Harrison, each contributing a chapter to the book. She may well have drafted them into their job, however, wanting to give the book academic weight by presenting it as a group effort.[73] Although Murray would have occasion to affirm the arguments he presented there, neither he nor Cornford expanded them directly on his own. Both were at the time engaged in other projects and throughout their careers continued to pursue scholarly work called forth by their own intellectual, cultural, and religious perplexities.

Alternative Ambivalences

What, then, were the individual religiocultural ambivalences of the three main Ritualists and the scholarly projects to which these gave rise? In a general sense, the three were wholehearted participants in the reaction against positivism that emerged in different irrationalist streams toward the turn of the twentieth century.[74] In the staid world of classics at the time, this meant looking for truths beyond variant readings and the correct construction of texts. What was "really true" in Greek religion—the depths that the Ritualists sought in part through anthropological and folkloristic comparisons—might then speak to people caught in contemporary cultural dilemmas. Given the different temperaments and upbringings of the three, however, those dilemmas presented themselves variously in the scholarship of each.

Harrison, as seen in chapter 2, combined an appreciation for the artistic and ritual forms of religion with a strong animus toward religious orthodoxy, which she knew firsthand from her devout evangelical stepmother. A woman of strong feelings, she was herself susceptible to religious experiences of the sort she described in Switzerland, and she referred occasionally to her mystical apprehensions. "The unseen is always haunting me," she wrote in *Alpha and Omega,* "surging up behind the visible."[75] For Harrison, ritual is primary in religion because for her it is something experienced, something felt. What is particularly Harrisonian about the year spirit, to whom the primordial ritual is dedicated, is its direct connection to affective life. A version of Frazer's familiar dying and rising vegetation god, it is transformed through Bergsonian élan and Durkheimian collective effervescence into a felt vital force.

Cornford, more philosophically inclined than Harrison, shared her rejection of traditional theology but not her animus toward orthodox traditions. Growing up the son of an Anglican cleric, he knew full well how impressive religious traditions could be and the affect they could have on the pious. That he rejected religion intellectually as a young man at Cambridge, where he was a cofounder of the Society of Heretics, seems in accord with his iconoclastic youthful character. But he doesn't tell of religious traumas in his childhood home, and there is no particular reason to think he had any. And when Frances, who grew up with Darwinian agnosticism, became "a good Anglican," Cornford went along to church with her and the family. Helen Fowler, a family friend, describes him as unorthodox but tolerant.[76] If Cornford had no theological stake in religious tradition, he nevertheless did not think it was such a bad thing; his scholarship, moreover, shows that he clearly understood the power of tradition over the way people conceive of their world.

The running theme of Cornford's works is "The Unwritten Philoso-

phy" (the title essay of a posthumously published volume)—that collection of unconscious religiocultural presuppositions that shape conscious thought. "If we look beneath the surface of philosophical discussion," Cornford proclaimed in his inaugural lecture as professor,
"we find that its course is largely governed by assumptions that are seldom, or never, mentioned. I mean that groundwork of current conceptions shared by all the men of any given culture and never mentioned
because it is taken for granted as obvious."[77] These remarks were made
in 1931, but Cornford's attitude is revealed most sharply in his earliest
works, written in the first decades of the twentieth century during his
active association with Harrison. *Thucydides Mythistoricus* (1906)
claims that even historical writing is shaped by a classical Greek sense
of life as tragedy, with Thucydides' narrative shaped by a pattern of
growth, hubris, and fall. *From Religion to Philosophy* (1912) then
traces philosophical concepts such as order and law back to the socioreligious concepts of an early tribe. Like Harrison, Cornford was
aware of the workings of subconscious patterns within tradition, but he
recognized them in the forms of rational thought and expression that
they shaped. These could then exert their own fascination, and even
when they served traditional religion, they could be respected for revealing important human truths.

The poles of Murray's personal dilemma were more extreme than
were those of the other two, although he often seemed to balance them
with greater finesse. On the one hand, Murray was a modern liberal rationalist, committed to progress and the common good, a very public intellectual active in political causes. On the other, he was psychically sensitive, over many years the principal actor in a series of experiments in
thought transference.[78] More than Cornford, Murray gave reason a high
positive value, but he also recognized something beyond it. "The Uncharted surrounds us on every side," he wrote in concluding a chapter of
The Five Stages of Greek Religion, "and we must have some relation toward it. . . . As far as knowledge and conscious reason will go, we
should follow resolutely their austere guidance. When they cease, as
cease they must, we must use as best we can those fainter powers of apprehension and surmise and sensitiveness" (106). Reason is best, but is
not all there is, and psychic sensitivity is sometimes all we have. Religiously, for Murray this attitude led to a lack of confessional belief married to a broad religious tolerance—the kind of stance seen in Cornford
(and many other interpretive writers) but with a greater sense of earnest
conviction. "As a rule," he writes, introducing the passage above, "each

individual belongs to some body which has received in writing the results of a divine revelation. I cannot share in any such feeling." Ending the chapter by admonishing us to remember "above all to walk gently in a world where the lights are dim and the very stars wander," Murray remains a "collector of religions" determined to act reasonably in the face of the inevitable unknown.

An important dimension of "the real truth" of ancient Greece that Murray wanted to bring to the public may well have been a version of the combination of religious tolerance and psychic openness that he saw reflected in classical Greek culture. Certainly, the Greek religion that he portrays is not the chthonic world of *Themis,* vital and primordial. Murray acknowledges his debt to Harrison in understanding the early stages of Greek religion but differs with her on the idealized divinities of the classical period: "She has by now made the title 'Olympian' almost a term of reproach, and thrown down so many a scornful challenge to the canonical gods of Greece, that I have ventured on this attempt to . . . plead for their religious value" (*Five Stages of Greek Religion,* xii).

The Olympian gods, "so calm, so perfect" in artistic portrayals, represent "the victory . . . of man over beast." Murray was enough of a collector of religions to know that religious ideals are not always accomplished; but even when not completely realized, the "Olympian Religion" was nevertheless a "superb endeavor . . . a movement and effort of life" (59). Modern humanity would do well to assimilate the ideals of classical Greece, which prized rationality but also recognized many gods and the great "uncharted"; those ideals could guide Murray's contemporaries on the necessary path toward progress. Something of this active liberal impulse seems to stand behind the popular accessibility of Murray's interpretive writing, his poetic translations, and his stagings of Greek drama. In Murray's view, more important for the general public than a knowledge of classical Greek was an appreciation of classical *Greece.*

The scholarly manifesto on which the three Ritualists all agreed was presented by Murray as an exclamation of Harrison's, whose favorite expressions he quotes: "what was then called 'sound scholarship' in itself, unilluminated by imagination, 'got you nowhere.' "[79] Specialists, added Harrison elsewhere, just "grub up the facts but don't see the relations."[80] To get at what was really true, it was worth being bold, taking chances, and shocking the staid classical establishment. The different personal contradictions of the three Ritualists, however, impelled their imaginations in alternative directions, which at times only barely converged.

Their mutual interaction was fertile because their (sometimes extreme) affection for one another helped them to enter into productive intellectual complementarities. But despite Harrison's occasional imperialistic designs,[81] the Cambridge Ritualists together had no coherent intellectual program.

TRUTHS AND CONSEQUENCES

The fruitful, sometimes stormy, interlude of the Ritualists ended abruptly with the outbreak of World War I, which severely disrupted academic life. Cornford surprised everyone by joining the British Army as an Instructor in Musketry (none of his academic colleagues had known that he was also an expert marksman). Murray became a much more public intellectual, first serving for a while as a government propagandist in the war effort, then regaining his credibility among radical pacifists by working for conscientious objectors. Harrison, staying in Cambridge, underwent the most radical personal change, effectively abandoning classical studies forever. Mixing with the local East European refugee community, she began to explore an interest in Russia that had lasted from her childhood, learning Russian well enough in her sixties to teach it at Newnham. After her move to Paris in 1922, she developed new working relationships—especially with Count V. S. Mirsky[82]—and published some translations from Russian with Mirrlees. Ties to older friends were loosened, which Murray and others noticed with consternation and puzzlement.[83] In a letter to Frances Cornford in the aftermath of her marriage, Harrison reflects on her feeling that "late in life—work & friendship come to be the whole of life."[84] With the advent of World War I, her old friends had gone, engaged in more urgent affairs, and with them her fertile way of working. For her life to remain whole, she needed to move on.

The Ritualist episode—although certainly not held up as an example to emulate in its excesses—still shows us how interpreters, not just explainers, have worked together productively. True, Harrison no doubt believed, for a time, that the year spirit was at least as true as any academic doctrine—a valid scholarly "explanation"—but her mode of working was, in our terms, eminently interpretive. In the Harrison archives at Newnham College, Robert Ackerman came across some jottings made by Jessie Stewart in preparation for her biography of Harrison. "Jane's urge [was] aesthetic," she noted, "not scientific"—a frequent, although not, I think, necessary, characteristic of an interpretive writer on religion. She "regarded Dörpfeld and Ridgeway [preeminent sound scholars of her day] as materials for pattern," Stewart continues, "i.e., her aesthetic sense [was] satisfied by conclusions elicited from masses of data." She embraced the stuff of religious life included in those "masses of data" and was a fine reader of artistic detail (her early works, remember, treated Greek art and architecture). But more important to her was the big picture, her "love of brilliant generalization." The year spirit was as true as anything for Harrison because she "desired a pattern, not the truth" in any scientific sense.[85]

And in the human sciences, it is often these interpretive patterns that last, finding new incarnations over academic generations, even as explanatory conjectures proved false are forgotten along with superseded text editions. If the historical migrations envisioned by the pan-Egyptianists now seem just fancy, the Panbabylonians' expansive patterns—eventually weakened by Jeremias into a broad "interpretation" in our sense—still reverberate: microcosm and macrocosm, sacred centers, primal mountains. Although originally constructed from faulty evidence,[86] that vision continues to point to pervasive dimensions of religious traditions, even if, becoming overfamiliar, it can blind one to other pertinent features of a tradition's shape. Similarly, Harrison's year spirit—never taken too seriously by many "sound scholars" in her day or later—found persisting life in literary criticism, where it suggests poetic truths that have interesting ramifications in historically attested literary forms. The Ritualists' influence is direct through the first half of the twentieth century: Jessie Weston explicitly attempted to explore the implications of Murray's chapter on tragedy in *Themis* for the Grail legend and romance in general; Maud Bodkin cited both Cornford and Harrison, taking the "year god" for granted in her examination of archetypes in literature.[87] In the myth criticism of the second half of the century, the reverberation of Ritualist thinking is more diffuse, but it is not too hard to see the year spirit also lurking in the seasonal archetypes of Northrop Frye.[88] Indeed, the lasting impression of Harrison's year spirit on Murray—it figured prominently in an article he wrote for the 1929 edition of the *Encyclopædia Britannica*—kept the term itself alive among literary scholars longer than many classicists might have preferred.[89]

As creative interpreters who also worked together, the Ritualists contrast with the Dutch phenomenologists, the great men who made individual syntheses of their own. In their own ways, of course, Harrison and Murray, if perhaps not quite Cornford, were also "great"—strong personalities accustomed to center stage in their respective worlds, which in

Murray's case also included literary and political circles. Although the phenomenologists and the Ritualists both had pronounced aesthetic sensibilities, the Ritualists did not share a concurrent ideal of descriptive phenomenological "science." With them there is more vivid imagination and less all-knowing pronouncement. No one would accuse Harrison of excessive humility, but in the case of Greek, at least, she knew her limits; she also, as seen in "Scientiae Sacra Fames," knew the necessity of sometimes restraining her imagination, if occasionally we wish she might have done so a bit more. Murray, too, as Bernard Shaw could see, hid a fierce determination behind his mild demeanor. Eminently capable of sound scholarship, he was still, like Cornford, receptive to new and imaginative ideas. The friends fertilized and restrained one another's thinking in different ways—even though, as Murray relates of Cornford, their sense of artistic craftsmanship did not always lead them to offer up works in progress to premature critique.[90] What we see among the Ritualists is not simply the bold conjectures and sharp criticisms of Popper's scientific fallibilism but a sympathy: an ability to listen, respond, and take away an insight to develop; an openness and give-and-take that normally only comes with a degree of trust and affection.

CHAPTER 11

Concepts of Collectivity and the Fabric of Religiohistorical Knowledge

If, as in other humanistic fields, long-lived collaborative projects are rare in religious studies, small-scale collaborative volumes often seem all too common. Many of these begin with a core of like-minded intellectual friends—working together, perhaps, in ways recalling the intellectual (although not usually the emotional) dynamics among the Cambridge Ritualists. Others derive from the interaction of personal networks and public institutions, emerging out of individual panels at large academic meetings or from smaller, more intimate conferences for which an enthusiastic colleague has managed to find sponsorship. In their origins, then, edited volumes often take shape from scholars interacting in some of the personalized, unstructured ways seen in the last chapter as characteristic of interpretive writers.

As a finished publication, however, an edited volume usually bears the stamp of its individual editor, and its design—the ostensible basis of its organization—often displays a particular understanding of how knowledge in religious studies develops.[1] If the detailed dialectic of group interaction in the study of religion found in chapters 8, 9, and 10 ends on a note of vague, perhaps disconcertingly personalized, informality, the editorial frameworks discussed in chapter 11 will at least suggest some of that interaction's possible public intellectual results. As warps for the weaving-together of different personal visions into a fabric of public knowledge, moreover, each of the editorial frames to be treated seems to generate a characteristic texture of its own.

Following one of the Frazerian threads evident in the Cambridge Ritualists, I will examine four edited volumes on sacred kingship, paying
particular attention to what these suggest about visions of collective
knowledge in religious studies.[2] As scholars frequently do with the data
of religious traditions, in discussing edited volumes on kingship I will
treat ideals in tension with realities. Like many scriptural collections, edited volumes frequently must reckon with the realities of patronage and
make do with the materials at hand. Like ritual priests, editors may find
themselves creating an exemplary design that represents the ways things
should be but rarely can be in the everyday world.[3] In looking at the edited volumes, I will examine both their design and their fulfillment: the
collective project as ideally conceived and the real sum of individual contributions. For through the scope of its project and the planning of its
chapters, each volume promises the possibility of a particular dynamic
in the growth of religiohistorical knowledge—a promise, however, that
is difficult to keep. Understanding the reasons why these promises usually remain unkept, if not all the means to fulfill them, may give us a better sense of the roots of public religiohistorical knowledge in private insight and what these mean for its distinctive texture.

A LAYERED TAPESTRY

The four volumes I will examine differ in both historical origin and academic significance. Two have emerged from international conferences:
The Sacral Kingship, from the International Congress for the History of
Religions held in Rome in 1955, one of the first major conferences in
postwar history of religions; and *Kingship in Asia and Early America,*
from a seminar at the International Congress of the Human Sciences in
Asia and North Africa, held in Mexico City in 1976.[4] The first, although
edited with the very lightest of hands, has remained significant in part
through its sheer bulk and the importance of the meeting from which it
emerged. The second, although more carefully ordered and executed, has
received less notice. The other two volumes were originally conceived as
projects for which an edited work was deemed a particularly appropriate format. *Myth, Ritual, and Kingship,* a series of lectures given at Manchester in 1955 and 1956 and originally prepared for publication, presents a treatment of kingship within a specific tradition of scholarship,
the English Myth and Ritual School—later intellectual cousins of the
Cambridge Ritualists, with a focus shifted to the Ancient Near East.[5] *Rituals of Royalty,* instead of working within a specific school, is deliber-

ately cross-disciplinary, exploring relationships between history and social sciences still fertile today.[6] Although the first and third of these volumes may now sooner be of interest to historiographers of religious studies than to current researchers, the types of collective dynamic presented
by all of them continue, each reflecting a process through which public
knowledge in religious studies takes shape. Together, the problems in the
interconnection of knowledge intimated by the four volumes recall an intricately constructed tapestry, layered with different types of fabric that
are themselves complexly joined one to the other. Each of the four volumes suggests a different layer of the tapestry, with its own coherence
and appeal.

A Gossamer Net

The first of the four volumes to appear, *The Sacral Kingship* reveals an
overlay in our fabric of knowledge that still remains particularly characteristic of religious studies. Emerging from a midsized and moderately
focused international conference, the volume does indeed represent a
meeting of scholarly minds. Although many interesting debates may have
taken place at the gathering, these have not left their traces on the published essays, which in some cases consist only of précis of papers presented or of papers sent in but not read (xii). Thus, the meeting of minds
revealed by *The Sacral Kingship,* like that exemplified by many conference volumes (and conferences), is less a fruitful interchange than an as-
semblage of views.[7] At the same time, the volume is explicitly presented
as a "collective work." The term is emphasized, repeated in the very brief
avant-propos,[8] and reinforced by the lack of a signature on the avant-
propos and of a named editor for the volume.[9] What is the force of the
term here? It certainly does not imply group deliberations: "the collective work was not realized according to any systematic plan established
in advance. . . . [The authors] have all worked independently of one another" (xi–xii). The term instead seems to emphasize the power of plural authorship, which, it is implied, can produce a collective wisdom
overshadowing the vision of any editor. Indeed, this kind of collectivity,
we are told, can give rise to some extraordinary dynamics, potentially
producing a work whose "unity . . . comes from the completely spontaneous convergence" of essays produced "on the communally proposed
subject" (xii). Although flashes of insight from this sort of spontaneous
convergence may appear only infrequently to many of us, they still remain alluring to some. Moreover, the random intersections of disparate

threads of learning from which those insights usually emerge remain very much with us: much cumulative knowledge in the study of religion continues to appear as a loose concatenation of separate efforts, a gossamer net spread over any more substantial knowledge we may share. *The Sacral Kingship* shows us how this net is woven and what it can hold.

Two basic principles are apparent in the weave. One is conscious and deliberate: the unity of *The Sacral Kingship* would be "supported . . . by procedures of presentation, like the division of materials among the different sections of the collection" (xii)—sections straightforwardly ordered by geographical and historical area. The other is unordered and accidental: the intersection of the articles at academic problems topical at the time. Both this substantial organization by area and collective attention to topical issues continue to shape the study of religion today. But the volume shows just how light and variegated a fabric these principles create when they work together haphazardly at a general meeting of the field.

The areal threads, to begin with, are of widely diverging lengths and uneven breadth. Of the fifty-seven scholars agreeing to write on the theme of "the king-god and the sacral character of kingship," only seven wrote explicitly general comparative essays, which were placed in an introductory section; the other fifty addressed the theme in their specific area of expertise. As might be expected, the areal interests of the contributors were not evenly distributed, producing long sections on Christianity and Israel; smaller ones on ancient Egypt, Greece and Rome, and pre-Christian Europe; and a solo paper[10] on Islam. The sections on Asia and nonliterate peoples were middle-length but inclusively broad.

Further, these areal threads are not spun together tightly from the fibers of the separate articles. This is because, in some cases, of the very breadth of the threads but more often because of the brevity and independence of the fibers: the papers were short and not explicitly related to one another. Although sometimes referring briefly to the work of earlier scholars, writers for the most part offered a straightforward sketch of the meanings of sacred kingship in their particular domain. Those working in the same area could then emphasize different, apparently contradictory, aspects of their subject. J. Gonda, for example, says that in ancient India, the king is not seen as uniquely divine but as a *deva,* one of a large class of deities (172). A. Basu, on the other hand, says that the ancient Indian king himself is not taken as divine at all; rather, the institution of kingship is (167). Someone trying to take in both views of ancient Indian kingship at once may then come away wondering about the paradox of the *deva* who is not divine. Here, then, as in much of comparative religion, areal threads are offered as an explicit warp. But they are very difficult to discern coherently, composed of articles that do not quite tie together. At the same time, articles only loosely entwined with those in their area may connect with others from different places. Thus, among articles running awry from major threads, wispy links are formed.

The interconnections among articles from different areas often come into focus at points of definition, and definitional questions about divine kingship are a major theme in several pieces.[11] These definitional questions, moreover, are likely to entail more substantial issues of the king's religious meaning and role. In the early 1950s, the Frazerian paradigm of the king as dying and rising god, having gone through diverse transformations in academic traditions of Myth and Ritual, was still a live issue in the study of divine kingship. It thus linked a number of the essays here through common motifs, although much less tightly than in the Myth and Ritual volume to be discussed below. Scholars working on Christian England, pagan Ireland, and Old Norse materials extend the paradigm matter-of-factly;[12] scholars of early Christianity muster evidence to refute it.[13] In hindsight, the contretemps is instructive for revealing some of the swings of scholarship: the paradigm is applied boldly and naively in new domains but is examined critically in an area where it has already been widely pursued. Connected in the fixed time of the volume, however, these different strands of argument give us no coherent answers but rather a web of related, frequently contrasting, patterns.

Thus, through a succession of constructions, sometimes complementing one another, often not, our understanding becomes formed and refined but achieves no definite shape. As a motif contained in all the essays, divine kingship reveals different patterns, depending on which essays we view together and from what perspective. Certainly, the uneven areal warp provides some order to the overall design we see. Some of the individual fibers, moreover, manage to stand out—articles still occasionally cited and useful as brief surveys of a topic or concise presentations of a particular scholarly view.[14] Yet the shifting shapes presented by the essays together will give different readers their own impressions of the whole, abstract and subjective. Nevertheless, the collective weight of the essays—their number, as well as their manifold diversity—may convince many that the pattern each sees does indeed reflect some reality.

Its gossamer webs representing the eternally abiding, ethereal heights of history of religions, *The Sacral Kingship* reveals the discipline at its characteristic extremes as a collective endeavor. The volume highlights the kind of cross-cultural concept that lets the study of religion flourish as a comparative enterprise and offers plenty of the individual insights that give it depth. By presenting many intriguing arguments on its subject while keeping it aloof from any one, the volume gives us rational reflection but lets our subject stay numinous, too. The problem is that in revealing the numinous subject as a vague and shifting presence, the collective scholarship of *The Sacral Kingship* makes that subject impossible to pin down. We get fine rational reflection but no firm rational precision. In their brevity and lack of coordination, the individual essays fail to offer a coherent descriptive picture of what sacral kingship might be even in a limited regional domain. Focusing on their own presentations, the authors, for the most part, build little on past scholarship and collectively present no interpretive coherence. The volume thus does not harness the power of its collectivity either descriptively or theoretically.

Instead, *The Sacral Kingship* promises to generate new knowledge through the results of a sort of collective effervescence: "the completely spontaneous convergence of essays" touted in the introduction. Indeed, the volume shows us how, when scholars of religion come together, they are wont to celebrate a topic's diversity and their own. But the results of this celebratory magic remain chimerical. True, through the very number of thematic strands they contribute, with the inevitable overlapping that takes place, the collected scholars give the topic a discernible presence. The image of sacral kingship here, however, is elusive and amorphous—a shifting, abstract pattern visible through a loose, inadvertent, weave. We are aware of the divine king as a translucent, shimmering presence: now a god, now an institution, sometimes dying and rising again. But, taken together, these loosely woven images reveal no coherent phenomenological picture of him. Spun from arguments at odds with one another, even individual thematic strands are supported by no common theoretical frame: what dies and rises in England and Ireland does definitely *not* do so in the early Christian world. Readers are thus left to form their own judgments on the basis of a diverse array of apparently contradictory articles that are themselves, for the most part, fairly thin: short, descriptive, and restricted to a single topic. Phenomenologically vague, theoretically indecisive, and produced from thin pieces, the collective religiohistorical knowledge that thus emerges can sometimes seem lustrous but cannot hold up on its own. Each of the other volumes to be examined adds a layer to our tapestry that adds strength in one of these areas: historical precision, theoretical coherence, and a thick complexity that can add conceptual depth.

A Set of Tableaus

In *Kingship in Asia and Early America,* reasonably uniform threads come together in a coherent historical phenomenology. Deriving from a focused symposium, not a large conference, the volume reveals the results of ordered cooperation. Contributors were asked to address not kingship generally but the "ideology" of kingship in a particular area. The papers were rewritten, "in the light of often vigorous discussion," and some additional ones were added as problems in coverage were seen: a contributor on ancient India "misinterpreted his briefing" and editor A. L. Basham, himself an expert in the area, prepared a supplementary article; a paper from another symposium at the same meeting also seemed suitable for inclusion (3). Shaped to similar patterns and altered to fit together, the combined papers appear as a continuous panorama, even though the seams between them are evident. Whereas the Rome conference produced a gossamer net over our tapestry, this symposium produced an ordered set of tableaus as backdrop.

With single, longer essays devoted to kingship in each area, this volume yields more coherent pictures than *The Sacral Kingship,* and the broad but definite focus on ideology gives all the pictures similar perspectives. We are thus left with fewer perplexities, and the paradox of the king as *deva* who is not divine is here, in fact, resolved. In his essay on Indian kingship, Basham, like Gonda in *The Sacral Kingship,* regularly refers to the king as a *deva,* a god; but, like Basu in the same volume, he also focuses on the limits of the king's personal power. At the same time, he reminds us that the term *deva* can be used not only of kings but most perfunctorily in reference to husbands and teachers, too: just because a king is a god, he needn't be *particularly* divine. Instead of a vague, potentially awesome, religious paradox, we are left with a satisfied, if mundane, semantic understanding.[15]

In its connected pieces, the volume offers a panoramic vision that is reasonably clear and detailed but suggests only the broadest of general comparative patterns. The essays themselves contain few cross-cultural references, and Basham's introduction is brief and cursory, noting a few structural similarities in kingship across the areas and describing historical links. There is a brief nod toward one of the more controversial theoretical writers of the day—Wittfogel on oriental despotism—and a middling stand taken (11–12). Theory is not seriously engaged, even at middle levels; no striking comparisons are made. We are left to see the obvious.

What we get here is a backdrop to our knowledge, something substantial, a sense that, within the limits we have set, we have encompassed the globe. All the papers, Basham reminds us, "are very valuable for the information they contain, and the reader who carefully works through them all will have acquired most valuable background knowledge of theories of government of the major civilizations of Asia and America" (5). In seeking "authoritative survey[s]" (5), Basham also realizes some nascent postcolonialist insights, consciously commissioning essays from informants with origins in the culture on which they write.[16] Yet this innovation fails to spark the interest it might evoke today, in part because of the homogeneity in attitude of the scholars selected. Basham, writing in an academy just awakening to postorientalist anxieties, is clear on this. Although he expresses concern about "nationalism" (3), his motive was sensitivity to political controversy, not to the concern, more current today, that peoples should be represented by scholars of their own.[17] In fact, all the scholars write in the same discursive academic style. The cumulative effect here is to show us that modern scholars all over the world can present reasonable descriptions in similar ways. Thus, even with all the national voices represented, we come away with fewer perspectives—fewer doubts and fewer questions—than from the much more multivocal *Sacral Kingship*. Yet if we are looking here for coherent historical grounding, this can be taken as a strength.

The reasonableness of the volume's discourse, its clarity, and the many details it takes into account all give strength to the fabric of knowledge it creates. But this is a fabric designed for *coverage,* not depth. The volume itself remains intellectually flat. Despite the fact that several well-respected authors contributed to it—including Basham and J. Kitagawa[18]—the book itself is not well known. If *The Sacral Kingship* sought for the emergence of new knowledge from a collective effervescence—the romantic spark in Durkheim's largely positivist vision—*Kingship in Asia and Early America* really does look to a sensible positivist grounding for study. Its essays planned, coordinated, and organized, it promises a sturdy historical backdrop—which is, more or less, what it delivers. Unfortunately, that backdrop alone has not attracted the interests of many historians of religion. Scholars realize that the type of knowledge *Kingship in Asia and Early America* contains is useful, even necessary, but they do not usually find it very exciting.

A Patterned Brocade

Myth, Ritual, and Kingship, by contrast, represents a later flowering of a school of scholarship that did in fact excite the interests of many when it first appeared. By the end of the 1920s, scholars in biblical studies began to see continuities among myths and rituals of the ancient Near East, Israel, and early Christianity. Using methods of philological, form-critical, and folkloric scholarship, these scholars reined in some of the freewheeling visions of historians of religions who preceded them: Frazer's vastly elaborate narrative of dying and rising gods and the pan-Egyptian diffusionism of Perry and Elliot Smith.[19] They focused particularly on the royal New Year's ritual, identifying concrete patterns throughout the Near East. Influential in England and Scandinavia from the 1930s into the 1950s, they were together known broadly as the Myth and Ritual School. If several prominent members of the school had a personal stake in some Christian church (as many working in biblical studies do), their findings might nevertheless be read from secularizing as well as theologizing perspectives: on the one hand, the Christian history of redemption could be extended back beyond the prophets of Israel into a world that understood the truths of ritual; on the other, the figure of Christ the King could be seen as just another myth.[20]

In either case, definite patterns in ancient Near Eastern myth and ritual needed to be demonstrated. Scholarly excitement was generated by the sense that there were important new truths that could be *proved*. As among the diffusionists of chapter 9, real explanations seemed possible and led to collective effort. In this case that effort took two forms. In Scandinavia, cooperation was more informal: philologically trained scholars, familiar with one another's projects, worked on common problems in related Near Eastern materials.[21] In England, the Myth and Ritual School took the form of a de facto working group with an acknowledged leader: Samuel Hooke of the University of London long provided academic impetus for a number of biblical scholars and folklorists, editing three volumes over thirty-five years.[22] *Myth, Ritual, and Kingship*, the last of these, reveals—together with the ritual importance of the ancient Near Eastern king—the maturity of the group as a school. The volume includes two essays offering strong critiques of the group's collective endeavor—critiques that are (along with others) specifically addressed by Hooke in his introduction.[23] While pointing to the theoretical confidence of the group, the inclusion of these essays shows, even more significantly, that the group developed an explanatory theory that could be discussed, one that aroused debating partners who shared not only its concerns but access to its data, too. Here, truly, was a nascent science.

The possibility of a science emerges more readily here than in many other religiohistorical fields because of the limited academic domain of debate. Although the geographical and historical areas covered are very extensive, the data left to us from them are less so—a situation particularly true in the prewar years in which the Myth and Ritual School flourished. Moreover, the relevance of those data to Western religion lent them early to philological and historical scrutiny. More than in many humanistic fields, there are common bodies of evidence from which to marshal arguments. In the volume, then, specialists in ancient Egyptian, Hittite, and Ugaritic are joined by scholars dealing with several aspects of Hebrew Scriptures to present a common Near Eastern pattern from which the ancient Israelite annual festival could be reconstructed. The common ritual, they maintain, included recitations of creation and divine law; ritual humiliation, murder, and marriage of the king; ritual combat and triumphal procession; and more.[24] Members of the school showed how different biblical passages reflect this pattern. Critics attempt, with mixed success, to unravel the various strands, wondering if they ever did really come together in ancient Israel and emphasizing the differences among Near Eastern societies.[25]

The fabric of knowledge that emerges here is certainly more thickly woven and sharply defined than any we have seen in the other two volumes. Standing out in bold relief from the flat and uniform backdrop portrayed by our historical tableau, it offers a dimension that adds depth to our vision. Distinctly drawn, but with magical proportions that included elements of combat, murder, and humiliation, the divine king could surely capture the imaginations of scholars and public alike. Nevertheless, although the ideal royal pattern was deemed significant in part just because of its wide extent, it sometimes seemed only loosely affixed to the historical backdrop on which it was identified. As Jonathan Z. Smith suggested through a Melanesian comparison in "A Pearl of Great Price" (discussed in chapters 5 and 6), the ritual humiliation in the Babylonian New Year's festival—a crucial piece of the Myth and Ritualists' puzzle—may have had a crucial religious and political significance completely unsuspected by them. The Myth and Ritualists emphasized "the importance of the king for the well-being of the community,"[26] with the various elements of the presenting reenactments of archetypal patterns around a presumably native king; Smith, by contrast, examining specific historical contexts, suggested instead that the humiliations ritually rectify the incongruous reality of a *foreign* king. In its dissent, Smith's article also shows us how an established pattern, striking and apparently firm, can at the same time be a basis for new discovery: Smith draws loose strands from the ethereal net overlying our tapestry—strands, in this case, all the way from Melanesia—to give a new twist to what seemed like an established truth. In this way a segment of thickly patterned brocade can thus serve to link the other two layers of the tapestry seen so far. It serves as a piece of visibly structured, if still tentative, knowledge against which scholars can reflect according to the particular webs of knowledge they wispily perceive and the historical tableau they recognize as firmly genuine.

Myth, Ritual, and Kingship derived from a scholarly program that at its outset promised exciting new discovery, a definitive demonstration of a new mythic paradigm through coordinated effort. The program produced, in fact, a thick pattern that was indeed bold and exciting when it first appeared but that has never seemed as historically grounded as its creators envisioned. Particularly when attached to areas beyond its Near Eastern center, the Myth and Ritualists' brocade no longer lay flat against its historical backdrop and tended to unravel. Hardly new and bold any more, the pattern still remains woven into the texture of collective religiohistorical knowledge, continuing subtly to inform scholars' views and, recast in new ways, sometimes consciously evoking thought. Still, the texture it once added to our knowledge has, with the years, worn pretty thin. Beyond a patterned brocade, are there any other ways of tying the data of religious studies together that can connect them thickly, deeply, and complexly?

The Strengths of Knot Work

The connections offered by *Rituals of Royalty* offer more complexity, if less coherence. The most recent of our four edited volumes, it is of them the type of volume most actively produced today and presents the dimension of collective knowledge in religious studies now pursued most vigorously. The previous three volumes were focused around a single subject presented in various contexts. Both subject and context saw increasing specification: from any sort of kingship in any sort of context (our gossamer webs), to the ideology of kingship in certain ancient societies (our historical tableau), to the pattern of kingship in the ancient Near East (our patterned brocade). In *Rituals of Royalty*, instead of one subject, we get two: ritual as well as royalty. Our focus is now explicitly on the *relationship* between the two. In volumes of this type, the two strands of the subject are tied together in a number of highly specific historical milieus. The individual knots that develop can thus become very intricate. The editor's challenge is to identify the similarities in the ways the knots are tied. This general design runs through a great many edited volumes published from the mid-1980s on, a large number of which have titles featuring two abstract nouns connected by *and*: *Myth and Philosophy, Colonialism and Culture*.[27]

For the dynamics of the growth of knowledge, this focus on relationship between two subjects is significant. As seen in chapter 7, a commonsensically realist Popperian view tells us that knowledge appears particularly new and striking when it is *comprehensible* within a larger order but not *logically predicted* by it.[28] It is difficult to deal seriously with the last part of this proposition when we focus on single subjects, for then we are, for the most part, only refining our logical types, trying to make them cohere more closely to the apparent historical order. We develop definitions and taxonomies and examine related phenomenological categories. We may encounter some surprises, but we are largely interested in identifying the order we see. Explicitly talking about the relationship between taxonomically unrelated types, however, offers potential for a further dynamic, one of opposition and unexpected tangents. We can now conjoin our logical types—grammatical nominals—with interesting verbal phrases, bringing them together in statements that may be unexpected, as well as significant.

From a broader religious studies perspective, the significance of our statements will still derive largely from the logical types in which we frame them: Ritual, Royalty, Colonialism. At the same time, much of their initial freshness will derive from unexpected turns in their relationships revealed by a historical situation. *Really* significant new knowledge emerges when an unexpected historical turn appears in other historical situations, too, that is, when our new knowledge is also generalizable. *Rituals of Royalty*, however, shows us that in practice, the knowledge we are likely to get from generalizing about complex historical cases is likely to be both abstract and spare.

Focusing on traditional societies, *Rituals of Royalty* represents a collaboration of anthropologists with historians. Although the historians who contributed have interests differing from those of most in their profession, which "are overwhelmingly concentrated in Europe since the sixteenth century" (7), the book remains in good part an enterprise of Western-oriented specialists. Thus, several of the patterns that do recur seem historically related, the legacy of extended Roman tradition in Rome itself, Byzantium, and Carolingian Europe. But beyond these historical continuities (and even within them), the most evident conclusion

drawn by editor David Cannadine is the sheer diversity of the relationships between power and ceremonial across the societies covered, which
include the ancient Near East, China, Nepal, Madagascar, and Ghana.

The diversity presented—a factor of the writers' perspectives, as well
as of the societies—has two effects. One is to reinforce the historian's
emphasis on particularity: "all history, all anthropology, all sociology, is
ultimately a case-study of something," and there are no easy generalizations (13). But Cannadine does not want to abandon totally the generalizing dimensions of the project and alternatively suggests that the diversity itself raises some interesting questions: how can we explain the
contrasting relationships between power and ceremonial revealed in the
historical cases? "Why does spectacle sometimes accompany royal (and
national) power, and sometimes go with royal (and national) weak-
ness? . . . What is the connection between the overthrow of royalty and
the overthrow of ritual?" (17–18).

When Cannadine tries to move beyond diversity, his results seem less
intriguing. First of all, as he points out, most of the writers provide some
support for one or more of several familiar, intersecting academic theories: any royal ceremony is likely to sustain a ruler's authority in a functionalist way; the same ceremony may also evoke some Durkheimian collective effervescence; and the ruler almost always serves as a Geertzian
exemplary center (15). But these theories are all already as established as
they are likely to get, and the new knowledge we receive from closely analyzing the relationships between kingship and ritual recurring in the
chapters seems both abstract and evident: royal ceremonials, Cannadine
tells us, convey power precisely because they are made up of cultural
components that may already suggest power. Somewhat circular in its argument, this statement is hardly striking, containing just the barest mod-
icum of the logical unpredictability that gives new knowledge weight.[29]

Because the generalizations apparent from knot work are usually
spare, its most interesting dividends very often derive from the questions
provoked in attempting to penetrate its thick and intricately clustered diversity. The knots we find are indeed dense and multidimensional, penetrating all the other layers of the religiohistorical tapestry so far seen:
Amélie Kuhrt's contribution to Rituals of Royalty,[30] for example, examining the significance of the Babylonian royal New Year's festival for Persian kingship, is sewn neatly into the established historical tableau represented by Basham's volume, adding to the breadth of its backdrop. But
since the article deals at the same time with an important version of the
ancient Near Eastern rite that occupied Hooke's Myth and Ritualists, it

contributes as well to their patterned brocade, giving it an interesting historical turn. The loose ends Kuhrt leaves, finally, also become enmeshed in the ethereal filigree. Not, like Jonathan Z. Smith, offering a radical revision of a ritual's significance suggested by distant comparison, Kuhrt touches on wispy threads from closer at hand: she alludes to similar rites in ancient India and a possible Old Persian ritual that is "*totally* hypothetical" (53). The knot between power and ceremonial she ties is thus well grounded and thick but also suggestive. Yet, as in most knot work, it is *only* suggestive—tentative and probing—offering merely the possibility of leading to general knowledge by slowly expanding from one situation to another.

Indeed, aside from any links through definite historical traditions, the threads joining the individual knots tied in *Rituals of Royalty* blend in indistinguishably with others in the general religiohistorical panorama: the different examples stand alone, with little specifically to connect them. What the knots have in common is, at most, something about the way they are tied. But created from different historical elements, the individual knots themselves are all somewhat different, and frequently their resemblance is difficult to see: when compared to, say, the ceremonial gift giving by the early-nineteenth-century Nepali king analyzed in Richard Burghart's contribution to *Rituals of Royalty*,[31] the relationships between ritual and royal power described by Kuhrt in ancient Persia seem to lie in a totally different world—as lie, at least from the historical standpoint, they most certainly do. Indeed, given that the only similarity Cannadine can find among the cases in his book is the existence of already established culturally specific representations of power in royal ceremonial, there is little reason to expect that the many possible variants of power and ceremonial, ritual and royalty, that are evident in complex historical situations are likely to be tied together in ways that are particularly similar. Attention to knot work may give us a helpful initial view of specific new religiohistorical problems, but it rarely gives us any detailed formulas for neatly unraveling them.

Knot work, then, examining the complex interrelationships between concretely imaginable types in specific contexts, promises the possibility of generating knowledge from the unexpected conjunction of recognizable categories; in doing so, further, it builds on the interplay of mythic ideas and historical realities. These interstitial, middle-range domains are just the kind of areas where, as I suggested in chapter 6, religiohistorical knowledge is wont to grow. But in contrast to the brocaded pattern presented by the Myth and Ritualists and other reasonably co-

herent schools, knot work offers no overall design, no method leading
to an expected result. As a way of approach to specific material, knot
work in itself only intimates. Suggestive, hinting at possible relationships, it leads inevitably from the collective project back to individual
reflection.

ENVELOPING FABRICS

When even knot work—which today draws the most public attention—
relies on individual reflection, we might do well to take a new perspective on our tapestry, one that examines how it emerges as a broad network of public knowledge from the interpretive visions of individual
scholars. Each having a particular view of the public tapestry, individual
scholars may be inspired to take private ruminations to specialized materials in order to spin some new public threads; thus, when a researcher
comprehends, say, Bengali devotional song both within earlier religiohistorical speculation about liturgical music and against his or her own
continuing participation in church choirs, the result may be a tentative
new theoretical statement about liturgical song.[32] If, when grasped by
others, the new theoretical thread seems to have substance, it may then
be woven back into the public whole: knotted into someone else's comparison of two different forms of religious music, perhaps, or appearing
as a recurring detail in an elaborate tableau of Indian devotional religion.
Reflected in and deriving from the personal perceptions of individuals,
the same four layers of the tapestry of public knowledge discussed above
thus also have counterparts in private vision as well. At each of these layers, however, we find a different interplay of private with public—of personal insights and presuppositions with the collective development of
knowledge.

   The extremes of private and public appear at the surfaces. At the top
of the tapestry, an individual net of privately perceived, inexplicit connections wafts down on a gossamer web of diverse relations sketched by
others among publicly available materials: thus, private ruminations on
experience in Episcopal church choirs and Bengali devotional songfests
might interact diffusely with anthropological theory of African drum rituals or theological reflections on Gregorian chant. At the bottom, new
research—say, the careful recording of a Bengali or African performance—may produce additions to historically grounded, apparently public facts, adding somewhat to the coverage of an ever-extending tableau.
Yet in themselves, the stray wisp of insight touching the common web or

the bare fact added to the general store is not likely to seem particularly significant. The first is too privately flighty; the second, though public, is in context usually infinitesimal. To yield something of general scholarly interest, the interplay of individual and collective that is found at the two surfaces of the tapestry needs to be less extreme, to become coherently entwined with some distinguishable pattern in the middle. How does this happen?

On the upper surface, the transformation of the private into something strikingly more public often appears as an accidental event. An individual scholar's inexplicit web of knowledge is woven from the many strands of information he or she meets in pursuing a career: from research done, books read, or academic conversations. To the extent that these remain in consciousness, such discrete strands of knowledge are likely to have some relationship to one another, usually vague and shifting. Occasionally, however, a few of these strands, enveloped by a new perspective, may get caught by a strong thread that pulls in a particular direction, leading the way toward a complex knot or vivid pattern suitable for general display. Thus, we have seen Jonathan Z. Smith's ruminations on Melanesia and the ancient Near East pull apparently disparate strands of scholarship together to give a striking turn to an established pattern. Through training, intuition, and happenstance, vague private vision stumbles onto a situation that it can manage to present as new knowledge of interest to a broader public.

Interest at the factual lower surface is aroused when new evidence also gives our basic grounding new shape. The materials of historical and ethnological record, barely woven together in their most publicly accepted guise, become intriguing only through the narrative texture given to them by a scholar. History, as Hayden White has shown us, draws us in as it develops a plot, which is up to individual scholars to envision.[33] Certainly, the more a scholar can shape a believable story through his or her own individual insights, the more intriguing it is likely to become. At the same time, there are practical limits to the believable stories that can be produced from available evidence. Compelling new stories are likely to emerge from imaginative interpretations of *new* data. Thus, archeological evidence gained over the last twenty years has brought into serious question at least the preamble to the background story of ancient Indian kingship presented in Basham's volume. Instead of a straightforward tale of the invasion of a ruling "Aryan" elite from the West—an account admittedly subject to postcolonialist suspicions—we now have a wide range of competing metanarratives: from slightly altered versions of the old story, to the moderate suggestion of early slow, peaceful migrations, to a radical counterhypothesis of Aryan origins in the Indian subcontinent and a later spread to the West.[34] New facts thus become exciting when they give focus to larger shapes drawn on the historical tableau.

The general scholarly interest that develops from the surfaces of our tapestry, although striking when it occurs, is relatively rare: the few apparently brilliant insights that in fact pan out; the occasional new facts that really do have revolutionary implications. Most of the tapestry's interesting texture is regularly provided by its other two elements. Involving more regular modes of give-and-take among individual scholars and their public fund of knowledge, these present more obvious dynamics in the sociology of comparative studies. The interactions of public and private entailed in the creation of religiohistorical brocade and knot work, however, are not the same.

A patterned brocade takes shape through a sociological process that can be easily typified. The general uniformity in the process derives in good part from the *situation* of neatly constructed religiohistorical patterns in our larger tapestry. Like kingship in the ancient Near East, a pattern usually lies between the two surfaces in a particular place, bringing together extended strands from above—kingship was in the air at least since Frazer—with patches of the historical tableau below. The process is usually started by a scholar who has managed to link the new brocade neatly to the two surfaces at a particular historical or geographical point. Thus Hooke, in the first essay in the first of his three edited anthologies, invoked Frazer and then outlined his basic myth and ritual pattern through Babylonian and Egyptian evidence.[35] Dealing with Canaanite materials in his own contribution to that volume, he then started to work outward, and the apparent success of his own work and that of his early colleagues attracted scholarly attention. As the Myth and Ritual brocade gained greater definition, wispy Frazerian ideas about kingship appeared firmer and the flat historical tableau achieved striking new depth. The Myth and Ritual School progressed as other scholars decisively joined in, thickening the weave here, spreading it out there, producing a substantial core of work. Following a similar pattern in the sociology of their development, different religiohistorical schools have emerged along their own intellectual trajectories: Indo-European studies in the Dumézilian tradition spread a historically grounded pattern over a wider geographical area than the Myth and Ritual School; the Eliadean "patterns of comparative religion" point to psychic structures of apparently universal scope that might be located anywhere. Nevertheless, within each school, the patterns that are woven are taken as valid public knowledge, deep, interesting, and having some definite substance. Outside the school, however, the same patterns often soon appear insubstantial, shallow, and tiresome. The school's contribution to public knowledge, as well as its acceptance by a broad public, is contained.

The clusters of knots in our fabric of knowledge, on the other hand— through offering complex, grounded truths—may appeal widely to a broad public; at the same time, the significant knowledge they offer collectively, less precise, becomes ultimately more private: insights into seeing diverse relationships between ritual and royalty, myth and philosophy, or colonialism and culture. Although the patterned brocade of a school spreads laterally between wispy filigree and historical tableau, connecting them through sometimes tenuous links, individual knots penetrate both surfaces, joining them intricately and deeply. Certainly, they can aid our understanding of concrete historical situations. Yet however much we may be fascinated by individual knots, the specific public truths we can generalize from a collection of them are, as we have seen in the Cannadine volume, usually abstract and obvious. Most of the depth we may find in their collectivity remains inexplicit, sensed through our scholarly intuition but not easily expressed. Pulling wisps of insight down into historical understanding in highly diverse ways, the collective knowledge created by knot work certainly appears to have more weight than our individual religiohistorical visions, but it is usually only through those visions that this knowledge can be grasped.

Comprehended together, the knots thicken our own individual nets of knowledge in particular directions, giving us an acuteness toward particular types of cases, helping us to understand nuances and ask good questions of our materials and of one another. They thus point to the benefit of constructive scholarly interchange and collaboration—even to the virtues of the conferences out of which many edited volumes continue to emerge! Moreover—especially when deriving from an organized collective endeavor—a piece of knot work may help us better see the general contours of a complex problem that has aroused current interest. Nevertheless, the value of knot work is usually found less in the establishment of any significantly generalizable collective knowledge than in the sharpening of individual insight. Thus, even in what seems to be its most successful current collective dimension, religiohistorical knowledge points back inevitably to the individual. In religious studies especially, public science is driven by private vision.

The Future of
Modern Dilemmas

The individual insights crucial to public knowledge in history of religions have undergone some shifts in course at the beginning of the twenty-first century, impelled by some brisk theoretical currents of the 1980s and 1990s: postcolonial studies, literary poststructuralism, postmodern thinking on and within religion. Although those currents do not play on the surface of my discussions, they have, in varying degrees, contributed to their emergence—as they have more forcefully and obviously to the sources of approaches taken by other writers in the field. As an afterword, let me recount the way I find my own line of thought moving with and against some recent theoretical streams, the directions in which these appear to be taking some other religiohistorical writers, and what seems to me most crucial for writers to remember as they interpret religious traditions anew.

ON THE RELIGION IN "WRITING RELIGION"

In the last decades of the twentieth century, when "writing" and "the other" were key critical terms, someone thinking about scholarly writing on others' religions could not help but be drawn to then-current critical work. Both literary studies and postcolonial thought have in fact at times excited me, and have been discussed at places in the text.[1] What I learned from these fields, moreover, has been crucial to the arguments here. Exploring literary studies led me to the aesthetic of the sublime and suggested a way it might be taken to religiohistorical writing. Postcolonial thought, in demonstrating a history of politically skewed representations of the other, made emphasizing the need to reveal the complex humanity of our subjects seem all the more imperative. In their different ways, these two discoveries seemed individually important—but even more so when taken together.

Since the religiohistorical sublime is experienced when a complex imaginative response is evoked through a rational analysis of the materials of a tradition, those materials cannot appear as simple representations of an exotic other of the sort that have haunted orientalist texts. They must instead resonate expansively enough for us somehow to relate to them as our own: myths of broad significance, say, or human actors in existential distress. One-dimensional stereotypes may beguile us for a while, but the complex imaginative reflection that builds to the religiohistorical sublime demands complicated human materials that keep pulling us in new directions. For only when readers (and writers) feel pulled to extremes will their own sense of self be given a jolt. It is then that our art and science together really can lead to "writing religion"—in the sense of creatively evoking in the reader a feeling for the religiohistorical object in a way that can seem deeply and personally profound.

The sense of "writing" in "writing religion" here differs, I think, from that in *Writing Culture*—the influential 1986 anthropological volume edited by James Clifford and George Marcus.[2] There the term was used more closely in its Derridean sense of "inscription" (6): recording an authorial view necessarily bound by historical, institutional, and personal prejudgments that together inform the "metaphor, figuration, and narrative" (4) of the text. Subtitled "The Poetics and Politics of Ethnography," that volume and subsequent ones offer essays that presume "poetics and . . . politics are inseparable," that "reach beyond texts to contexts of power, resistance, institutional constraint, and innovation" (2). This regular concern with the political is not one I have shared, having dealt with it here only in the most egregious individual cases. My emphasis has been sooner on the poetics of translating religion to an intellectually oriented modern in a way that recreates something of the force of distant traditions: how can we in fact "write religion" in the sense of producing something approaching a religious impact on readers? Just what this impact is, of course—or at least how it is understood—will depend on the kind of ambivalence readers have toward religion itself.

Those drawn to interpretive writing on religion, we recall, generally *like* religion, at least as it reflects important human truths, but *believe* in science—with *science* here used as a tag for some post-Enlightenment, more-or-less-materialist way of seeing the world. But this pithy statement was meant to encapsulate a dilemma, not to limit a field—and at the start of the twenty-first century the contrary horns of liking and believing both present some intricate twists. In examining what the impact of effective interpretive writing might mean for those taking alternative paths between those horns, I will begin, as I did with the work as a whole, in the middle—considering scholars like Harrison and Goodenough, who are secular-minded to be sure but still appreciative of religious texts.

In describing the existential situation of contemporary secular humanity, the postmodern theologian Charles Winquist draws on some psychoanalytic insights: modern worldviews have repressed our capacities to be religious, but since these still lie dormant, we often have "the peculiar feeling that religious life is always elsewhere."[3] However broadly we might take this insight as a general truth, it does seem suggestive for many of our scholars-in-the-middle: regularly fascinated by a religious life they sense elsewhere, they try to bring it into their consciousness through rational and imaginative faculties they recognize in themselves. As a response to a modern condition, moreover, this attempt does seem to present real parallels to personal experimentation with non-Western religions. Writing of "the popular interest in the religion of others," Winquist continues: "What is sought is a defamiliarization of ordinary life that would fissure its repressive surfaces and give access to new intensities and forces."[4] In interpretive writing, these intensities and forces seem sometimes to break through with the religiohistorical sublime.

Is religiohistorical practice, then, simply an ersatz religion—something seen as sadly insufficient on the theological side and a potentially pernicious escape on the (social-)scientific? Perhaps it sometimes is. But let us not be too quick to load our own perspectives (and problems) onto creative scholars who themselves seem reasonably satisfied in their work. Although many of the theologically inclined may not find interpretive writing a satisfactory resolution to a dilemma they see as religious, most decidedly secular practitioners of the craft would probably give other definitions to their personal problems. Jane Harrison, we recall, had her share of dilemmas in life, but most didn't seem to be particularly religious. Nevertheless, as a self-confessed "hopeless worldling" she found considerable fulfillment in using imaginative argument to bring the Greek ritual she loved forward onto an academic stage. Other writers—even as they dodge toward one or another of the dilemma's horns—similarly exercise their imaginative and intellectual faculties to extremes to probe what seems, for the moment, to be especially real and important for them. And attempting somehow to keep in touch with "the real and important," for a postmodern theologian like Winquist, is about as religious as anyone can get.[5]

Most religiously oriented interpretive writers, however—those who like religion enough to let it loosen somewhat their belief in "science"— have an outlook that differs from Winquist's. Postmodern thinkers like him, who have peered into the abyss at the edges of radical constructivism and still attempt to find something of the religious, can only end up locating it somewhere in transformed attitudes toward present realities: in "the signifying play," as Winquist (and others) write, of a "new subjectivity"[6]—in freshly realized, important immediacies of life. From this perspective, anyone who finds her or his work really important and pursues it with a certain self-consciousness and enthusiasm might be seen as engaged in religious endeavor. But most interpretive writers who have thought-out theologies would probably have a different view of the situation—even when they do in fact see religious purpose in their work. For historians of religion, we recall from chapter 7, attuned to the mindsets of the analytic scientist and the sympathetic believer, tend to be by temperament not radical constructivists but fallibilists of different sorts—sensing that there are truths out there to be understood, if only imperfectly. Trying to comprehend others' worlds might then help in understanding real truths that may impinge on the divine as well as on the human. Taking realized truths as bordering the divine, it is true, can lead to some hasty theologizing, but those who are fallibilist enough to recognize the limits of any knowledge are not likely to feel compelled to tie separate analyses into a neatly totalizing system. Indeed, writers fascinated by the stuff of other worlds will sooner find imagination moving ahead of reason in glimpsing supramundane truths, the evocative power of separate details outpacing rational syntheses. The religiohistorical sublime then marks the limit, for the moment, of truths that can be grasped. If these are seen as somehow religious, they are also recognized as partial.

What, then, of those writers on religion who negotiate their dilemma via its scientific horn, which can give a pointed twist to their fascination with their subject? Just as happily secular writers might scoff at being told they have religious problems, many of these writers might resist the modern dilemma I have posed for them: even though most will hold with "science" as we have taken it, not all seem really to like religious traditions very much. Still, from my perspective a few of these sometimes

seem to suffer from particularly acute cases of the modern repression discussed by Winquist—with religious capacities that return as moral out-
rage at less than perfect instances of religious life. And a majority of critical writers also demonstrate some fondness in their fascination. They
bring reason and imagination together, as interpretive writers tend to do,
but are apt to give more priority to critical reason, wedding them both
more closely to political understandings and privileging a hermeneutic of
suspicion over the more familiar reflective openness. An experience of
the religiohistorical sublime that emerges here may well leave in its wake
a sense of profound dissatisfaction with human religious institutions or
perhaps a sad, sometimes amused, irony. Unraveling the fabric of religiohistorical knowledge where it has become thin, these writers have also
made places for their own work within it.

WEAKENED THREADS AND COUNTERPATTERNS

Some of the most visible critical unravelings in history of religions have
also been the messiest. Both Eliade and Dumézil, two of the field's great
men, have had their greatness materially diminished. Particularly in the
case of Eliade, who had stood on a very high pedestal, the fall has been
dramatic. And in both cases, as mentioned in chapter 5, reassessments
have been complicated by possible disturbing relationships between
each scholar's political and intellectual lives. Although Eliade's historical wartime transgressions seem at this point much less deniable than
Dumézil's, their relationship to his work seem more questionable—evident, if at all, mostly in his large-scale trivialization of history in favor
of broad mythic pattern.[7] And it is more for that trivialization of history
itself, with all its broader intellectual implications, that Eliade's influence
has waned than for its possible origin in a shameful episode of his historical past. The relationships between Dumézil's political views and academic work, as Bruce Lincoln has shown us, are at once more complex
and specific, traceable in his shifting treatment of Indo-European myths
during the war years.[8] But among those scholars who have always taken
Dumézil's work seriously, that work has, with its structure and precision,
stood up better than Eliade's in the latter's own admittedly wider religiohistorical world.

The critical reevaluation of the fathers, moreover, has gone beyond
Eliade and Dumézil, although with less sense of shock and loss. The ideological biases of many past and present thinkers on religion have been
vigorously examined by several writers, with Lincoln going all the way

back to the ancient Greeks.[9] Also explored have been partialities in perspective whose significance is sooner cultural than political. Eliade was not alone in demonstrating particular interests in the esoteric and mystical dimensions of tradition. As Steven Wasserstrom has underscored, the scholarly interests of the Judaist Gershom Scholem and the Islamist Henri Corbin were also oriented in the same direction. All three great men in their fields, they were, if not as personally intimate as the three Cambridge Ritualists, also close intellectual friends, encouraging one another in their separate expositions of religion's inward aspects. But in the ethical monotheisms studied by the last two, these aspects are arguably less than crucial.[10] If we take these scholars to have presented a skewed view of the larger traditions they studied, however, our critique is one of balance in perspective, not moral or political error. If their emphases now appear distorted, the popularity of their work during the mid-twentieth century seems to be a sign of the contemporary ambivalences toward religion explored throughout this book. Given their modern dilemmas, their strong scholarly interest in the esoteric—itself no sin—is easily comprehensible.

Perceiving the links between great religion scholars' works and lives not only impresses on us the inevitable role of personal perspectives in our field but also, as Wasserstrom and others emphasize, helps give us the freedom to go beyond our forebears. For even when cultural moments pass, idealizations of their heroes can remain. And it now has become all too clear that even in the study of religion, the fathers were not themselves divine beings but very human ones. Yes, like most of us, Eliade was not of the toughest moral fiber and was unfortunately swayed by the political currents and racial prejudices of a very nasty era; but when the currents passed, so, it seems, did Eliade's prejudices, and many—myself included—will testify to Eliade's very apparent lack of anti-Semitic attitudes during his later years.[11] Like everybody else—and perhaps even more so—scholars in religious studies present contradictory aspects, change, and grow. Historians of religion have long taught about the ways in which images of gods derive from those of men. Deconstructing the fathers brings that lesson home to our own tribe.

Not just individuals, but specific religious traditions, too, have been deconstructed—if not as widely as might be expected given general developments in the humanities over the last decades. The most successful sustained work in a deconstructive genre on the Asian traditions regularly treated by historians of religion has been Bernard Faure's studies on Chinese Chan/Zen Buddhism.[12] Intent on upsetting familiar ideas about

Zen, Faure plays with familiar binaries—enlightenment that can be sudden and/or gradual, truth that is immanent and/or transcendent. Taking up different aspects of Buddhist religion and Chinese culture, Faure unsettles Zen from many sides at once. His approach thus inverts the strategy, seen in chapter 4, that Geertz used to describe the Balinese cockfight. Geertz constructed an object out of an event whose existence we never suspected; Faure shakes up a religiocultural object that we thought we already knew. In doing this he exercises his rationality vigorously to display vagaries of religious imagination both subtle and striking, potentially eliciting the religiohistorical sublime in a particularly exciting way. Some comparable achievements can be found as well in the field of Greek religion, also by French scholars who are really at home with their theory.[13]

On a larger scale, the quickening of critical rationality in the humanities generally has led to a wider academic recognition of the perspectival nature of all discourse, with two significant consequences for religious studies. First, it makes the coherentist logical ploys inevitably found in religiohistorical argument, discussed in chapters 4 and 7, more readily acceptable to scholars appreciative of a nicely made case. Although a very critical rationality intent on finding motives in all discourse will no doubt still find them in writing of and on religion, the styles of argument natural to religious studies are at least now more generally familiar. Second, a perspectival view, holding that all points of reference may yield a partially valid truth, is more likely than one sure of its foundations to be open to voices from the academic margins, where religious studies frequently finds itself. Although a theologically oriented study of religion was once at the center of many American church-affiliated universities, the religious studies that has flourished from the mid-twentieth century has never been preeminent in the academy. Like Ethnic Studies, or Gay and Lesbian Studies, Religious Studies programs are sometimes seen as filled with people who aren't quite in sync with the mainstream, whose ways of seeing things are a little off center. But, increasingly, off-center perspectives are now granted their own share of truth and in their freshness can seem especially perceptive. More and more, voices from the academic margins are being listened to in the larger academy—thus often, for better or worse, becoming less marginal. Some of the most widely heard of these voices—including, as just seen, some from religious studies—critique institutional injustices and authors' ideologies. The challenge for critical writers on religion who want to keep their voice distinctively religiohistorical too is to marry their critique to imaginative depth.

SOFT HEARTS AND HARD MINDS

Charles Taylor, at the conclusion of his monumental *Sources of the Self*—a treatise on the moral sources of contemporary humanity, among other topics—emphasizes the importance of "personal resonances" in finding one's way at a time when "a publicly accessible cosmic order of meanings is an impossibility."[14] Yet despite the necessity for personal resonance, Taylor stresses, most people like to have a sense of objective order, too. The last two centuries have thus witnessed a continuing "search for moral sources *outside* the subject through sources which resonate *within* him or her, the grasping of an order which is inseparably indexed to a personal vision" (510). Certain kinds of art, he continues, have been effective in the mediating role demanded in this search, bringing a larger, external order of meanings into the personal sensibilities of the individual. Pointing to works by Mann, Rilke, and Lawrence, he calls art that serves this role "epiphanic." But epiphanic works are not limited to art per se; they can include "other efforts, in philosophy, in criticism, which attempt the same kind of search." At its best, "the great epiphanic work can actually put us in contact with the sources it taps. It can *realize* the contact" (512). It seems to me that certain types of interpretive writing on religion, too, when inspired, are especially suited to play this epiphanic role.

By presenting others' religious worlds from their own modern standpoints, interpretive writers ideally open a contemporary sensibility to realms of moral order that regularly present that quality of external reality taken by Taylor as crucial. Writers make reference to materials that are eminently outside the reader and felt to be such: historically attested and often very other. But interpreting these materials imaginatively can make distant moral worlds reverberate *within* the reader as well. The writer's art here comes through making his or her own personal resonances vibrate at once with that distant world and the present contemporary one. Any sense of the sublime elicited by a work may help readers "realize the contact" between their world and the other at an essential human level. But the moral order of that other cosmos will resonate, as in literature, through the suggestive elaboration of details. Romantic excess is of course certainly possible here, but the believability essential to religiohistorical art is enhanced when honest critique and ironic observation temper sympathetic imagination. Since this kind of scholarly writing does not depend on a general *religionswissenschaft*, it can easily go on outside departments of religion, and it does. Indeed, one of the most gifted contemporary writers in the genre has been Peter Brown, most often identified as a historian, whose books on early Christian life pull us into a world of felt religious values but let us have our modern ironies, too. Thus, even if unbridled critical reason succeeds in unraveling any coherent fabric of general religiohistorical knowledge as we know it, individual works of interpretive writing on religion, playing a real cultural role, will continue.

Odds are, though, that history of religions will continue as well, transformed with time, to be sure, but recognizable. Writers on religious traditions who like to integrate their knowledge are learning from critical approaches and pushing on, unafraid to make daring comparisons to make points about their materials or suggest some common contours of human religious behavior.[15] And for readers of interpretive writing, some general religiohistorical knowledge can enhance the pleasure of the text, letting its personal resonances reverberate more broadly in mind and heart. Where postmodern critical understandings may in fact have their most serious impact in any science of religion is less on the texture of religiohistorical knowledge than on modern ideas of its growth and progress. Perhaps our collective understandings about religious traditions are not really moving onward and upward but just changing their shape somewhat, adjusting to the cultural and intellectual exigencies of a new century. Just what the fabric of religiohistorical knowledge will look like over the next decades I do not know, but I do have some ideas about the qualities it will need to maintain its peculiar strengths.

Partly through artifice, partly by accident, the striking figure of Jane Harrison appears toward the end of this book as well as the beginning. Like many of those who have recently written about Harrison, I admire her gumption and her style, but I have let her frame my book because she also seems to me to embody in her typically dramatic fashion two characteristic traits shared by some of the best interpretive writers on religion in the past century. Standing, like many of us, at the margins of the academy, she excelled through harnessing together her imaginative spirit and her inquisitive intellect—cardinal features, respectively, of the soft heart and hard mind presented in the introduction as poles of disciplinary opposition in religious studies. Although by no means the foremost interpretive writer on religion in the twentieth century (but perhaps the first), Harrison vividly displayed crucial aspects of the heart and mind it takes to be one. By "soft heart" here I mean an ability to empathize imaginatively with religious actors together with a willingness to let the intuitions thus engendered guide the intellect. By "hard mind" I mean not one that is inflexible but one that is sharp, able to penetrate material analytically if not always critically in that word's most contemporary sense. If, as in *Themis,* Harrison sometimes seemed to lean more toward the soft heart, her hypotheses stretched by imaginative enthusiasms, that direction seems to me to be more potentially fruitful for a historian of religion than the opposite, toward an unrelenting reason that constrains intuition. Although soft hearts and hard minds sometimes appear contradictory, I hope by now to have shown that most successful historians of religion have in fact demonstrated vital qualities of both. As the twenty-first century progresses, some hard minds taking critical turns can make the fabric of our knowledge truer and more exciting. But only from soft hearts can come the richness of imaginative comprehension that has made it seem special.

Notes

INTRODUCTION. MODERN DILEMMAS
IN WRITING ON RELIGION

1. For a fine example of this type of work, see Peter Homans, *The Ability to Mourn* (Chicago: University of Chicago Press, 1989).

2. The novel is available in English as *Bengal Nights,* trans. Catherine Spencer (London: Carcanet, 1993). For Eliade's work on yoga, see Mircea Eliade, *Yoga: Immortality and Freedom* (New York: Pantheon, 1958).

3. See Mircea Eliade, *The Quest: History and Meaning in Religion* (Chicago: University of Chicago Press, 1969), chaps. 1 and 4.

4. See Geertz's "Thick Description: Toward an Interpretive Theory of Culture," in his *The Interpretation of Cultures* (New York: Basic Books, 1973), 3–30. On Geertz's life, see his autobiographical essay, "Passage and Accident, a Life of Learning," in his *Available Light: Anthropological Reflections on Philosophical Topics* (Princeton, N.J.: Princeton University Press, 2000), 3–20.

5. See the essays in Mark C. Taylor, ed., *Critical Terms for Religious Studies* (Chicago: University of Chicago Press, 1998); and in Willi Braun and Russell T. McCutcheon, eds., *Guide to the Study of Religion* (London: Cassell, 2000).

6. See, e.g., Timothy Fitzgerald, *The Ideology of Religious Studies* (New York: Oxford, 2000) together with its reviews by Benson Saler, Gustavo Benavides, and Frank Korom and a response by Fitzgerald in *Religious Studies Review* 27, no. 2 (Apr. 2001): 103–15.

CHAPTER 1. FASCINATED SCIENTISTS
AND EMPATHIZING THEOLOGIANS

1. This program has been admirably presented by J. Samuel Preus, *Explaining Religion: Criticism and Theory from Bodin to Freud* (New Haven, Conn.: Yale University Press, 1987).

2. See, e.g., ibid., chap. 5; and Frank E. Manuel, *The Eighteenth Century Confronts the Gods* (Cambridge, Mass.: Harvard University Press, 1959), 168–83.

3. This is a Deist vision. See Manuel, *Eighteenth Century,* chap. 2. The work of Lord Herbert of Cherbury, whom Thomas Halyburton called "the Father of English Deism," has been recently translated by John Anthony Butler: *Pagan Religion: A Translation of "De religione gentilium"* (Ottawa, Canada: Dovehouse Editions, 1996), citation from p. 21. Also preceding Hume were Euhemerists, finding the origins of myth in historical persons and events, often through complex historical and scientific argument. The most famous of these was the scientist Isaac Newton; see Manuel, *Eighteenth Century,* chap. 3. For Newton's religion see Frank E. Manuel, *The Religion of Isaac Newton* (Oxford, U.K.: Clarendon Press, 1974).

4. David Hume, *The Natural History of Religion and Dialogues Concerning Natural Religion,* ed. A. Wayne Colver and John Valdimir Price (Oxford, U.K.: Clarendon Press, 1976).

5. For the world as known in the eighteenth century, see P. J. Marshall and Glyndwyr Williams, *The Great Map of Mankind: Perceptions of New Worlds in the Age of Enlightenment* (Cambridge, Mass.: Harvard University Press, 1982).

6. Several diffusion theories are treated below in chapter 9. For some of the cultural contexts of Müller's solar mythology, see J. B. Bullen, *The Sun Is God: Painting, Literature, and Mythology in the Nineteenth Century* (Oxford, U.K.: Clarendon Press, 1989). Steven Connor's article in that volume makes an interesting comparison: "Conclusion: Myth and Metamyth in Max Müller and Walter Pater," 199–222. Müller's views on myth derive from his theory of the degeneration of language and are discussed at length in his *Lectures on the Science of Language,* 2 vols. (London: Longman Green Longman and Roberts, 1861–64), esp. vol. 2.

7. Edward Burnett Tylor, *Primitive Culture,* 2 vols. (1873; reprint, Gloucester, Mass: Peter Smith, 1970).

8. For a short version of the story, see Sir James George Frazer, *The Golden Bough,* abr. ed. (1922; reprint, New York: Collier, 1963), 1–2. This edition has no notes but reveals Frazer's theses more sharply than the twelve-volume 3d edition of 1913–15 (London: Macmillan).

9. See Richard Crouter's introduction to his new translation of Friedrich Schleiermacher, *On Religion: Speeches to Its Cultured Despisers* (Cambridge, U.K.: Cambridge University Press, 1996), xi. Crouter's translation (to which my in-text citations refer) presents the first edition of Schleiermacher's text—the rhetorical force of which had been toned down in the third edition, on which the earlier standard translation was based: Friedrich Schleiermacher, *On Religion: Speeches to Its Cultured Despisers,* trans. John Oman (New York: Harper and Row, 1958). One of the most readable expositions of Schleiermacher is a set of university lectures by probably his most ardent twentieth-century theological adversary: Karl Barth, *The Theology of Schleiermacher: Lectures at Göttingen, Winter Semester of 1923/24,* ed. Dietrich Ritschl, trans. Geoffrey W. Bromiley (Grand Rapids, Mich.: Eerdman's, 1982).

10. For the relationship between Otto and Schleiermacher, see Philip Almond, *Rudolf Otto: An Introduction to His Philosophical Theology* (Chapel Hill: University of North Carolina Press, 1984), 38–42. Otto himself discusses Schleiermacher in his introduction to Schleiermacher's *Speeches,* given in Oman's translation (see note 9 above).

11. Rudolf Otto, *Das Heilige: Über das Irrationale in der Idee des Göttlichen und sein Verhältnis zum Rationalen* (München: Verlag C. H. Beck, 1963); Rudolf Otto, *The Idea of the Holy,* trans. John W. Harvey (London: Oxford University Press, 1923). For a reading of *Das Heilige* as a theological argument, see Gregory D. Alles, "Toward a Genealogy of the Holy: Rudolf Otto and the Apologetics of Religion," *Journal of the American Academy of Religion* 69, no. 2 (2001): 323–41.

12. Otto presents his Friesian philosophy in *The Philosophy of Religion Based on Kant and Fries,* trans. E. B. Dicker (London: Williams and Norgate, 1931), esp. chaps. 1–4; it is discussed in Almond, *Rudolf Otto,* 46–54; and in Robert F. Davidson, *Rudolf Otto's Interpretation of Religion* (Princeton, N.J.: Princeton University Press, 1947), chap. 5. For Fries in English, see Jakob Friedrich Fries, *Dialogues on Morality and Religion,* ed. D. Z. Phillips, trans. David Walford (Totowa, N.J.: Barnes and Noble, 1982).

13. For the continuing discourse on "the holy" in the study of religion, see Carsten Colpe, ed., *Die Diskussion um das "Heilige," Wege der Forschung CCCV* (Darmstadt: Wissenschaftliche Buchgesellschaft, 1977). For the continuing impact of Rudolf Otto on religious studies, see Ernst Benz, ed., *Rudolf Otto's Bedutung für die Religionswissenschaft und die Theologie Heute* (Leiden: E. J. Brill, 1971), with articles by Reinhard Schinzer, Ernst Benz, Gustav Mensching, Søren Holm, and Gotthard Nygren. Gregory D. Alles discusses Otto's reception among theologians and historians of religion in his introduction to Rudolf Otto, *Autobiographical and Social Essays,* trans. Gregory D. Alles (Berlin: Mouton de Gruyter, 1996). The most recent treatment of Otto and his reception in English is Todd A. Gooch, *The Numinous and Modernity: An Interpretation of Rudolf Otto's Philosophy of Religion* (New York: W. de Gruyter, 2000).

14. William Brede Kristensen, *The Meaning of Religion: Lectures in the Phenomenology of Religion,* trans. John Carman (The Hague: Martinus Nijhoff, 1960), 17.

15. Hendrik Kraemer, Kristensen's successor at Leyden, quoting Kristensen in Kraemer's introduction to *The Meaning of Religion,* xxii.

16. Wilfred Cantwell Smith, "Comparative Religion: Whither—and Why?" in *The History of Religions: Essays in Methodology,* ed. Mircea Eliade and Joseph M. Kitagawa (Chicago: University of Chicago Press, 1959), 32. The essay has been republished in Smith's *Religious Diversity,* ed. Willard G. Oxtoby (New York: Crossroad, 1982), 139–57.

17. Andreas Grünschloß, *Religionswissenschaft als Welt-Theologie: Wilfred Cantwell Smiths Interreligiöse Hermeneutik* (Göttingen: Vandenhoeck und Ruprecht, 1994), 32.

18. See Wilfred Cantwell Smith's *Modern Islam in India: A Social Analysis* (Lahore: Minerva Book Shop, 1943)—still valuable for insights into late colonial South Asian Islam.

19. W. C. Smith, "Comparative Religion: Whither—and Why?" 44.
20. Ibid.

CHAPTER 2. FINDING MIDDLE GROUNDS

1. Full-length studies of Lang include Eleanor de Selms Langstaff, *Andrew Lang* (Boston: Twayne, 1978); and Roger Lancelyn Green, *Andrew Lang: A Critical Biography with a Short-Title Bibliography of the Works of Andrew Lang* (London: Edmund Ward, 1946), which contains useful appendices of articles on him. For reminiscences of Lang from different perspectives, see A. Blyth Webster and J. B. Salmond, eds., *Concerning Andrew Lang: Being the Andrew Lang Lectures Delivered before the University of St. Andrews, 1927–1937* (Oxford, U.K.: Clarendon Press, 1949), esp. the articles by George Gordon ("Andrew Lang") and R. R. Marett ("The Raw Material of Religion"). For a short analysis of Lang, see Richard M. Dorson, *The British Folklorists: A History* (Chicago: University of Chicago Press, 1968), 206–20.

2. Lang's *The Making of Religion* (London: Longmans, Green, 1898) is dedicated to arguing this claim.

3. Lang's anthropological theories are expounded, with numerous examples, in *Myth, Ritual, and Religion,* 2 vols. (London: Longmans, Green, 1887); *Modern Mythology* (London: Longmans, Green, 1897) presents attacks against Müller.

4. Lang's best-known children's story is *Prince Prigio,* found in many editions—some with elaborate illustrations, such as those by Robert Lawson in *Prince Prigio* (Boston: Little, Brown, 1942). For an example of Lang's engaging speaking style, see his *How to Fail in Literature: A Lecture* (London: Field and Tuer, the Leadenhall Press, 1890).

5. Langstaff, *Andrew Lang,* 12, 130. Lang became president of the Society for Psychical Research in 1911.

6. Frederick Myers, an early leader of the Society, to the editor of *The Psychological Review* 5 (Nov. 1882): 459; cited in Samuel Hynes, *The Edwardian Turn of Mind* (Princeton, N.J.: Princeton University Press, 1968), 139–44. On the Society for Psychical Research, see also John J. Cerullo, *The Secularization of the Soul: Psychical Research in Modern Britain* (Philadelphia: Institute for the Study of Human Issues, 1982); and Alan Gauld, *The Founders of Psychical Research* (London: Routledge and Kegan Paul, 1968). For a popular Edwardian manual, see W. F. Barrett, *Psychical Research* (New York: Holt, 1911); the Society for Psychical Research is treated on pp. 32–43.

7. Hynes, *Edwardian Turn of Mind,* 143.

8. See Lang's *Cock Lane and Common Sense* (London: Longmans, Green, 1894) and *The Book of Dreams and Ghosts* (London: Longmans, Green, 1897).

9. *Longman's Magazine,* Nov. 1895, 104–5; cited in Dorson, *The British Folklorists,* 215.

10. From "Protest of a Psycho-Folklorist," *Folk-Lore* 6 (Sept. 1895), 247; cited in Dorson, *The British Folklorists,* 215.

11. See Philip Almond, *Rudolf Otto: An Introduction to His Philosophical Theology* (Chapel Hill: University of North Carolina Press, 1984), 62.

12. R. R. Marett, *The Threshold of Religion* (London: Methuen, 1909), 32.

13. Ibid.

14. Ibid., 13

15. Gerardus van der Leeuw, *Religion in Essence and Manifestation,* trans. J. E. Turner, 2 vols. (New York: Harper and Row, 1963); Marett's view is commended in 1:27n4.

16. Joachim Wach, *Sociology of Religion* (Chicago: University of Chicago Press, 1944). Gregory D. Alles, "Transmission and Transformation: Reflections on Translating Joachim Wach," *Cresset* (Mar. 1988): 10–18, offers insights on Wach's early personal and intellectual life.

17. Important works in the field available in English include Johannes Pedersen, *Israel: Its Life and Culture,* 2 vols. (1926–40; reprint, Atlanta, Ga.: Scholars Press, 1991); and Sigmund Mowinckel, *He That Cometh,* trans. G. W. Anderson (Oxford, U.K.: Basil Blackwell, 1956). Within the Scandinavian tradition, the so-called Uppsala school placed a particular stress on myth and ritual studies. A set of essays by one of the later exponents of that tradition, Ivan Engnell, has been translated into English as *A Rigid Scrutiny: Critical Essays on the Old Testament,* trans. and ed. John T. Willis (Nashville, Tenn.: Vanderbilt University Press, 1969); in addition to chapters on specific Old Testament topics, it includes treatments of the "Traditio-Historical Method" and "Science of Religion." A readable introduction in English to the issues in Scandinavian biblical scholarship as they were defined in the late 1940s is Aage Bentzen, *King and Messiah,* ed. G. W. Anderson, 2d ed. (Oxford, U.K.: Basil Blackwell, 1970). The Scandinavian scholarly tradition is discussed as a "school" in chapter 11 below.

18. See esp. his "Psalmenstudien II: Das Thronbesteigungsfest Jahwäs und der Ursprung der Eschatologie," *Skrifter utgit av Videnskapsselskapet i Kristiania* 2 (1921): 1–347; and *The Psalms in Israel's Worship,* trans. D. R. Ap-Thomas (Sheffield: JSOT Press, 1992). Mowinckel's early emphasis on the cultic background of the psalms gave an impetus to myth and ritual studies in Scandinavia, but he differed from many of his colleagues at Uppsala on important details. See Helmer Ringgren, "Mowinckel and the Uppsala School," *Scandinavian Journal of Theology* 2, no. 2 (1988): 36–41.

19. *The Old Testament as Word of God,* trans. Reidar B. Bjornard (New York: Abingdon, 1959); and *Religion und Kultus* (Göttingen: Vandenhoeck und Ruprecht, 1953), respectively. For some relationships between Mowinckel's theology and his scholarship, see Nils A. Dahl, "Sigmund Mowinckel: Historian of Religion and Theologian," *Scandinavian Journal of Theology* 2, no. 2 (1988): 8–22.

20. See Hynes, *Edwardian Turn of Mind,* chap. 5. On the beginnings of new religious outlooks in Britain toward the end of the nineteenth century (with some chapters on early leaders of the Society for Psychical Research), see Frank Miller Turner, *Between Science and Religion: The Reaction to Scientific Naturalism in Late Victorian England* (New Haven, Conn.: Yale University Press, 1974). Turner has a good feel for the religious conflicts of the age.

21. Compare the autobiographical reflections of contemporary scholars of religion collected in Jon R. Stone, ed., *The Craft of Religious Studies* (New York: St. Martin's, 1998).

22. The best short account of Harrison's ideas is Renate Schlesier, "Prolegomena to Jane Harrison's Interpretation of Ancient Greek Religion," in *The Cambridge Ritualists Reconsidered,* ed. William M. Calder III, Illinois Classical Studies, Supplement 2 (Atlanta, Ga.: Scholars Press, 1991). The most cogent outline of the development of her thought is in Robert Ackerman, *Myth and Ritual School: J. G. Frazer and the Cambridge Ritualists* (New York: Garland, 1991), chaps. 5–7. The main published sources for her life are her memoir—Jane Ellen Harrison, *Reminiscences of a Student's Life* (London: Hogarth, 1925)—and a collection of her letters: Jessie Stewart, *Jane Ellen Harrison: A Portrait from Letters* (London: Merlin Press, 1959). Based on these and other sources, Sandra Peacock has written a full and interesting psychobiography: *Jane Ellen Harrison: The Mask and the Self* (New Haven, Conn.: Yale University Press, 1988). Mary Beard's research adds revealing insights on Harrison's personal, scholarly, and cultural worlds: *The Invention of Jane Harrison* (Cambridge, Mass.: Harvard University Press, 2000).

23. Harrison, *Reminiscences,* 17, 19.

24. Ibid., 19.

25. Ibid., 87. In the same volume, she comments patronizingly on the "Psychical Research" circle she knew in Edwardian Cambridge: "their quest, scientific proof of immortality. To put it thus seems almost grotesque now; then it was inspiring" (ibid., 55). Harrison's condescension here ignores the fact that Henri Bergson, whom she would cite as one of her main intellectual inspirations, was president of the Society for Psychical Research in 1913, two years after Andrew Lang (Hynes, *Edwardian Turn of Mind,* 142).

26. Jane Ellen Harrison, *Unanimism: A Study of Conversion and Some Contemporary French Poets, Being a Paper Read before "The Heretics" on November 25, 1912* (Cambridge, U.K.: "The Heretics," 1913), 19–20.

27. Jane Ellen Harrison, *Epilegomena to the Study of Greek Religion and Themis: A Study of the Social Origins of Greek Religion,* 2d ed. (1927; reprint New Hyde Park, N.Y.: University Books, 1962), 542.

28. Harrison, *Reminiscences,* 91–92.

29. Ibid., 82.

30. Harrison, *Unanimism,* 40.

31. Jane Ellen Harrison, *Prolegomena to the Study of Greek Religion* (Cambridge, U.K.: The University Press, 1903); Jane Ellen Harrison, *Themis: A Study of the Social Origins of Greek Religion* (Cambridge, U.K.: The University Press, 1912). In 1962, the second edition of *Themis* (1927) was reprinted together with Harrison's short *Epilegomena to the Study of Greek Religion* (1921) and Gilbert Murray's memorial tribute to her (see note 27 above). Page references to *Themis* are to this reprint edition.

32. On these contexts of Harrison's early work, see Ackerman, *Myth and Ritual School,* 77–79; for a more extensive account, see Beard, *Invention,* esp. chaps. 5–8.

33. *Themis,* 542.

34. Ibid. Gilbert Murray's memorial lecture for Harrison gives a succinct account of the development of Harrison's interests: *Jane Ellen Harrison: An Address Delivered at Newnham College, October 27th, 1928* (Cambridge, U.K.: W. Heffer and Sons, 1928 [reprinted with Harrison's *Epilegomena,* 559–77]).

35. Harrison, *Reminiscences*, 63.

36. Jane Ellen Harrison, *Alpha and Omega* (London: Sidgewick and Jackson, 1915), 184–85.

37. Harrison, *Unanimism*, 21.

38. Ibid., 22. Harrison uses similar language to state the thesis of her essay "Alpha and Omega" in her volume of the same name: "The object of the following paper is to show that if we are to keep our hold on religion, theology must go" (179).

39. Some affective links between Harrison's attitude toward evangelical religion and her resented stepmother are explored psychoanalytically in Peacock, *The Mask and the Self*, 11–22.

40. Erwin Ramsdell Goodenough, *The Psychology of Religious Experiences* (New York: Basic Books, 1965), jacket biography.

41. In addition to Erwin Ramsdell Goodenough, *Toward a Mature Faith* (New York: Prentice-Hall, 1955), for Goodenough's life see also Robert S. Eccles, *Erwin Ramsdell Goodenough: A Personal Pilgrimage* (Chico, Calif.: Scholars Press, 1985).

42. Goodenough, *Toward a Mature Faith*, 9–10.

43. Eccles, *Goodenough*, 8.

44. Erwin Ramsdell Goodenough, *Jewish Symbols in the Greco-Roman Period*, 13 vols. (New York: Bollingen Foundation/Pantheon Books, 1953–68). An overview of Goodenough's argument can be found in the one-volume abridgement: Erwin Ramsdell Goodenough and Jacob Neusner, *Jewish Symbols in the Greco-Roman Period*, abr. ed. (Princeton, N.J.: Princeton University Press, 1988). Goodenough's views on the psychology of religion are presented in his *The Psychology of Religious Experiences*.

45. Goodenough, *Jewish Symbols*, 12:3.

46. On these questions, see Goodenough and Neusner, *Jewish Symbols*, 42–44.

47. Goodenough, *Toward a Mature Faith*, 15. All citations in this paragraph and the next are from this source.

48. Harrison, *Reminiscences*, 84.

49. Goodenough, *Toward a Mature Faith*, 1.

50. *Themis*, xlix–l.

51. Goodenough, *Toward a Mature Faith*, 2.

52. Ibid., 13.

53. Harrison, *Reminiscences*, 86.

54. The classic study is, of course, Edward W. Said, *Orientalism* (New York: Vintage, 1979). Two of Said's later essays of particular interest to religionists are "Representing the Colonized: Anthropology's Interlocutors," *Critical Inquiry* 15, no. 2 (1989): 205–25; and "Secular Interpretation, the Geographical Element, and the Methodology of Imperialism," in *After Colonialism: Imperial Histories and Postcolonial Displacements*, ed. Gyan Prakash (Princeton, N.J.: Princeton University Press, 1995), 21–39. Religionists might also consult Richard King, *Orientalism and Religion: Postcolonial Theory, India, and "the Mystic East"* (London: Routledge, 1999); and David Chidester, *Savage Systems: Colonialism and Comparative Religion in Southern Africa* (Charlottesville: Uni-

versity Press of Virginia, 1996). For a collection of influential essays in the field, see Patrick Williams and Laura Christen, eds., *Colonial Discourse and Post-colonial Theory* (New York: Columbia University Press, 1994).

55. J. J. Clarke, *Oriental Enlightenment: The Encounter between Asian and Western Thought* (London: Routledge, 1997), gives a revisionist account of orientalism emphasizing the more benign aspects of intercultural transmission suggested here. A less benign perspective on current romanticized enthusiasms with Tibetan traditions is given in Donald Lopez Jr.'s critique, *Prisoners of Shangri-La: Tibetan Buddhism and the West* (Chicago: University of Chicago Press, 1998). Contrasting views of that work are given by David Germano, Tsering Shakya, Robert A. F. Thurman, and Donald S. Lopez Jr., "Symposium on *Prisoners of Shangri-La*," *Journal of the American Academy of Religion* 69, no. 1 (2001): 161–213.

56. An egregious picture of colonialist stereotypes in South Asia was presented by Katherine Mayo in *Mother India* (New York: Harcourt, 1927); their continuing postcolonial internalization has been studied by Ashis Nandy in *The Intimate Enemy: Loss and Recovery of Self under Colonialism* (Delhi: Oxford University Press, 1983).

57. On the development of modern occultism, see Bradford J. M. Verter, "Dark Star Rising: The Emergence of Modern Occultism, 1800–1950" (Ph.D. diss., Princeton University, 1997). The continuities between esoteric traditions and history of religions have been emphasized by Steven M. Wasserstrom, *Religion after Religion: Gershom Scholem, Mircea Eliade, and Henry Corbin at Eranos* (Princeton, N.J.: Princeton University Press, 1999).

58. For other theological contexts of Otto's affirmation, see Alles, "Toward a Genealogy of the Holy."

59. This passage from one of Rudolf Otto's 1911 letters from North Africa is telling: "[T]here are probably a thousand ways in which the aesthetic experience of nature modulates into religious experience, for it is related to religious experience in its very depths. But aesthetics is not religion, and the origins of religion lie somewhere completely different. They lie . . . —" The resonances between aesthetics and religion seem to be clearer to Otto in this writing than the distinction between the two, for he breaks off at this point, confessing that he can't think about "such weighty matters now." He was aesthetically distracted: the "roses smell too sweet and the deep roar of the breaking waves is too splendid" (Otto, *Autobiographical and Social Essays*, 73). For some historical background to the theological issues here, see Todd A. Gooch, *The Numinous and Modernity: An Interpretation of Rudolf Otto's Philosophy of Religion* (New York: W. de Gruyter, 2000), 28–32.

60. Harrison, *Reminiscences*, 84.

61. For a classic statement of this displacement see M. H. Abrams, *Natural Supernaturalism: Tradition and Revolution in Romantic Literature* (New York: Norton, 1971), 13.

CHAPTER 3. A CREATIVE PROCESS

1. M. H. Abrams, *The Mirror and the Lamp: Romantic Theory and the Critical Tradition* (London: Oxford University Press, 1953), 30–69. For an interest-

ing historical study of aesthetic theory, see Lucian Krukowski, *Aesthetic Legacies, the Arts and Their Philosophies* (Philadelphia: Temple University Press, 1992); for an accessible philosophical survey, see Dabney Townsend, *An Introduction to Aesthetics* (Malden, Mass.: Blackwell, 1997).

2. Quoted in Charles Taylor, *Sources of the Self: The Making of the Modern Identity* (Cambridge, Mass.: Harvard University Press, 1989), 379; from Schlegel's 1817 *Vorlesungen uber dramatische Kunst und Literatur.*

3. John Dennis, "The Advancement and Reformation of Modern Poetry" (1701), in *The Critical Works of John Dennis,* ed. Edward Niles Hooker (Baltimore, Md.: Johns Hopkins University Press, 1939), 1:202 (quoted in Abrams, *Mirror and the Lamp,* 17). In another essay, Dennis elaborates further on the importance of formal order in poetry (see "Chap II—That Poetry is to be establish'd, by laying down the rules" [Hooker, 1:335]); most crucial here, Dennis emphasizes at the outset, is the mutual relationship of poetry and religion: "the use of Religion in Poetry was absolutely necessary . . . and on the other side . . . Poetry was requisite to Religion" (Hooker, 1:325); see also "The Grounds of Criticism in Poetry" (1704) (Hooker, 1:325–73).

4. More than just a stance in interpretive writing, "scientific" has become a label adopted by sociologically oriented scholars: see the *Journal for the Scientific Study of Religion.*

5. For the role of significant form in aesthetics, see Clive Bell, *Art* (1913; reprint, London: Chatto and Windus, 1949).

6. Jane Ellen Harrison, *Ancient Art and Ritual* (New York: Holt, 1913).

7. As Abrams points out, even though the eighteenth-century neoclassicists all began, at least, with imitation, many ended up in a more rhetorical stance: "Art, it was commonly said, is an imitation—but an imitation which is only instrumental toward producing effects upon an audience" (*Mirror and the Lamp,* 14).

8. For the impact of the market on romantic poets, see Martha Woodmansee, *The Author, Art, and the Market: Rereading the History of Aesthetics* (New York: Columbia, 1994). Foundational works on art and institutions include Theodor W. Adorno, *Aesthetic Theory,* trans. C. Lenhart, ed. Gretel Adorno and Rolf Tiedemann (London: Routledge and Kegan Paul, 1984); and Walter Benjamin, *Illuminations* (New York: Schocken Books, 1986).

9. See chapter 10 below.

10. For Coleridge's writing on imagination, see John Spencer Hill, ed., *Imagination in Coleridge* (Totowa, N.J.: Rowman and Littlefield, 1978). Exemplary works featuring imagination as an analytical idea in literary studies and anthropology, respectively, include John Livingstone Lowes, *The Road to Xanadu: A Study in the Ways of Imagination* (Princeton, N.J.: Princeton University Press, 1986); and James W. Fernandez, *Bwiti: An Ethnography of the Religious Imagination in Africa* (Princeton, N.J.: Princeton University Press, 1982). For different perspectives on imagination in religious studies, contrast the variety of theological and philosophical views found in James P. Mackey, ed., *Religious Imagination* (Edinburgh: Edinburgh University Press, 1986) with the more analytical one of Jonathan Z. Smith discussed in the text below.

11. Jonathan Z. Smith, *Imagining Religion: From Jonestown to Babylon* (Chicago: University of Chicago Press, 1982), xi.

12. The phrase "religious imagination," e.g., is used by Fernandez in the subtitle to his *Bwiti* and is itself taken as the title for Mackey's edited volume. On the "religiohistorical imagination," see my "Approaching Some Householder Yogis: To Visit or Move In?" *Journal of Ritual Studies* 2, no. 2 (1988): 185–94.

13. Taylor, *Sources of the Self,* 374.

14. As a graphic representation of a known philosophical view, the UFO metaphor seems most of all to develop some Crocean insights—which have been highly influential in twentieth-century aesthetics. For Croce, "intuitions" become defined by their "expression," and "impressions" are "objectified" into a work of art. See Benedetto Croce, *Aesthetic as Science of Expression and General Linguistic,* trans. Douglas Ainslie (London: Macmillan, 1909), 35. The classic exposition and development of the Crocean perspective is R. G. Collingwood, *The Principles of Art* (New York: Oxford University Press, 1958). For a philosophical discussion of the concept of horizon in hermeneutics, see Hans-Georg Gadamer, *Truth and Method* (New York: Seabury Press, 1975), 269–74. UFOs of a sort also seemed to frequent the religious horizons of Schleiermacher himself: "That first mysterious moment that occurs in every sensory perception, before intuition and feeling have separated . . . I know how indescribable it is and how quickly it passes away. . . . Would that I could and might express it, at least indicate it, without having to desecrate it!" (*On Religion,* 31–32).

15. On mythic lenses as "microscopes and telescopes" in religiohistorical work, see Wendy Doniger, *The Implied Spider: Politics and Theology in Myth* (New York: Columbia University Press, 1998), 7–25.

16. Joachim Wach, e.g., talked about the use of ideal exemplars in religious studies as "classical"—using the term, to be sure, in a somewhat different way than I do here. See "The Concept of the Classical," in Wach's *Types of Religious Experience: Christian and Non-Christian* (Chicago: University of Chicago Press, 1951), 48–57.

17. Ronald Bruzina, *Logos and Eidos: The Concept in Phenomenology* (The Hague: Mouton, 1970), 55.

18. For the outlines of a sympathetic study of religion that invokes the idea of phenomenology, see Ninian Smart, *The Phenomenon of Religion* (New York: Herder and Herder, 1973). In *The Seeing Eye: Hermeneutical Phenomenology in the Study of Religion* (University Park: Pennsylvania State University Press, 1982), Walter L. Brenneman Jr., Stanley O. Yarian, and Alan M. Olson attempt seriously to integrate philosophical phenomenology into the phenomenology of religion. On Dutch phenomenology as a tradition in religious studies, see chap. 8 below.

CHAPTER 4. OTHER SCHOLARS' UFOS

With apologies to Wendy Doniger and her *Other Peoples' Myths* (Chicago: University of Chicago Press, 1995).

1. For a simple introduction to foundation strategies, see Roderick M. Chisholm, *Theory of Knowledge,* 2d ed. (Englewood Cliffs, N.J.: Prentice-Hall, 1977). In classical Western epistemology, important "foundations" have included Descartes's cogito and Locke's sense impressions.

2. For a sober discussion treating problems of foundationalism in modern intellectual culture, see Richard J. Bernstein, *Beyond Objectivism and Relativism: Science, Hermeneutics, and Praxis* (Philadelphia: University of Pennsylvania Press, 1983), 1–49. For more radical antifoundationalist views, see Linda J. Nicholson, *The Play of Reason: From the Modern to the Postmodern* (Ithaca, N.Y.: Cornell University Press, 1999), 117–28; and Barbara Herrnstein Smith, *Belief and Resistance: Dynamics of Contemporary Intellectual Controversy* (Cambridge: Harvard University Press, 1997), 83–104.

3. For an example from religious studies, see Ivan Strenski, *Four Theories of Myth in Twentieth-Century History: Cassirer, Eliade, Lévi-Strauss, Malinowski* (Iowa City: University of Iowa Press, 1987). See also my treatment of Eliade and Dumézil in chap. 5 and of Wilhelm Schmidt in chap. 9.

4. For a twentieth-century theory of knowledge from a coherence perspective, see Brand Blanshard, *Reason and Analysis* (La Salle, Ill.: Open Court, 1962). For revised versions of coherence theories, see Nicholas Rescher, *The Coherence Theory of Truth* (Oxford, U.K.: Oxford University Press, 1973); Keith Lehrer, *Knowledge* (Oxford, U.K.: Oxford University Press, 1974); and Lehrer's more recent textbook, *Theory of Knowledge* (Boulder, Colo.: Westview Press, 1990). *Coherence* is a term used in philosophical theories of justification (Lehrer, *Theory of Knowledge,* 13–16); culture theorists proposing alternatives to foundationalism may talk of "skepticism" (B. H. Smith, *Belief and Resistance,* 88–104) or of alternative forms of rationality (Nicholson, *Play of Reason,* 117–28). For an early articulation of some practical principles of coherence in theological studies, see David Friedrich Strauss, *The Life of Jesus Critically Examined,* trans. George Eliot, ed. Peter Crafts Hodgson (Philadelphia: Fortress Press, 1973; reprint, Ramsey, N.J.: Sigler Press, 1994), introduction, esp. 78, 86–92 (page citations are to the reprint edition).

5. Wendy Doniger O'Flaherty, *Śiva, the Erotic Ascetic* (New York: Oxford University Press, 1981); first published as *Asceticism and Eroticism in the Mythology of Śiva* (London: Oxford University Press, 1973).

6. See William C. Wimsatt, "Robustness, Reliability, and Overdetermination," in *Scientific Inquiry and the Social Sciences: A Volume in Honor of Donald T. Campbell,* ed. Marilynn B. Brewer and Barry E. Collins (San Francisco: Jossey-Bass, 1981), 124–71.

7. Clifford Geertz, "Thick Description: Toward an Interpretive Theory of Culture," in *The Interpretation of Cultures* (New York: Basic Books, 1973), 3–30.

8. Ibid., 15.

9. Dumézil's writings on Indo-European myth are vast. Most are collected in his multivolume *Mythe et Épopée* (Paris: Gallimard, 1968–73). Sections of his opus have been translated under different titles, including *Archaic Roman Religion,* trans. Philip Krapp, 2 vols. (Chicago: University of Chicago Press, 1970); *Gods of the Ancient Northmen* (Berkeley: University of California Press, 1973); *The Destiny of the Warrior,* trans. Alf Hiltebeitel (Chicago: University of Chicago Press, 1970); and *Mitra-Varuna: An Essay on Two Indo-European Representations of Sovereignty,* trans. Derek Coltman (New York: Zone Books, 1988)—one of Dumézil's earliest works. On Dumézil's achievement, see C. Scott

Littleton, *The New Comparative Mythology: An Anthropological Assessment of the Theories of Georges Dumézil,* rev. ed. (Berkeley: University of California Press, 1973). On continuing work in Indo-European mythology, see Jaan Puhvel, *Comparative Mythology* (Baltimore, Md.: Johns Hopkins University Press, 1987). For short, recent assessments, see Cristiano Grottanelli, "Dumézil, the Indo-Europeans, and the Third Function," in *Myth and Method,* ed. Laurie Patton and Wendy Doniger (Charlottesville: University Press of Virginia, 1996), 128–46; and Dean A. Miller, "Georges Dumézil: Theories, Critiques, and Theoretical Extensions," *Religion* 30, no. 1 (2000): 27–40. For an insightful critique, see Bruce Lincoln, *Theorizing Myth: Narrative, Ideology, and Scholarship* (Chicago: University of Chicago Press, 1999), 121–37.

10. The term originated with Gilbert Ryle (see Geertz, "Thick Description," 6).

11. Richard Levins, "The Strategy of Model Building in Population Biology," *American Scientist* 54 (1966): 423; quoted by Wimsatt ("Robustness," 125), who gives a clear explanation of principles of robustness.

12. Le Corbusier (Charles-Édouard Jeanneret), *Towards a New Architecture,* trans. Frederick Etchells (1927; reprint, New York: Praeger, 1960), 15.

13. Doniger O'Flaherty, *Śiva, the Erotic Ascetic,* 3.

14. Ibid., 4. Classic essays by Claude Lévi-Strauss can be found in his *Structural Anthropology* (New York: Basic Books, 1963).

15. It is true that Lévi-Strauss (and other classical structuralist anthropologists) sometimes treated the mythologies of the West, but they gave them flat rational social significances similar to those they found in the myths of small-scale cultures. See Lévi-Strauss's "The Structural Study of Myth," in his *Structural Anthropology,* 206–31, for an important comparison of the Oedipus myth with Pueblo mythic thought; and Edmund R. Leach, "Lévi-Strauss in the Garden of Eden: An Examination of Some Recent Developments in the Analysis of Myth," *Transactions of the New York Academy of Sciences,* 2d ser., 23 (1961): 386–96.

16. Mircea Eliade, *Patterns in Comparative Religion,* trans. Rosemary Sheed (New York: Meridian, 1963). For some recent evaluations of Eliade, see Bryan Rennie, ed., *Changing Religious Worlds: The Meaning and End of Mircea Eliade* (Albany: State University of New York Press, 2001).

CHAPTER 5. THE RELIGIOHISTORICAL SUBLIME

1. Paul Crowther, *Critical Aesthetics and Postmodernism* (Oxford, U.K.: Oxford University Press, 1993). This volume continues the author's project begun in his *The Kantian Sublime: From Morality to Art* (Oxford, U.K.: Clarendon Press, 1989).

2. The *urtexts* are Edmund Burke, *A Philosophical Enquiry into the Origin of Our Ideas of the Sublime and Beautiful,* 2d ed. (1759; reprint, New York: Garland, 1971); and Immanuel Kant, *Critique of Judgment,* trans. Werner S. Pluhar (Indianapolis, Ind.: Hackett, 1987).

3. For different usages, see Joseph Tabbi, *Postmodern Sublime: Technology and American Writing from Mailer to Cyberpunk* (Ithaca, N.Y.: Cornell University Press, 1995), with his expression of exasperation on p. xi; David B. Mor-

ris, *The Religious Sublime: Christian Poetry and Critical Tradition in Eighteenth-Century England* (Lexington: University Press of Kentucky, 1972); Thomas Weiskel, *The Romantic Sublime: Studies in the Structure and Psychology of Transcendence* (Baltimore, Md.: Johns Hopkins University Press, 1976); Mary Arensberg, ed., *The American Sublime* (Albany: State University of New York Press, 1986); Vijay Mishra, *Devotional Poetics and the Indian Sublime* (Albany: State University of New York Press, 1998). Arensberg, pp. 1–19, gives a cogent summary of the broad theoretical lineages on which these authors draw, and Weiskel's early extensive critical discussion offers insight into the family resemblances among them. Some interesting implications of the sublime for religious studies, featuring the work of Rudolf Otto, have been explored by Lynn Poland, "The Idea of the Holy and the History of the Sublime," *Journal of Religion* 72 (1992): 175–97. For cultural studies, the most influential theorist on the sublime has been Jean-François Lyotard, *Lessons on the Analytic of the Sublime: Kant's Critique of Judgment, Sections 23–29* (Stanford, Calif.: Stanford University Press, 1994). On a dynamic of the sublime in the creation of tradition, see Sanford Budick, *The Western Theory of Tradition: Terms and Paradigms of the Cultural Sublime* (New Haven, Conn.: Yale University Press, 2000).

4. Kant, *Critique of Judgment*, 23:225, 98. Here and in subsequent citations of the *Critique* the first number refers to the *Critique*'s section, the second to the page of the standard German *Akademie* edition, and the third to the page of Pluhar's translation.

5. For the centrality of limits in a general theory of the sublime, see Lap-Chuen Tsang, *The Sublime: Groundwork Towards a Theory* (Rochester, N.Y.: University of Rochester Press, 1998), xix–xx, 31.

6. Crowther, *Critical Aesthetics and Postmodernism*, 60.

7. Kant, *Critique of Judgment*, 26:256, 113.

8. This presentation of Kant's sublime, adapted from Crowther, is tailored to my own critical aims. Kant's formal definition seems to emphasize the second pole of this dynamic, the inability of imagination to keep up with reason: "The sublime can be described thus: it is an object (of nature) *the presentation of which determines the mind to think of nature's inability to attain to an exhibition of ideas.*" This definition, however, also describes reason and imagination in a complex dialectic: the "presentation" of an *image* causes the *rational* "mind to think" of the impossibility of nature's "exhibition" to *imagination* of *rational* "ideas." Kant emphasizes that this dialectic is one of aesthetic sensibilities, not a logical regression, for "[i]f we speak literally and consider the matter logically, ideas cannot be exhibited." Thus when, "in intuiting nature" our imagination begins to expand, "then reason . . . never fails to step in and arouse the mind to an effort, although a futile one, to make the presentation of the senses adequate to . . . [reason's idea of] totality" (ibid., 29:268, 127–28). Given Kant's intellectual priorities, the breakdown in the dynamic between reason and imagination occurs with imagination, not reason; but the force of the sublime moment seems to derive from the intensity of the mutual interplay between the two that precedes it.

9. The sublime "is produced by the feeling of a momentary inhibition of the vital forces followed immediately by an outpouring of them that is all the stronger" (ibid., 23:245, 98).

10. Immanuel Kant, *Observations on the Feeling of the Beautiful and Sublime*, cited by Pluhar in his translation of Kant's *Critique of Judgment*, 98n4. For a readable version of *Observations* in English, see John T. Goldthwait's translation (Berkeley: University of California Press, 1981); the passage cited is on p. 47. Kant sometimes presents the sublime as the result of an awesome, primordially fearful experience of self-loss: something "excessive to the imagination . . . is . . . an abyss in which the imagination is afraid to lose itself" (Kant, *Critique of Judgment*, 27:258, 115). On feelings of respect inspired by the sublime see *Critique of Judgment*, 27:257, 114.

11. "[T]he mind is not just attracted by the object but is alternately always repelled as well" (Kant, *Critique of Judgment*, 26:245, 98).

12. For a valuable history of the concept of imagination in modern thought, see Mary Warnock, *Imagination* (Berkeley: University of California Press, 1976); Warnock examines the role of imagination in perceptual psychology (13–34). On Kant's understanding of imagination see Rudolf A. Makkreel, *Imagination and Interpretation in Kant: The Hermeneutical Import of the "Critique of Judgment"* (Chicago: University of Chicago Press, 1990). For an extensive history of the imagination informed by a postmodern perspective, see Richard Kearney, *The Wake of Imagination: Ideas of Creativity in Western Culture* (London: Hutchinson, 1988).

13. See, e.g., Erwin Ramsdell Goodenough and Jacob Neusner, *Jewish Symbols in the Greco-Roman Period*, abr. ed. (Princeton, N.J.: Princeton University Press, 1988), 40.

14. Suggestive titles include David Gordon White, *Myths of the Dog-Man* (Chicago: University of Chicago Press, 1991); and Wendy Doniger, *Tales of Sex and Violence: Folklore, Sacrifice, and Danger in the Jaiminya Brahmana* (Chicago: University of Chicago Press, 1985).

15. William Brede Kristensen, *The Meaning of Religion: Lectures in the Phenomenology of Religion*, trans. John Carman (The Hague: Martinus Nijhoff, 1960), 22.

16. See Geertz's famous characterization, "Religion as a Cultural System," in Clifford Geertz, *The Interpretation of Cultures* (New York: Basic Books, 1973), 87–125.

17. For an earlier formulation of this thesis, see my "The Paradox in Writing on Religion," *Harvard Theological Review* 83, no. 3 (1990): 321–32.

18. Eliade used the term *archetype* throughout *Patterns* but later dropped it, no doubt because his usage too easily suggested the different Jungian one.

19. See, e.g., the essays in James Hillman, ed., *Facing the Gods* (Dallas, Tex.: Spring Publications, 1988).

20. Bruce Lincoln, *Death, War, and Sacrifice: Studies in Ideology and Practice* (Chicago: University of Chicago Press, 1991), 252; pp. 231–43 present a good short introduction to the political controversy surrounding Dumézil. See also Lincoln's *Theorizing Myth: Narrative, Ideology, and Scholarship* (Chicago: University of Chicago Press, 1999), chap. 6. Perhaps the most influential article on Dumézil's politics was published by the Italian historian Carlo Ginzburg in 1984; it is available in English as "German Mythology and Nazism: Thoughts on an Old Book by Georges Dumézil," in Carlo Ginzburg, *Clues, Myths, and the*

Historical Method, trans. John and Anne C. Tedeschi (Baltimore, Md.: Johns Hopkins University Press, 1989), 126–45. Dumézil is defended vigorously by Didier Eribon, *Faut-il Brûler Dumézil: Mythologie, Science, et Politique* (Paris: Flammarion, 1992), who gives abundant bibliographical notes on Dumézil's detractors. For a judicious presentation of the academic and cultural background of the debate, see Stefan Arvidsson, "Aryan Mythology as Science and Ideology," *Journal of Religion* 67, no. 2 (1999): 327–54.

21. See David Lehman, *Signs of the Times: Deconstruction and the Fall of Paul De Man* (New York: Poseidon Press, 1991).

22. One of the earliest and most balanced political critiques of Eliade is given in Ivan Strenski, *Four Theories of Myth in Twentieth-Century History: Cassirer, Eliade, Lévi-Strauss, Malinowski* (Iowa City: University of Iowa Press, 1987), 70–128. The implications of a supposed anti-Semitic outlook in Eliade's work is developed by Daniel Dubuisson, *Mythologies du XXe Siècle (Dumézil, Lévi-Strauss, Eliade)* (Lille: Presses Universitaires de Lille, 1993), 217–303 (tellingly, Dubuisson singles out Eliade for political critique and does not present a parallel perspective in his ample treatment of Dumézil in the same volume [23–128]). Personally pointed charges of anti-Semitism against Eliade are given by Adriana Berger, "Mircea Eliade: Romanian Fascism and History of Religions in the United States," in *Tainted Greatness: Antisemitism and Cultural Heroes,* ed. Nancy A. Harrowitz (Philadelphia: Temple University Press, 1994), 51–74. Leon Volovici, *Nationalist Ideology and Antisemitism: The Case of Romanian Intellectuals in the 1930s* (Oxford, U.K.: Pergamon, 1991), provides a context for understanding Eliade's nationalist politics and a sober assessment of them (see esp. 83–85). Excerpts from Mihail Sebastian's memoirs suggest that Eliade was indeed personally caught up in the anti-Semitic nationalism of the times but make no specific accusations: Mihail Sebastian, "Friends and Fascists: What the Author Saw in Wartime Bucharest," *New Yorker,* Oct. 2, 2000, 106–13. For the journal itself, see Mihail Sebastian and Radu Ioanid, *Journal, 1935–1944* (Chicago: Ivan R. Dee, 2000). A vigorous defense of Eliade is provided by Bryan S. Rennie, *Reconstructing Eliade: Making Sense of Religion* (Albany: State University of New York Press, 1996), 143–78, which includes valuable bibliographical notes.

23. Geertz, *Interpretation of Cultures,* 28–29.

24. On "like us," see Jonathan Z. Smith, "Adde Parvum Parvo Magnum Acervus Erit," in his *Map Is Not Territory: Studies in the History of Religions* (Leiden: Brill, 1978; reprint, Chicago: University of Chicago Press, 1993), 240–64.

25. Geertz, *Interpretation of Cultures,* 142–69.

26. See, e.g., P. B. Medawar, *Induction and Intuition in Scientific Thought* (Philadelphia: American Philosophical Society, 1969); and Geoffrey Vickers, "Rationality and Intuition," in *On Aesthetics in Science,* ed. Judith Wechsler (Cambridge, Mass.: MIT Press, 1978), 143–64.

27. See Burke, *Ideas of the Sublime and Beautiful,* part 4, secs. 5–8, pp. 252–58.

28. Crowther, *Critical Aesthetics and Postmodernism,* 125–28.

29. Gonzalo Fernández de Oviedo y Valdés, "Histoire du Nicaragua," in *Voyages, Relations et Memoires Originaux pour Servir a l'Histoire de la De-*

couverte de l'Amerique, ed. Henri Ternaux-Compans (Paris: Arthur Bertrand, 1840). Cited in Tylor, *Primitive Culture,* 2:293. Citations in this paragraph are from Fernández de Oviedo's text.

30. See Michel-Rolph Trouillot, "Anthropology and the Savage Slot," in *Recapturing Anthropology,* ed. Richard Fox (Santa Fe, N.M.: School of American Research, 1991), 17–44.

31. Philip P. Arnold's presentation of Aztec child sacrifice in a drought ritual presents a striking example of vivid description integrated into rational interpretation: the children's tears represent rain. See his *Eating Landscape: Aztec and European Occupation of Tlalocan* (Niwot: University Press of Colorado, 1999), 78–92.

32. Tzvetan Todorov, *The Fantastic: A Structural Approach to a Literary Genre,* trans. Richard Howard (Ithaca, N.Y.: Cornell University Press, 1975). The first chapter of Todorov's book has been cited frequently in studies of literary genre; see, e.g., Adena Rosmarin, *The Power of Genre* (Minneapolis: University of Minnesota Press, 1985), 32–33.

33. Jonathan Z. Smith, *Imagining Religion: From Jonestown to Babylon* (Chicago: University of Chicago Press, 1982), 90–101 ("A Pearl of Great Price and a Cargo of Yams: A Study in Situational Incongruity"—originally published in *History of Religions* 16 [1976]: 1–19); J. Z. Smith, *Map Is Not Territory,* 190–207, 289–309.

34. J. Z. Smith, "A Pearl of Great Price."

35. For more on German diffusionist thought, see below, chapter 9, on Wilhelm Schmidt's Vienna school; Jensen represents another branch of the school from which Schmidt drew his anthropological (but not theological) lineage. On the British Myth and Ritual school see chap. 11 below, where the school appears as a "patterned brocade" in the fabric of religiohistorical knowledge.

36. For what Crowther has to say on genius in this respect, see *Critical Aesthetics and Postmodernism,* 62–71, 160–61.

37. For a classic study of this question, see Thomas S. Kuhn, "The Essential Tension: Tradition and Innovation in Scientific Research," in *The Essential Tension: Selected Studies in Scientific Tradition and Change* (Chicago: University of Chicago Press, 1977), 225–39.

PART 3. TWO TRUTHS

1. On the ways in which aesthetics functions in natural science, see the essays in Judith Wechsler, ed., *On Aesthetics in Science* (Cambridge, Mass.: MIT Press, 1978).

2. The mutual embeddedness of the two truths is expressed in the famous Mahayana maxim: Samsara is Nirvana. On the doctrine of two truths in Indian philosophy generally, see the essays in Mervyn Sprung, ed., *The Problem of Two Truths in Buddhism and Vedånta* (Boston, Mass.: Reidel, 1973). For a classical Indian Buddhist text on the doctrine, see Jñānagarbha and Malcolm David Eckel, *Jñānagarbha's Commentary on the Distinction between the Two Truths: An Eighth-Century Handbook of Madhyamaka Philosophy* (Albany: State University of New York Press, 1987). On the import of the two truths in a currently in-

fluential school of Tibetan Buddhism, see Guy Newland, *The Two Truths: In the Madhyamika Philosophy of the Ge-luk-pa Order of Tibetan Buddhism* (Ithaca, N.Y.: Snow Lion, 1992).

3. Gavin Flood, *Beyond Phenomenology: Rethinking the Study of Religion* (London: Cassell, 1999), gives a clear presentation of the issues, offering some detailed analysis of the scholarship in religious studies, critical theory, and philosophy; see esp. his chap. 3. The fallibilist philosophical position I articulate in chapter 7 is similar to Flood's, the dialogism less so. Voices speaking from decided critical perspectives include Robert A. Segal, *Explaining and Interpreting Religion: Essays on the Issue* (New York: Peter Lang, 1992); Russell T. McCutcheon, *Manufacturing Religion: The Discourse on Sui Generis Religion and the Politics of Nostalgia* (New York: Oxford University Press, 1997); Donald Wiebe, *The Politics of Religious Studies: The Continuing Conflict with Theology in the Academy,* 1st ed. (New York: St. Martin's Press, 1999); Timothy Fitzgerald, *The Ideology of Religious Studies* (New York: Oxford University Press, 2000). A number of interesting critical views are presented in Armin W. Geertz and Russell T. McCutcheon, eds., *Perspectives on Method and Theory in the Study of Religion* (Leiden: Brill, 2000).

CHAPTER 6. RELATING STORIES
ABOUT RELIGIOUS TRADITIONS

1. The ocular metaphor, of course, also has a long history in Western thinking about philosophical and scientific truths. See Richard Rorty, *Philosophy and the Mirror of Nature* (Princeton, N.J.: Princeton University Press, 1980), esp. 11, 38–39.

2. Literature on interpretation and explanation is legion; the senses I give to the terms here emphasize one of the basic distinctions they are often used to make. On interpretation, the classical accounts cited most by students of religion remain Hans-Georg Gadamer, *Truth and Method* (New York: Seabury Press, 1975); and Clifford Geertz, "Thick Description: Toward an Interpretive Theory of Culture," in *The Interpretation of Cultures* (New York: Basic Books, 1973), 3–30. For the roles of explanation in religion studies, see J. Samuel Preus's intellectual history, *Explaining Religion: Criticism and Theory from Bodin to Freud* (New Haven, Conn.: Yale University Press, 1987); Donald Wiebe's philosophical study, *Religion and Truth: Toward an Alternative Paradigm for the Study of Religion* (The Hague: Mouton, 1981); and Hans H. Penner's outline of a methodological program, *Impasse and Resolution: A Critique of the Study of Religion* (New York: Peter Lang, 1989). Some interesting observations on the dialectic between interpretation and explanation are given by Paul Ricoeur in his short *Interpretation Theory: Discourse and the Surplus of Meaning* (Fort Worth: Texas Christian University Press, 1976).

3. Karl Popper, *Objective Knowledge: An Evolutionary Approach* (Oxford, U.K.: Oxford University Press, 1972), 188. Popper's remarks here are based on a lecture given in Vienna in 1968.

4. Gavin Flood, *Beyond Phenomenology: Rethinking the Study of Religion* (London: Cassell, 1999), 68.

5. See Marvin Harris, *Cultural Materialism: The Struggle for a Science of Culture* (New York: Random House, 1979). The phrase "cultural materialism" has been adopted as a label by like-minded anthropologists; see, e.g., Eric B. Ross, *Beyond the Myths of Culture: Essays in Cultural Materialism* (London: Academic Press, 1980).

6. Marvin Harris, *Cows, Pigs, Wars, and Witches: The Riddles of Culture* (New York: Random House, 1974; reprint, New York: Vintage, 1989), 3. Harris had earlier published a substantial history of anthropology from a materialist perspective: *The Rise of Anthropological Theory: A History of Theories of Culture* (New York: Crowell, 1968). Nor did he keep quiet in the wake of critical theory: *Theories of Culture in Postmodern Times* (Walnut Creek, Calif.: AltaMira Press, 1999). For a critique with comments, rejoinders, and a long bibliography see Drew Westen, "Cultural Materialism: Food for Thought or Bum Steer?" *Current Anthropology* 25, no. 5 (1984): 639–53.

7. Marvin Harris, *Good to Eat: Riddles of Food and Culture* (New York: Simon and Schuster, 1985); chap. 3 (47–87) is entitled "The Riddle of the Sacred Cow."

8. Harris notes, "It's important that the chapters in this book be seen as building on each other and as having a cumulative effect" (*Cows, Pigs,* vi).

9. Harris devotes the last chapter of his *Cultural Materialism* to an exposé of "obscurantism": "a research strategy whose aim is to subvert the possibility of achieving a science of human social life" (315). Included among varieties of obscurantism are the "phenomenological" and the "reflexive"—both of which have had currency in religious studies.

10. See Jessie L. Weston, *From Ritual to Romance* (1920; reprint, Garden City, N.Y.: Doubleday, 1957); and Maud Bodkin, *Archetypal Patterns in Poetry: Psychological Studies of Imagination* (London: Oxford University Press, 1934). Both are discussed at the end of chap. 10 below.

11. Classic volumes in the discussion include Thomas S. Kuhn, *The Structure of Scientific Revolutions,* 2d ed. (Chicago: University of Chicago Press, 1970); Imre Lakatos and Alan Musgrave, eds., *Criticism and the Growth of Knowledge* (Cambridge, U.K.: Cambridge University Press, 1970); and Paul Feyerabend, *Against Method* (London: Verso, 1978). The correspondence between Lakatos and Feyerabend has recently been published in Imre Lakatos, Paul K. Feyerabend, and Matteo Motterlini, *For and against Method: Including Lakatos's Lectures on Scientific Method and the Lakatos-Feyerabend Correspondence* (Chicago: University of Chicago Press, 1999). For a sober assessment of issues in the sociology of science, see Helen Longino, *Science as Social Knowledge* (Princeton, N.J.: Princeton University Press, 1990). For a critique of the sociology of science from the political left, see Christopher Norris, *Against Relativism: Philosophy of Science, Deconstruction, and Critical Theory* (Oxford, U.K.: Blackwell, 1997).

12. Harris, *Cultural Materialism,* 287–314. Interestingly, Harris describes eclecticism as "a prescription for . . . middle-range theories"—which I take as the characteristic level at which religiohistorical discourse occurs but which he sees as "perpetual scientific disaster" (288). So Harris and I can agree on eclecticism's results if not on those results' value.

13. Donald Wiebe, *The Politics of Religious Studies: The Continuing Conflict with Theology in the Academy* (New York: St. Martin's, 1999), 155, 148.

14. The phrase "middle-range theory" was used in the mid-twentieth century by Robert K. Merton in something like the sense I am using it in here. See Robert K. Merton, *Social Theory and Social Structure* (New York: Free Press, 1968), esp. chap. 2, "On Sociological Theories of the Middle Range." The idea of a middle ground continues to appear in religious studies; see, e.g., Dean A. Miller, "Georges Dumézil: Theories, Critiques, and Theoretical Extensions," *Religion* 30, no. 1 (2000): 27.

15. On the different intellectual dynamics of intersubjectivity and consensus, see Charles Taylor, "Interpretation and the Sciences of Man," in his *Philosophy and the Human Sciences* (Cambridge, U.K.: Cambridge University Press, 1985), 36–37.

16. Clifford Geertz, *Islam Observed: Religious Development in Morocco and Indonesia* (Chicago: University of Chicago Press, 1971), 23.

17. See, e.g., McKim Marriott, "Constructing an Indian Ethnosociology," in *India through Hindu Categories,* ed. McKim Marriott (New Delhi: Sage Publications, 1990), 1–40.

18. Georges Dumézil, *Mitra-Varuna: An Essay on Two Indo-European Representations of Sovereignty,* trans. Derek Coltman (New York: Zone Books, 1988), 17.

19. See, e.g., ibid., 12–14; and Georges Dumézil, *Gods of the Ancient Northmen* (Berkeley: University of California Press, 1973), xlv.

20. Clifford Geertz, *Negara: The Theatre State in Nineteenth-Century Bali* (Princeton, N.J.: Princeton University Press, 1980).

21. Geertz, *Interpretation of Cultures,* 453.

22. Geertz, *Islam Observed,* 54.

23. The article is discussed briefly in chapter 5 under "compact frames."

24. For classic studies of cargo cults, see Kenelm Burridge, *Mambu: A Melanesian Millennium* (London: Methuen, 1960); and Peter Lawrence, *Road Belong Cargo: A Study of the Cargo Movement in the Southern Madang District, New Guinea* (Manchester, U.K.: Manchester University Press, 1964).

25. For a somewhat different sense of truth in a moderate sense see Barbara Herrnstein Smith, *Belief and Resistance,* xvii–xviii, where she presents a principle of "more-or-less."

CHAPTER 7. AESTHETIC OBJECTS AND OBJECTIVE KNOWLEDGE

1. This is actually a paraphrase of Geertz paraphrasing himself—"Is knowledge possible? . . . Objectivity a sham? . . . Is it power, pelf and political agendas all the way down?" (Clifford Geertz, *Available Light: Anthropological Reflections on Philosophical Topics* [Princeton, N.J.: Princeton University Press, 2000], 18); the *original* text paraphrased is quoted above under "compact frames" in chap. 5. For an incisive account of the political agendas in writing on myth, see Bruce Lincoln, *Theorizing Myth: Narrative, Ideology, and Scholarship* (Chicago: University of Chicago Press, 1999).

2. Richard Rorty notes a similar common juxtaposition of an "epistemological antifoundationalism" and metaphysical realism among analytic philosophers. See Richard Rorty, *Truth and Progress* (Cambridge, U.K.: Cambridge University Press, 1998), 2–3. Summarizing this stance, which he does not hold himself, he writes, "Granted that the *criterion* of truth is justification, and that justification is relative, the *nature* of truth is not" (3).

3. Thomas Nagel, *The View from Nowhere* (New York: Oxford University Press, 1986), 11; cited in Richard Rorty, *Objectivity, Relativism, and Truth* (Cambridge, U.K.: Cambridge University Press, 1991), 7. Barbara Herrnstein Smith makes a similar observation from the opposite camp. In her levelheaded presentation of a postmodern communication theory, she discusses charges of cynicism against it by moral theorists and pessimism by Marxists: "The reason for the charge in each case seems to be pretty much the same, namely the failure of accounts to endorse a redemptive script—either religious, moral, or political—of underlying human unity and ultimate human transcendence" (Barbara Herrnstein Smith, *Belief and Resistance: Dynamics of Contemporary Intellectual Controversy* [Cambridge, Mass.: Harvard University Press, 1997], 70). I think the large stories of most interpretive writers have at least one of the last two elements.

4. The context of the passage cited from Peirce under "Consensus and Fascination" below presents a cheerful, energizing hope as a pragmatic value of a sense of reality: "all the followers of science are animated by a cheerful hope that the process of investigation, if only pushed far enough, will give one certain solution to each question to which they apply it. . . . This great hope is embodied in the conception of truth and reality" (Charles S. Peirce, *Collected Papers,* ed. Charles Hartshorne and Paul Weiss [Cambridge, Mass.: Belknap Press of Harvard University Press, 1960], 5:268 [par. no. 407]). For the practical value of a sense of realism in research, see Karl Popper, *Objective Knowledge: An Evolutionary Approach* (Oxford, U.K.: Oxford University Press, 1972), 203.

5. Although Husserl himself refrained from ontological claims behind the appearances he aims to describe, some scholars simply seem to be presenting religious "phenomena," which they take as unproblematically real; see Gavin Flood, *Beyond Phenomenology: Rethinking the Study of Religion* (London: Cassell, 1999), 91–116, 169.

6. For procedural objectivity see Allan Megill, ed., *Rethinking Objectivity* (Durham, N.C.: Duke University Press, 1994), 10–11. In his introductory essay, Megill describes "four senses of objectivity," which differ somewhat from those presented here, although his "dialectical" sense is close to my "dialogic."

7. On the place of this objectivity in natural science, see Helen Longino, *Science as Social Knowledge* (Princeton, N.J.: Princeton University Press, 1990), 62–82.

8. For a version of this sense of objectivity in historiography, see Thomas L. Haskell, *Objectivity Is Not Neutrality: Explanatory Schemes in History* (Baltimore, Md.: Johns Hopkins University Press, 1998), 161; in anthropology, see James A. Boon, "Ultraobjectivity: Reading Cross-Culturally," in *Objectivity and Its Other,* ed. Wolfgang Natter, Theodore R. Schatzki, and John Paul Jones (New York: Guilford Press, 1995), 179–205.

9. On objectivity as an attribute of persons, "a cluster of intellectual virtues" (137), see Theodore R. Schatzki, "Objectivity and Rationality," in Natter, Schatzki, and Jones, *Objectivity and Its Other,* 137–60.

10. On this sense of objectification, see Charles Taylor, *Hegel* (Cambridge, U.K.: Cambridge University Press, 1975), 9–10. For more on objectification, the Enlightenment, and rational analysis, see Foucault's afterword to Hubert L. Dreyfus and Paul Rabinow, *Michel Foucault: Beyond Structuralism and Hermeneutics* (Chicago: University of Chicago Press, 1982), 208–16.

11. B. H. Smith, *Belief and Resistance,* xvii.

12. See Rorty, *Objectivity, Relativism, and Truth,* esp. part 1.

13. Peirce, *Collected Papers,* 5:268, par. no. 407. The immediate passage is cited in Peter Novick, *That Noble Dream: The "Objectivity Question" and the American Historical Profession* (Cambridge, U.K.: Cambridge University Press, 1988), 571. For the epistemological value of community in Peirce, see Thomas L. Haskell, "Professionalism versus Capitalism: R. H. Tawney, Émile Durkheim, and C. S. Peirce on the Disinterestedness of Professional Communities," in *The Authority of Experts: Studies in History and Theory,* ed. Thomas L. Haskell (Bloomington: Indiana University Press, 1984), 180–225, esp. 203–15.

14. See Peirce, *Collected Papers,* 5:1, par. no. 2.

15. Nicholas Rescher, *Objectivity: The Obligations of Impersonal Reason* (Notre Dame, Ind.: University of Notre Dame Press, 1997), 8.

16. Ibid.

17. For one of the most outspoken of such arguments, see Gananath Obeyesekere, *The Apotheosis of Captain Cook: European Mythmaking in the Pacific* (Princeton, N.J.: Princeton University Press, 1992). Obeyesekere argues against Marshall Sahlins's views as stated in Sahlins's *How "Natives" Think: About Captain Cook, for Example* (Chicago: University of Chicago Press, 1995). For a review of their debate, see Geertz, *Available Light,* 97–107; Geertz notes the irony of "the offended and injured 'native subject' as Enlightenment universalist" (106).

18. On W. C. Smith's statement, see chapter 1 above. On some new directions in this mutually participative approach in religious studies, see Flood, *Beyond Phenomenology,* chaps. 6–8. On anthropologists' reading of ethnographical texts to those texts' subjects, see Steven Feld, "Dialogic Editing: Interpreting How Kaluli Read *Sound and Sentiment,*" *Cultural Anthropology* 2, no. 2 (1987): 190–210; and The Hajj, Smadar Lavie, and Forest Rouse, "Notes on the Fantastic Journey of the Hajj, His Anthropologist, and Her American Passport," *American Anthropologist* 20, no. 2 (1993): 363–84.

19. See, e.g., Flood, *Beyond Phenomenology,* 68, 144. Popper on historical explanation is discussed in the opening section of chap. 6 above.

20. Popper, *Objective Knowledge,* 197. All quotations in this paragraph are from this source.

21. Karl Popper, *Conjectures and Refutations: The Growth of Scientific Knowledge,* 4th ed. (London: Routledge and Kegan Paul, 1972), 233.

22. Ibid., 237.

23. See the distinctions between context of discovery and context of justification in classical philosophy of science in Longino, *Science as Social Knowledge,*

64–65. Judith Wechsler, in her introduction to *On Aesthetics in Science* (Cambridge, Mass.: MIT Press, 1978), makes the point that in natural science aesthetic judgments operate in the process of discovery, not in understanding the finished product (4).

PART 4. WORKING TOGETHER

1. On possibilities for the integration of knowledge, see Louis O. Mink, *Historical Understanding,* ed. Brian Fay, Eugene O. Golob, and Richard T. Vann (Ithaca, N.Y.: Cornell University Press, 1987), 35–41. For its inevitable uneasinesses, see Barbara Herrnstein Smith, *Belief and Resistance: Dynamics of Contemporary Intellectual Controversy* (Cambridge, Mass.: Harvard University Press, 1997), 86.

CHAPTER 8. INTERPRETING ANEW AND ALONE

1. Strictly speaking, "phenomenology of religion" best translates "*Religionsphänomenologie,*" but it has sometimes been used as a general term for comparative studies in religion.

2. For the application of the later French phenomenology of Merleau-Ponty to religious studies, see Ariel Glucklich, *The Sense of Adharma* (New York: Oxford University Press, 1994).

3. George Alfred James, *Interpreting Religion: The Phenomenological Approaches of Pierre Daniël Chantepie de la Saussaye, W. Brede Kristensen, and Gerardus van der Leeuw* (Washington, D.C.: Catholic University of America Press, 1995), 22–46.

4. On the different English and German usages of the term *phenomenology* by the Dutch religionist Jouco Bleeker, see ibid., 29. For alternative versions of phenomenology as it is relevant to religionists, see Thomas Ryba, *The Essence of Phenomenology and Its Meaning for the Scientific Study of Religion* (Toronto: Peter Lang, 1991). For a short survey of phenomenological approaches in religion, see Olof Pettersson and Hans Åkerberg, *Interpreting Religious Phenomena: Studies with Reference to the Phenomenology of Religion* (Stockholm: Alkvist and Wiksell International, 1981), 9–66. A sustained integration of Husserlian insights into a phenomenology of religion is attempted in Walter Brenneman, Stanley Yarian, and Alan Olson, eds., *The Seeing Eye: Hermeneutical Phenomenology in the Study of Religion* (University Park: Pennsylvania State University Press, 1982). Sigurd Hjelde, ed., *Man, Meaning, and Mystery: One Hundred Years of History of Religions in Norway—The Heritage of W. Brede Kristensen* (Leiden: Brill, 2000) offers analytical essays on the phenomenology of religion by Dutch and Scandinavian scholars. Richard Schmitt, "Phenomenology," in *Encyclopedia of Philosophy,* ed. Paul Edwards (New York: Macmillan, 1967), 135–51, provides a short incisive survey of philosophical phenomenology. The standard long survey remains Herbert Spiegelberg, *The Phenomenological Movement: A Historical Introduction,* 2 vols. (The Hague: Martinus Nijhoff, 1960).

5. C. P. Tiele, *Elements of the Science of Religion,* 2 vols. (New York:

Charles Scribner's Sons, 1897–99), 1:289. On Tiele's historical evolutionism in the context of his theology, see L. Leertouwer, "C. P. Tiele's Strategy of Conquest," in *Leiden Oriental Connections, 1850–1940,* ed. Willem Otterspeer (Leiden: E. J. Brill, 1989), 153–67.

6. Tiele himself belonged to the Remonstrant tradition, whose liberal, progressive, and scholarly heritage looks back to the late-sixteenth-century Dutch reformer Arminius.

7. Tiele, *Science of Religion,* 2:14, 15.

8. Of Tiele's specialized works, *The Religion of the Iranian Peoples* (Bombay: "The Parsi" Publishing Co., 1912) is available in English, among others; see also his *Outlines of the History of Religion to the Spread of the Universal Religions,* trans. J. Estlin Carpenter, 3d ed. (London: Trübner, 1884).

9. On Kristensen's understanding of rationality, see John B. Carman, "Kristensen, W. Brede," in *Encyclopedia of Religion,* ed. Mircea Eliade (New York: Macmillan, 1987), 8:382–83.

10. James, *Interpreting Religion,* 141.

11. William Brede Kristensen, *The Meaning of Religion: Lectures in the Phenomenology of Religion,* trans. John Carman (The Hague: Martinus Nijhoff, 1960), 2.

12. Ibid., 1.

13. Jacques Waardenburg, "P. D. Chantepie de la Saussaye," in *Encyclopedia of Religion,* 3:203.

14. P. D. Chantepie de la Saussaye, *Manual of the Science of Religion,* trans. Beatrice S. Colyer-Fergusson (née Müller) (London: Longmans, Green, 1891). The German original, *Lehrbuch der Religionswissenschaft,* has gone through many editions. The later ones have been posthumously edited and expanded into substantially new volumes, capitalizing on the classical status of the work. The English translation of the first edition was prepared by the daughter of the Oxford-based German Sanskritist Max Müller.

15. Jacques Waardenburg, "Gerardus van der Leeuw," in *Encyclopedia of Religion,* 8:493–95.

16. For an appreciation of van der Leeuw as a "universal man" in the tradition of Leonardo and Goethe, see Eliade's preface to van der Leeuw's *Sacred and Profane Beauty: The Holy in Art,* trans. David E. Green (Nashville, Tenn.: Abingdon Press, 1963). For an appreciation by a student, see Hubertus G. Hubbeling, "Religion, Religionsphilosophie und Theologie bei Gerardus van der Leeuw," in *Religion im Denken unserer Zeit,* ed. Wilfried Härle and Eberhard Wölfel (Marburg: N. G. Elwert Verlag, 1986), 73–88. A short survey of van der Leeuw's life is given by Jacques Waardenburg, *Reflections on the Study of Religion: Including an Essay on the Work of Gerardus van der Leeuw,* ed. Jacques Waardenburg (The Hague: Mouton, 1978), 187–92.

17. For a fuller description of Van der Leeuw's phenomenology, see chap. 6 above; on Marett, see chap. 2 above.

18. The German original was published in Tübingen in 1933; it was first published in English in 1938 (Allen and Unwin), reprinted as a paperback in 1963 (Harper and Row) and again in hardcover in 1986 (Princeton University Press).

19. Chantepie de la Saussaye, *Manual,* 50–59.

20. Van der Leeuw, *Religion in Essence and Manifestation,* 2:695.

21. Although Kraemer speaks in the spirit of Barthian Christian revival, his position differs from Barth's on important particulars. In *Kraemer Towards Tambaram: A Study in Hendrik Kraemer's Missionary Approach* (Uppsala: Gleerup, 1966), Carl F. Hallencreutz notes that Kraemer didn't even study Barth until after his first missionary experience (99); Hallencreutz locates Kraemer, along with other important Dutch phenomenologists of religion, in the tradition of Dutch "ethical theology" (88–99). For Kraemer as a Barthian, see Bert Hoedemaker, "Kraemer Reassessed," *Ecumenical Review* 41, no. 1 (1989): 41–49; for a survey of Dutch phenomenologists' theological views on studying "non-Christian" religions, see Hallencreutz, *Kraemer Towards Tambaram,* 107–18.

22. For some observations on the preparation of the background book for the conference, see Hallencreutz, *Kraemer Towards Tambaram,* 272–74.

23. Ibid., 46, 49. A short sketch of Hurgronje's work in an unabashed survey of Dutch orientalism can be found in J. Ph. Vogel, *The Contribution of the University of Leiden to Oriental Research: Lecture Delivered to the Royal India and Pakistan Society on Thursday, June 23, 1949* (Leiden: E. J. Brill, 1954), 12–14.

24. Hallencreutz, *Kraemer Towards Tambaram,* 78.

25. Ibid., 272.

26. Willem Bijlefeld, "Kraemer, Hendrik," in *Encyclopedia of Religion,* 8:380–81.

27. See Hendrik Kraemer, *The Communication of the Christian Faith* (Philadelphia: Westminster Press, 1956); on Wilfred Cantwell Smith, see chapter 1.

28. In 1988–89, the anniversary year of the Tambaram conference, two missiology journals devoted issues to retrospectives on it and reassessments of Kraemer: *International Review of Mission* 78, no. 307 (July 1988); and *Ecumenical Review* 41, no. 1 (1989). Contributing to the first were prominent historians of religions Wilfred Cantwell Smith, "Mission, Dialogue, and God's Will for Us," 360–74; and Diana L. Eck, "The Religions and Tambaram: 1938 and 1988," 375–89. Valuable articles from the second include Philip A. Potter, "WCC and the World of Religions and Cultures," 4–19; and Bert Hoedemaker, "Kraemer Reassessed," 41–49.

29. Hendrik Kraemer, *Religion and the Christian Faith* (Philadelphia: Westminster Press, 1956); Hendrik Kraemer, *World Cultures and World Religions* (Philadelphia: Westminster Press, 1960).

30. Gilbert Murray, *Five Stages of Greek Religion,* 3d ed. (New York: Doubleday, 1955); quoted in Hendrik Kraemer, *The Christian Message in a Non-Christian World,* 3d ed. (Grand Rapids, Mich.: Kregel Publications, 1956), 13.

31. Kraemer, *Christian Message,* 13.

32. Ibid., 1. Joseph M. Kitagawa, *The History of Religions: Understanding the Human Experience* (Atlanta, Ga.: Scholars Press, 1987), 311–27, gives a brief history of the missiological controversies in which this statement figures and contrasts Kraemer's views on "other religions" with those of his theological contemporary Paul Tillich.

33. Kraemer, *World Cultures,* 19–20; for an appreciation of Kraemer's apparent moderation of his position later in his career see Bijlefeld, *Hendrik Kraemer.*

34. Hallencreutz, *Kraemer Towards Tambaram,* 102, quoting Kraemer in the Christian students' journal *Eltheto,* 1918–19, 238.

35. Kraemer, *Christian Faith,* 110. In giving the Vedas authority as revelation, Kraemer is in fact following an orthodox Hindu position that contrasts with Radhakrishnan's Hindu modernism: see Anantananda Rambachan, *Accomplishing the Accomplished: The Vedas as a Source of Valid Knowledge in Śankara* (Honolulu: University of Hawaii Press, 1991).

36. Hallencreutz discusses the evolutionary tendencies in Kraemer's thesis in *Kraemer Towards Tambaram,* 76–77.

37. Jacques Waardenburg, "Religion between Reality and Idea: A Century of Phenomenology of Religion in the Netherlands," *Numen* 19 (1972): 201n183.

38. For the theological import of van der Leeuw's phenomenological work, see Jan Hermelink, *Verstehen und Bezeugen: Der Theologische Ertrag der "Phänomenologie der Religion" von Gerardus van der Leeuw* (München: Chr. Kaiser Verlag, 1960).

39. Harold Bloom, *The Anxiety of Influence: A Theory of Poetry* (New York: Oxford University Press, 1973).

40. See Kraemer's introduction to Kristensen's *The Meaning of Religion.* On Kristensen's attitude toward Tiele, see Leertouwer, "Tiele's Strategy of Conquest," 167; Leertouwer cites an article written by Kristensen in *Nieuw Nederlands Biografisch Woordenboek* (Leiden, 1918), 1332–34, to which I have not had access.

CHAPTER 9. EXPLAINING TOGETHER

1. See Dean A. Miller, "Georges Dumézil: Theories, Critiques, and Theoretical Extensions," *Religion* 30, no. 1 (2000): 27–40.

2. See, e.g., Glyn Daniel, *The Idea of Prehistory* (Cleveland, Ohio: World Publishing, 1963), 107.

3. See the discussion by Reinhard G. Lehmann, *Friedrich Delitzsch und der Babel-Bibel-Streit* (Freiburg, Schweiz: Universitätsverlag: Vandenhoeck und Ruprecht, 1994), 38–39. Delitzsch, whom Lehmann sees as a Neo- not a Panbabylonian, was involved in the most public controversy of the age: the "Bibel-Babel Streit," in which Kaiser Wilhelm II became involved. For a contrast between the "Babylonians" and "Panbabylonians" by a scholar contemporary with them, see Ditlef Nielsen, "Gemeinsemitische Götter," *Orientalistische Literaturzeitung* 16, no. 5 (1913): 199–203, esp. 200–201. Later scholarship sometimes does not distinguish between the two groups. In his encyclopedia article on Panbabylonianism, Jeremias defines the term as the "battle name" *(Trutzname)* adopted by Winckler and himself. See Alfred Jeremias, "Panbabylonismus," in *Die Religion in Geschichte und Gegenwart,* 2d ed., ed. H. Gunkel and L. Zscharnack (Tübingen: Mohr, 1927–31), 4:879–80. Most secondary writing on the Panbabylonians has been in German, to which the notes in Lehmann, *Friedrich Delitzsch,* 38–49, contain extensive references; for a moderately criti-

cal treatment in English by an American contemporary, see Crawford W. Toy, "Panbabylonianism," *Harvard Theological Review* 3, no. 1 (1910): 47–84.

4. Smith also points to the philological errors on which this Panbabylonian concept was founded. See Jonathan Z. Smith, *To Take Place: Toward Theory in Ritual,* ed. Jacob Neusner et al. (Chicago: University of Chicago Press, 1987), 15–16.

5. Jeremias, "Panbabylonismus," 879.

6. Wilhelm Schmidt, *The Origin and Growth of Religion: Facts and Theories,* trans. H. J. Rose (1931; reprint, New York: Cooper Square, 1972), 97 (page citations are to the reprint edition). Good examples of Siecke's interpretations are his *Die Liebesgeschichte des Himmels. Untersuchungen zur Indogermanischen Sagenkunde* (Strassburg: K. J. Trübner, 1892); and Ernst Siecke, *Götterattribute und Sogenannte Symbole* (Jena: H. Costenoble, 1909). For a manifesto of the "Gesellschaft für vergleichende Mythenforschung," see Heinrich Lessmann, *Aufgaben und Ziele der vergleichenden Mythenforschung* (Leipzig: J. C. Hinrichs, 1908), esp. chap. 5.

7. The most famous case is Max Müller's solar mythology; see, e.g., Müller's *Lectures on the Origin and Growth of Religion as Illustrated by the Religions of India* (London: Longmans, Green, 1880).

8. Eduard Stucken, *Astralmythen der Hebraër, Babylonier, und Aegypter* (Leipzig: Verlag von Eduard Pfeiffer, 1896–1907).

9. Quoted in Ingeborg Carlson, "Eduard Stucken: Eine Monographie" (Inaugural-Dissertation, Friedrich Alexander Universität zu Erlangen-Nurnberg, 1961), v–vi.

10. Clemens de Baillou, "Eduard Stucken: Eine Studie," *Kentucky Foreign Language Quarterly* 8, no. 1 (1961): 2–3.

11. Stucken's dual career brought criticism in both fields: his scholarship was too fanciful, his literature too fact-laden (Carlson, "Stucken," vii). The mythic element in his literary work is more obvious than in Eliade's—found in the elaboration of exotic detail and story, not in the transposition of mythic themes into modern life. He was also an artist whose drawings were published (he mentioned Blake as a major influence on his work [Carlson, "Stucken," x–xiii]) and an amateur pianist (de Baillou, "Stucken," 5).

12. On Bastian as an outspoken evolutionist, see Daniel, *Idea of Prehistory,* 107.

13. Hugo Winckler, *Geschichte Israels in Einzeldarstellungen,* 2 vols. (Leipzig: E. Pfeiffer, 1895, 1900), 2:276n1; cited in Carlson, "Stucken," x.

14. The story of Ishtar (Sumerian Inanna) is frequently taken as part of a cycle of death/regeneration/vegetation cycle myths; as an astral deity she is usually seen as Venus (William J. Fulco, "Inanna," in *Encyclopedia of Religion,* ed. Mircea Eliade [New York: Macmillan, 1987], 145–46).

15. Eduard Stucken, "Polynesisches Sprachgut in Amerika und in Sumer," *Mitteilungen der Vorderasiatisch-Aegyptischen Gesellschaft (E.V.)* 31, no. 2 (1927): 2.

16. de Baillou, "Stucken," 5; Carlson, "Stucken," 5.

17. The Neobabylonian Franz Delitzsch attributes Winckler's productivity to his lack of a university position (letter reproduced in Klaus Johanning, *Der Bibel-*

Babel-Streit: Eine forschungsgeschichtliche Studie [Frankfurt am Main: Peter Lang, 1988], 381).

18. See Otto Weber, "Hugo Winckler als Forscher: Gedachtnisrede," *Mitteilungen der Vorderasiatisch-Aegyptischen Gesellschaft (E.V.)* 20, no. 1 (1916): 18.

19. Winckler, *Geschichte Israels*, 2:275.

20. See letter from Delitzsch in Johanning, *Der Bibel-Babel-Streit*, 380–83; and Weber, "Gedachtnisrede."

21. Winckler's associate professorship, moreover, was not entirely regular: his appointment was as an "ausseretatsmässiger" faculty, someone "outside the budget," in an irregular, temporary line created especially for him (Felix E. Peiser, "Nachruf Hugo Winckler," *Orientalistische Literaturzeitung* 16, no. 5 [1913]: 198). Lehmann, *Friedrich Delitzsch*, 40, calls Winckler a Berlin *Privatdozent* and later *Extraordinarius* (associate professor) in Oriental Languages.

22. Peiser, "Nachruf Hugo Winckler," 198.

23. Alfred Jeremias, "Hugo Winckler: Gedachtnisrede (Memorial address)," *Mitteilungen der Vorderasiatisch-Aegyptischen Gesellschaft (E.V.)* 20, no. 1 (1915): 4.

24. Peiser, "Nachruf Hugo Winckler," 197. Peiser specifically mentions Winckler's conflict with the Wellhausen school.

25. Niebuhr, "Nachruf Hugo Winckler," *Orientalistische Literaturzeitung* 16, no. 5 (1913): 200. The name Carl Niebuhr was a pseudonym for Carl Krug.

26. Peiser, "Nachruf Hugo Winckler," 195.

27. Jeremias, "Gedachtnisrede," 5.

28. Hugo Winckler, "Himmels- und Weltenbild der Babylonier als Grundlage des Weltanschauung und Mythologie aller Völker," *Der Alte Orient* 3, nos. 2–3 (1902): 1–67.

29. Jeremias, "Panbabylonismus," 879.

30. W. Baumgartner, "Nachruf Alfred Jeremias," *Zeitschrift für Assyriologie* 43 (1936): 300.

31. See Alfred Jeremias, *Handbuch der altorientalischen Geisteskultur*, 1st ed. (Leipzig: J. C. Hinrichs'sche Buchhandlung, 1913).

32. Jeremias, "Gedachtnisrede," 8.

33. There are five main points in Jeremias's treatment, one with seven subheadings.

34. Jeremias, *Das Alte Testament*, 77–78; he refers the reader here to his argument about the host on p. 70.

35. On Jeremias as a conservative theologian, see Lehmann, *Friedrich Delitzsch*, 44–45.

36. Claude Lévi-Strauss, *Mythologiques*, 4 vols. (Paris: Plon, 1964). The four volumes of *Mythologiques* have been translated into English as *The Raw and the Cooked, Mythologiques 1* (New York: Harper and Row, 1975); *From Honey to Ashes, Mythologiques 2* (New York: Octagon Books, 1979); *The Origin of Table Manners, Mythologiques 3* (New York: Harper and Row, 1979); and *The Naked Man, Mythologiques 4* (New York: Harper and Row, 1981). On Lévi-Strauss, see "The Significance of Contradictions in Mythic Thought" in chapter 4 of this volume.

37. Unless otherwise noted, all direct quotes in this paragraph are from Jeremias, "Gedachtnisrede," 7–8.

38. Alfred Jeremias and Hugo Winckler, eds., *Im Kampfe um den alten Orient: Wehr- und Streitschriften,* 4 vols. (Leipzig: Hinrichs, 1907–14). One of the most noteworthy volumes in the series is the first: Jeremias's *Die Panbabylonisten: Der alte Orient und die aegyptische Religion* (1907). On the series itself, see Johanning, *Der Bibel-Babel-Streit,* 270. For a critique of one of the volumes in the series by a vehement opponent of the Panbabylonians and a brief reply by Jeremias, see Franz Xavier Kügler, "Auf den Trümmern des Panbabylonismus," *Anthropos* 4 (1909): 477–99; and Alfred Jeremias, "Vorläufige Antwort auf P. F. X. Kuglers Aufsatz 'Auf den Trümmern des Panbabylonismus,' " *Anthropos* 4 (1909): 823.

39. The Society was renamed the Vorderasiatisch-Aegyptische Gesellschaft in 1921: Johannes Renger, "Die Geschichte der Altorientalistik und der vorderasiatischen Archäologie in Berlin von 1875–1945," in *Berlin und die Antike: Architektur, Kunstgewerbe, Malerei, Skulptur, Theater und Wissenschaft vom 16. Jahrhundert bis Heute [Ausstellung],* ed. Willmuth Arenhövel and Christa Schreiber (Berlin: Deutsches Archäologisches Institut, 1979), 151–92, see esp. 162.

40. The *Mitteilungen der Vorderasiatisch-Aegyptischen Gesellschaft (MVAG)* constituted an important serial that lasted for 46 volumes; *Der alte Orient* lasted for 45 volumes; *Orientalistische Literaturzeitung (OLZ)* continues today, a bimonthly since 1976.

41. Alfred Jeremias, *Allgemeine Religions-Geschichte* (München: R. Pieper, 1918); in a prefatory comment, Jeremias notes that the work had sat completed with a publisher since before World War I. The work is discussed in Baumgartner, "Nachruf Alfred Jeremias," 300.

42. See Ernst F. Weidner, "Nachruf Alfred Jeremias," *Der Alte Orient* 6 (1935): 196.

43. Peter Jensen, "Kritik von Winckler's Himmels- und Weltenbild als Grundlage der Weltanschauung und Mythologie aller Völker," *Berliner Philologische Wochenschrift* 24, no. 8 (1904): 247–48.

44. Peter Jensen, *Das Gilgamesch-Epos in der Weltliteratur I: Die Ursprünge der alttestementlichen Patriarchen-, Propheten-, und Befreier-Sage und der neutestamentlichen Jesus-Sage* (Strassburg: Verlag von Karl J. Trübner, 1906), 1029; cited in Johanning, *Der Bibel-Babel-Streit,* 268.

45. See J. Z. Smith, who seems to be using the term in the wider "Babylonianist" sense in *To Take Place,* 15–16.

46. See Jeremias, *Handbuch,* 1st ed., 7n2, where Jeremias objects to Jensen's being termed a Panbabylonian: "this view is completely different from Jensen's," who is taken as an "opponent." But Jeremias is also ready to accommodate his friends, explicitly responding to Stucken's hypothesis of the South Sea origins of culture by suggesting the possible source there for the Sumerians. See Alfred Jeremias, *Handbuch der altorientalischen Geisteskultur,* 2d ed. (Berlin: W. de Gruyter, 1929), 4n1.

47. For the contributions of some other scholars, see the discussion in Lehmann, *Friedrich Delitzsch,* 38–49.

48. Jensen wrote in a weekly early in April 1904; Peiser responded in his monthly the same month: *Orientalistische Literaturzeitung* 7, no. 4 (1904): 142–45.

49. Jeremias was appointed ausserordentlicher Professor (associate professor) in Leipzig in 1922 (Baumgartner, "Nachruf Alfred Jeremias," 299); he had earlier lectured there as Privatdozent—an unsalaried instructor dependent on private tuitions.

50. See Lehmann's discussion in *Friedrich Delitzsch*, 39–40.

51. For interesting examples of writing from this esoteric perspective, see Frithjof Schuon, *The Transcendent Unity of Religions*, rev. ed. (New York: Harper and Row, 1975); and Seyyed Hossein Nasr, *Knowledge and the Sacred* (Albany: State University of New York Press, 1989). Schuon is an independent philosopher/sage, but Nasr is an established academic. For an analytic account of these writers, see William W. Quinn, *The Only Tradition* (Albany: State University of New York Press, 1997). For the role of this perspective in influencing modern history of religions, see Richard King, *Orientalism and Religion: Postcolonial Theory, India, and "the Mystic East"* (London: Routledge, 1999), 162–69; and Steven M. Wasserstrom, *Religion after Religion: Gershom Scholem, Mircea Eliade, and Henry Corbin at Eranos* (Princeton, N.J.: Princeton University Press, 1999).

52. Jeremias seems to have been more careful about his historical claims than Winckler. In his *Handbuch*, 1st ed., 7, he affirms that he "knows nothing of a primal time *(Urzeit)*" but only that "in a time prehistoric for us important elements of that 'Babylonian' spiritual culture wandered through the world." If that culture in fact originated somewhere else, "only the name Panbabylonian thesis would be lost, not its truth." Referred to in Lehmann, *Friedrich Delitzsch*, 44.

53. Jeremias, *Handbuch*, 2d ed., x.

54. C. M. Edsman, e.g., writing in 1959, notes that the English Myth and Ritual School (as well as its kindred scholars in Scandinavia) "had many points of contact with the Panbabylonians," even though they rarely made reference to them: see Carl-Martin Edsman, "Zum sakralen Königtum in der Forschung der letzten hundert Jahre," in *The Sacral Kingship: Contributions to the Central Theme of the VIIIth International Congress for the History of Religions (Rome, April 1955) [Alternative Italian Title: La Regalità Sacra]* (Leiden: E. J. Brill, 1959), 9. On the Myth and Ritualists, see chap. 11 below.

55. For a brief definition of the term by Elliot Smith, see his "On the Significance of the Geographical Distribution of the Practice of Mummification—a Study of the Migration of Peoples and the Spread of Certain Customs and Beliefs," *Memoirs and Proceedings of the Manchester Literary and Philosophical Society* 59, no. 9 (1915): 37.

56. Grafton Elliot Smith, *The Ancient Egyptians and Their Influence upon the Civilization of Europe* (London: Harper, 1911); reprinted as *The Ancient Egyptians and the Origin of Civilization* (London: Harper, 1923).

57. Lord Solly Zuckerman, ed., *The Concepts of Human Evolution* (London: Academic Press, 1973), 4; Misia Landau, *Narratives of Human Evolution* (New Haven, Conn.: Yale University Press, 1991) devotes chap. 5 to Elliot Smith's work.

58. Glyn Daniel, "Grafton Elliot Smith: Egypt and Diffusionism," in Zuckerman, *Concepts of Human Evolution*, 405–46, see esp. 411–12.

59. This narrative is abbreviated from Grafton Elliot Smith, *Human History* (New York: Norton, 1929), esp. 5–16, 292–303. Another long version of the heliolithic narrative is W. J. Perry, *The Children of the Sun: A Study in the Early History of Civilization*, 2d ed. (London: Methuen, 1927). For a positive contemporary assessment of Smith's work on cultural diffusion, see A. P. Elkin, "Elliot Smith and Diffusion of Culture," in *Grafton Elliot Smith: The Man and His Work*, ed. A. P. Elkin and N. W. G. Macintosh (Sydney: Sydney University Press, 1974), 139–59. For a pithy caricature of the position, see Daniel, "Egypt and Diffusionism," 413.

60. "The nucleus of the 'heliolithic' culture-complex—mummification, megalithic architecture, and the making of idols [were] three practices most intimately and genetically linked one with the other. But it was the merest accident that the people amongst whom these customs developed should also have been weavers of linen, workers in copper, worshipers of the sun and serpent, and practitioners of massage and circumcision" (G. E. Smith, "Practice of Mummification," 37).

61. G. E. Smith, *Human History*, 292.

62. Ibid., xiv. For Landau's discussion of Smith's hunch that civilization began with an early "anatomical genius," see her *Narratives of Human Evolution*, 136–37.

63. The most important of these publications are *Ancient Egyptians;* "Practice of Mummification"; and *The Evolution of the Dragon* (Manchester, U.K.: Manchester University Press, 1919). For a discussion by Elliot Smith of his writings as responses to critics, see *Evolution of the Dragon*, v.

64. G. E. Smith, *Human History*, 338.

65. G. E. Smith, "Practice of Mummification." See the discussion of the events in Elkin, "Elliot Smith and Diffusion of Culture," 142–43.

66. A. P. Elkin, "Sir Grafton Elliot Smith: The Man and His Work," in *Grafton Elliot Smith: The Man and His Work*, ed. A. P. Elkin and N. W. G. Macintosh (Sydney: Sydney University Press, 1974), 10.

67. Adam Kuper, *The Invention of Primitive Society* (London: Routledge, 1988), 153.

68. Introduction to W. H. R. Rivers, *Psychology and Politics, and Other Essays* (London: K. Paul, 1923), xi.

69. Ibid., xiii.

70. W. H. R. Rivers, *The Todas* (London: Macmillan, 1906), 7.

71. See discussion in George W. Stocking, *After Tylor: British Social Anthropology, 1888–1951* (Madison: University of Wisconsin Press, 1995), 189. Rivers, e.g., frequently received his information through intermediaries who were not native to the culture being studied and not highly conversant with the language. Rivers seems to have spent "several months" among the Todas, nowhere being explicit as to the length of his stay. See Richard Slobodin, *W. H. R. Rivers* (New York: Columbia University Press, 1978), 28n14.

72. Rivers, *The Todas*, 10–11.

73. Rivers's *The History of Melanesian Society* (Cambridge: The University

Press, 1914), e.g., comprises two volumes—one of which presents the data, the other an analysis.

74. Quoted in Kuper, *Invention of Primitive Society,* 153.

75. W. H. R. Rivers, *Psychology and Ethnology,* ed. G. Elliot Smith (1915; reprint, London: K. Paul, 1926), 167.

76. Rivers, *The Todas,* 717.

77. The address was published as "The Ethnological Analysis of Culture," in Rivers's *Psychology and Ethnology,* 120–40.

78. Robert H. Lowie, "Review of *The History of Melanesian Society,"* *American Anthropologist,* n.s., 17 (1915): 589. The British anthropologist A. M. Hocart, on the other hand, suggests in his review in *Man,* 1915, pp. 89–93, that the book would have been better had Rivers been a "whole-hogger" (92) as a historical ethnologist, not compromising with evolutionists. Both reviewers admire Rivers's compilation of facts in volume 1.

79. Rivers, "Distribution of Megalithic Civilization," 169.

80. Ibid., 170–71.

81. See, e.g., W. H. R. Rivers, *Conflict and Dream* (New York: Harcourt, Brace, 1923).

82. *Sherston's Progress,* published in Siegfried Sassoon's *The Memoirs of George Sherston* (New York: Literary Guild of America, 1937).

83. Quoted in Slobodin, *W. H. R. Rivers,* 58.

84. For Elliot Smith's early presentation in terms of racial ideas, see his *Ancient Egyptians;* for some (relatively) contemporary comments on them, see Edmund Leach's remarks on pp. 432–36 of the discussions appended to Daniel, "Egypt and Diffusionism," 405–46.

85. W. J. Perry, "The Relationship between the Geographical Distribution of Megalithic Monuments and Ancient Mines," *Memoirs and Proceedings of the Manchester Literary and Philosophical Society* 60 (1915): 1–28.

86. See Grafton Elliot Smith, "Remarks on Mr. W. H. Perry's Communication," *Memoirs and Proceedings of the Manchester Literary and Philosophical Society* 60 (1915): 29–36.

87. Perry, "Megalithic Monuments," 1.

88. W. J. Perry, *The Megalithic Culture of Indonesia* (Manchester, U.K.: Manchester University Press, 1918).

89. Perry, *Children of the Sun,* 4.

90. Perry, *Megalithic Culture of Indonesia,* 9.

91. Robert H. Lowie, in his review (*American Anthropologist,* n.s., 26 [1924]: 86–90), is very harsh, commenting that *The Children of the Sun* reveals its author's "unfamiliarity with both ethnological theory and ethnographic fact" (90); Alfred Haddon is also caustic, in remarks quoted in Stocking, *After Tylor,* 218. But the prehistorian V. Gordon Childe, reviewing two of Perry's later works, is more enthusiastic: "Everyone will welcome the restatement in a popular form of the startling results obtained by the same author in 'The Children of the Sun' " (27). Childe does, however, give more than the usual qualifications: "the synthesis would be more convincing if the facts on which Mr. Perry relies had been more carefully verified, if the unifying principles had been applied in a more scientific manner, and if the omissions had been less one-sided" (27–28). See his re-

view of Perry's *The Origin of Magic and Religion* and *The Growth of Civiliza-tion* in *Man* (Feb. 1925): 27–29.

92. Stocking, *After Tylor*, 215.

93. John Wilfrid Jackson, *Shells as Evidence of the Migrations of Early Cul-ture* (Manchester, U.K.: Manchester University Press, 1917).

94. Warren R. Dawson, ed., *Sir Grafton Elliot Smith: A Biographical Record by His Colleagues* (London: J. Cape, 1938). Dawson's *The Custom of Couvade* (Manchester, U.K.: Manchester University Press, 1929) is a compendium of sources on couvade without much analysis. Not a particularly heliolithic work (by 1929 these were not much published), it was dedicated to Elliot Smith "in friendship."

95. Stocking, *After Tylor*, 214.

96. See Rivers, *Psychology and Ethnology*; and Rivers, *Psychology and Pol-itics*.

97. Elkin, "Sir Grafton Elliot Smith: The Man and his Work," 11.

98. Daniel, "Egypt and Diffusionism," 419.

99. Wilhelm Schmidt, *Der Ursprung der Gottesidee: Eine historisch-kritische und positive Studie*, 2d ed., 12 vols. (Münster i W.: Aschendorff, 1926–55).

100. Now within Dortmund, Northwest Germany.

101. Ernest Brandewie, *When Giants Walked the Earth: The Life and Times of Wilhelm Schmidt, SVD* (Fribourg: University Press, 1990), 21. For a long ac-count of Schmidt's order—in Latin the Societas Verbi Divini (SVD)—see Fritz Bornemann, *A History of Our Society*, trans. Dermot Walsh (Rome: Apud Col-legium Verbi Divini, 1981).

102. Joseph Henninger, "P. Wilhelm Schmidt S. V. D. (1868–1954): Eine bi-ographische Skizze," *Anthropos* 51 (1956): 26.

103. Letter quoted at length in Brandewie, *When Giants Walked the Earth*, 36–37.

104. Bornemann, *History of Our Society*, 158; Fritz Bornemann, *Arnold Janssen: Founder of Three Missionary Congregations, 1837–1909* (Manila: Arnoldus Press, 1975), 364–65.

105. Schmidt had published a shorter draft of volume 1, dealing with theo-ries of religion, in *Anthropos*, in 1908–9: "L'Origine de l'Idée de Dieu," issued in eight installments. It was published in French to reach a larger missionary au-dience.

106. Wilhelm Schmidt, *Primitive Revelation*, trans. Joseph J. Baierl (St. Louis, Mo.: B. Herder, 1939), 291–92.

107. Brandewie, *When Giants Walked the Earth*, 55, quoting Wilhelm Schmidt, *Der Ursprung der Gottesidee*, 3:5–6, and Schmidt's unpublished mem-oirs.

108. Schmidt, "Invitation," 14–16; reprinted in Karl Josef Rivinius, Wilhelm Schmidt, and Georg Hertling, *Die Anfänge des "Anthropos": Briefe von P. Wil-helm Schmidt an Georg Freiherrn von Hertling aus den Jahren 1904 bis 1908 und andere Dokumente* (St. Augustin: Steyler, 1981), 190–92.

109. Rivinius, Schmidt, and Hertling, *Anfänge des "Anthropos,"* 23, 10–11; Rudolph Rahmann, "Fünfzig Jahre Anthropos," *Anthropos* 51 (1956): 112; Bornemann, *Janssen*, 14–35; citation from Ernest Brandewie, *Wilhelm Schmidt*

and the Origin of the Idea of God (Lanham, Md.: University Press of America, 1983), 40, where Brandewie gives an interesting account of Schmidt in the face of the modernist crisis. On the modernist crisis itself, see Lester R. Kurtz, *The Politics of Heresy: The Modernist Crisis in Roman Catholicism* (Berkeley: University of California Press, 1986); and David G. Schultenover, *A View from Rome: On the Eve of the Modernist Crisis* (New York: Fordham University Press, 1993). Rivinius discusses the Görres Society and its relationship to modernism, *Anfänge des "Anthropos,"* 20–40. Some implications of the modernist crisis also seem pertinent to the origin of contemporary religious studies: Alfred Loisy, seen as the most dangerous of the modernists, had been teaching at the College de France when he was excommunicated in 1907; he then took up the chair of History of Religions!

110. Lang's descriptive account begins with the Fuegians (Lang, *Making of Religion,* 187–88), an ethnologically early people studied by Schmidt's disciples Martin Gusinde and Wilhelm Koppers (see below).

111. Graebner discusses culture circles in his *Methode der Ethnologie* (Heidelberg: Carl Winter's Universitätsbuchhandlung, 1911), 151. For a tabular view of Schmidt's system of culture circles, see "Das System der Kulturkreise," in his *Wege der Kulturen: Gesammelte Aufsätze* (St. Augustin bei Bonn: Verlag des Anthropos-Instituts, 1964), 3–11. On "like us," see Jonathan Z. Smith, "Adde Parvum Parvo Magnum Acervus Erit," in his *Map Is Not Territory* (Leiden: Brill, 1978), 240–64.

112. See Schmidt's conclusion to book 6 of his *Der Ursprung der Gottesidee,* 491–508; the demonstration there is condensed and translated in Brandewie, *Origin of the Idea of God,* 280–88. See also Brandewie's comments on Schmidt's apologetics, *Origin of the Idea of God,* 24–31.

113. See A. L. Kroeber, *Cultural and Natural Areas of Native North America* (Berkeley: University of California Press, 1939).

114. Brandewie, *Origin of the Idea of God,* 89–105, 18–19; *When Giants Walked the Earth,* 111.

115. Wilhelm Schmidt, "Die psychologische Ausdeutung des Gottesbildes der Urzeit" (1923), in *Wege der Kulturen,* 133–36; and Schmidt, *Der Ursprung der Gottesidee,* 487–91. Mircea Eliade, commenting on the primacy of causal thinking in Schmidt's understanding of the psychology of religion, suggested during a seminar in the early 1980s that Schmidt, who said mass every morning, didn't understand his own religion. A clear presentation of a Thomistic world has been given by Thomas F. O'Meara, *Thomas Aquinas, Theologian* (Notre Dame: University of Notre Dame Press, 1997); on pp. 167–73, O'Meara gives an interesting critique of the later neoscholasticism in which Schmidt was schooled.

116. See Elliot Smith's *Human History,* xii. Meyer Fortes sees in Smith's diffusionism a commitment to "a monogenetic Darwinian type of biological evolutionism . . . and a habit of mind which prompts one always to seek explanations for contemporary states of affairs in terms . . . of remote and ultimate origins" (Daniel, "Egypt and Diffusionism," 428–29).

117. Robert H. Lowie, *The History of Ethnological Theory* (New York: Farrar and Rinehart, 1937), 191–92; for Lowie's tepid assessment of Rivers, see his remarks on p. 165; on his sharp criticism of Perry, see note 91 above.

118. For sympathetic critiques of Schmidt's science, see Brandewie, *Origin of the Idea of God,* 78–83; and *When Giants Walked the Earth,* 122–24, where he gives a long citation from Bornemann. For a critique of Schmidt's system as a formalism, see Karin R. Andriolo, "*Kulturkreislehre* and the Austrian Mind," *Man* 14 (1979): 133–44.

119. Brandewie, *Origin of the Idea of God,* 21.

120. Quoted in Rahmann, "Fünfzig Jahre Anthropos," 5. Along with information on the early years of *Anthropos,* Rahmann presents international contributors and endorsements on pp. 4–5, lists the volumes of the *Anthropos* library series on pp. 11–12, and gives one and a half pages of notes of articles from *Anthropos* devoted to ethnologically early cultures, published between 1920 and 1940 on pp. 8–10.

121. Schmidt gave some reasons for the formalization in "Die Errichtung des 'Anthropos Institutes,' " *Anthropos* 27 (1932): 275–77.

122. See Brandewie, *When Giants Walked the Earth,* 143–63; Fritz Bornemann, *P. Wilhelm Schmidt S. V. D., 1868–1954* (Rome: Apud Collegium Verbi Divini, 1982), 109–29. On the Vienna of the period, see William M. Johnston, *The Austrian Mind: An Intellectual and Social History, 1848–1938* (Berkeley: University of California Press, 1972).

123. Schmidt's anti-Semitism and his role during the first month of Nazi Austria have been discussed at length by the more recent scholars concerned with him. Brandewie, although admitting Schmidt's antipathy toward some groups of Jews, gives him the benefit of the doubt. Schmidt, he thinks, saw Jews as threatening traditional ideals of community through their liberal thought and capitalistic enterprise; this made him an economic and political anti-Semite but not a racial one. At the same time, Brandewie points to the convergence of Schmidt's views and Nazi doctrine in certain areas, especially pan-Germanism and certain areas of family policy (Schmidt had earlier founded the Family Welfare League, which promoted procreation and aid to poor families). Bornemann, whose writing may reflect some lasting animus toward Schmidt (he played a major role during Schmidt's difficult last years at Froideville), emphasizes the racial implications of some of Schmidt's statements about the Jews during the 1930s: after almost two thousand years the religious defects of the Jews have had a real, but secondary, effect on their physical race; converted Jews can belong to our church, Schmidt once said, but not to our people (paraphrased from Bornemann, *Schmidt,* 279–80, who quotes some 1934 remarks by Schmidt; these are also given and discussed by Edouard Conte, "Wilhelm Schmidt: Des letzten Kaisers Beichvater und das 'neudeutsche Heidentum,' " in *Volkskunde und Nationalsozialismus: Referate und Diskussionen einer Tagung der Deutschen Gesellschaft für Volkskunde,* ed. Helge Gerndt [München: Münchner Vereinigung für Volkskunde, 1987], 269). Bornemann also gives importance to the fact that even though Schmidt depicts the Nazi rule and the concentration camps in the edition of his book on race published (with an altered title) after the war, he is silent about the extermination of the Jews (Bornemann, *Schmidt,* 269). In fact, Schmidt does give a lengthy description of the persecution of a Jewish woman, but she had converted to Protes-

tantism, and he emphasizes the aid given her by Christian opponents of Nazism: *Rassen und Völker: In Vorgeschichte und Geschichte des Abendlandes,* 3d ed. (Luzern: Verlag Josef Stocker, 1949), 3:98–112. Conte points out that together with his Christian view of a single humanity, Schmidt also sees a hierarchical relationship among peoples ("Wilhelm Schmidt," 262) and is capable of an unrepentant religious vilification of the Jews that sounds almost medieval (267); he also notes that Schmidt's ethnologically slanted view of salvation history, highlighting "primitive revelation," implicitly minimizes the role of Israel (272–73).

124. See Schmidt, *Primitive Revelation,* esp. 265–73, which includes headings entitled "The Unity of the Human Race" and "Unity as to Bodily Origin."

125. Wilhelm Schmidt, *Rasse und Volk: Ihre allgemeine Bedeutung; Ihre Geltung in Deutschen Raum,* 2d ed. (Salzburg: Verlag Anton Pustet, 1935), 9–10. Brandewie, *When Giants Walked the Earth,* 239, 245; Bornemann, *Schmidt,* 332.

126. Schmidt, *Rasse und Volk,* 2d ed., 129; see also discussions in Bornemann, *Schmidt,* 279; and Edouard Conte, "Wilhelm Schmidt," 270. On Nazi religious policy and some possible ways in which scholars of religion might respond to it, see Gregory D. Alles, "The Science of Religions in a Fascist State: Rudolf Otto and Jakob Wilhelm Hauer during the Third Reich," *Religion* 32: 3 (2002), 177–204.

127. Brandewie, *When Giants Walked the Earth,* 214–15; Bornemann, *Schmidt,* 276–77.

128. Brandewie, *When Giants Walked the Earth,* 272; Bornemann, *Schmidt,* 289.

129. Bornemann, *Schmidt,* 56–58; Brandewie, *When Giants Walked the Earth,* 31, notes that "[o]bedience was the vow that gave him problems"; on pp. 60–62, he emphasizes the direct communication between Schmidt and Janssen, the Society's superior general, in the founding of *Anthropos.*

130. Joseph S. V. D. Henninger, "P. Wilhelm Koppers S. V. D.: Biographische Skizze und Würdigung seines wissenschaftlichen Lebenswerkes," *Mitteilungen der Anthropologischen Gesellschaft in Wien* 91 (1961): 9.

131. Ibid., 9, 2. See Wilhelm Koppers, "Grundsätzliches und Geschichtliches zur Ethnologischen Kulturkreislehre," in *Beiträge Österreichs zur Erforschung der Vergangenheit und Kulturgeschichte der Menschheit,* ed. Emil Britinger, Josef Haekel, and Richard Pettoni (Horn, Niederösterreich: Ferdinand Berger, 1959), 119. For a work in English by Koppers on his specialty, see Wilhelm Koppers, "The Oldest Forms of the State," in *Essays in Ethnology,* ed. John Vincent Ferreira, Stephen Fuchs, and Klaus K. Klostermaier (Bombay: New Literature, 1969), 340–59.

132. Koppers, "Grundsätzliches und Geschichtliches," 120, 121. Bornemann, *Schmidt,* 338–40; Arnold Burgmann, "Professor Dr. Wilhelm Koppers SVD," *Anthropos,* no. 56 (1961): 725. Koppers's remarks critical of Schmidt's theories can be found in Sol Tax, ed., *An Appraisal of Anthropology Today* (Chicago: University of Chicago Press, 1953), 79. The manuscript of Schmidt's new, exclusively authored edition of *Völker und Kulturen* was never published. For details on the manuscript, see Fritz Bornemann, "P. W. Schmidt's Vorar-

beiten für eine Neuauflage von 'Völker und Kulturen,' " *Anthropos* 51 (1956): 291–308.

133. For a short description of the development of the new Vienna school, see Burgmann, "Koppers," 726–27; for a longer description, see Sergej A. Tokarev, "Zum heutigen Stand der Wiener Schule der Völkerkunde," *Ethnogaphisch-Archäologische Zeitschrift* 1 (1960): 107–23. Robert Heine Geldern gives a brief perspective of the situation in English in his "Recent Developments in Ethnological Theory in Europe," in *Men and Cultures: Selected Papers of the Fifth International Congress of Anthropological and Ethnological Sciences,* ed. Anthony F. C. Wallace (Philadelphia: University of Pennsylvania Press, 1957), 49–53. There he declares about the end of the *Kulturkreislehre*: "It will suffice to say that the final blow came from archaeology" (49). Koppers's work on the Bhils is also available in English: Wilhelm Koppers and Leonard J. Jungblut, *Bowmen of Mid-India: A Monography of the Bhils of Jhabua [M. P.] and Adjoining Territories* (Wien: Elisabeth Stiglmayr, 1976).

134. Josef Haekel, "Zum heutigen Forschungsstand der historischen Ethnologie," in *Die Wiener Schule der Völkerkunde: Festschrift anlässlich des 25-jährigen Bestandes des Institutes für Völkerkunde der Universität Wien (1929–1954),* ed. J. Haekel, A. Hoenwart-Gerlachstein, and A. Slawik (Horn-Wien: Verlag Ferdinand Berger, 1956), 24, 20. Some of the most valuable more recent sources in English from Vienna historical ethnology have come from India, where Stephen Fuchs, SVD, settled before World War II, founding a branch of the Anthropos Institute in Bombay (later the Indian Institute of Culture). A student of Schmidt, and detached from later European developments, he seems to have valued the older Vienna thinking. Writing in 1983 for his seventy-fifth birthday *Festschrift*, he acknowledges the strengths of Haekel's article but thinks that he "underrates the strong conservatism of primitive man": Stephen Fuchs, Mahipala Bhuriya, and S. M. Michael, *Anthropology as a Historical Science: Essays in Honour of Stephen Fuchs* (Indore: Sat Prakashan Sanchar Kendra, 1984), 8. In 1969, a useful collection of translated extracts from Koppers's generation of Vienna ethnologists was published in Bombay: Ferreira, Fuchs, and Klostermaier, *Essays in Ethnology.*

135. Henninger, "Koppers," 4–5.

136. Mario Orellana Rodríguez sees Gusinde as one of the four great early anthropologists of Chile. See "La personalidad científica de Martin Gusinde," in Martin Gusinde and Mario Orellana Rodríguez, *Expedición a La Tierra Del Fuego, Imagen De Chile* (Santiago de Chile: Editorial Universitaria, 1980), 9. Gusinde's folklore collections remain valuable, with translations into English made as late as the mid-1970s.

137. The species he discovered, a Myrceugenia, he named "Johow-Gusinde," after a Santiago scientist and himself. See Fritz Bornemann, "P. Martin Gusinde S. V. D. (1886–1969): Eine biographische Skizze," *Anthropos* 65 (1970): 739.

138. Ibid., 743, 745.

139. Ibid., 744, 746–47.

140. Ibid., 747–48.

141. Ibid., 748–49. Bornemann, who lived in close quarters with Schmidt at Froideville for several years, gives no source for this quote.

142. Anton Vorbichler, "Professor Dr. Paul Schebesta, SVD," *Anthropos* 62 (1967): 668–69; Bornemann, "Gusinde," 753. Schebesta gives a short review of his research through the mid-1950s in "Die Pygmäenfrage," *Forschungen und Fortschritten* 30, no. 6 (1956): 161–63.

143. Paul Schebesta and Gerald Griffin, *My Pygmy and Negro Hosts* (London: Hutchinson, 1936); the original German title seems less benign: *Vollblutneger und Halbzwerge* (Full-blooded Negroes and little Pygmies). See also Paul Schebesta, *Among the Forest Dwarfs of Malaya* (Kuala Lumpur: Oxford University Press, 1973).

144. Bornemann, *Schmidt,* 300; Colin Turnbull, "Father Schebesta's Work among the Bambuti-Pygmies," in *Festschrift Paul Schebesta zum 75. Geburtstag, gewidmet von Mitbrüdern, Freunden und Schülern,* ed. Anton Vorbichler and Wilhelm Dupre (Wien: St. Gabriel-Verlag, 1963), 1–5. For Schebesta's academic differences with Schmidt, see Vorbichler, "Schebesta," 668.

145. On Schmidt's 1935 trip, see Bornemann, *Schmidt,* 230–38.

146. Rahmann, "Vier Pioniere," 263; Bornemann, "Gusinde," 738; Schmidt, "Die Errichtung des 'Anthropos Institutes,' " 276–77.

147. Bornemann, *Schmidt,* 325–31; Brandewie, *When Giants Walked the Earth,* 281–332. One of the major actors in Schmidt's final bitter days was Fritz Bornemann, then editor of *Anthropos* and director of the Anthropos Institute at Fribourg. Later to become the historian of the Society, he has written much of the source material used here. Most of Bornemann's work seems either evenhanded or, on occasion, eulogistic, but much of his treatment of Schmidt, particularly in his last years, is ironic, to say the least. On Bornemann's relationship with Schmidt, see Brandewie, *When Giants Walked the Earth,* 297–303.

CHAPTER 10. INTERPRETING TOGETHER

1. On the cultural and institutional background of English classical studies during the Ritualists' day, see Christopher Stray, *Classics Transformed: Schools, Universities, and Society in England, 1830–1960* (Oxford, U.K.: Clarendon Press, 1998).

2. The most important researcher has been Robert Ackerman, who has written an insightful survey: *Myth and Ritual School: J. G. Frazer and the Cambridge Ritualists* (New York: Garland, 1991). Papers from a conference on the Ritualists held at the University of Illinois in 1989 have been published as *The Cambridge Ritualists Reconsidered,* ed. William M. Calder III (Atlanta, Ga.: Scholars Press, 1991). More recent works include Annabel Robinson, "A New Light Our Elders Had Not Seen: Deconstructing the 'Cambridge Ritualists,' " *Echos du Monde Classique* 42 [n.s. 17] (1998): 471–87; and Mary Beard, *The Invention of Jane Harrison* (Cambridge, Mass.: Harvard University Press, 2000). For a long and generally favorable review article on Beard by Ackerman, see his "Jane Ellen Harrison: By Myth Begotten," *Religion* 31 (2001): 67–74. For a reader that places the Ritualists in their twentieth-century intellectual contexts, see Robert Alan Segal, ed., *The Myth and Ritual Theory: An Anthology* (Malden, Mass.: Blackwell, 1998). A 414-page bibliography of works by and about the Ritualists has been prepared by Shelley Arlen, *The Cambridge Ritualists: An An-*

notated *Bibliography of the Works by and about Jane Ellen Harrison, Gilbert Murray, Francis M. Cornford, and Arthur Bernard Cook* (Metuchen, N.J.: Scarecrow Press, 1990).

3. Robert Ackerman, "The Cambridge Group: Origins and Composition," in Calder, *Cambridge Ritualists Reconsidered*, 3.

4. See Stephen Toulmin, *Human Understanding: The Collective Use and Evolution of Concepts* (Princeton, N.J.: Princeton University Press, 1972), 378–95.

5. These include Harrison's *Prolegomena* and *Themis;* Murray's *The Rise of the Greek Epic: Being a Course of Lectures Delivered at Harvard University* (Oxford, U.K.: Clarendon Press, 1907) and *Five Stages of Greek Religion,* 3d ed. (New York: Doubleday, 1955 [1st ed. 1912, as *Four Stages of . . .*]); and Cornford's *Thucydides Mythistoricus* (London: E. Arnold, 1907) and *From Religion to Philosophy; A Study in the Origins of Western Speculation* (1912; reprint, New York: Harper and Row, 1957).

6. Gilbert Murray, *Jane Ellen Harrison: An Address Delivered at Newnham College, October 27th, 1928* (Cambridge: W. Heffer and Sons, 1928; reprinted in Harrison, *Epilegomena* [1962], 560–61).

7. When Harrison's fellowship expired in 1903, she remained at Newnham as a lecturer, receiving room and board for light duties. This was economically feasible since she had a modest independent income (Sandra J. Peacock, *Jane Ellen Harrison: The Mask and the Self* [New Haven, Conn.: Yale University Press, 1988], 91).

8. William M. Calder III, "Jane Harrison's Failed Candidacies for the Yates Professorship (1888–1896): What Did Her Colleagues Think of Her?" in Calder, *Cambridge Ritualists Reconsidered,* 56.

9. Beard, *Invention of Jane Harrison,* 86; see Gladys Scott Thomson, *Mrs. Arthur Strong: A Memoir* (London: Cohen and West, 1949), 24–25.

10. Murray, *Jane Harrison,* 575.

11. Ibid., 576.

12. Peacock, *The Mask and the Self,* 97–98.

13. Cornford remembers the bull-roarer in his biographical note on Harrison for the *Dictionary of National Biography, supp. 4 (1922–30),* 408–9; Beard describes the slides in *Invention of Jane Harrison,* 55.

14. Harrison also shared rooms for many of her seventeen years in London with someone named "Get" Wilson, a working woman with a good sense of humor with whom she did not seem to have an intellectual relationship. There is no particular reason to think this was anything more than a convenient living arrangement, however. See Peacock, *The Mask and the Self,* 64.

15. On the relationship between Harrison and Sellers in London and the meaning of "G. A.," see Beard, *Invention of Jane Harrison,* 81–87.

16. See ibid., 87, for Mirrlees's description; and Thomson, *Mrs. Arthur Strong,* 24–25, who writes: "There followed a friendship, with intense admiration on one [that is, Sellers's] side, and then disaster."

17. Hope Mirrlees, *Madeleine: One of Love's Jansenists* (London: Collins, 1919). On Mirrlees as a personality in her own right, see Beard, *Invention of Jane Harrison,* 138–41.

18. Tina Passman, "Out of the Closet and into the Field: Matriculture, the

Lesbian Perspective, and Feminist Classics," in *Feminist Theory and the Classics,* ed. Nancy Sorkin Rabinowitz and Amy Richlin (New York: Routledge, 1993), 181. On the sexual contradictions of scholars of mystical traditions, with particular reference to homosexuality, see Jeffrey John Kripal, *Roads of Excess, Palaces of Wisdom: Eroticism and Reflexivity in the Study of Mysticism* (Chicago: University of Chicago Press, 2001).

19. Hugh Lloyd-Jones, "Jane Harrison, 1850–1928," in *Cambridge Women: Twelve Portraits,* ed. Edward Shils and Carmen Blacker (Cambridge, U.K.: Cambridge University Press, 1996), 49.

20. Mirrlees to Jessie Stewart, quoted in Peacock, *Mask and the Self,* 247.

21. D. S. Mirsky, "Jane Ellen Harrison and Russia," *Jane Harrison Memorial Lecture* 2 (Cambridge: W. Heffer and Sons, 1930), 7.

22. Patricia E. Easterling, in a recent assessment, sees Murray's interest in Euripides as intersecting with his larger concerns for social issues as well as poetry: "Gilbert Murray's Reading of Euripides," *Colby Quarterly* 33, no. 2 (1997): 113–27. These concerns are visible in his *Carlyon Sahib* (London: W. Heinemann, 1900), about a personally powerful but morally flawed officer from British India. Although produced, it was too dark for a successful run. Sybil Thorndyke remembers Murray's theatrical life in "The Theatre and Gilbert Murray," in *An Unfinished Autobiography—with Contributions by His Friends,* ed. Jean Smith and Arnold Toynbee (London: George Allen and Unwin, 1960), 149–75 (in collaboration with Lewis Casson).

23. Murray writes about his early life in his *Unfinished Autobiography,* which doesn't extend much beyond his marriage.

24. Dorothy Howard Eden Henley, *Rosalind Howard, Countess of Carlisle* (London: Hogarth, 1958), 80, 115–16.

25. Lloyd-Jones, "Harrison," 40. Dorothy Henley, Mary Murray's younger sister, wrote of her mother as possessing "An Eye like Mars, to threaten and command"—an observation with which Bertrand Russell, Lady Carlisle's nephew, agrees. See Henley, *Rosalind Howard,* 13. But Mary was a match for her mother. Henley describes a confrontation between the two: "Mary, always unafraid, always definite," had accused Lady Carlisle of being selfish. The latter denied the charge: "I don't think of *my* pleasure, but of other people's." "No," said Mary, "it's not that kind of selfishness; but you are an Egotist. You *must* do what *you* want to do *for* other people. It's your will, not theirs that must be done" (40). Murray himself, reflecting on his early relationship with Lady Carlisle, is more charitable: "People who knew Lady Carlisle in her later years only, when her masterful nature was exasperated by troubles and ill health, will scarcely understand the inspiration she brought into the lives of us eager young men" (*Unfinished Autobiography,* 100).

26. Henley, *Rosalind Howard,* 61.

27. Cusins calls himself a "collector of religions" twice: Bernard Shaw, *Major Barbara* (1913; reprint, Baltimore: Penguin, 1960), 92, 117 (page citations are to the reprint edition): "The fact is, I am sort of a collector of religions, and the curious thing is that I find I can believe them all" (92). On Murray's friends' use of the term to describe him, see Duncan Wilson, *Gilbert Murray, OM, 1866–1957* (Oxford, U.K.: Oxford University Press, 1987), 117.

28. See Wilson, *Gilbert Murray*, 112, who also quotes Murray's reaction to a performance of *Major Barbara* in a letter to his daughter Rosalind: "the caricature of me . . . is outrageously personal, but not a bit offensive or malicious."

29. Shaw, *Major Barbara*, 62, cited in Wilson, *Gilbert Murray*, 112. (Citations in this and the following paragraph are from this source.) Murray seems to have kept this sense of refinement throughout his life. A description of the older Murray is given by Virginia Woolf: "[T]he cleanliness of Gilbert was remarkable; a great nurse must rub him smooth with pumice stone every morning; he is so discreet, so sensitive, so low in tone & immaculate in taste that you hardly understand how he has the boldness to beget children" (Virginia Woolf, *The Diary of Virginia Woolf*, 5 vols., ed. Anne Olivier Bell [New York: Harcourt Brace Jovanovich, 1977], 1:210, quoted in Peacock, *The Mask and the Self*, 126).

30. E. R. Dodds, *Missing Persons: An Autobiography* (Oxford, U.K.: Clarendon Press, 1977), 29.

31. Peacock, *The Mask and the Self*, 139, sees the Murrays as a surrogate family for Harrison, whose general ambivalences about family life affected her attitude toward the Murray household.

32. Wilson, *Gilbert Murray*, 119.

33. See ibid., 144–45. Peacock, *The Mask and the Self*, 133–35, discusses the mutual jealousy between Harrison and Mary Murray.

34. Quoted in Wilson, *Gilbert Murray*, 120. Murray's reflections to his wife on the visit reveal another contrast between his character and Harrison's: "The Berensons were very interesting, and just as I was beginning to lose my temper with them (for their fatuous artisticness and intellectual foppery) Miss Harrison arrived and lost hers so instantly and violently that I felt perfectly serene again" (ibid., 102).

35. Ibid., 121.

36. Ibid., 142–43.

37. Peter Stansky and William Miller Abrahams, *Journey to the Frontier: Julian Bell and John Cornford: Their Lives and the 1930s* (London: Constable, 1966), 139.

38. Having become an assistant lecturer in 1902 and a lecturer in 1904, Cornford did not become Laurence Professor of Ancient Philosophy until 1931. He twice stood unsuccessfully for the Regius Professorship of Greek at Cambridge, losing the second time to his former student D. S. Robertson. See Douglas Kellogg Wood, "F. M. Cornford," in *Classical Scholarship: A Biographical Encyclopedia*, ed. Ward W. Briggs and William M. Calder III (New York: Garland, 1990), 31–32.

39. See Hugh Cornford, "Memoir," in *Selected Poems of Frances Cornford*, ed. Jane Dowson (London: Enitharmon Press, 1996), xxxi.

40. Kellogg Wood, "F. M. Cornford," 27–28.

41. Francis Macdonald Cornford, *Microcosmographia Academica* (Cambridge, U.K.: Bowes and Bowes, 1908). Reprinted several times, *Microcosmographia Academica* was published in 1994 with a sociohistorical introduction by Gordon Johnson—"University Politics: F. M. Cornford's Cambridge and His Advice to the Young Academic Politician" (Cambridge, U.K.: Cambridge University Press, 1994); quote in the text is from p. 99 of this reprint edition.

42. Johnson, "University Politics," 6.

43. Kellogg Wood, "F. M. Cornford," 24.

44. This passage is much quoted in the literature on Harrison. See, e.g., Jessie Stewart, *Jane Ellen Harrison: A Portrait from Letters* (London: Merlin Press, 1959), 20; Peacock, *The Mask and the Self*, 99; and Kellogg Wood, "F. M. Cornford," 24.

45. A. C. Benson, quoted in Helen Fowler, "Frances Cornford, 1886–1960," in Shils and Blacker, *Cambridge Women*, 140.

46. This is Frances Cornford's phrase, quoted in Peacock, *The Mask and the Self*, 151.

47. Quoted in ibid., 158.

48. Ibid., 153.

49. Stewart, *Portrait*, 109.

50. Peacock, *The Mask and the Self*, 158.

51. Stewart, *Portrait*, 110.

52. Frances would battle depression throughout her life (it seemed to run in her family on both sides). See Helen Fowler, "Frances Cornford," and the memoir of her youngest son, Hugh, in her *Selected Poems*. After Cornford's death Frances remembered her often silent husband in a poem called "The Scholar": "You often went to breathe a timeless air / And walk with those you loved, perhaps the most / You spoke to Plato. You were native there" (*Selected Poems*, 40). The Cornfords' son John was a brilliant young leftist in the 1930s, a poet and essayist who died in the Spanish Civil War (see John Cornford, *Understand the Weapon, Understand the Wound: Selected Writings of John Cornford, with Some Letters of Frances Cornford*, ed. Jonathan Galassi [Manchester: Carcanet New Press, 1976]). Some glimpses into the Cornfords' family background and later family life can be found in Stansky and Abrahams's book about John, *Journey to the Frontier*, esp. 131–51.

53. Stewart, *Portrait*, 106.

54. Ibid., 106, 107. See also Hugh Cornford, *Memoir*, xxx. Peacock, *The Mask and the Self*, 157, offers some psychological motives for Harrison's unconscious matchmaking.

55. Stewart, *Portrait*, 113.

56. Ibid., 109, 112.

57. Ibid., 112.

58. Gilbert Murray, "Francis Macdonald Cornford, 1874–1943," in *Proceedings of the British Academy* (London: Oxford University Press, 1943), 421–22.

59. From an unpublished biography quoted in Robinson, "Deconstructing the 'Cambridge Ritualists,' " 485n.

60. Ackerman, *Myth and Ritual School*, 164–65; he quotes Stewart, *Portrait*, 102.

61. Arthur Bernard Cook, *Zeus: A Study in Ancient Religion*, vol. 1 (Cambridge, U.K.: The University Press, 1914), xiv–xv; quoted in Hans Schwabl, "A. B. Cook, *Zeus: A Study in Ancient Religion*," in Calder, *Cambridge Ritualists Reconsidered*, 231.

62. Charles Seltman, "Arthur Bernard Cook, 1868–1952," *Proceedings of the British Academy* 38 (1952): 298.

63. From the title essay of Harrison's *Alpha and Omega*, 126.

64. Ibid., 130–31.

65. Murray, "Cornford," 422.

66. Quoted in Robinson, "Deconstructing the 'Cambridge Ritualists,' " 483; from *Newnham College Letter* (Jan. 1929): 75.

67. Robert Ackerman, "Some Letters of the Cambridge Ritualists," *Greek Roman and Byzantine Studies* 12, no. 1 (1971): 135.

68. Robinson, "Deconstructing the 'Cambridge Ritualists,' " 481.

69. Ibid., 472n8.

70. Quoted in Wilson, *Gilbert Murray*, 154.

71. See Robinson, "Deconstructing the 'Cambridge Ritualists,' " 486.

72. Stewart, *Portrait*, 102.

73. Robinson, "Deconstructing the 'Cambridge Ritualists,' " 484–85.

74. For a neat summation of the "new intellectual concerns of the 1890's," see H. Stuart Hughes, *Consciousness and Society: The Reorientation of European Social Thought, 1890–1930* (New York: Knopf, 1958), 63–66.

75. Harrison, *Alpha and Omega*, 206, quoted in Thomas W. Africa, "Aunt Glegg among the Dons: Or Taking Jane Harrison at Her Word," in Calder, *The Cambridge Ritualists Reconsidered*, 27. Africa gives a catalogue of similar observations and remarks; e.g., "I am by nature rotten with superstition and mysticism" (from Stewart, *Portrait*, 38).

76. Helen Fowler, who calls Frances Cornford an Anglican ("Frances Cornford," 144), writes of staying with the Cornfords at the outbreak of World War II (142). On Frances's early religious background, see Hugh Cornford, "Memoir," xxviii.

77. Quoted in Guthrie's introduction to *The Unwritten Philosophy and Other Essays* (Cambridge, U.K.: Cambridge University Press, 1950), viii, where Guthrie, Cornford's student, adds, "In his later years [Cornford] said that it sometimes seemed to him as if he had been all his life writing one and the same book."

78. Rosalind Heywood gives a most readable account of Murray's experiments in *The Sixth Sense: An Inquiry into Extra-Sensory Perception* (London: Chatto and Windus, 1959), 132–40. They were discussed as genuine phenomena by Murrray's student and successor, E. R. Dodds, in *Proceedings of the Society for Psychical Research* 55 (1972): 371–402. E. J. Dingwall refutes Dodds in the next year's *Proceedings* 56 (1973): 21–39. The debate provoked a number of letters to the Society's journal: see the June 1973 issue, pp. 123–35. Murray was president of the Society for Psychical Research in 1915 and again in 1952.

79. Murray, "Cornford," 424.

80. Stewart, *Portrait*, 85.

81. In ibid., 84–85, Stewart cites Harrison's conclusion to her short *The Religion of Ancient Greece* (London: Archibald Constable, 1905), 62–63, where she notes that the history of ancient Greek religion is yet to be written. The questions remaining, she continues, include (1) the early mutual interaction of philosophy and religion, and (2) the "difficult and delicate task" of determining the attitude of different literary authors to their religious tradition: "How far did each modify the religious material ready to his hand?" The first, philosophical,

task she had set for Cornford and the second, literary, one for Murray. When Murray cancelled his proposed Gifford Lectures on "The Religion of the Poets," the writing of which Harrison had told him was "just what I had longed for," she wrote him of her "crushing disappointment."

82. Mirsky was one of the great twentieth-century scholars of Russian literature; his two-volume history of Russian literature was originally dedicated to Harrison. A classic, first published in 1926, it has gone through many editions, with an abridgement reprinted by Northwestern as late as 1999: D. S. Mirsky and Francis J. Whitfield, *A History of Russian Literature: Comprising a History of Russian Literature and Contemporary Russian Literature* (New York: Knopf, 1958).

83. Peacock, *The Mask and the Self*, 230, 235, 243.

84. Ackerman, "Some Letters," 123.

85. Robert Ackerman, "Jane Ellen Harrison: The Early Work," *Greek, Roman and Byzantine Studies* 13, no. 2 (1972): 221; the essay also forms a chapter of his *Myth and Ritual School*.

86. See Jonathan Z. Smith, *To Take Place: Toward Theory in Ritual*, (Chicago: University of Chicago Press, 1987), 15–17.

87. Weston, *Ritual to Romance*, xiii. Maud Bodkin, *Studies of Type-Images in Poetry, Religion, and Philosophy* (London: Oxford University Press, 1951), refers to Cornford's *From Ritual to Philosophy* on pp. 10 and 17, where his distinctions between Olympian and Dionysian elements of Greek religion are central to one of her chapters; she draws on Harrison on pp. 2–3 and 13–14, referring to the "year-god" on pp. 68–69. Bodkin's classic *Archetypal Patterns in Poetry* begins with a discussion featuring Murray (1–5). For a study of the legacy of Harrison in English literature, see Martha C. Carpenter, *Ritual, Myth, and the Modernist Text: The Influence of Jane Harrison on Joyce, Elliot, and Woolf* (Amsterdam: Gordon and Breach, 1998).

88. Northrop Frye, *Anatomy of Criticism: Four Essays* (Princeton, N.J.: Princeton University Press, 1957).

89. See Ackerman's discussion (*Myth and Ritual School*, 170) of Murray's "Greek Drama," a section of the multiauthored article "Drama" in the *Encyclopædia Britannica*, 14th ed., 1929. Duncan Wilson, Murray's otherwise admiring biographer, notes uncharacteristically that "unfortunately for his later reputation as a scholar," Murray gave his "whole-hearted backing" to the concept of the year spirit; Wilson continues by commenting that Murray's "simplistic" presentation of the year spirit in his popular *Euripides and His Age* (New York: Holt, 1913) "shows the influence of Jane Harrison . . . at its most pernicious" (*Gilbert Murray*, 154–55).

90. Murray, "Cornford," 431.

CHAPTER 11. CONCEPTS OF COLLECTIVITY AND THE
FABRIC OF RELIGIOHISTORICAL KNOWLEDGE

1. A clear and now classic debate on the growth of knowledge in science is presented in Imre Lakatos and Alan Musgrave, eds., *Criticism and the Growth of Knowledge* (Cambridge, U.K.: Cambridge University Press, 1970). A daring

and rigorous application of some of Lakatos's insights to theology can be found in Nancey Murphy, *Theology in the Age of Scientific Reasoning* (Ithaca, N.Y.: Cornell University Press, 1990).

2. Thorough reviews of the literature on kingship, which I make no attempt here to provide, can be found in Gillian Feeley Harnick, "Issues in Divine Kingship," in *Annual Review of Anthropology*, ed. Bernard J. Siegel, Alan R. Beals, and Stephen A. Tyler (Palo Alto, Calif.: Annual Reviews, 1985), 273–313; and John D. Kelly and Martha Kaplan, "History, Structure, and Ritual," in *Annual Review of Anthropology*, ed. Bernard J. Siegel, Alan R. Beals, and Stephen A. Tyler (Palo Alto, Calif.: Annual Reviews, 1990), 119–50.

3. On this role of ritual in the history of religions, see Jonathan Z. Smith, "The Bare Facts of Ritual," *History of Religions* 20 (1980): 112–27, reprinted in his *Imagining Religion: From Jonestown to Babylon* (Chicago: University of Chicago Press, 1982), 53–65.

4. *The Sacral Kingship: Contributions to the Central Theme of the VIIIth International Congress for the History of Religions (Rome, April 1955) [alternative Italian title: La Regalità Sacra]* (Leiden: E. J. Brill, 1959); and A. L. Basham, ed., *Kingship in Asia and Early America* (Mexico City: El Colegio de Mexico, 1981).

5. Samuel Henry Hooke, ed., *Myth, Ritual, and Kingship: Essays on the Theory and Practice of Kingship in the Ancient Near East and in Israel* (Oxford, U.K.: Clarendon Press, 1958).

6. David Cannadine and Simon Price, eds., *Rituals of Royalty: Power and Ceremonial in Traditional Societies* (Cambridge, U.K.: Cambridge University Press, 1987).

7. For some trenchant remarks on this subject, see Wendy Doniger's introduction in Wendy Doniger O'Flaherty and J. Duncan M. Derrett, eds., *The Concept of Duty in South Asia* (Columbia, Mo.: South Asia Books, 1977).

8. The *avant-propos* speaks of a *travail collectif* twice (xi, xii), as well as of a *monographie collective* (xi).

9. There is a dedication to Raffaele Pettazzone signed by eighteen scholars, listed in no apparent order, with Geo Widengren first. If Widengren was the first among equals at the time—and thus sometimes listed as editor by default (as by Walter Harrelson, "The Myth and Ritual School," in *The Encyclopedia of Religion*, ed. Mircea Eliade [New York: Macmillan, 1987], 282–85), he is still very much represented as part of a collectivity.

10. Helmer Ringgren, "Some Religious Aspects of the Caliphate," 737–48.

11. See, e.g., Paul Radin, "The Sacral Chief among the American Indians," 83–97; and M. Murray, "The Divine King," 595–608.

12. See Murray, "Divine King"; Maartje Draak, "Some Aspects of Kingship in Pagan Ireland," 651–63; and Ake V. Strom, "The King God and His Connection with Sacrifice in Old Norse Religion," 702–15.

13. See S. G. F. Brandon, "The Effect of the Destruction of Jerusalem in A.D. 70 on Primitive Christian Soteriology," 471–77; and F. C. Grant, "The Idea of the Kingdom of God in the New Testament," 437–46.

14. See, e.g., the *Encyclopedia of Religion* article by Harrelson, "The Myth and Ritual School."

15. A. L. Basham, "Ideas of Kingship in Hinduism and Buddhism," in Basham, ed., *Kingship in Asia and Early America,* 115–32.

16. The exceptions to this rule were papers on Vedic civilization and the ancient Near East—seen as "long vanished civilizations"—and Basham's own contribution, which was to be taken as an addendum to another "misinterpreted brief" on Hindu tradition included in the volume (Basham, *Kingship in Asia,* 3).

17. "I feared that remarks made by foreign scholars in their papers might in some cases be taken as disparaging or politically loaded by others indigenous to the civilizations being discussed" (ibid.).

18. Joseph M. Kitagawa, "Monarchy and Government: Traditions and Ideologies in Pre-Modern Japan," 217–32.

19. Hooke discusses the influences on him at the beginning of his introductory chapter (1–2). For a survey of the school, see Harrelson, "The Myth and Ritual School."

20. In his concluding critical contribution to the volume ("The Myth and Ritual Position Critically Considered," 261–91), S. G. F. Brandon traces the British school's focus on ritual to the renewed interest in Christian liturgical heritage underway in the country at the time (263–64).

21. The foremost of these scholars was the Norwegian Sigmund Mowinckel, whose work begins in the 1910s (see chap. 2). Geo Widengren includes a survey of the Scandinavian scholarship on kingship in his "Die Religionswissenschaftliche Forschung in Skandinavien in den Letzten Zwanzig Jahren," *Zeitschrift für Religions- und Geistesgeschichte* 5, nos. 3 and 4 (1953): 193–222, 320–34.

22. In addition to the volume under discussion, Hooke edited *Myth and Ritual: Essays on the Myth and Ritual of the Hebrews in Relation to the Culture Pattern of the Ancient Near East* (London: Oxford University Press, 1933); and *The Labyrinth: Further Studies in the Relation between Myth and Ritual in the Ancient World* (London: Society for Promoting Christian Knowledge, 1935).

23. Brandon, "Myth and Ritual Position"; and H. H. Rowley, "Ritual and the Hebrew Prophets," 236–60.

24. For concise descriptions of the pattern, see Harrelson, "Myth and Ritual School," 283; and Brandon, "Myth and Ritual Position," 269.

25. The chapters by Brandon and Rowley in *Myth, Ritual, and Kingship* reveal the ways in which the myth and ritual patterns can be unraveled. The best-known alternative theory was that of Henri Frankfort, who emphasized the differences in natural terrain of Egypt and Mesopotamia: *Kingship and the Gods* (1948; reprint, Chicago: University of Chicago Press, 1978).

26. Samuel H. Hooke, "The Myth and Ritual Pattern of the Ancient East," in Hooke, *Myth and Ritual,* 7.

27. Frank E. Reynolds and David Tracy, eds., *Myth and Philosophy: Toward a Comparative Philosophy of Religions* (Albany: State University of New York Press, 1990); Nicholas B. Dirks, ed., *Colonialism and Culture* (Ann Arbor: University of Michigan Press, 1992). Similar titles also frequently add a limiting phrase "x and y in z": *Ritual and Speculation in Early Tantrism,* ed. Teun Goudriaan (Albany: State University of New York Press, 1992).

28. For Popper's "commonsense realism," see Karl Popper, *Objective Knowl-*

edge: An Evolutionary Approach (Oxford, U.K.: Oxford University Press, 1972). Popper, of course, is concerned with "novel facts," not "striking appearances"; but in history of religions, unexpected appearances often lead us to striking new—if tentative—explanations: see Jonathan Z. Smith's "small explanation," discussed toward the end of chapter 6. On "novel facts" in Lakatos, see Murphy, *Theology,* 66–68.

29. The significance of the statement derives in good part from the theoretical debate that generated it. Cannadine builds his argument from the critique of the Geertzian theater state found in Maurice Bloch's essay in the volume: Maurice Bloch, "The Ritual of the Royal Bath in Madagascar: The Dissolution of Death, Birth, and Fertility into Authority," 271–97. In representing Bali as a theater state that reflects a superhuman order, Bloch contends, Geertz refrains from showing how royal ritual derives from "symbolic systems which organize the life of lesser mortals" (Bloch, 295). Bloch, and Cannadine, want to look at these two in closer relation to one another.

30. Amélie Kuhrt, "Usurpation, Conquest, and Ceremonial: From Babylon to Persia," 20–55.

31. Richard Burghart, "Gifts to the Gods: Power, Property, and Ceremonial in Nepal," 237–70.

32. This hypothetical example is inspired by Donna Marie Wulff, *Drama as a Mode of Religious Realization: The Vidagdhamadhava of Rupa Gosvami* (Chico, Calif.: Scholars Press, 1984); Guy L. Beck, *Sonic Theology: Hinduism and Sacred Sound* (Columbia: University of South Carolina Press, 1993); and Joyce L. Irwin, *Sacred Sound: Music in Religious Thought and Practice* (Chico, Calif.: Scholars Press, 1983).

33. Hayden White, *The Content of the Form: Narrative Discourse and Historical Representation* (Baltimore, Md.: Johns Hopkins University Press, 1987).

34. For an extensive treatment, see Edwin Bryant, *The Quest for the Origins of Vedic Culture: The Indo-Aryan Migration Debate* (Oxford, U.K.: Oxford University Press, 2001); for a review of the discussion, see Klaus Klostermaier, "Questioning the Aryan Invasion Theory and Revising Ancient Indian History," *ISKCON Communications Journal* 61 (1998): 5–16.

35. See Hooke, "Myth and Ritual Pattern," 1–14.

AFTERWORD. THE FUTURE OF MODERN DILEMMAS

1. See above pp. 86–88, 113–14; 37–41, 118–20.

2. James Clifford and George E. Marcus, *Writing Culture: The Poetics and Politics of Ethnography* (Berkeley: University of California Press, 1986). See also E. Valentine Daniel and Jeffrey M. Peck, *Culture/Contexture: Explorations in Anthropology and Literary Studies* (Berkeley: University of California Press, 1996).

3. Charles E. Winquist, *Desiring Theology* (Chicago: University of Chicago Press, 1995), 5.

4. Ibid., 14.

5. Ibid., 4: "The more modest definition I propose is that religion can be indexed in the flux of life by what we value as real and important."

6. Ibid., 16. See also Mark C. Taylor, *Erring: A Postmodern a/Theology* (Chicago: University of Chicago Press, 1984). For Derrida himself on religion (not theology), see his *Acts of Religion,* ed. Gil Anidjar (New York: Routledge, 2002). For other critical perspectives in the same spirit, see Jacques Derrida and Gianni Vattimo, eds., *Religion* (Stanford, Calif.: Stanford University Press, 1998).

7. See Ivan Strenski, *Four Theories of Myth in Twentieth-Century History: Cassirer, Eliade, Lévi-Strauss, Malinowski* (Iowa City: University of Iowa Press, 1987), 70–128. Robert S. Ellwood, by contrast, more generous toward Eliade, finds the most important biographical component of his mature religiohistorical work in the prominence it gives to religious humanity's nostalgia for a timeless past, a nostalgia that reflects Eliade's sense of exile from the Romania of his youth. See Robert S. Ellwood, *The Politics of Myth: A Study of C. G. Jung, Mircea Eliade, and Joseph Campbell* (Albany: State University of New York Press, 1999), 97–104.

8. Bruce Lincoln, *Theorizing Myth: Narrative, Ideology, and Scholarship* (Chicago: University of Chicago Press, 1999), 121–37.

9. See ibid., 3–43, on the Greeks, and passim; Russell T. McCutcheon, *Manufacturing Religion: The Discourse on Sui Generis Religion and the Politics of Nostalgia* (New York: Oxford University Press, 1997); Strenski, *Four Theories of Myth;* Tomoko Masuzawa, *In Search of Dreamtime: The Quest for the Origin of Religion* (Chicago: University of Chicago Press, 1993).

10. Steven M. Wasserstrom, *Religion after Religion: Gershom Scholem, Mircea Eliade, and Henry Corbin at Eranos* (Princeton, N.J.: Princeton University Press, 1999).

11. See, e.g., Lincoln, *Theorizing Myth,* 146.

12. The references are to Bernard Faure, *The Rhetoric of Immediacy: A Cultural Critique of Chan/Zen Buddhism* (Princeton, N.J.: Princeton University Press, 1991); but see also his *Chan Insights and Oversights: An Epistemological Critique of the Chan Tradition* (Princeton, N.J.: Princeton University Press, 1993).

13. See the many works of Marcel Detienne and Jean-Pierre Vernant, including their coauthored *The Cuisine of Sacrifice among the Greeks* (Chicago: University of Chicago Press, 1989). Vernant gives interesting autobiographical reflections in his *Entre Mythe et Politique, la Librairie du XXe Siècle* (France: Seuil, 1996).

14. Charles Taylor, *Sources of the Self: The Making of the Modern Identity* (Cambridge, Mass.: Harvard University Press, 1989), 512.

15. See two recent anthologies: Kimberley C. Patton and Benjamin C. Ray, eds., *A Magic Still Dwells: Comparative Religion in the Postmodern Age* (Berkeley: University of California Press, 2000), with reflective essays; and Francois Boespflug and Francoise Dunand, eds., *Le Comparatisme en Histoire des Religions: Actes du Colloque International de Strasbourg (18–20 Septembre 1996)* (Paris: Cerf, 1997), with examples of recent comparative practice.

Frequently Cited Sources

This bibliography is intended primarily as an aid for readers who become curious about a reference cited in short form in the notes. At the same time, as a list of works to which I have returned in my discussions, it should also give readers a sense of the threads of scholarly tradition running through my arguments.

Abrams, M. H. *The Mirror and the Lamp: Romantic Theory and the Critical Tradition.* London: Oxford University Press, 1953.

Ackerman, Robert. *Myth and Ritual School: J. G. Frazer and the Cambridge Ritualists.* New York: Garland, 1991.

———. "Some Letters of the Cambridge Ritualists." *Greek Roman and Byzantine Studies* 12, no. 1 (1971): 113–36.

Alles, Gregory D. "Toward a Genealogy of the Holy: Rudolf Otto and the Apologetics of Religion." *Journal of the American Academy of Religion* 69, no. 2 (2001): 323–41.

Almond, Philip. *Rudolf Otto: An Introduction to His Philosophical Theology.* Chapel Hill: University of North Carolina Press, 1984.

Arlen, Shelley. *The Cambridge Ritualists: An Annotated Bibliography of the Works by and about Jane Ellen Harrison, Gilbert Murray, Francis M. Cornford, and Arthur Bernard Cook.* Metuchen, N.J.: Scarecrow Press, 1990.

Basham, A. L., ed. *Kingship in Asia and Early America: XXX International Congress of Human Sciences in Asia and North Africa.* Mexico City: Colegio de México, 1981.

Baumgartner, W. "Nachruf Alfred Jeremias." *Zeitschrift für Assyriologie* 43 (1936): 299–301.

Beard, Mary. *The Invention of Jane Harrison.* Cambridge, Mass.: Harvard University Press, 2000.

Bodkin, Maud. *Archetypal Patterns in Poetry: Psychological Studies of Imagination.* London: Oxford University Press, 1934.

Bornemann, Fritz. *Arnold Janssen: Founder of Three Missionary Congregations,* *1837–1909.* Manila: Arnoldus Press, 1975.

———. *A History of Our Society.* Trans. Dermot Walsh. Rome: Apud Collegium Verbi Divini, 1981.

———. "P. Martin Gusinde, S. V. D. (1886–1969): Eine Biographische Skizze." *Anthropos* 65 (1970): 737–57.

———. *P. Wilhelm Schmidt, S. V. D., 1868–1954.* Rome: Apud Collegium Verbi Divini, 1982.

Brandewie, Ernest. *When Giants Walked the Earth: The Life and Times of Wilhelm Schmidt, SVD.* Fribourg: University Press, 1990.

———. *Wilhelm Schmidt and the Origin of the Idea of God.* Lanham, Md.: University Press of America, 1983.

Brandon, S. G. F. "The Myth and Ritual Position Critically Considered." In *Myth, Ritual, and Kingship: Essays on the Theory and Practice of Kingship in the Ancient Near East and in Israel,* ed. Samuel Henry Hooke, 261–91. Oxford, U.K.: Clarendon Press, 1958.

Burgmann, Arnold. "Professor Dr. Wilhelm Koppers SVD." *Anthropos,* no. 56 (1961): 721–36.

Burke, Edmund. *A Philosophical Enquiry into the Origin of Our Ideas of the Sublime and Beautiful.* 1759. 2d ed. Reprint, New York: Garland, 1971.

Calder, William M., III, ed. *The Cambridge Ritualists Reconsidered.* Atlanta, Ga.: Scholars Press, 1991.

Cannadine, David, and Simon Price, eds. *Rituals of Royalty: Power and Ceremonial in Traditional Societies.* Cambridge, U.K.: Cambridge University Press, 1987.

Carlson, Ingeborg. "Eduard Stucken: Eine Monographie." Inaugural-Dissertation, Friedrich Alexander Universität zu Erlangen-Nurnberg, 1961.

Chantepie de la Saussaye, P. D. *Manual of the Science of Religion.* Translated by Beatrice S. Colyer-Fergusson (née Max Müller). London: Longmans, Green, 1891.

Conte, Edouard. "Wilhelm Schmidt: Des letzten Kaisers Beichvater und das 'neudeutsche Heidentum.' " In *Volkskunde und Nationalsozialismus: Referate und Diskussionen einer Tagung der Deutschen Gesellschaft für Volkskunde,* ed. Helge Gerndt, 261–78. München: Münchner Vereinigung für Volkskunde, 1987.

Cornford, Frances. *Selected Poems.* Ed. Jane Dowson. London: Enitharmon Press, 1996.

Cornford, Francis Macdonald. *From Religion to Philosophy; a Study in the Origins of Western Speculation.* 1912. Reprint, New York: Harper and Row, 1957.

———. *Microcosmographia Academica.* 1908. Reprint, Cambridge, U.K.: Cambridge University Press, 1994.

———. *Thucydides Mythistoricus.* London: E. Arnold, 1907.

Cornford, Hugh. "Memoir." In *Selected Poems of Frances Cornford,* ed. Jane Dowson, xxvii–xxxvii. London: Enitharmon Press, 1996.

Crowther, Paul. *Critical Aesthetics and Postmodernism.* Oxford: Oxford University Press, 1993.

Daniel, Glyn. "Grafton Elliot Smith: Egypt and Diffusionism." In *The Concepts of Human Evolution,* ed. Lord Solly Zuckerman, 405–46. London: Academic Press, 1973.

———. *The Idea of Prehistory.* Cleveland, Ohio: World Publishing, 1963.

de Baillou, Clemens. "Eduard Stucken: Eine Studie." *Kentucky Foreign Language Quarterly* 8, no. 1 (1961): 1–6.

Doniger, Wendy. *Siva, the Erotic Ascetic.* New York: Oxford University Press, 1981. First published as *Asceticism and Eroticism in the Mythology of Shiva,* by Wendy Doniger O'Flaherty. London: Oxford University Press, 1973.

Dorson, Richard M. *The British Folklorists: A History.* Chicago: University of Chicago Press, 1968.

Dumézil, Georges. *Gods of the Ancient Northmen.* Berkeley: University of California Press, 1973.

———. *Mitra-Varuna: An Essay on Two Indo-European Representations of Sovereignty.* Trans. Derek Coltman. New York: Zone Books, 1988.

Eccles, Robert S. *Erwin Ramsdell Goodenough: A Personal Pilgrimage.* Chico, Calif.: Scholars Press, 1985.

Eliade, Mircea. *Patterns in Comparative Religion.* Trans. Rosemary Sheed. New York: Meridian, 1963.

Elkin, A. P. "Sir Grafton Elliot Smith: The Man and His Work." In *Grafton Elliot Smith: The Man and His Work,* ed. A. P. Elkin and N. W. G. Macintosh, 8–15. Sydney: Sydney University Press, 1974.

Elkin, A. P., and N. W. G. Macintosh, eds. *Grafton Elliot Smith: The Man and His Work.* Sydney: Sydney University Press, 1974.

Encyclopedia of Religion. Ed. Mircea Eliade. 16 vols. New York: Macmillan, 1987.

Fernandez, James W. *Bwiti: An Ethnography of the Religious Imagination in Africa.* Princeton, N.J.: Princeton University Press, 1982.

Fernández de Oviedo y Valdés, Gonzalo. "Histoire du Nicaragua." In *Voyages, Relations et Memoires Originaux pour Servir a L'histoire de la Decouverte de l'Amerique,* ed. Henri Ternaux-Compans. Paris: Arthur Bertrand, 1840.

Ferreira, John Vincent, Stephen Fuchs, and Klaus K. Klostermaier, eds. *Essays in Ethnology.* Bombay: New Literature, 1969.

Fitzgerald, Timothy. *The Ideology of Religious Studies.* New York: Oxford University Press, 2000.

Flood, Gavin. *Beyond Phenomenology: Rethinking the Study of Religion.* London: Cassell, 1999.

Fowler, Helen. "Frances Cornford, 1886–1960." In *Cambridge Women: Twelve Portraits,* ed. Edwards Shils and Carmen Blacker, 137–57. Cambridge, U.K.: Cambridge University Press, 1996.

Geertz, Clifford. *Available Light: Anthropological Reflections on Philosophical Topics.* Princeton, N.J.: Princeton University Press, 2000.

———. *The Interpretation of Cultures.* New York: Basic Books, 1973.

———. *Islam Observed: Religious Development in Morocco and Indonesia.* Chicago: University of Chicago Press, 1971.

———. *Negara: The Theatre State in Nineteenth-Century Bali.* Princeton, N.J.: Princeton University Press, 1980.

———. "Ritual and Social Change." In *The Interpretation of Cultures,* 142–69. New York: Basic Books, 1973.

———. "Thick Description: Toward an Interpretive Theory of Culture." In *The Interpretation of Cultures,* 3–30. New York: Basic Books, 1973.

Gooch, Todd A. *The Numinous and Modernity: An Interpretation of Rudolf Otto's Philosophy of Religion.* New York: W. de Gruyter, 2000.

Goodenough, Erwin Ramsdell. *Jewish Symbols in the Greco-Roman Period.* 13 vols. New York: Bollingen Foundation/Pantheon, 1953–68.

———. *The Psychology of Religious Experiences.* New York: Basic Books, 1965.

———. *Toward a Mature Faith.* New York: Prentice-Hall, 1955.

Goodenough, Erwin Ramsdell, and Jacob Neusner. *Jewish Symbols in the Greco-Roman Period.* Abr. ed. Princeton, N.J.: Princeton University Press, 1988.

Hallencreutz, Carl F. *Kraemer Towards Tambaram: A Study in Hendrik Kraemer's Missionary Approach.* Uppsala: Gleerup, 1966.

Harrelson, Walter. "The Myth and Ritual School." In *The Encyclopedia of Religion,* ed. Mircea Eliade, 282–85. New York: Macmillan, 1987.

Harris, Marvin. *Cows, Pigs, Wars, and Witches: The Riddles of Culture.* New York: Vintage, 1989.

———. *Cultural Materialism: The Struggle for a Science of Culture.* New York: Random House, 1979.

Harrison, Jane Ellen. *Alpha and Omega.* London: Sidgewick and Jackson, 1915.

———. *Epilegomena to the Study of Greek Religion; and Themis: A Study of the Social Origins of Greek Religion.* 1921, 1927 (2d ed.). Reprint, with a preface by John C. Wilson, New Hyde Park, N.Y.: University Books, 1962.

———. *Prolegomena to the Study of Greek Religion.* Cambridge, U.K.: The University Press, 1903.

———. *Reminiscences of a Student's Life.* London: Hogarth, 1925.

———. *Themis: A Study of the Social Origins of Greek Religion.* Cambridge, U.K.: The University Press, 1912. [Page references to *Themis* in the text refer to the 1962 reprint of the 2d edition, in Harrison's *Epilegomena,* cited above.]

———. *Unanimism: A Study of Conversion and Some Contemporary French Poets, Being a Paper Read before "the Heretics" on November 25, 1912.* Cambridge: "The Heretics," 1913.

Henley, Dorothy Howard Eden. *Rosalind Howard, Countess of Carlisle.* London: Hogarth, 1958.

Henninger, Joseph, S. V. D. "P. Wilhelm Koppers, S. V. D.: Biographische Skizze und Würdigung seines wissenschaftlichen Lebenswerkes." *Mitteilungen der Anthropologischen Gesellschaft in Wien* 91 (1961): 1–14.

Hoedemaker, Bert. "Kraemer Reassessed." *Ecumenical Review* 41, no. 1 (1989): 41–49.

Hooke, Samuel Henry, "The Myth and Ritual Pattern of the Ancient East." In *Myth and Ritual: Essays on the Myth and Ritual of the Hebrews in Relation to the Culture Pattern of the Ancient Near East,* ed. Samuel Henry Hooke, 1–14. London: Oxford University Press, 1933.

———, ed. *Myth and Ritual: Essays on the Myth and Ritual of the Hebrews in Relation to the Culture Pattern of the Ancient Near East.* London: Oxford University Press, 1933.

———. *Myth, Ritual, and Kingship: Essays on the Theory and Practice of Kingship in the Ancient Near East and in Israel.* Oxford, U.K.: Clarendon Press, 1958.

Hume, David. *The Natural History of Religion and Dialogues Concerning Natural Religion.* Ed. A. Wayne Colver and John Valdimir Price. Oxford, U.K.: Clarendon Press, 1976.

Hynes, Samuel. *The Edwardian Turn of Mind.* Princeton, N.J.: Princeton University Press, 1968.

James, George Alfred. *Interpreting Religion: The Phenomenological Approaches of Pierre Daniël Chantepie de la Saussaye, W. Brede Kristensen, and Gerardus van der Leeuw.* Washington, D.C.: Catholic University of America Press, 1995.

Jeremias, Alfred. *Das Alte Testament im Lichte des alten Orients.* Leipzig: J. C. Hinrichs'sche Buchhandlung, 1904.

———. *Handbuch der altorientalischen Geisteskultur.* 1st ed. Leipzig: J. C. Hinrichs'sche Buchhandlung, 1913.

———. *Handbuch der altorientalischen Geisteskultur.* 2d ed. Berlin: W. de Gruyter, 1929.

———. "Hugo Winckler: Gedachtnisrede." *Mitteilungen der Vorderasiatisch-Aegyptischen Gesellschaft (E. V.)* 20, no. 1 (1915): 3–12.

———. "Panbabylonismus." In *Die Religion in Geschichte und Gegenwart,* 2d ed., ed. H. Gunkel and L. Zscharnack, 879–80. Tübingen: Mohr, 1930.

Johanning, Klaus. *Der Bibel-Babel-Streit: Eine forschungsgeschichtliche Studie.* Frankfurt am Main: Peter Lang, 1988.

Johnson, Gordon. *University Politics: F. M. Cornford's Cambridge and His Advice to the Young Academic Politician.* Cambridge, U.K.: Cambridge University Press, 1994.

Kant, Immanuel. *Critique of Judgment.* Trans. Werner S. Pluhar. Indianapolis: Hackett, 1987. [In in-text citations, the first number refers to the section of the *Critique,* the second to the page of the German *Akadamie* edition (ed. Wilhelm Windelband, 1908–13), the third to the page of Pluhar's English translation.]

Kellogg Wood, Douglas. "F. M. Cornford." In *Classical Scholarship: A Biographical Encyclopedia,* ed. Ward W. Briggs and William M. Calder III, 23–36. New York: Garland, 1990.

King, Richard. *Orientalism and Religion: Postcolonial Theory, India, and 'the Mystic East.'* London: Routledge, 1999.

Koppers, Wilhelm. "Grundsätzliches und Geschichtliches zur ethnologischen Kulturkreislehere." In *Beiträge Österreichs zur Erforschung der Vergangenheit und Kulturgeschichte der Menschheit,* ed. Emil Britinger, Josef Haekel, and Richard Pettoni, 110–26. Horn, Niederösterreich: Ferdinand Berger, 1959.

Kraemer, Hendrik. *The Christian Message in a Non-Christian World.* 1938. 3d ed. Grand Rapids, Mich.: Kregel Publications, 1956.

———. *World Cultures and World Religions.* Philadelphia: Westminster Press, 1960.

Kristensen, William Brede. *The Meaning of Religion: Lectures in the Phenomenology of Religion.* Trans. John Carman. The Hague: Martinus Nijhoff, 1960.

Kuper, Adam. *The Invention of Primitive Society.* London: Routledge, 1988.

Lakatos, Imre, and Alan Musgrave, eds. *Criticism and the Growth of Knowledge.* Cambridge, U.K.: Cambridge University Press, 1970.

Landau, Misia. *Narratives of Human Evolution.* New Haven, Conn.: Yale University Press, 1991.

Lang, Andrew. *The Making of Religion*. London: Longmans, Green, 1898.

Langstaff, Eleanor de Selms. *Andrew Lang*. Boston: Twayne, 1978.

Leertouwer, L. "C. P. Tiele's Strategy of Conquest." In *Leiden Oriental Connections, 1850–1940*, ed. Willem Otterspeer, 153–67. Leiden: E. J. Brill, 1989.

Lehmann, Reinhard G. *Friedrich Delitzsch und der Babel-Bibel-Streit*. Freiburg, Schweiz: Universitätsverlag/Göttingen: Vandenhoeck und Ruprecht, 1994.

Lehrer, Keith. *Theory of Knowledge*. Boulder, Colo.: Westview Press, 1990.

Lévi-Strauss, Claude. *Structural Anthropology*. New York: Basic Books, 1963.

Lincoln, Bruce. *Theorizing Myth: Narrative, Ideology, and Scholarship*. Chicago: University of Chicago Press, 1999.

Lloyd-Jones, Hugh. "Jane Harrison, 1850–1928." In *Cambridge Women: Twelve Portraits*, ed. Edward Shils and Carmen Blacker, 29–72. Cambridge, U.K.: Cambridge University Press, 1996.

Longino, Helen. *Science as Social Knowledge*. Princeton, N.J.: Princeton University Press, 1990.

Mackey, James P., ed. *Religious Imagination*. Edinburgh: Edinburgh University Press, 1986.

McCutcheon, Russell T. *Manufacturing Religion: The Discourse on Sui Generis Religion and the Politics of Nostalgia*. New York: Oxford University Press, 1997.

Miller, Dean A. "Georges Dumézil: Theories, Critiques, and Theoretical Extensions." *Religion* 30, no. 1 (2000): 27–40.

Murphy, Nancey. *Theology in the Age of Scientific Reasoning*. Ithaca, N.Y.: Cornell University Press, 1990.

Murray, Gilbert. *Five Stages of Greek Religion*. 3d ed. New York: Doubleday, 1955.

———. *Four Stages of Greek Religion*. New York: Columbia University Press, 1912.

———. "Francis Macdonald Cornford, 1874–1943." In *Proceedings of the British Academy*, 421–32. London: Oxford University Press, 1943.

———. *Jane Ellen Harrison: An Address Delivered at Newnham College, October 27th, 1928*. Cambridge, U.K.: W. Heffer and Sons, 1928 [reprinted in Harrison, *Epilegomena*, 559–77].

———. *An Unfinished Autobiography—with Contributions by His Friends*. Ed. Jean Smith and Arnold Toynbee. London: George Allen and Unwin, 1960.

Natter, Wolfgang, Theodore R. Schatzki, and John Paul Jones. *Objectivity and Its Other*. New York: Guilford Press, 1995.

Nicholson, Linda J. *The Play of Reason: From the Modern to the Postmodern*. Ithaca, N.Y.: Cornell University Press, 1999.

Niebuhr, Carl. "Nachruf Hugo Winckler." *Orientalistische Literaturzeitung* 16, no. 5 (1913): 198–99.

Otto, Rudolf. *Autobiographical and Social Essays*. Trans. Gregory D. Alles. Berlin: Mouton de Gruyter, 1996.

———. *The Idea of the Holy*. Trans. John W. Harvey. London: Oxford University Press, 1923.

Passman, Tina. "Out of the Closet and into the Field: Matriculture, the Lesbian Perspective, and Feminist Classics." In *Feminist Theory and the Classics,* ed.

Nancy Sorkin Rabinowitz and Amy Richlin, 181–208. New York: Routledge, 1993.

Peacock, Sandra J. *Jane Ellen Harrison: The Mask and the Self*. New Haven, Conn.: Yale University Press, 1988.

Peiser, Felix E. "Nachruf Hugo Winckler." *Orientalistische Literaturzeitung* 16, no. 5 (1913): 195–98.

Perry, W. J. *The Children of the Sun: A Study in the Early History of Civilization*. 2d ed. London: Methuen, 1927.

———. *The Megalithic Culture of Indonesia*. Manchester, U.K.: Manchester University Press, 1918.

———. "The Relationship between the Geographical Distribution of Megalithic Monuments and Ancient Mines." *Memoirs and Proceedings of the Manchester Literary and Philosophical Society* 60 (1915): 1–28.

Popper, Karl. *Objective Knowledge: An Evolutionary Approach*. Oxford, U.K.: Oxford University Press, 1972.

Preus, J. Samuel. *Explaining Religion: Criticism and Theory from Bodin to Freud*. New Haven, Conn.: Yale University Press, 1987.

Rahmann, Rudolph. "Fünfzig Jahre Anthropos." *Anthropos* 51 (1956): 1–18.

———. "Vier Pioniere der Völkerkunde: Den Patres Paul Arndt, Martin Gusinde, Wilhelm Koppers, und Paul Schebesta Zum Siebzigsten Geburtstag." *Anthropos* 52 (1957): 264–76.

Rivers, W. H. R. "Distribution of Megalithic Civilization." 1915. In *Psychology and Ethnology*, ed. G. Elliot Smith, 167–72. London: K. Paul, 1926.

———. *The History of Melanesian Society*. 2 vols. Cambridge, U.K.: The University Press, 1914.

———. *The Todas*. London: Macmillan, 1906.

Rivers, W. H. R., G. Elliot Smith, and Charles Samuel Myers. *Psychology and Politics, and Other Essays*. London: K. Paul, 1923.

Rivinius, Karl Josef, Wilhelm Schmidt, and Georg Hertling. *Die Anfänge des "Anthropos": Briefe von P. Wilhelm Schmidt an Georg Freiherrn von Hertling aus den Jahren 1904 bis 1908 und andere Dokumente*. St. Augustin: Steyler, 1981.

Robinson, Annabel. "A New Light Our Elders Had Not Seen: Deconstructing the 'Cambridge Ritualists.'" *Echos du Monde Classique* 42, n.s., 17 (1998): 471–87.

Rorty, Richard. *Objectivity, Relativism, and Truth*. Cambridge, U.K.: Cambridge University Press, 1991.

Rowley, H. H. "Ritual and the Hebrew Prophets." In *Myth and Ritual: Essays on the Myth and Ritual of the Hebrews in Relation to the Culture Pattern of the Ancient Near East*, ed. Samuel Henry Hooke, 236–60. London: Oxford University Press, 1933.

The Sacral Kingship: Contributions to the Central Theme of the VIIIth International Congress for the History of Religions (Rome, April 1955) [Alternative Italian Title: La Regalità Sacra]. Leiden: E. J. Brill, 1959.

Schleiermacher, Friedrich. *On Religion: Speeches to Its Cultured Despisers*. Trans. and ed. Richard Crouter. Cambridge, U.K.: Cambridge University Press, 1996.

Schmidt, Wilhelm. "Die Errichtung des 'Anthropos Institutes.' " *Anthropos* 27 (1932): 275–77.

———. *Primitive Revelation.* Trans. Joseph J. Baierl. St. Louis, Mo.: B. Herder, 1939.

———. *Rasse und Volk: Ihre allgemeine Bedeutung; Ihre Geltung in deutschen Raum.* 2d ed. Salzburg: Verlag Anton Pustet, 1935.

———. *Der Ursprung der Gottesidee: Eine historisch-kritische und positive Studie.* 2d ed. 12 vols. Münster i W.: Aschendorff, 1926–55.

———. *Wege der Kulturen: Gesammelte Aufsätze.* St. Augustin bei Bonn: Verlag des Anthropos-Instituts, 1964.

Shaw, Bernard. *Major Barbara.* 1913. Reprint, Baltimore: Penguin, 1960.

Slobodin, Richard. *W. H. R. Rivers.* New York: Columbia University Press, 1978.

Smith, Barbara Herrnstein. *Belief and Resistance: Dynamics of Contemporary Intellectual Controversy.* Cambridge, Mass.: Harvard University Press, 1997.

Smith, Grafton Elliot. *The Ancient Egyptians and the Origin of Civilization.* London: Harper, 1923. [Originally published as *The Ancient Egyptians and Their Influence upon the Civilization of Europe.* London: Harper, 1911.]

———. *Human History.* New York: Norton, 1929.

———. "On the Significance of the Geographical Distribution of the Practice of Mummification—a Study of the Migration of Peoples and the Spread of Certain Customs and Beliefs." *Memoirs and Proceedings of the Manchester Literary and Philosophical Society* 59, no. 9 (1915): 1–143. [Published separately as *The Migrations of Early Culture.* Manchester, U.K.: Manchester University Press, 1915.]

Smith, Jonathan Z. "Adde Parvum Parvo Magnum Acervus Erit." In *Map Is Not Territory,* by Jonathan Z. Smith, 240–64. Leiden: Brill, 1978. [Originally published in *History of Religions* 11, no. 1 (1971): 67–90.]

———. *Imagining Religion: From Jonestown to Babylon.* Chicago: University of Chicago Press, 1982.

———. *Map Is Not Territory: Studies in the History of Religions.* Leiden: Brill, 1978. Reprint, Chicago: University of Chicago Press, 1993.

———. "A Pearl of Great Price and a Cargo of Yams: A Study in Situational Incongruity." In *Imagining Religion,* by Jonathan Z. Smith, 90–101. Chicago: University of Chicago Press, 1982. [Originally published in *History of Religions* 16 (1976): 1–19.]

———. *To Take Place: Toward Theory in Ritual.* Chicago: University of Chicago Press, 1987.

Smith, Wilfred Cantwell. "Comparative Religion: Whither—and Why?" In *The History of Religions: Essays in Methodology,* ed. Mircea Eliade and Joseph M. Kitagawa, 31–58. Chicago: University of Chicago Press, 1959.

Stansky, Peter, and William Miller Abrahams. *Journey to the Frontier: Julian Bell and John Cornford: Their Lives and the 1930s.* London: Constable, 1966.

Stewart, Jessie. *Jane Ellen Harrison: A Portrait from Letters.* London: Merlin Press, 1959.

Stocking, George W. *After Tylor: British Social Anthropology, 1888–1951*. Madison: University of Wisconsin Press, 1995.

Strenski, Ivan. *Four Theories of Myth in Twentieth-Century History: Cassirer, Eliade, Lévi-Strauss, Malinowski*. Iowa City: University of Iowa Press, 1987.

Stucken, Eduard. *Astralmythen der Hebräer, Babylonier, und Aegypter*. Leipzig: Verlag von Eduard Pfeiffer, 1896–1907.

———. "Polynesisches Sprachgut in Amerika und in Sumer." *Mitteilungen der Vorderasiatisch-Aegyptischen Gesellschaft (E. V.)* 31, no. 2 (1927): 1–127.

Taylor, Charles. *Sources of the Self: The Making of the Modern Identity*. Cambridge, Mass.: Harvard University Press, 1989.

Thomson, Gladys Scott. *Mrs. Arthur Strong: A Memoir*. London: Cohen and West, 1949.

Tiele, C. P. *Elements of the Science of Religion*. 2 vols. New York: Charles Scribner's Sons, 1897–99.

Tylor, Edward Burnett. *Primitive Culture*. 2 vols. 1873. Reprint, Gloucester, Mass.: Peter Smith, 1970.

van der Leeuw, G[erardus]. *Religion in Essence and Manifestation*. Trans. J. E. Turner. New York: Harper and Row, 1963. [Original German edition 1933; first English edition 1938.]

Vorbichler, Anton. "Professor Dr. Paul Schebesta, SVD." *Anthropos* 62 (1967): 665–85.

Wasserstrom, Steven M. *Religion after Religion: Gershom Scholem, Mircea Eliade, and Henry Corbin at Eranos*. Princeton, N.J.: Princeton University Press, 1999.

Wechsler, Judith, ed. *On Aesthetics in Science*. Cambridge, Mass.: MIT Press, 1978.

Weston, Jessie L. *From Ritual to Romance*. 1920. Reprint, Garden City, N.Y.: Doubleday, 1957.

Wilson, Duncan. *Gilbert Murray, OM, 1866–1957*. Oxford: Oxford University Press, 1987.

Wimsatt, William C. "Robustness, Reliability, and Overdetermination." In *Scientific Inquiry and the Social Sciences: A Volume in Honor of Donald T. Campbell*, ed. Marilynn B. Brewer and Barry E. Collins, 124–63. San Francisco: Jossey-Bass, 1981.

Winckler, Hugo. *Geschichte Israels in Einzeldarstellungen*. 2 vols. Leipzig: E. Pfeiffer, 1895, 1900.

———. "Himmels- und Weltenbild der Babylonier als Grundlage des Weltanschauung und Mythologie aller Völker." *Der Alte Orient* 3, nos. 2–3 (1902): 1–67.

Zuckerman, Lord Solly, ed. *The Concepts of Human Evolution*. London: Academic Press, 1973.

Index

Abrams, M. H., 47, 247n7
Ackerman, Robert, 190, 208, 275n175
aesthetics: of extent, 79–81, 137, 153, 168; historically considered, 47–49; importance for religious studies, 1–2, 53, 107; Kant's, 6, 53, 70–71, 74, 87; and objectivity, 116–19; and postmodernism, 9, 229–33; of religiohistorical reception, 75–85; of religiohistorical writing, 38, 40–41, 45, 69, 75–77, 87, 95, 127; and science, 91–92, 103–4, 120–23, 210; of the sublime (*see* sublime, the); and theology, 40; and truth, 97–99, 114
aesthetics of specific writers: Doniger, 66, 73, 84; Dumézil, 63, 79–80, 84; Eliade, 67–68, 74, 80–81; Faure, 234–35; Geertz, 61, 73, 83, 84; Harris, 100, 102; Harrison, 208–9; van der Leeuw, 137; Panbabylonians, 152–54; Perry, 168; Schmidt, 174–75; Schmidt's students, 187; Smith, J. Z., 90–91, 112
agnosticism, 205; of historians of religion, 31, 35
Alles, Gregory, 26, 241n13, 273n126
anthropology: British, 23–25, 159–60, 163–66; German-speaking (*see* ethnology: German-speaking); and Harrison, 30, 201; and history, 222–23; influences on religious studies, 60–61, 64–65, 133, 110, 118–19, 142, 190; materialist, 100–102, 107;

objectivity in, 115, 119–20; postmodern, 230
Anthropos Institute, 179, 182, 186, 187
Anthropos (journal): and Catholic traditions, 173, 175, 181; concept of, 172, 174; history of, 172, 179, 182, 184; success of, 179
anti-Semitism, 82; and Eliade, 234, 253n22; Schmidt's, 180, 272–73n123
architecture, 8, 33–34, 57, 63, 162, 209
argument, religiohistorical, 9, 41; coherence in, 56–57, 81, 165, 235; four types of, 58–59; imagination and, 84, 71, 90, 231; local, 59–63, 80, 83; objectivity in, 114–20, 122–23; and religious belief, 133–34, 138–41, 170, 172, 176, 177; science and, 84, 107; universal, 63–64, 66–68, 80
Arnold, Philip, 254n31
astral mythology, 146, 152, 156

Basham, A. L., 217–18, 223, 226
Beard, Mary, 190, 192, 193
Bergson, Henri, 28–29, 30, 191, 204
Bible, the: construed historically, 16, 141, 145, 173–74, 176–77; in Panbabylonian theory, 146–47, 148, 149, 151–52; as subject of study, 2, 26, 150, 151, 157, 175, 219
Bodkin, Maud, 209
Bornemann, Fritz, 275n275
bracketing, phenomenological, 54–55

Compositor: Binghamton Valley Composition, LLC
Text: 10/13 Sabon
Display: Sabon
Printer and binder: Maple-Vail Manufacturing Group